Individualizing Instruction in the Elementary School

CONSULTING EDITOR: **PAUL NASH**
BOSTON UNIVERSITY

Individualizing

Instruction in the

Elementary School

GEORGE I. THOMAS and
NEW YORK STATE EDUCATION DEPARTMENT

JOSEPH CRESCIMBENI
JACKSONVILLE UNIVERSITY

RANDOM HOUSE NEW YORK

TO OUR WIVES

MAVIS and ALYNE

who demonstrated patience, stamina, and
encouragement in the preparation of this book

Acknowledgments

. . . . are extended to all professional colleagues who made definitive suggestions; to Angela Holland for typing the complete manuscript and assisting in the proofreading; and to Elizabeth Taylor, Linda Hurley, and Suzanne Judd who assisted in parts of its revision. Special recognition is given to Robert Weiss and members of his editorial staff at Random House for their valued recommendations and their perseverance from beginning to end.

PREFACE

Educators are taking a new look at the curriculum of the elementary school and the many ways teachers are trying to realize their goals. There has been an increased interest in *homogeneous grouping, departmentalization,* and *grouping within the classroom.* Old ideas and methods are being adopted under new names or with different labels, because teachers and the public want to improve the quantity and quality of education.

This book is aimed at young prospective teachers and teachers already in the field who want to do a better job. It recognizes the need for quality and quantity, but tries to show that good education cannot be offered on an assembly-line basis. There will be times when large groups of children can be exposed to a learning situation if the chief goal is the acquisition of factual knowledge. But individual differences in learners and teachers make it imperative that the learning group be small enough to guarantee that each child will have opportunities to react and respond with the teacher.

The hypothesis is presented that learning must be continuous and that children must have opportunities to progress at their own rates of speed. This means that teachers must meet the needs of slow maturing boys and girls through varied teaching methods. In the past, educators tried to meet the challenge of individual differences by some form of ability or homogeneous grouping. Teachers and parents have often been willing to adopt homogeneous grouping plans, but their goals are not usually realized because of the lack of "real homogeneity" in children. An outstanding reader may not be very competent in mathematics. A good mathematics student may have no interest in science. A brilliant boy may have no creative ability of any kind, but a boy who is merely high average in intelligence may show every indication that he has the capabilities of becoming an artist, a musician, or a mechanical wizard.

Unless the school can be organized on a flexible basis to meet the varying social, emotional, physical needs of boys and girls, as well as different academic needs, it will be impossible for the teacher to help each pupil develop to the maximum of his potentialities. This can best be done in classrooms where the teacher can work with children individually and in small groups, as well as on an all-class basis, with the understanding that many needs of children can be met if the teacher: (1) recognizes the basic needs of children; and (2) is able and willing to make the effort to help individual children grow.

Teachers and school administrators must set the stage for helping fast learners move ahead, but this will call for teachers' using a wide variety of materials and going beyond the ordinary limits of a graded textbook. Teachers must be prepared to measure the individual's level of learning and base their instruction on helping each boy and girl to progress steadily in terms of his potential. One of the points made in this book is that many boys and girls drop out of high school or college because they have not been given the kind of work-study skills necessary for success. They need to learn the meaning of independent work and self-discipline; and they must learn to assume a greater share of the leadership responsibilities in the world about them. The teacher acts as a leader, but she does not monopolize the role to the point that pupil initiative is thwarted. By working in small groups and in areas where both need and interest exist, the learner has many opportunities to be both a leader and a follower.

Many of the principles expounded here have been tried in the authors' schools and have been applied in other school systems by teachers who were sincerely interested in good education for all children.

G.I.T.

J.C.

Spring, 1967

CONTENTS

PREFACE

Introduction: The Challenge of Teaching   3

    Grouping and Scheduling   4
    Challenges for Tomorrow   6

PART ONE

CHAPTER
1.   Regimentation in Graded Elementary Schools   11

    The Evolution of the Graded School: A New
       Frontier in Education   12
    Early Attempts to Provide for Individual
       Differences in the Graded School   24

2.   Innovations in Elementary Education   31

    New Concepts Develop to Modify
       Educational Practices   32
    The Changing Nature of the Elementary School   36
    Innovations Affecting the Teacher-Learner Situation   50

3. **Setting the Stage for Effective Learning**   65

Establishing Goals for More Effective Learning
    and Teaching   66
Putting These Goals into Effect   67

4. **Observing and Understanding Pupil Behavior**   79

Teaching Children by Understanding Their Basic Needs
    as Influenced by Their Background   80

5. **Interpreting Standardized Test Results**   107

Educational Statistics Used by Teachers in Getting
    to Know Their Children   107
The Use of Standardized Tests to Ascertain
    Instructional Levels   126

6. **Improving Evaluation and Reporting of
Pupil Progress and Promotion**   133

Developing Effective Measures   134
Understanding Promotional Policies   154

7. **Recognizing the Need for Creativity**   161

Creativity Is the Teacher's Responsibility   161
Children's Need for Opportunities to Share
    Creative Efforts   172

PART TWO

CHAPTER
8. **Developing More Effective Work-Study
Skill Patterns**   187

New Responsibilities for the Modern Teacher   187
Types of Work-Study Skill Activities   199

9. **Meeting Individual and Group Needs in
the Field of Reading**   213

An Overview of Reading Instruction   213
Providing for Individual Differences in Reading
    Through Subgrouping   227
The Nature of the Reading Lesson   243
Individualizing the Reading Process   252

10. **Developing Handwriting Skills**   267

   Setting the Stage for Writing Proficiency   268
   Helping Children to Become More Proficient
       Manuscript and Cursive Writers   277

11. **Improving Spelling Techniques**   294

   Elementals of Teaching Spelling   294
   Individualizing the Teaching of Spelling   301

12. **Meeting Individual and Group Needs
    in Mathematics**   317

   Children's Reactions to Arithmetic and the Need
       to Stimulate Them   317
   Setting the Stage for Arithmetic Instruction
       by Grouping Pupils   326
   Meeting the Mathematical Needs of Children with
       Different Learning Abilities   335

13. **Helping Children Discover the World
    of Science**   349

   Implications for Instruction   349
   Updating Elementary School Science   363

14. **Meeting Individual and Group Needs in
    Social Studies**   374

   Defining Social Studies   374
   Unit Teaching—One Approach to
       Individual Differences   375
   Meeting Individual Needs by Approaches Other
       Than Unit Teaching   394
   Helping Pupils Find Themselves Through
       Social Studies   397

   BIBLIOGRAPHY   409

   INDEX   417

Figures

CHAPTER 4

FIGURE 1.   First, Second, and Third Choices for Girls in Grade 6.   103

FIGURE 2.   First, Second, and Third Choices for Boys in Grade 6.   104

CHAPTER 6

FIGURE 1.   Areas Included in a Modern Report Card Designed to Show Basic Skills Taught.   151

CHAPTER 9

FIGURE 1.   The Reading Tree.   218

CHAPTER 10

FIGURE 1.   Forming Manuscript Letters.   282

CHAPTER 13

FIGURE 1.   The Problem-solving Method.   356

Tables

CHAPTER 1

TABLE 1. Patterns of School Organization in the United States Extending from the Ungraded Schools of the 1830s to the Graded Schools of Today   22

CHAPTER 2

TABLE 1. A Comparison Between Block Scheduling and Flexible Scheduling   62

CHAPTER 4

TABLE 1. Planning a Program of Education for Intermediate Grade Children Based on Recognition of Their Needs and Stages of Mental, Physical, Social, and Emotional Development   82

TABLE 2. Pupil Reactions to Parents' Behavior   86

CHAPTER 5

TABLE 1. A Descriptive Classification of Intelligence Quotients   109

TABLE 2. Grade Level Expectancy for Given Mental Ages   112

TABLE 3. Reading Ages and Grade Equivalents for Pupils with Above-average Intellectual Quotients   121

TABLE 4. Mental Age–Grade Conversion Table for Children with Average Potential   123

TABLE 5. Estimating Reading Expectancy Level Based Upon Refined Measure   125

CHAPTER 6

TABLE 1. Sample Marking Codes Used on Report Cards   137

TABLE 2.   Establishing Ability Levels for Pupils   *143*

CHAPTER 9

TABLE 1.   Reading Skills Taught in a Sound Developmental Reading Program   *216*

TABLE 2.   Guidelines for Teachers Who Must Subscribe to Grade Standard Restrictions   *223*

TABLE 3.   Activities of Children in Sixth Grade During Reading Instruction   *232*

TABLE 4.   A Guide for Teachers in Identifying Appropriate Reading Levels   *235*

TABLE 5.   A Typical Informal Reading Inventory   *236*

TABLE 6.   A Composite List of Oral and Silent Reading Deficiencies   *240*

CHAPTER 10

TABLE 1.   Paper Standards for Elementary School Children   *276*

TABLE 2.   Standards for Good Handwriting in Grades 1 Through 8   *287*

CHAPTER 11

TABLE 1.   Study-Guide Questions to Help Pupils Study Words Independently   *308*

TABLE 2.   Rinsland's 100 Most Commonly Used Spelling Words   *312*

TABLE 3.   100 Words Most Often Misspelled by Children in the Elementary Grades   *313*

TABLE 4.   Fitzgerald's Master List of 220 Spelling Demons, a Useful Core Vocabulary for Children's Writing   *314*

CHAPTER 13

TABLE 1.   What Children Learn from Scientific Method and Attitude   *356*

CHAPTER 14

TABLE 1.   Typical Outlines for a Unit of Work   *378*

TABLE 2.   Types of Classifications of Learning Skills in Social Studies Textbooks   *403*

Individualizing Instruction in the Elementary School

Introduction:
The Challenge of Teaching

The cardinal tenet of American education is to provide a comprehensive education for *all* children. The increasing birth rate and the widespread acceptance of the school's role have made this challenge a formidable one in the conventional elementary schools in America. Educators have recognized for some time that the graded elementary school *fails* to meet the educational needs of the wide variety of children found in the typical elementary classroom. Ability grouping or homogeneous grouping is often recommended as a solution to this perplexing problem. Popular in the 1920s and 1930s, less favored in the 40s and 50s, homogeneous grouping is again being championed in the mid-1960s.

During the closing years of the nineteenth century a number of leading educators began to see dangers in the patterns of school organization which had become commonplace. There were advantages to be found in the graded school which defied all attempts to break away from it. Parents and teachers alike found a security in the compartmentalization of the curriculum that has defied numerous attacks upon it.

Modern attempts to provide for individual differences in the classroom may be seen in the various parts of the country in the nongraded school. Unfortunately, most of these new programs tend to center around reading, especially in the primary school. One can find a few scattered nongraded intermediate or middle schools plus a small handful of nongraded junior high and senior high schools. These schools bravely operate under the banner of nongradedness, but thousands of other teachers are working diligently to individualize their programs to minimize claims that their students will be frustrated by the lockstep of mass teaching and a fixed curriculum.

In some schools teachers can be found who actually treat boys and girls as individuals and try to meet their educational needs through a one-to-one relationship. One of the best illustrations of this can be found in the individualized reading program, where classes of children continue to bear grade labels but teachers guide individual students in learning activities usually taught at lower or upper learning levels of the elementary school curriculum. This type of teaching often resembles that found in small rural schools where grade lines are nonexistent for the most part.

Since boys and girls have many common interests and needs, teachers are able to break with the concept of mass education without going to the extreme of individualization by bringing together children who are ready for a particular stage of learning. Subgrouping, or clustering, of children for instruction is fairly commonplace in some parts of the country. Yet, those who speak of "grouping" may not be referring to the same approach used for individualizing instruction.

Grouping and Scheduling

Ability or homogeneous grouping is often referred to in literature or educational circles as a solution to the problem of individual differences. Homogeneous grouping generally refers to the assignment of boys and girls to different classrooms on the basis of a common trait or characteristic. In many schools reading achievement may be the basis. However, principals in other schools may attempt to form homogeneous groups on the basis of innate ability or a culmination of factors which should narrow the range of achievement in the classroom, thereby making it easier for the teacher to meet the needs of individual students. During its early period of prominence, homogeneous grouping found favor at the junior and senior high school levels, but more recently elementary school teachers have turned to homogeneous grouping as a solution to the wide range of differences commonly found in the average classroom. Their argument centers around a belief *that teaching should be easier and children should learn better* if grouping provides for a separation of the faster learners from the average and the slow learners in a particular grade.

Effective teachers have been trying to differentiate instruction for many years, but many of them favor the organization of classes on a heterogeneous basis rather than a homogeneous basis. Homogeneity is generally recognized by the practice of subdividing the class for instruction in *different* subject fields. While primary grade teachers have been grouping children in reading for years, the general concept of *subgrouping* has seldom been understood or practiced in the intermediate and secondary school levels. It is here where wide ranges of differences in achievement and interest became a threat to the teacher attempting to divide classes into subgroups. It is at this point that teachers, regardless of whether students have been assigned to them on a heterogeneous or homogeneous basis, must consider their role as instructors and strive for *reasonable,* teachable groups.

Individually, teachers may resort to multiple texts, mixed texts, and unit teaching. Collectively, they may work as teaching teams or in a framework that permits cross-grade grouping or a nongraded approach. How far they go depends upon the philosophy of education supported by the entire school staff. Thus, continuous progress must carry with it the implication that some students will complete the work of a given grade or class in less than a chronological year while other students will require more than a year.

This concept carries with it the implication that up to a fourth of a class or grade may complete the traditional thirteen-year (kindergarten plus 12 grades) curriculum in less than thirteen years unless something is done to retard pupil progress. One solution advocated in some schools may be described in terms of "enrichment." This all-inclusive term may be interpreted as "marking time" by some pupils, but it can also mean new doorways to the world of knowledge. In the latter sense the students take part in what may be described as a truly broadened curriculum which provides challenges and new approaches to the world of modern man.

Many teachers have successfully worked within the confines of a structured graded curriculum through the use of units of study. Actually, the broad resource unit gives teachers latitude to recognize individual competencies and interest without fear that students will be frustrated by involvement in activities which may be too difficult for their accomplishment quotient. The unit permits accomplished grouping without the homogeneous or heterogeneous labels, but an effective program of this type calls for careful planning by the teacher, a wide variety of instructional materials, plus the teacher's ability to identify the varying needs of the students assigned to her and then provide the instruction necessary to meet these needs and match the pupils' different response patterns.

The authors recognize the differences that exist in teaching philosophies as well as in school organization patterns; however, the book will attempt to bring about a greater unity by stressing the need for a consistent educational philosophy among teachers who represent grade or school divisions. Good teachers have always made use of a variety of techniques to meet the basic needs of their children. However, the school organization patterns have frequently worked against them. This is where a common philosophy along with a flexible school organization becomes essential. For example, many schools assign students to teachers in blocks which remain fixed for the day. A number of factors may go into the decision to assign a student to a class section, but one criterion will not suffice for a full program of study.

Some educators are concerned about grouping plans that keep the children together for all subjects because children from low socio-economic levels tend to end up in the lower level class sections. This results in a form of segregation that follows social, economic, and racial lines as well as academic and intellectual lines. Thus block scheduling, when tied in with homogeneous grouping, tends to foster segregation.

Most teachers will subscribe to the principle of fostering creativity in their classrooms, but much that falls into the realm of the creative tends to be highly individual. This means that the setting for learning must encourage individual or small group activity, regardless of whether pupils are assigned to class sections heterogeneously or homogeneously. The day must provide large blocks of time for some creative activities as well as experiences which excite the imagination or provide background for creative thought and action.

The true test of an effective school organization will ultimately be reflected in what transpires in the classroom. What teachers do when they are with their pupils is the important issue. If they know the nature of their children and their stages of growth, they can plan a program of effective school experiences. If teachers will make the effort to identify pupil needs in stages of readiness for learning, the ultimate end should be purposeful activity on the part of teacher and learner, and an end to what may be considered as a wasteful expenditure of teacher and student time and energy. In today's world we cannot afford a "shotgun" approach to education because each boy or girl currently in our primary grades will spend a portion of his life in the twenty-first century. As a result, each individual student must acquire a full and rich background in knowledge plus a command of the functional skills which will help him cope with the vast changes anticipated in tomorrow's world.

Challenges for Tomorrow

There is an attempt in every society to hang on to its past and to protect itself in the present. We are currently concerned with ourselves and what we believe in, but we must also be concerned with the perpetuation of what we believe in. This great responsibility of perpetuating heritage, of broadening knowledge, of creating conditions leading to critical thinking, of shaping marketable skills becomes the challenge of the classroom teacher.

The school is a unity of experiences. It is the "thinking and doing" battleground of ideas involving personalities from all corners of the community. The school becomes the unification process for creating quality education for quality children, regardless of the children's social, racial, or economic levels. The school becomes the center for personal success and for personal failure.

And this is the challenge—the challenge of boys and girls and their teacher-guides working together, planning together, thinking together, and doing together those selected experiences that form the elementary curriculum. It is the challenge also of preserving the identity of the individual in a mass society that leans toward conformity.

The cornerstone to quality education and a teacher's personal challenge of teaching lies in commitment. It is the very first principle of quality education for, without commitment, the efforts of children and their dedicated teachers can become a wasteland of misguided effort. The question of educational funds, adequate instruction materials, and competent personnel are secondary factors in the challenge of quality education, for the lack of commitment will breed the lack of these other necessary resources.

We have now reached the crossroads of decision in American education. The Elementary and Secondary Education Act and the Higher Education Act passed in 1965 by Congress have indicated to the American people the national commitment to education. State legislators are now recognizing education as the foremost state problem. National, state, and local teacher organizations are becoming unified in their efforts to champion quality education in every community.

Thus the instructional challenge now falls to the teacher. The teacher must choose whether to remain part of the problem—by using sterile and traditional teaching methods and materials inconsistent with new discoveries in the field of learning and human behavior—or to *elect to become part of the solution*—by adopting new teaching and grouping techniques, using new and varied instructional materials, and developing thinking and creativity in children rather than memorization and routine.

The ideas presented in this book become meaningless unless they produce action. This action must be in the form of experimentation and solution, and the daily challenge of developing an *attitude of inquiry* in children which will be rewarding and continuous.

Each teacher should frequently re-examine her goals and values, her purposes and objectives, and her philosophy in a world that is changing daily. Perhaps she should ask herself these questions:

1. *Is it not true* . . . that quality education means the most out-

standing experiences that we can provide for our children: instructional, social, psychological, and emotional?

2. *Is it not true* . . . that quality education means quality teachers who are perceptive, intelligent, alert, creative, committed, and professional in their experiences with children, parents, and other teachers?

3. *Is it not true* . . . that outstanding school experiences, initiated by outstanding teachers, will produce boys and girls of vision, understanding, insight, appreciation, and in fact, "world" men and women who can cope successfully with the discoveries and the problems of our scientific future?

4. *And is it not true* . . . that the alternative to the world man is no man at all?

The challenge begins with you.

one

CHAPTER **1**

Regimentation in
Graded Elementary Schools

There are many critics of our modern school system. Some would like to have it resemble school systems in other countries. These critics see qualities in foreign education which are not found in ours. However, they sometimes forget that our schools evolved to meet some basic needs of Americans, that we are the nation which we are *because* of our schools. Much that we hold precious in American life today can be traced back to the development of our American graded school system. If we look at our schools as separate units, it is easy to see where changes can and should be made. But if one looks at them as a whole, we must admit that no country duplicates what we have for an educational system. Our schools are not perfect. Many of them are still "evolving," which means that educators are still trying to resolve issues which were controversial over a century ago. The elementary school came into existence after many struggles. Once a pattern had been established, regimentation set in.

Much of the controversy over our modern schools develops because educators are struggling to break away from this regimentation. Different philosophies of education and of living are involved. What to teach, whom to teach, and how to teach are questions which are not easily resolved, because we are living in a different world than our forebears lived in. Today, education is an essential for both individual and national survival. Therefore, the role of the elementary school must be looked at in the light of the problems of living in a new type of social, political, and economic world. Children receive a foundation in the elementary school which will influence their whole pattern of living for the rest of their lives! This means that the curriculum which they face, along with the way it is presented to them, must be considered a continuation of the evolutionary process which began so long ago.

The Evolution of the Graded School: A New Frontier in Education

The graded school system which came into existence with the opening of the Quincy Grammar School in 1848 had come a long way since the early colonial period. Its uniqueness was the result of a revolution in the way people lived, acted, and thought, based upon various political, economic, and social changes which had occurred in a short number of years. While many Americans like to point with pride to the early interest in public education, as expressed by the Puritans who established our first common schools and grammar schools through the "Old Deluder Satan Act" of Massachusetts in 1647, the fact remains that thousands of soldiers who fought for independence under Washington's leadership had never learned to read or write. The American Revolution did more than free a people from restrictive political and economic bonds. It set forces into motion that were to free men from the shackles of ignorance throughout the rapidly expanding young nation.

Before the American Revolution, schools were few and restrictive. New England still had its town schools, but everyone did not go to them for an education. In Virginia and in the South, educational opportunities were not available to those who did not belong to the upper classes. Children from higher levels of the social order usually had tutors or went to England for their education. Children from the lower classes could prepare for the trades through an apprenticeship system. Theoretically, this was a means of providing for the children of the very poor, the orphans, and the illegitimate. Parents and masters of apprentices in both the North and the South had the obligation of seeing that these children could read and understand the principles of religion and the laws of the country, but the primary purpose of the early colonial statutes was economic or vocational, since artisans and workers were needed throughout the colonies.

During this period education was primarily a church and family responsibility, with an occasional assist from private individuals who sponsored schools as a philanthropic endeavor. The schools were patterned after practices found in England where free education for all was unknown. While some laws called for the establishment of grammar schools, the lack of interest in education was evident in the way people evaded the law with random building of schools. For a long time the basic teaching tool was the "Catechism" or a Bible. In New England, the Puritans did stress the importance of reading since it was essential if people were to understand the word of God. Many parents and teachers tried to teach children to read, but failed because the children could not obtain the reading proficiency necessary to understand the prose style of the Bible. Children needed more preliminary reading experiences, but they lacked the reading materials to build a vocabulary or facility for reading.

Today's critics of the reading program in our schools had their counterparts in the homes and schools of the seventeenth century. Something was remiss in the early schools. Children were constantly failing to show progress in reading even when they had the assistance of such teaching aids as the *Hornbook*, the *Battledoor*, and one or more *Catechisms* before they were introduced to the Bible. The *Catechism* was a basic teaching tool throughout the colonies. Children learned to read all the questions and answers. They learned to copy it word for word, and they memorized the answers to the questions to absorb the prevailing religious doctrine. The *Catechism* was the primer of that period of history. An educational revolution took place in 1690 with the printing of a new teaching aid, namely, the *New England Primer*. While this new textbook was still religious in its content and included much that had been used before to teach the children to read, it had an appeal which made it the "best seller" of its day.

In the span of a century and a half, at least 3 million copies of the *New England Primer* were sold. It found its way into almost every home in the colonies and was used in the schools and churches. It did not guarantee success in reading for all who possessed a copy, but it was a step forward. The book was adorned with illustrations to give meaning to such common words as "apple," "cat," "dog," "king," "lion," "lamb," "top." Rhyming passages were illustrated to promote interest and to give greater understanding. Children were introduced to the letters of the alphabet and some syllabification procedures, but there was no controlled vocabulary. Within a few days after starting to read the new book, children were exposed to two- and three-syllable words. Since there was little understanding by the learner, reading success frequently consisted largely of name calling and repetition of words or a series of words. In learning to read the *New England Primer*, the children were given only one instructive bit of advice, "Memorize these four lines." Despite its limitations—the contrast between the new book and other texts of the time—teachers adopted it for their beginning reading text in all schools in the colonies except those under the direct control of the Church of England. It soon replaced the old *Hornbook* and remained as the basic beginning reader for over 125 years in the schools of the Dissenters and Lutherans. Numerous imitations were made, but none of them had the appeal of the original. For over a century the *New England Primer* was a basic tool for the teaching of reading, writing, and spelling, although its value began to diminish by the middle of the eighteenth century with the decline of much of the religious fervor of the previous century.

EMERGENCE OF THE TEXTBOOK

Prior to the American Revolution the schools used teaching techniques and textbooks which had been transported to the colonies. There was nothing which could be truly called "American" about the colonial schools until a few decades after the battles of Lexington and Concord. The outbreak of war between the colonies and the mother country was a mortal blow to education. Schools were burned and destroyed, teachers became a nonexistent commodity, and money for education disappeared. Suddenly, all the language books, the spellers, the basic textbooks which were used in the grammar schools and other schools disappeared from the market. The war curtailed the financial support for some of the colleges and most of the early parochial and charity schools, but even where money was available, it was impossible to secure textbooks since they had all been written and printed in England.

The lack of textbooks was a blow to the postwar educators who survived the period of economic, social, and political upheaval which resulted from the conflict with England, but American ingenuity came to the foreground and the catastrophe led to the development of new concepts of education and new types of schooling. Change was to come slowly for educators, but a start was made with the writing of new books which were American in both format and authorship. In 1783 a young Connecticut school teacher published one of the first distinctly American textbooks. Webster's new book was a combination spelling book and reader. It was easier to follow than the classic *New England Primer* or Dilworth's *A Guide to the English Tongue.* New moral reading lessons were substituted for the English prayers. American historical and geographic terms replaced English words used by Dilworth, so the new book had a unifying effect on the language which was taught in the schools for several generations. As Noah Webster's *Blue Back Speller* went from one printing to another, other American educators began to use their talents to help educate our youth through the writing of new textbooks. Many of them tried to imitate Webster's *Speller,* but none of them could match his in popularity.

Later, Webster wrote what has been called America's first school reader. The book, *An American Selection,* contained patriotic orations of early Americans including Hancock, Ames, Livingston, and Barlow. While few of today's pupils would find enjoyment in this reader, it was considered in its day a book which molded character and instilled in the minds of its readers the meaning of the "new democracy." While popular, its fame was not as lasting as Webster's *Speller.* Caleb Bingham's *American Precepter,* which was a graded reading book, reached a wider audience than Webster's reader. In 1806 Bingham published an advanced *Reader* which included more interesting reading selections, such as poetry and prose which could be read for enjoyment or declamation.

The number of textbooks increased rapidly, though for several decades there was a shortage of books in the increasing number of schools. However, the new textbooks gave new meaning and life to traditional subjects and led to the introduction of new subjects and a new type of teaching. Education was no longer dominated by the strong religious motives which had been popular during the first part of the eighteenth century. For the first time there was an interest in the preservation of man's freedom and individuality. Education for the masses began to assume a new importance. The schools became a means of preserving the new democratic form of government which was struggling for recognition.

INDIVIDUALIZED INSTRUCTION IN THE
POST-REVOLUTIONARY PERIOD

Modern educators who advocate a greater individualization of pupil instruction are not trying to return to the type of schooling commonplace before and after the American Revolution in the ungraded schools of the city, town, and frontier villages. While the dearth of textbooks in colonial times was partially responsible for the individualized teaching in the schools, it was not a strong reason for its continuance after 1800. In the earlier schools teachers never had enough books. Pupils shared meager materials. Memory and drill became the avenues of learning. The teacher made assignments, and the pupils memorized the materials until it was time to recite back what they had studied. Usually, learning consisted of studying questions and memorizing the answers. At that time understanding or comprehension was not considered important in the learning process.

For many years the teacher was a person who heard recitations. Each recitation was an individual lesson. Theoretically, this procedure should have helped the teacher meet the problem of individual differences, but when one considers the large numbers of students who were literally clamoring for a chance to recite, the amount of individual attention given to pupils was negligible. If a pupil needed special help, he could not obtain it because time was a limiting factor. Pupils who did not memorize assignments went back to their seats for another period of memory work, and then waited hopefully for a turn at re-reciting the answers to the teacher.

As long as the schools remained reading and writing schools, teachers could cope with their problems; but increasing enrollments and additional subjects made the teacher's role too complex. Schooling began to be a meaningless affair with pupils waiting in idleness for an opportunity to tell the teacher what they had learned from their text-books. The teachers were ready for a change, but they were startled when they heard about a new approach to teaching. Jesse Olney gave them food for thought when he wrote a new geography and atlas (1828) which proved to be easy on the child. As one of Pestalozzi's followers, he advocated having teachers introduce children to geography through a study of the known world. He insisted that children begin with a study of their own town or community. With leadership from men like Olney, teaching techniques began to change.

The movement from individual recitations to class recitations was another revolutionary step, but it was handicapped by the continuance of the ungraded school form of organization. As long as children continued to be assigned to the teacher en masse, the teacher remained a taskmaster who made individual assignments and heard individual recitations. Under the pressure of time and work, the teachers began to rely upon having older pupils hear the lessons of younger pupils. Finally, assistant teachers, largely women, were brought in to relieve the master of some responsibilities. The women assistants were expected to teach the youngest children in the class or the beginning children, thus freeing the teacher to work with older pupils or more advanced students. This division of labor was a forward step toward the adoption of a graded school and had its origin in the city schools, although the practice of using older pupils to teach younger pupils is still not uncommon in today's rural schools.

RISE OF THE MONITORIAL SCHOOL

Education by slow, individualized teacher-pupil recitation was not very popular. People did not like to dig deeper into their pockets to support schools of this type, but a break came with the introduction of the new monitorial school which made education inexpensive by doing away with the individualized form of teaching. Group instruction became the mode, and for the first time people began to support common, public schools. A revolution in American education began in

1806 with the opening of the first Lancastrian or monitorial school in New York City.

A few years earlier, Dr. Andrew Bell and Joseph Lancaster had become the proponents of a type of schooling which was based upon the use of pupil monitors, who assisted teachers in schools which were too poor to pay for additional teachers. Their ideas led to the establishment of monitorial schools throughout England because it was soon found to be both cheap and effective. In the United States, Lancaster's monitorial schools spread like wildfire. Private societies started new monitorial schools as fast as teachers could be trained to teach in them. The first public schools of Philadelphia (1818) reflected the Lancastrian influence. The new plan made it possible to bring together hundreds of pupils at little expense since a single teacher with numerous pupil monitors could teach from 300 to 1,000 pupils. For a time it looked as though a perfect method of educating children had been developed.

Though the monitorial schools flourished, all was not perfect in them. The discipline was strict and pupils kept busy, with little time for idleness. Pupils who finished the work of a section and passed an examination were promoted to another class. The schools were organized on a military scale with monitors checking on monitors. The schools became centers of activities and operated with considerable noise, although successful master teachers were able to demand instant attention and absolute quiet from every pupil and monitor in the room. One can visualize the factory-like appearance of a monitorial school where hundreds of children worked at their seats or clustered at stations along the wall for a lesson with a pupil monitor.

Lancastrian schools brought education to thousands of children who would never have had an opportunity to receive any. Once these schools were established, there was no turning back, and more schools led to a recognition that the public had to do more to support public education. Educational problems provoked controversy and discussions which led to the development of a graded school system as a means of improving the education given to the children.

CHANGES THAT INFLUENCED THE PATTERN
OF AMERICAN EDUCATION

The colonial and nationalist periods were transition periods during which old ways of life and thinking were modified. Public education was slow in coming until vestiges of an early social caste system could be eliminated. From 1790 to 1848, the young nation was changing from one which had been largely rural to one which began to feel the impact of cities. This ruralization was often a barrier to the elimination of the ungraded school. New innovations in education came largely as the result of experiments in the schools which were opened in the cities, where young labor movements had begun to press for a system of public education. Many changes had to occur before a pattern of education could evolve which modern educators would approve and follow. Some of the following factors influenced the pattern American education was to take.

1. Man's views concerning the nature of children had to change. Modern teachers try to recognize children as individuals by respecting their wishes and trying to avoid thwarting them or frustrating them. This was not the case two or three centuries ago. Child psychology and the nature of learning, as we understand it, did not exist. At that time children existed in a world which depicted them as necessary evils.

2. Disciplinary measures reflected a way of life which was passing. Many children in the early days of our nation grew up in homes where they learned the meaning of love and kindness. However, men and women who lived in a world which accepted slavery, tolerated branding of criminals or condoned their being put to death publicly, and put wrongdoers in a pillory or stocks for mistreatment by anyone who cared to abuse them tolerated a type of discipline which modern parents would never condone.

3. The public had to accept the concept that girls were educable. The concept of educational opportunity for girls was unacceptable for a great part of the nineteenth century. For a long time parents gave girls their first rudiments of education. A few private schools helped give some of them a taste of refinement—perhaps reading, crocheting, some music, dancing—but mostly things to help them become better managers of the home.

4. The influence of the church upon early schools diminished. New England's first schools owed their existence to an early church-state concept of life. Education was desired as a means of interpreting the Bible. At times these first schools were barriers to people who professed a different belief or religion. For a time the state was the representative of the church, but a break came when a division of responsibility for schools was established. Gradually the civil authorities took over taxation for civil responsibilities, of which schooling was one.

With the separation of the church and the state and the opposition of the Founding Fathers to a strong central government, the ultimate control over the newly formed public schools became a responsibility of the individual states.

5. Equality meant the end of the caste system. For many years the effects of an old European type social caste system were to be felt in America even though the Constitution seemed to have settled that issue. As late as 1860, one could find a general resistance to publicly

supported schools because many people preferred to send children to private schools where social barriers eliminated the chance that a child would have to mix with lower class children.

6. The extension of male suffrage created a new interest in education. Andrew Jackson's arrival in the White House was a turning point for the common man. Up to this period the right to vote had been restricted in all but a few states to men who owned property. Full suffrage came into existence in the frontier states and with it came a demand for the end to property and other restrictions on voting in other states.

7. Children had to learn to read before they could start school. During the colonial and much of the nationalist periods, children were not allowed to enter school until they had learned to read. Where they acquired this skill was inconsequential, as long as they could meet the requirement on entry. This led to a starting age of about eight in cities like Boston, Hartford, Philadelphia, New York, and Baltimore until the early 1800s.

MCGUFFEY'S READERS PLAYED AN IMPORTANT ROLE

Textbook writers were numerous during the early 1800s but many of the books published were poorly written, and up to about 1860 there was no such thing as a uniform set of books in most classrooms. With parents purchasing textbooks at will or children using hand-me-downs, a teacher could find almost every pupil possessing a different book for a given subject, making group instruction difficult. In an attempt to eliminate poor texts and as an aid in the classification of children, state school authorities compiled recommended lists of books for selected subjects. One of the most popular and universally recommended sets of books was the McGuffey *Readers*.

Since some early writers had tried to set the stage for the graded school with the development of so-called graded readers, it is difficult to see how or why the McGuffey *Readers* became as popular as they did shortly after they arrived on the scene. One answer seems to be that McGuffey was able to appeal to a new group of people with materials they could understand and appreciate. Other writers had borrowed heavily from England's writers for stories and illustrations, which meant that their books lacked the natural appeal of McGuffey's. He wrote and collected stories which introduced boys and girls to the world about them, replacing stories of death and the grave with those which helped children visualize the beauty of the fields, the streams, the garden, and the woods.

McGuffey's *First* and *Second Readers* met a basic need in the new small schools of the West when they came out in 1836, although many

The first free kindergarten, established by the Society for Ethical Culture, New York City, 1878.

of the children in these schools did not remain in school long enough to make use of the *Third* and *Fourth Readers* which were published in 1837. McGuffey's *First Reader* was quite difficult since children were supposed to know how to read when they started school. There was some question about the need for the *Primer* which came out in 1838, but this was revised and made into two separate volumes, with the *Pictorial Electric Primer* becoming the *First Reader* in the revisions of 1857. The books were revised and a *Fifth Reader* was added in 1844, followed in 1857 by a *Sixth Reader* and a *High School Reader* to give teachers and children a collection of progressively more difficult reading materials which could be adapted to the new graded school which was beginning to take form. A *Spelling Book* completed the series which was to influence the lives of more than half of the children who attended school up to the turn of the century. Rival writers and their eastern publishers fought to keep the McGuffey *Readers* from becoming too popular in New England and the East, but they could not prevent their spread through the western and southern states.

The McGuffey *Readers* did not bring about the graded school system, but they gave it a big boost. Their popularity led to the elimination of many books of poor quality which had been retarding education. As parents bought books, brothers and sisters studied them in turn. They knew what was going to be used as a book when one reached a particular stage of learning. Teachers with vested textbook interests found it difficult to resist the pressure to use the McGuffey *Readers,* so there was a unifying of textbooks in many school systems. McGuffey's new methods of teaching and the natural appeal of the selections used in the textbooks made a lasting mark on education which time has not been able to erase.

SCHOOL DIVISIONS WERE FORMED

From 1830 to 1850, city schools began to form a school organization around a number of distinct schools or school divisions. Common labels were often given to a school division, but this did not mean that they were alike since some school divisions duplicated the work taught in other schools or overlapped in some academic areas. Table 1 shows some of the classifications which were found in different parts of the country. At the top of the educational ladder were the colleges with the pupils feeding into them from the new public high schools which were replacing the old academies and the last of the Latin grammar schools. The initial reading and writing schools became known as the "common" or "grammar" schools in some communities, and in others as the "intermediate" or "junior" school. As the "primary" school became popular, it was added to the bottom of the new educational structure to give communities a seven-, eight-, or nine-year elementary school system.

Teachers in the large ungraded primary schools of this period began to divide their pupils into instructional levels. In Boston, the primary program called for six instructional levels, with each teacher in charge of a group of pupils, teaching the full six instructional levels extending from the youngest beginner to the more mature pupils who were getting ready for admission to the grammar school. Even with these early attempts at grade classification, teachers had problems which interfered with attempts to bring continuity to their teaching—for example, absenteeism. Large numbers of children would not attend school for days at a time, thus disrupting any plans to keep children together. Again, there was the lack of uniform textbooks. And the books, when they had them, were designated as beginner or advanced books before publishers began to try to grade them in a sequential order the way McGuffey did. Discipline was a problem in the large rooms, so teachers made continued use of harsh methods and often beat or mistreated their children. Teachers found themselves wasting time, children were miserable, and the achievement or progress of individual children tended to be slow.

Educators like Henry Barnard and Horace Mann were disturbed by these school conditions. They objected to the placement of 200 or more

TABLE 1

Patterns of School Organization in the United States Extending from the
Ungraded Schools of the 1830s to the Graded Schools of Today

	Colleges and Universities	*Colleges and Universities* *Graduate School* *College* *Junior College*	
	THE EARLY PERIOD (1830–1860)	**THE LATER PERIOD** (1860–1910)	**THE PRESENT PERIOD** (1910 TO PRESENT)
The District School or Ungraded Rural School	Secondary School Types: 1. High school (3–4 yr.) 2. Academies (3–4 yr.) 3. Latin grammar schools (5–6)	American senior high school (4 yr.) Grade 12, Grade 11, Grade 10, Grade 9	Senior high school (3–4–6 yr.)
	Upper Elementary School Types: 1. Grammar schools (3-4-5-6-7) 2. Common schools (6-7-8) 3. Master's schools (4-6) 4. Middle school (4-6) 5. Senior school (3) 6. Intermediate school (3) 7. Writing school (3-4) 8. Reading school (3-4)	Grade 8, Grade 7, Grade 6, Grade 5, Grade 4, Grade 3, Grade 2, Grade 1	Junior high school (2–3 yr.) Elementary school Grades 1–6, 1–8, K–6, K–8 or Elementary schools with experimental (a) ungraded primary, (b) ungraded intermediate grades (Grades 4-5-6)
	Lower Elementary School Types: 1. Intermediate school (3) 2. Junior school (3) 3. Secondary school (2) 4. Second grade (2)		
	Primary school (2-3-4)	Kinder	garten*
			Nursery school†

* Many schools are incorporating the kindergarten as a part of the elementary school, making a K–6 or a K–8 school.

† A few school systems now operate their own nursery schools, but most nursery schools are still operated on a private basis.

pupils in a classroom. They did not like the way children were taught or treated. Horace Mann was one of several educators who visited schools in Europe and reported on their advanced type of education. In his annual report of 1844, Mann praised German schools and recommended the classification of children into some form of graded school system. He advocated the use of Pestalozzian methods, better trained teachers, intelligent supervision, and a milder form of discipline. While others had criticized American teaching procedures, it wasn't until Mann's *Seventh Report* was printed that the public really became aware of what was going on. Boston teachers disagreed with Mann and issued a reply to his report, but he came back with a rejoinder. The victory belonged to Mann, because many of his recommendations were adopted in Massachusetts and in other states. There are some who attribute the grade system which followed soon afterwards to the ideas brought over from Prussia by Mann and other educators; however, others believe that the grade system was coming into its own, due to changes occurring in various city schools. The inefficiency and duplication of activity in the old ungraded schools of the first half of the nineteenth century could not have survived. So the new graded schools which did come into existence should be classified as truly American, rather than just imitations of European schools.

THE OPENING OF THE QUINCY GRAMMAR
SCHOOL SETS A PATTERN

A number of attempts had been made to classify children into a graded school prior to the opening of the Quincy Grammar School in 1848, but the school organized and built under the direction of John D. Philbrick is considered the blueprint for numerous schools which were to be established as grade schools all over the United States. Up to this point, educators had been floundering under the handicaps of inadequate facilities and too many children. Some forms of graded classes had been started in the Latin schools with the division of children based on their mastery of their Latin readers and grammar. With the addition of new subjects and better textbooks, teachers had begun to divide children into rough groups, using chronological age and pupil progress as the basis.

Philbrick's school was reportedly the result of Mann's recommendations and was unique in many ways. Not only was it erected to provide children and teachers with facilities for teaching in small graded classrooms, but it had individual seats and chairs for pupils. This school became a pattern for new elementary schools. For the first time schools were built four stories high to accommodate the larger number of pupils, and to allow assignment of pupils to different classrooms on a grade basis. Each of the twelve classrooms had seats for 55 pupils and its own cloakroom. The assembly hall on the top floor could accommodate the whole school population.

Division of children into separate schools was eliminated as the new united school was established under the direction of a principal who could give teachers guidance. Six years after the Quincy Grammar School was opened, Boston placed the primary schools under the direction of the grammar school principal. This unifying action and the new pattern of school organization was duplicated everywhere. By 1860 the graded school was virtually universal in city schools and the idea of grading was fairly well accepted in small school systems, although many rural schools were to continue as ungraded schools for some time due to the lack of facilities and pupils.

Early Attempts to Provide for
Individual Differences in the Graded School

The adoption of the graded school and its rapid extension to the most remote rural school was progress, but it was not long before many teachers and school administrators became aware of imperfections in the new schools. The graded school was based upon a *grade standard concept* of education which resulted in frustration for the pupil who learned at a slower rate than his chronological-aged peers. It was soon found to be an obstacle to growth on the part of pupils who could learn at a rapid rate. Because educators recognized the individual differences in children, some of them soon began to look for ways to break away from the regimentation which the graded school had fostered. Unfortunately the grade system had only recently come into its own and was something which could not easily be tampered with. Administrators found strong parent and teacher resistance to innovations, and while some new patterns developed, the changes were not always lasting.

Although the elementary schools of the 1960s are quite different from those of a century ago, the grade standard concept of education is still popular with the general public. However, many communities are now swinging toward a form of nongraded primary or ungraded elementary school in an attempt to meet the challenge of individual differences. Under the grade standard concept a pupil is supposed to master selected skills or complete the study of prescribed material during the course of a school year. *Thus the grade standard becomes a goal for all children.* Each pupil is expected to master the skills and content outlined without too much consideration for his past experiences or intellectual capacity. Frequently, citizen groups get excited when they hear that boys and girls in a fifth grade are not all able to read at the same level or compute with the same facility. "How could a boy get to fifth grade if he is still reading on a third- or fourth-grade level?" A common complaint is made that we need to return to the good old days when such pupils would have repeated the grade until they were ready to do the work of the next grade.

Sorting pupils into grades was a revolutionary step in educational circles, but early educators failed to see the unique nature of children. All children were considered alike in capacity. Pupils who failed to make progress were essentially failures because they would not behave or follow directions. Laziness or a lack of interest were frequent excuses for failures. The diligent scholar would succeed through mere perseverance. There was little recognition of the need to vary the rate or method of instruction for individual pupils. Since imparting knowledge was the chief purpose of education, textbooks became the driving force in the classroom. Education in the 1870s and the 1880s outlined courses of study in great detail, with the textbook frequently becoming the basis for what the teacher taught at a given grade level. The fixed curriculum was the basis for pupil progress. How much work, the nature of the work, the probable time for the various phases of study, and the sequence of skills and knowledge were all prescribed. Success was measured in terms of the pupil's ability to pass oral or written examinations.

ATTEMPTS TO BREAK FROM THE MECHANISTIC PATTERN
OF ELEMENTARY SCHOOL ORGANIZATION

Almost from the inception of the graded elementary school one finds educators who were not satisfied with some phase of it. This led to the introduction of innovations to bring about a school organization which would provide more adequately for the varying needs of pupils and teachers. Some innovations received wide acceptance, while others were classified as passing fads, even though they had a widespread popularity for a time and were accepted as good educational practice in many school systems. Brief descriptions of some of these experiments in school organization and teaching follow:

The St. Louis Plan. William T. Harris, superintendent of schools in St. Louis, encouraged the development of the kindergarten and introduced the teaching of elementary school science. In an attempt to break with the rigidity of the graded school and to facilitate grading and pupil classification, Dr. Harris divided the elementary school year into four quarters of ten weeks each. Bright pupils and rapid learners were able to move into advanced classes at the end of each quarter. The plan which was put into effect in 1868 was the forerunner of semiannual or quarterly promotion plans which were adopted in many other cities.

The Cambridge Plan. Elementary schools of Cambridge, Massachusetts, were reorganized about 1910 to allow bright pupils to progress faster than slow or average learners. Two parallel courses of study were prepared which allowed fast learners to study one-third more work in a given period than average pupils. Thus bright pupils could complete their elementary schooling in six years instead of eight.

Multitrack Grouping. Many school systems attempted to provide for individual differences through multitrack programs; only they went further than Cambridge or St. Louis. In order to meet the needs of slow learners a third track was added. Pupils were then assigned to slow, average, or fast moving classes. Baltimore had a multitrack program about 1898 which did not allow acceleration. This was also true for Santa Barbara. Both programs depended upon three different courses of study, with slow learners following a minimum-essentials program, average students going beyond them, and bright pupils going into extra studies and enriching activities. The program for the gifted was considered a forward step because it took them out of the category of mediocrity.

The Dalton Plan. Hundreds of schools in the United States and thousands of foreign schools have been organized on the Dalton plan. Helen Parkhurst, who introduced the plan in the high school at Dalton, Massachusetts, in 1919, described it as an attempt to socialize the school and keep its life from becoming too mechanical. Soon it was in use in elementary schools starting with the fourth grade, where it extended upward through high school. Grades were not abolished, and the plan could be used with any curriculum. In essence, the Dalton laboratory plan called for the division of the work of several subjects into monthly job classifications. Each job classification was subdivided into twenty days' work per subject. These individual work units would be prepared by the teacher, the pupil, or teacher and pupil working together. At the beginning of the month or twenty-day period, each pupil signed up for a job contract. He was then free to work on the completion of the job at his own rate of speed. He could work in each of several subjects each day, or he could work for an extended period in order to complete the outlined program in that field. There was only one stipulation: He could not start an advanced work program in one subject until he had completed the units outlined for all phases of a job. Bright pupils could finish a "job" in less than twenty days, while slow learners would need additional time, although they were supposed to complete them within the designated twenty-day period.

Morning hours were devoted primarily to academic work; a typical morning program follows:

Period	Time	Nature of Activity
Organization time	15–20 min.	Pupils meet with homeroom teacher to plan day's activities.
Laboratory period	2–3 hr.	Pupils go to subject laboratory to work on job contract. They may go to one or more laboratories to work alone or with teachers who can help them.
Conference time	30–40 min.	Pupils meet daily to discuss a specific part of the job, according to a posted conference schedule by subject. During these periods they can debate, report, or review any work which relates to the subject called in the conference.

Afternoons were reserved for nonacademic studies. Here pupils worked in groups in art, music, physical education, industrial arts, homemaking, and the like.

The Winnetka Plan for Individualizing Instruction. Instruction for each pupil was individualized in Carleton Washburne's school system at Winnetka through a division of the curriculum into two parts: The most important phase of the program called for the establishment of individual work centers about the "common essentials" or the body of knowledge and basic skills which everyone had to master. The second phase provided each pupil with opportunities to be self-expressive along with a chance to contribute something of his own special interests and abilities. In describing the Winnetka plan, Carleton Washburne [14] says:

> Under the first head, come the common essentials—the three R's and similar subject matter. . . . Since every child needs these things, and since every child differs from others in his ability to grasp them, the time and amount of practice to fit each child's needs must be varied.

The day was divided into four quarters, with half the morning and half the afternoon being devoted to the common essentials. A pupil did not go to teachers to recite, but worked out his own program starting with a very simple skill or idea and then worked to higher levels. The course of study was broken into minute learning steps so the pupil could test himself repeatedly until he could show 100 per cent mastery. If the pupil did not master the skill or material, he would go back to restudy, then ask for another test. No pupil was considered a failure, nor was he allowed to skip grades. Grade lines, as such, disappeared. Pupils who completed the prescribed units of a subject for a grade level would be free to continue at higher grade levels though his progress in other subject fields could be a grade or two behind.

When pupils worked on creative or group activities, they were free from predetermined goals. Children were encouraged to contribute their special abilities to this group welfare in such courses as social studies and literature, as well as in art, music, dramatics, newspapers, self-governing assemblies, shopwork, and play activities.

The basic class structure in the Winnetka plan called for heterogeneous grouping with progress in each subject depending upon pupil initiative, ability, and interest. Common essentials were learned through "self-instructional materials." Each pupil kept his own record of progress as a motivating factor. From time to time the teacher worked with individual pupils and with small groups of children, but she was not apt to be found teaching the common essentials on an all-class basis.

The Activity Movement. In the beginning, the "activity" movement seemed to be the answer to those who wanted to do something about the varying needs and abilities of children. For a time it was a threat to the ability grouping movement, but as extremists swung too far to the left, the word "progressive" fell into disrepute. As a result, many outstanding teachers and administrators who could have done something worthwhile for and with children returned to standard classroom procedures which were less controversial.

Many mistakes had been made in the name of homogeneous grouping, so it was a relief to some educators to turn to the activity movement as a partial solution to their problems. Teachers began to move away from the formal teaching with mass sitting and listening and began to bring children together to work on what were called "meaningful activities." Children began to get away from fixed seat activities. Construction work, research, class trips took on new meaning. Teachers were able to demonstrate that these children could take standardized tests and hold their own with students still taught under the old textbook stand-and-recite methods. Growth by slow, average, and rapid learners was evident as children worked collectively and democratically together.

The Platoon School. Many school systems have operated some form of the platoon school initiated by William A. Wirt in Gary, Indiana. The typical platoon school organization calls for the division of children into two sections or platoons, with one platoon using the basic classrooms for the study of the basic academic subjects, while the second platoon is engaged in nonacademic activities in the special classrooms, the auditorium, and the gymnasium.

The Cooperative Group Plan. Under a plan sponsored by James F. Hosic in the early 1920s, teachers worked together under a team chairman. The teachers would jointly plan activities for children from their subject fields to make up a unified learning experience for the children. While the teachers appeared to be mere subject matter specialists, they were actually called "specialists in teaching children." Through their group conferences the teachers were able to develop cooperative programs of work with and for children.

The Batavia Plan. Dissatisfaction with children's progress in the graded school led many school systems to adopt John Kennedy's Batavia plan, which consisted of using special assistant teachers to give slow learners extra help so that everyone could be promoted together semiannually or annually.

The Departmentalized Elementary School. Departmentalization appeals to some teachers because it tends to promote teacher specialization. Usually it is found in secondary schools, but it has been extended down to the primary grades. Recently, some form of departmentalization in the elementary school has been adopted to improve the teaching of reading and arithmetic. Through departmentalization, teachers become subject matter specialists. Theoretically, a teacher should be able to do a better teaching job, because she does not have to diffuse herself trying to teach the whole elementary school curriculum. To meet the criticism that teachers do not know their pupils, many schools require the teaching of two related subjects. By becoming a subject specialist, the teacher is supposed to become familiar with the latest theory or approaches to teaching. Unfortunately, many teachers have become merely subject matter specialists who simplify teaching through using the same basic textbook over and over again regardless of the needs of their pupils. Departmentalization also develops new regimentation, since time becomes a governing factor in the elementary school using it.

REFERENCES

1. Arthur Combs, *The Professional Education of Teachers* (Boston: Allyn and Bacon, 1965).
2. James B. Conant, *Shaping Educational Policy* (New York: McGraw-Hill, 1964).
3. Harry Dunn, *The School Teacher's Manual Containing Practical Suggestions on Teaching and Popular Education* (Hartford, Conn.: Reed and Barber, 1838).
4. Educational Policies Commission, *The Purposes of Education in American Democracy* (Washington, D.C.: National Education Association, 1938).
5. Harry G. Good, *A History of American Education*, 2nd ed. (New York: Macmillan, 1962).
6. Maxine Greene, *The Public School and the Private Vision* (New York: Random House, 1965).
7. Maurie Hillson, *Change and Innovation in Elementary School Organization* (New York: Holt, Rinehart & Winston, 1965).

8. Duane Manning, *The Qualitative Elementary School* (New York: Harper & Row, 1963).
9. Adolph Meyer, *An Educational History of the American People,* 2nd ed. (New York: McGraw-Hill, 1965).
10. Mehdi Nakosteen, *The History and Philosophy of Education* (New York: Ronald Press, 1965).
11. Helen Parkhurst, "The Dalton Plan," *Twenty-fourth Yearbook of the National Society for the Study of Education,* Part II, *Adapting the Schools to Individual Differences* (Bloomington, Ill.: Public School Publishing, 1925).
12. V. T. Thayer, *Formative Ideas in American Education* (New York: Dodd, Mead, 1965).
13. I. N. Thut, *The Story of Education* (New York: McGraw-Hill, 1957).
14. Carleton Washburne, "Burke's Individualized System as Developed at Winnetka," *Twenty-fourth Yearbook of the National Society for the Study of Education,* Part II, *Adapting the Schools to Individual Differences* (Bloomington, Ill.: Public School Publishing, 1925).

CHAPTER 2

Innovations in
Elementary Education

I n spite of rapid technological advances and social, economic, and political revolutions, significant changes in thought tend to come about slowly. However, changes do occur which ultimately alter schools and teaching practices. Some may be very pronounced, but others may be scarcely noticed unless one studies the schools carefully. Furthermore, education goes through periods or cycles in which an idea or practice long since abandoned is resurrected. Sometimes old practices reappear under a different name, or a new twist is added so that the old is scarcely noticed in its new dress. Educational changes are seldom revolutionary, although so-called frontiers of educational thought and action may appear. A new idea or practice may be in operation in a whole school system, but in many instances it is limited to a selected school or number of schools within a system.

The ultimate nature of a school system—its curriculum, its organization, and the type of teaching—is affected by many external forces. Teachers react to national and world tensions as well as to changing conditions or pressures in their own communities. Similarly, some educators are swayed by new practices adopted in other school systems. Some innovations are not scientifically sound, and so have to be tested, modified, and retested before they will stand the pressure of criticism. Then too, changes are resisted by vested interests. Traditional practices and thinking often hold back new ideas which are educationally sound.

Modern schools have been influenced by a number of new concepts about how children learn and the role the school should play in their education. Some of these concepts have been fairly well accepted, although individual teachers frequently do not subscribe to all of them. The fact that educators will not agree to all or part of a new educational pattern can cause the general public confusion over this apparent discord. The conflict may sometimes be only on the surface, but at other times it can be significant, because acceptance or rejection of a concept may mean a difference in basic philosophy that cannot easily be resolved.

New Concepts Develop to Modify Educational Practices

Modern teachers have at their disposal a wide variety of teaching aids to help them do a better job. Audiovisual aids can be of great help if they are used properly to enrich the curriculum and to save hours of labor. Records, film strips, motion pictures, tape recordings, and an ever-increasing number of teaching machines can be used to give depth to a program and to motivate pupils to greater activity. Through careful use of television, children can be taught by specialists in selected fields where a small school would lack the staff or facilities to put on a technical program. Today's textbooks are attractively illustrated and have an appeal that was missing in yesterday's. Through advances in the testing programs teachers can readily determine where children stand in selected fields and can better plan the work in terms of pupil needs. New schools are light and airy, making the teaching environment a pleasurable and stimulating one. With modern movable furniture, teachers can rearrange classrooms to reflect their own personalities and to gain flexibility. Successful teaching in the modern school is often based on the readiness of the teacher to use teaching aids, to make education challenging to pupils, and to use resource people to help her understand her pupils.

Good teaching is more than the use of new materials and equipment, unless one is willing to accept a very narrow interpretation of the meaning of education. Unfortunately, many people conceive of education in just this narrow sense. Essentially, they are chiefly interested in the rapid mastery of basic skills and the accumulation of standard bodies of knowledge. Supporting this view are numerous elementary, secondary, and college teachers. These teachers work steadily and conscientiously at the job of teaching, believing in what they do and resisting the attempts of educators they classify as "theorists" or "progressives" to impose a different type of teaching on the schools.

One finds many of these teachers very satisfied with the teaching of the same classics advertised by the publishers of McGuffey back in 1879. Their teaching methods are only slightly different in the 1960s from the methods used before the turn of the century. They may accept a "gimmick," such as the teaching machine, because it seems like an easy method to cram more facts into their pupils in a shorter period of time. On the surface these teachers may favor some new changes, but they are reluctant to accept real educational advances because they have not prepared themselves to teach such things as the "new science" or the "new mathematics."

Essentially, a school system is as good as its teaching staff. Most teachers want to do the best possible job, but they may not know how to go about improving their procedures unless they receive help from sympathetic supervisors or administrators. If conflicts arise within a school or school system, they may be due to a lack of common agreement on a number of basic concepts of education.

Therefore, let us review the new concepts of education which have helped change or modify educational thinking and practices:

The Belief in Fundamental Education. Teachers must be ready to accept the belief that fundamental education for all children is a prerequisite for survival and success in the modern world. Citizens from one section of the country may get quite concerned about their own educational problems, but may not worry if children in another section of the nation are not receiving quality education. In view of the mobility of Americans, this inequality of educational opportunity can be a serious handicap to everyone. The boy or girl who missed out on his education can be tomorrow's neighbor or employee.

Lip service to quality education is not sufficient. Fundamental education is more than mere textbook education. Something is basically wrong with a nation which allows millions of boys and girls to drop out of school before they terminate a complete educational program. Educators have been partially to blame for many pupil failures in finding success in the schools. Teacher attitudes, as well as ineffective teaching, have helped contribute to the flow of dropouts. Educators who believe in fundamental education must take a new look at what they are offering in the way of group and individual guidance and leadership to pupils as they progress through school.

Recognition of Relation between Interest and Effort. A belief in the importance of interest is one of the educational principles which make modern schools different from old time schools. Modern educators recognize the relationship between pupil effort and interest—an importance that was largely ignored until Herbert and then Dewey recognized that it had a positive effect upon the conduct of the learner. Teachers have learned to capitalize on real interests of children, and where they are lacking to generate interest which then becomes a driving force in the learning situation.

The Structured Curriculum Versus the Child-centered Curriculum. A child-centered curriculum has often resulted from attempts to recognize children's interests. The curriculum may change from day to day, or week to week and be built around their interests. No two classes or grades need be alike, since pupils may not need the same educational experiences. This curriculum is in decided contrast with the structured curriculum of the grade standard school. While good teachers capitalize upon pupil interests, one is less likely to find schools which are fully child-centered. Some educators have attempted to break with the traditionally structured curriculum by developing a teacher-guided type of child-centered curriculum.

Educating Youth for Democracy. Educators are frequently pressured to teach children self-governing principles. This is not new, but many vested interests insist that the schools try to place democracy on a higher plane through a textbook approach. Teaching about people and the problems of living is an essential part of the responsibilities teachers have, but educating youth for democracy is more than reading and talking about it. Sometimes children have to live in a setting where they can work together before there is any real understanding of other children's problems. The authors have seen classes where children did not know who sat behind them because they were dealt with so strictly that they did not dare to turn around. One does not obtain true democracy without giving children opportunities to work together to accept and share responsibilities.

Teaching Children To Think Critically. Educators do not agree on how children learn to think. To some, thinking is a natural process. They believe that one can fill the pupil's mind with facts, figures, and rules, and thinking will develop as a natural outcome of the learning process. On the other hand, there are those who believe in the *experience* approach. Children need to have experiences and must work with problems which have some significance to them. Actually, both approaches are necessary. Children do need a background of data or skill if they are going to progress. At times first-hand experiences are the best way to sense and solve problems, but there are times when secondary experiences can be a time saver.

The Acceptance of the Testing Movement. Modern educators place more and more reliance on a variety of research techniques plus many types of tests in the study of pupil ability and progress. This is a far cry from the attitude of educators at the turn of the century who belittled men like J. M. Rice, an early advocate of testing. For example, Rice was told that one could not measure educational results when he advocated consideration of *how* to teach spelling instead of *the amount* *of time* devoted to the teaching of spelling. Critics of the testing movement still claim that tests fail to have value because of the many intangibles in education. However, the fact remains that the public has been indoctrinated to the point where tests seem to be the ultimate in education.

The Theory of Mental Discipline. During the early twentieth century, research by E. L. Thorndike in the psychology of learning led to a revolution in the thinking of leading educators. For years teachers had been defending a principle known as the theory of mental discipline and the concept of transfer of training. They argued that the harder a subject, the better it was for the pupil. The mere addition, for example, of pictures in Latin textbooks was considered a deterrent to successful teaching because the illustrations made the textbooks too interesting. It took time to get teachers to accept the ideas of Thorndike, and even today one encounters die-hards who still believe that pupils who study one hard subject will do better in another subject because of the disciplining of the mind. While this group is now in a minority, their type of thinking can be a barrier to the acceptance of a different form of teaching and learning.

Recognition of Differences in Children and their Effects on Curriculum. For many years every pupil in a class was presumed capable of doing the work of the grade. Here and there educators protested over the lack of attention given to pupils who, because they were different, did not conform to the common grade standards and the single approach to instruction, but they were islands of light in a great sea of darkness. The great mass of teachers did not recognize individual differences in children until fairly recently.

Educators who have studied differences in children recognize the need to use different approaches. They find that a mass approach often fails to challenge some children, while it frustrates others. Teachers who try to keep children on the same instructional level find that "age" differences create problems. As a result many teachers group pupils homogeneously on the basis of chronological age. When this is done, children tend to go through school without much retardation or acceleration. Individual differences are taken into account through a modification of the curriculum and through differentiation of teaching methods. Other teachers use different approaches to bring children together with common needs. IQ or mental age is one basis for grouping. Progress in reading may be another. However, there is a danger that these bases will lead to a curriculum which is appealing only to one side of the pupil's total growth pattern. As teachers study their children, plan special programs, and use different approaches to cope with problems of unequal growth, they have made teaching a science.

The Changing Nature of the Elementary School

Education in the elementary schools has been characterized by a change in the philosophy of education underlying our schools and the way teachers teach. The elementary school of today is not the same school it was two decades ago. Teachers have many more teaching aids. They can make learning more interesting and more effective when they base their methods upon a knowledge of the "nature of the children." Children are more likely to be recognized as human beings with strong feelings and drives. They have many more opportunities to acquire good work-study habits, because more teachers are interested in a type of teaching which calls for multiple textbooks and references. Also, children today are encouraged to work both independently and cooperatively.

Teachers in many schools are interested in individualizing the teaching process, but they are not going back to the type of individualized teaching found before the start of the graded school. There are times when teachers find it highly desirable to work with boys and girls individually; however, children have many common needs, abilities, and interests which should enable them to share group experiences. So today we are seeing a modified return to the ungraded school.

UNGRADED ELEMENTARY SCHOOLS

A large number of school systems have been exploring the ungraded elementary school concept, but have restricted themselves to the ungraded primary stage. In such school systems children in Grades 1, 2, and 3 of the traditional school are grouped together without grade levels. These ungraded primary groups allow children to make continuous progress through the ungraded unit until it is time for them to move into the intermediate grades. When the children leave the ungraded primary school, they may go into a regular fourth grade or they may advance to a new ungraded unit which extends through the equivalent of Grades 4, 5, and 6. A school which takes children through the primary and intermediate levels without actual grade designations may be called the ungraded elementary school, but the true test of ungradedness will depend upon the philosophy of the teachers as they work with children in the classroom.

Advantages of the Ungraded School. Since many factors influence the achievement or growth of boys and girls, it is not always easy to prove claims for the ungraded school pattern. However, educators who have been experimenting and working to improve the ungraded pattern of organization believe that achievement has improved and that the amount of failure and pupil dropout has decreased in their schools. Some of the specific advantages claimed for the ungraded school are:

1. It recognizes the individuality of children. Due to emotional, mental, physical, and social differences, boys and girls progress at their own rates of speed, even at junior high school levels. The ungraded program provides better than the graded school for the lags and spurts which accompany children's growth.

2. It attempts to provide a program of continuous and sequential learning experiences. Children gain confidence and satisfaction from success at each learning level.

3. Pupil academic progress has been reportedly faster. (Further studies may be desired here since many teachers in the ungraded school are using teaching techniques which are not new, but which have just been neglected in all but the better graded schools. This advantage may not be real where comparable teaching methods are used.)

4. Slow pupils are not pressured to work beyond their normal rate of growth. They do not have to contend with the problem of repeating grades since they always move on to new levels from the point where they left off the previous year. Bright pupils or fast learners are not held back to await slower-progressing pupils, nor are they accelerated. They work in higher levels or special enrichment levels where they can continue to find challenge as they work and grow.

5. Pupil achievement is more likely to be considered in terms of expectancy levels for the pupil's *mental age* than in terms of normal grade standards, since pupils and teachers may work with materials extending over several years.

6. A higher quality of reading results from more complete mastery, leading to better achievement in other subjects. For example, problem solving has improved where children really mastered reading comprehension.

7. There is greater flexibility of movement within and between classes. Pupils can be transferred to higher or lower learning levels during the school year without having a major adjustment problem.

8. Teachers are not restrained from using textbooks and work materials normally reserved for higher grade levels. They use materials appropriate for given learning levels regardless of grade designations by publishers and others. Teachers are expected to work with pupils with advanced materials if they are ready for such experiences.

9. The ungraded school is easy to administer and is no more expensive than the traditional graded school, yet it gives children opportunities to grow with fewer frustrations.

10. Experience with the ungraded school organization shows that parents favor it once they understand its goals.

The Ungraded Primary Easy to Adapt. The curriculum of the first, second, and third grades can be adapted, without too much difficulty, to meet the format of the ungraded primary unit as long as the teachers are prepared to think in terms of *continuous progress* instead of grade standards. Since reading is frequently used to group boys and girls in the ungraded primary school, progress through the school is related to the speed with which pupils move through the developmental reading material. The average pupil goes through the ungraded primary unit in the space of three years, fast learners in less time, while slow learners may require four years.

After they complete kindergarten, children are usually assigned to the primary unit, but without grade designation. In some schools, parents are asked to refer to the child as being in his first or second year of school rather than in a specific grade. In other schools the parents merely refer to the fact that a pupil is in the primary division, e.g., "Johnny is in Miss Howell's primary section."

When children attend kindergarten prior to starting to work in an ungraded primary, the ungraded school teachers have a pupil record to guide them. Where a school system does not have a kindergarten, the teachers have to work very slowly with their new children. They have to (1) expose the pupils to readiness activities and (2) accumulate a fairly complete record about each pupil.

Continuous Progress in the Ungraded School. The theme of this book will stress the concept that children should be grouped so that progress can be continuous for *all children,* even within the confines of a graded school, although the nongraded approach may be ideal for individualizing the learning process. The ungraded school organization owes its success to the fact that children progress through these various achievement levels at their own rate of speed. Bright pupils or fast learners do not have to wait for slower pupils, nor do they have to read and reread books or special materials which no longer challenge them. Average pupils do not have to keep up with faster learners, nor do they have to wait for the slower.

The issue of promotion or nonpromotion can be eliminated in the ungraded elementary school since there is never a question about where the pupils are going to be in the fall. Each individual is expected to continue with the learning stages at the point where he left off when

school closed for the summer. In many graded schools teachers feel
pressure to get their boys and girls through a prescribed series of
learning activities by the close of the year. With true grouping, neither
the pupil nor the teacher feels this pressure. The children tend to
continue their work with other pupils who are similar in ability and
achievement. If a pupil is overachieving in terms of the other pupils in
his group, he is phased out and put into the next higher level. There
is no question about "skipping" grades as such.

If these pupils are socially and physically mature, they may leave
the primary unit a year earlier than their chronological peers, but many
schools have introduced extra achievement levels or an enrichment
level to challenge such pupils before they are allowed to move ahead to
another group. Thus, one may find the brighter pupils reading fewer
preprimers, first readers, second readers, or third readers. To occupy
their time, they may read from a wide variety of advanced books with
the teacher or independently. In other cases, their vertical growth will
be slowed only for a short time before they are allowed to move into
higher levels of instruction. In such schools one may find pupils leaving
the primary unit who have mastered the fourth-, fifth-, and even sixth-
grade curriculum. There may be some pupils leaving the intermediate
unit who have mastered the books normally assigned to the seventh-
and eighth-grade classes.

Pupils who complete the books of a designated level, but who show
that they have not mastered them, are not asked to repeat the book
they have read. The pupil works with a reinforcement reader to
develop skills essential to his continued growth. Surprisingly enough,
studies of schools which have adopted the ungraded primary program
show that many pupils who may be labeled "slow starters" catch up
with pupils who progressed at a faster rate in their first year in the
primary grade unit. Through a program of continuous progress there
seems to be a decrease in the amount of actual retardation in the three-
year span. In some schools this may be due to the elimination of mass
reteaching when specific children in a learning group have trouble. If a
child seems to be making slow progress in a learning level, the teacher
tries to identify what is responsible for the slow progress. Thus, a
teacher may work with a child on the improvement of auditory recognition of sounds that are causing trouble, or place the pupil in learning
situations that stretch out the program.

To guarantee that all pupils are making continuous progress, the
teachers must study carefully the achievement of their children and in
some instances shift them to higher or lower levels. Each child should
be placed in a learning situation which will enable him to achieve a
continued measure of success. The teacher who is working with 25 to
30 pupils will have two or three reading or arithmetic groups, so

children may be shifted from one group to another at almost any time during the year. Occasionally, however, some children may be shifted from one teacher to another during the school year to place them in a desired learning level without forcing the teacher to form another instructional group. Teachers often try to group children so no child is more than one year younger or older chronologically within a classroom, and some pupil shifting may therefore result from other than academic achievement.

Children in ungraded primary classes reportedly are happier and make better progress due to the absence of the pressures encountered in schools where grade standards have to be met by the close of the school year. By breaking the curriculum into small segments or steps, boys and girls experience success at more frequent intervals and then proceed to the next learning stage when they are ready for it.

Reading Is Often the Basis for Grouping in the Ungraded Primary School. A pupil's placement in an ungraded primary unit is usually determined by his reading accomplishment. Where the pupil stands at the end of a given year of schooling depends upon the speed with which he masters the *sequence of learning skills* of the various reading levels established by the teachers. There is considerable variation in the number of levels established by different school systems, but a typical reading program may resemble the following:

Levels of Learning	Representative Reading Levels of a Basic Reading Program	Probable Rate of Progress of Children		
		FAST LEARNER	AVERAGE LEARNER	SLOW LEARNER
Level 11	Fourth reader or reading for independence	3rd year	4th year	5th year
Level 10	Third reader—hard (3–2)		3rd year	4th year
Level 9	Third reader—easy (3–1)			
Level 8	Reading for enrichment	2nd year		
Level 7	Second reader—hard (2–2)		2nd year	3rd year
Level 6	Second reader—easy (2–1)			
Level 5	First reader (1–2)	1st year	1st year	2nd year
Level 4	Primer (1–1)			
Level 3	Preprimer			1st year
Level 2	Chart reading			
Level 1	Readiness or prereading			
Kindergarten	Orientation and readiness			

Each child works with other children on a given level until he masters the skills of that level. The work is sequential, so he does not skip nor repeat a level if his readiness to go to higher levels has been properly evaluated. Each pupil's success is carefully measured through regular reading tests. In one school where some pupils failed to pass the tests, provisions were made for work in a parallel reader. Pupils rating high on the tests could bypass the reinforcement materials, but pupils who rated low would have to work with them until they mastered the skills outlined for their reading levels. In other schools, slow learners skip the enrichment levels which rapid learners complete before going into higher reading levels. The enrichment levels allow bright pupils to broaden their background and strengthen their skills before going too far ahead of their peers. Enrichment reading should not be reserved for only bright pupils, because all children would be exposed to a program of enrichment at each reading level. For example, some schools develop reading lists composed of basic readers, supplementary books, and library books to guide teachers at each level.

Some teachers have advocated the ungraded primary plan in hopes of eliminating subgrouping. In terms of achievement, the number of groups that have to be taught is decreased with the ungraded primary, but teachers are still expected to work with their children in small groups for reading and other subjects. The difference lies in the narrower range between the top and bottom reading subgroups within a section. This range may be kept small by transferring pupils to other sections if they are isolated in a given classroom. If a school is large, teachers will often teach overlapping reading levels to give greater flexibility in grouping. Thus, one teacher may be working with levels 4–5–6 while another is working with levels 3–4–5 and still another is working with levels 5–6–7. This overlapping makes it easy to place transfer students from another classroom or another school.

Transfers Not Made Without Considering the Impact. Studies seem to indicate a tendency to transfer *groups* of children from one teacher to another much more readily than to transfer *individual* pupils. This does not mean that individual children are not transferred —because they are. With subgrouping in each classroom, the teacher has some flexibility when it comes to placing pupils in an appropriate learning situation. In some schools, children are changed at the end of a semester or at the conclusion of the work in a given level. Special changes are made, but the transfers are based upon consultation with the principal, other teachers, and, frequently, the parents.

Other Criteria Besides Reading Used to Assign Children to Ungraded Sections. Some educators reject the idea of using reading as a basis for assigning children to ungraded sections since it connotes or resembles a form of homogeneous grouping. To achieve a more heterogeneous pattern, children are assigned to teachers on the basis of random selection or chance. Other educators study kindergarten records and then make selective pupil assignments to ensure balanced heterogeneity. A few schools use chronological age as the basis of assignment. For example, the younger-aged kindergarten children are placed together in a beginning primary section, and the older pupils go to another section. Through chronological age grouping, educators attempt to keep together those children who should have common needs. Some educators consider such grouping as too unrealistic. They prefer a balanced heterogeneity which takes into account the interests, personalities, and backgrounds of the children assigned to given sections. Unfortunately, the amount of information about six-year-olds is often sparse and not too reliable for truly balanced groupings of this sort. Apparent differences disappear due to the leveling influence of the school. Yet other differences become noticeable when pupils are in learning situations which call for decisions and actions based upon physical and mental exercise plus different experiential backgrounds.

A number of schools attempt to place children into class sections on the basis of mental age or expectancy levels for their mental age. Group intelligence tests are administered in an attempt to determine the readiness of individual children for learning levels. As children work together, the teacher observes their growth in terms of their actual progress in various subject fields and their expected progress for their intellectual capacity. From time to time pupils are transferred to other class sections to bring together children who have common educational needs. IQs are not used for grouping since they do not tell a pupil's potential at a given period of time. However, if the mental age is used to compute expectancy levels, and if achievement test scores are interpreted in terms of these expectancy levels, parents and teachers can more effectively follow the progress of children through a sequence of learning activities. Pupils who are working close to expectation levels should not be pushed, whereas pupils who are working one or more years below expectation levels may need extra help in one or more academic areas.

Standardized achievement test results may be used to determine the level to which boys and girls should be assigned as they go through an ungraded primary unit. Thus:

LEVEL 1. Pupils whose tests scores range from 1.0 to 1.4 (grade equivalents)

LEVEL 2. Scores from 1.0 to 1.4

LEVEL 3. Scores from 1.5 to 1.9

LEVEL 4. Scores from 2.0 to 2.4

LEVEL 5. Scores from 3.0 to 3.4

LEVEL 6. Scores from 3.5 to 3.9
LEVEL 7. Scores from 4.0 to 4.4
LEVEL 8. Scores from 4.5 to 4.9

The authors are reluctant to recommend achievement test results for placement unless flexibility is guaranteed through consideration of factors other than a single test score. This is especially true of children at beginning levels.

TWO-TEACHER CLASSES

When space is at a premium, large numbers of children are frequently assigned to a classroom. In an attempt to provide them with a more individualized program, experimentation with two teachers to a classroom has proved highly effective. Excellent results have been obtained when two teachers worked together as partners, planned

Courtesy of the Ford Foundation

Teaching intern gives a helping hand to pupil while regular teacher (in rear) supervises rest of class.

together, and divided their responsibilities equally. This is a form of team teaching, because the success of the program depends upon constant cooperation of two teachers whose educational goals are compatible. The authors have seen success with such a program with kindergarten children and third- and fourth-grade pupils. While not advocating this type of organization, the authors do feel it is possible to provide children with a broad enriched program if two average-sized classes are combined to work in a large-sized classroom, with the teachers making every effort to teach subgroups elsewhere in the building at some other time of day.

For this type of organization to be effective, the two teachers must understand their responsibilities and must be willing to share them under conditions that can be most trying. Work must be divided so that no teacher feels that she is doing more than her share. There will be times when all children will work together with one teacher. At such times the other teacher can correct papers, confer with parents, put assignments on the board, study test results and cumulative records, plan activities for special subject teachers, or prepare materials for demonstrations and experiments. During skill development periods the class is divided into groups on the basis of homogeneity or readiness for an activity, with each teacher taking two to three groups. In arithmetic there will be times when all pupils work together in introductory activities; then they may be divided in terms of need for additional practice, need for review of lower-level skills, or ability to work with higher-level concepts or skills. In any case, pupils requiring remedial help should be taken out of the class.

Fifty children can work together in some areas of the curriculum where numbers are insignificant, but for activities that call for free expression, teachers find it advantageous to divide their work so that one teacher can work in the classroom with a limited number of pupils. During the course of the week there are many free areas in a building if one looks for them. This is especially true if recess and lunch periods are staggered for a two-teacher class. For example, half the class may go to the gym or cafeteria while the other children work in their homeroom. Study groups may go to the library to work with research materials. Thus small groups are left behind to work on creative activities or to engage in discussion. In one school, large second-grade groups found it advantageous to go to the cafeteria because they could spread out art materials.

MULTILEVEL ASSIGNMENTS

Pupils from all ability levels gain in general achievement when teachers individualize their teaching by making multilevel assignments.

Teachers have been most successful in meeting the needs of pupils in homogeneous or heterogeneous classes when they have planned the work in terms of ability, interest, achievement, attitude, and drive. Varied assignments can meet these differences within a class without having to subdivide it into intermediate and upper grade pupils. Some teachers have been most successful with assignments which called for work in one of three different level social studies books. The pupils in one such class never had assignments given in terms of *pages* to be studied. History books of different degrees of difficulty were used, and the pupils learned to locate the appropriate pages using the index.

DEPARTMENTALIZATION AND TEAM TEACHING

For more than half a century, educators have been arguing about the pro and con of departmentalized teaching versus the self-contained classroom. While upper grade and high school teachers are firmly committed to departmentalized teaching, elementary school teachers have been divided as to its merits. It has an appeal to subject-matter-minded teachers and parents; so one finds pressure exerted from time to time to departmentalize the teaching in the intermediate and even the primary grades. Between 1910 and 1930 there was considerable experimentation with departmentalized teaching in the elementary schools. During the 1930s feelings ran high between teachers favoring or opposing the plan, but during the 1940s many schools gave up departmentalization only to see a new surge of interest appear during the 1950s and 1960s. Recent attempts to narrow the range of reading or arithmetic instruction at the intermediate grade levels have helped to stimulate interest in some form of departmentalized teaching.

Opposition to departmentalized teaching is often based on the following arguments:

Departmentalization tends to develop subject matter specialists who fail to see the relationship between what they teach and what the next teacher teaches. There is no continuity in the curriculum when several teachers teach separate subjects. Their work cannot be integrated so that children can see and understand relationships between subjects or studies.

Teachers work with so many children that they fail to get to know their students as individuals. By not seeing the children working under different conditions, it is impossible for teachers to understand thoroughly their children's basic needs.

Departmentalized teachers think in terms of adult needs more than they do in terms of children's needs.

Some of these arguments, however, can be met through a form of team teaching that has been used successfully in some elementary schools. While there are a number of departmentalized school systems which claim to have adopted a team teaching approach, the concept may vary within these schools. In its simplest form it may consist of nothing more than two or three teachers meeting together regularly to plan their work and to talk about the progress of the children with whom they work in a departmentalized program. If the teachers are conscientious about their work and can get together fairly regularly, they can counter some of the arguments listed above. Through repeated evaluations and through joint planning teachers can get acquainted with boys and girls and can interpolate their own subject matter with what the other teachers are teaching. They can see the desirability for continuity as pupils go from class to class or even to the next grade. This is possible at the elementary school or junior high school level where the teachers assigned to a team work with the same children as they teach different subjects. It is not necessarily true where the teams consist of teachers teaching the same subjects to different groups of children.

Team teaching should be used as a means to improve the quality of education. It should be ignored if the objective is to save money. In a proper setting, team teaching at the elementary school level can help eliminate some of the handicaps under which the teachers work in a departmentalized program. There are some persons who are opposed to bringing large groups of children together for lectures or motion pictures, but this can be one way to free teachers from routine so they may give special instruction to pupils who need it. Better teacher planning and cooperative planning can result from team teaching, particularly where large-group activities are alternated with small-group seminars and individual work or study periods.

TEAM TEACHING IN A GIVEN SUBJECT

Team teaching can be considered a much higher phase of joint teacher activity than team planning. Here teachers who work in a common subject field plan a program which may be based on both large group and small group instruction. Thus, a social studies teacher with a special interest or background may elect to teach all of the students from four, five, or more classes. The large group of children may be supervised with the assistance of one of the other members of the team. This releases the other social studies teachers to prepare their own lessons or to work with small groups of students or with individuals. When the large group instruction is over, the pupils may then discuss the lecture, picture, or demonstration in their regular classrooms with their regular teacher.

TEAM PLANNING

In its simplest form teachers may be assigned to teach four classes of students. The pupils go to a different teacher for reading, arithmetic, social studies, and language arts where instruction may be directed to the elimination of problems identified in the weekly or biweekly planning session of the teaching team. In this school the teachers do not combine classes; however, they will try to direct their efforts to the basic problems they identify when they meet to discuss their work with the children assigned to their teams, as the following illustration shows:

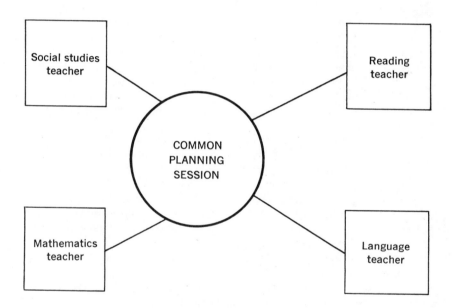

TEAM LEARNING

Parents and teachers have a tendency to frown upon having children work together when they do their work, yet many boys and girls find that it helps to work with others. Teachers will find that they often assume added burdens by not taking advantage of what may be described as team learning. There are times when teachers have to teach, but there also are times when boys and girls can teach each other if they are left to themselves or are encouraged to help each other. Teachers who are overly concerned about the wide range within an intermediate class can delegate some of the responsibility for learning to pupil learning teams without reverting to the faults of the old pupil monitorial system. This was illustrated in a group experiment conducted at Dedham, Massachusetts, under the direction of Dr. Donald D. Durrell of Boston University:[6]

In the Dedham experiment, forty-five teachers worked with 1200 intermediate grade pupils in a special team learning approach. Each class was divided into two or three work teams for instruction in subjects like arithmetic, spelling and social studies. The pupils in each classroom were divided into sub-groups or work teams on the basis of ability, with the understanding that they could move ahead as fast as they were able to do so. As a result, about one-third of the fourth, fifth, and sixth graders finished the equivalent of two years of arithmetic in one year.

A report on pupil performance based on the result of comparative tests showed growth in all subjects beyond the normal rate for pupils in a given grade. Fourth graders exceeded the normal growth for the year by 4.3 months, fifth graders by 5.3 months, and sixth graders by 3.4 months. As a result of the team learning approach, there was a definite increase in the proportion of pupils making a full year's growth in school. It was estimated that team learning had resulted in a jump of from about 50 to 74 per cent in achievement. This growth was not limited to selected classrooms. Every class which was involved in the experiment showed an increase in the percentage of pupils making at least a full year's growth.

The experiment called for flexible grouping with all pupils working on a team in terms of ability and congeniality. Some of the pupils were on different teams for arithmetic, spelling, history, or geography. Instead of competing with each other, team members provided mutual help and support to each other. Discussion frequently took the place of drill. Because pupils continued to help each other in team learning activities, classroom teachers often had fewer papers to correct. While group activities were stressed, each pupil was always on his own when it came time to take the tests which were given every ten days to judge their mastery of basic skills.

From time to time the teachers instructed the whole class as a unit, but most of the class work was performed by small teams of pupils working at their own rates of speed. Individual pupils or groups of pupils did not spend their time waiting for the teacher. As a result, they did not waste time with busy-work. Teachers found that they had less disciplinary problems to cope with than formerly. Usually, discipline was meted out by the working unit. Pupils who acted up were isolated by the learning team. This was most effective since team learning capitalized upon the natural desire of the students to work together. Most pupils accepted the leadership of the other students and learned to carry their own share of work and responsibility rather than lose the respect of their classmates.

Here one finds another illustration of what happens when boys and girls in a learning situation are encouraged to progress at their own pace. They can, under the right stimulus, make a mockery of traditional grade standards. The problem is what to give these fast learners who demonstrate their ability to master traditional bodies of knowledge or skill at twice the rate of speed of average-learning pupils. Educators have often used the term "enriched curriculum" for the faster learners, but the term is inadequate to express what is desired. Modern children are living in a world which is changing daily. To live in it they must be prepared to solve problems undreamed of by their fathers and mothers when they went to school. To solve them they must have a background of information and skill far beyond traditional grade standards, yet it is virtually impossible to think of this new knowledge and skill in terms of grade levels or age levels. One has to cope with elements of interest and background or readiness for new learning at all levels of our schools; therefore, it may be necessary to think in terms of optional units or even new courses of study for our faster learners.

Team learning is another example of what happens when continuous progress becomes the accepted pattern. Grade lines, as such, tend to be eliminated. Unless the teachers teach a multiple-track curriculum, some of them will find themselves hard pressed to challenge their faster learners. Furthermore, team learning points up a possibility that many classes have been too teacher-dominated in the past. Teachers have to see that boys and girls often learn from each other as well as from the teachers. This does not mean that a teacher can ignore his leadership role in the classroom, but if the right type of environment is created, many of the pupils can help him extend the range of pupil interests and achievement and, in doing so, may help him resolve the issue of grouping or balancing out classes in an artificial attempt to narrow the teaching range.

For decades the good disciplinarians were teachers who could keep children quiet and orderly in class. This problem has plagued most teachers from time to time in their teaching careers. One of the complaints about group instruction has been that teachers have to interrupt good group activity to quiet the talkers or to stop some pupils who are working together from copying or wasting time. In spite of the desirability of modern movable school furniture, one still finds desks and chairs lined up in rows, largely to keep pupils from getting too close to one another. Teachers reason that it is easier to preserve discipline by separating children as much as possible in order to discourage talking and copying.

This philosophy fails to recognize a natural tendency of both children and youths to work together on many types of projects or problems. Team learning calls for an end to the silent classroom. Pupils in the new setting are not only going to be permitted to talk and work together, but they are actually going to be encouraged to talk out their problems without teacher intervention. Studies have shown that boys and girls not only prefer to work in teams or in small groups, but they can work successfully without constant admonitions to be quiet while they are working. Students have shown that they prefer to work in small teams instead of on an all-class or a large subgroup basis. If they can be given an opportunity to work in meaningful activities, the teacher does not have to worry so much about problems of discipline such as those that haunt teachers in the traditional teacher-dominated classroom. Much of the need or desire to copy or waste time with idle talk will disappear once pupils have experience working closely with selected students with similar problems and learning needs.

How children react to the new rules and procedures becomes a matter of training and experience. Pupils can learn to work coopera-tively with each other and with the teacher from the day they start school in the kindergarten or first grade. They can learn that there is a time for individual work as well as a time for all-class or large group activity. If, after three or four years of close work, boys and girls have not learned to accept responsibility for the way they work, one may question whether they have learned the true meaning of words such as "responsibility," "self-discipline," "leadership," and "cooperation."

Innovations Affecting
the Teacher-Learner Situation

How one teaches and what one teaches depends on the individual teacher's educational philosophy. For many years educators have been divided over the question of what to teach and how to teach it. To some, education is essentially a mechanical process consisting largely of someone feeding accumulated knowledge and demonstrating skills to a willing or unwilling learner whose job is to digest, memorize, and imitate until he can repeat what he has heard and seen. Good teachers have been ridiculed because they have talked in terms of intangibles or because they have used what the public may think of as the "soft sell" approach to learning. Methodology has been considered as an over-emphasized phase of a teacher's training or background, yet if the truth were known, a large number of our educational problems are the result of poor teaching by teachers who were never trained to teach either subjects or children at lower grade levels. We also get poor results because a large number of teachers have been caught in the controversy of *what and how to teach*. Some of these teachers were exposed to good teaching principles and methods of improving instruc-tion, but they never made the effort to apply their knowledge. Other teachers were content to take the path of least resistance, which usually meant avoiding taking sides where possible. This has often resulted in their ignoring educational research and in a general resistance to what may appear to be new and drastic approaches to the problems of teaching children. Some of these teachers are confused and afraid when they hear educators talk about ungraded schools, individualized teaching, team teaching, subgrouping, or machine teaching and programmed learning. And even teachers who support one or more of these new approaches to teaching often find themselves in a quandary when it comes to realizing the basic objectives of education. For example, team teaching can result in a better understanding of children and greater attention to individual pupil needs, but at the same time it may promote an overemphasis upon mass teaching based upon lectures to pupils working in a departmentalized framework. If this happens, the individual and his needs may be forgotten. Let us examine here some of the innovations that have brought teaching to a sort of crossroads.

USE OF PROGRAMMED LEARNING

Educators may find themselves at a crossroads when they consider the possibilities of various programmed learning aids prepared and publicized by vested interests. They may find themselves hard pressed to cope with parent requests to promote a type of learning based upon the use of teaching machines. This may be especially true when the parents present articles with endorsement by college professors. The teacher's problem may be complicated by some parents' purchasing a machine for their own children on the basis of high-pressure advertisements or salesmen. For years, educators have been trying to individualize the learning process, so the popularization of teaching machines or programmed textbooks becomes a force that is hard to resist. [4, 7] The idea of accelerating learning with a minimum of teacher effort appeals to the teachers in many schools, as well as to the parents of the children.

In theory, at least, individual pupils can progress at their own rates of speed. With programmed learning they do not have to wait for others to master mechanical skills such as vocabulary drill or routine factual presentations. This means that persevering students can quickly complete a program of study with little, if any, teacher help in order to set the stage for study at an advanced level or to free themselves for study in other fields. Teachers have found that the rapidity of student learning with teaching machines has forced instructors to offer new and additional material. This has enabled teachers to enrich programs or courses which were dry and encyclopedic due to time pressures. With the new types of programmed learning, the teacher is released from the tedious chore of correcting homework or test papers, with the result that she has the time to prepare herself to supplement what the pupils learn through the teaching machine or programmed textbook. She now has the time to be more creative in her approach.

How far educators go with programmed learning depends upon their goals and their educational philosophies. Some educators see this type of learning as a threat to the self-contained classroom with its intimate by-play and cooperative teacher-learning relationship based upon an understanding of children as individuals. On the other hand, teachers who are concerned with individual differences in their class-rooms will find that some forms of programmed learning will offer greater challenge to boys and girls than teacher worksheets or work-books. One can, for example, see teachers in the self-contained class-room having time to work with small groups of pupils who need attention. They do not have to worry about the progress of the more capable pupils engrossed in intensive study at the teaching machines in the back of the room.

The Nature of Programmed Learning. Good teachers are able to break down basic skills or the component parts of the content material essential for full understanding of a subject; this allows them to take pupils step by step to higher learning levels. Up until recent times this ability of selected gifted teachers was lost to children other than those in their classes, but with the development of programmed learning, thousands of students can benefit from their skill. Essentially, pro-grammed learning may take many forms; however, to many educators it is best represented through the use of teaching machines to present carefully-prepared sequential materials. The program which is studied by the pupils contains many separate items and skills, leading the pupil through an orderly progression of learning skills or divisions of subject matter much the same as the master teacher did as she worked to meet individual differences in her classroom.

Most teaching machines are simple devices which control the flow of information or skills through allowing pupils to study a sequence of stimulus frames. Each frame contains a minute amount of information which may be described as the stimulation. Before the student can go to another frame he is expected to answer a question or complete a statement. This is known as the pupil's response to the stimulation. In using some machines the pupil reads a question and then writes his answer on the blank paper which moves past a small window. By pressing a button or lever, the correct answer is revealed and the pupil's answer is covered. If the pupil's answer has been correct, he may move on to another frame and a new question. If his answer is wrong, he may be told why. The pupil is expected to correct his answer before he is allowed to move to a new stimulus frame, thus the answer is a means of reinforcing his response. The machines are so constructed that the learner does not see any answer beforehand, nor can he change his answer once the correct response has been revealed.

Teaching machines come in various sizes and shapes and price ranges. Programs offered range from the preschool child to the graduate student in the university. Young children may use programmed material to learn to read, to spell, or to compute. Older students may use programmed material to study higher mathematics, physics, Russian, French, Spanish, German, psychology, music, logic, statistics, chemistry, and a variety of other subjects. The preparation of these programs requires a great deal of skill and is most time-consuming, and as a result, the programs for a teaching machine can be quite costly.

Advantages and Disadvantages of Teaching Machines and Programmed Textbooks. Thus far, educators have not considered teaching machines or programmed textbooks in the light of *replacing* teachers in the classroom. However, they have a definite value in lightening the load of teachers who have large classes and multiple responsibilities. Following are some of the advantages and disadvantages of programmed instruction materials:

Advantages	*Disadvantages*
1. Boys and girls can work at their own rate of speed. Some pupils can complete a program of studies in one-half the time by using a teaching machine. Pupils acquire new skills or new knowledge with less effort.	1. Some students have found the repetition of written answers boring and fatiguing.
2. Students are exposed to only a small amount of material in a given frame, so that the learner does not go to more difficult material until he is ready to do so and is thus less apt to be frustrated.	2. Pupils who miss or forget earlier sequences find it hard to go back with a teaching machine.
3. Programmed materials are developed to give a sequence to learning activities that go from the known to the unknown.	3. Pupils may learn skills or knowledge based upon memory, but they may not always acquire the understanding of the principles studied. (They may still require practice in working with concrete materials.)
4. Learning is reinforced through carefully planned questions.	4. Some pupils may still feign success by copying answers from programmed texts.

Closed-circuit television lesson in basic Spanish.

One hundred children get TV lesson in basic Spanish (see photo above). In classroom, regular teacher writes the words the television teacher is speaking, using an overhead projector.

Advantages	Disadvantages
5. Pupils can see the answers as soon as they complete a question. This leads to increased pupil interest in teaching machines or programmed textbook.	5. Teaching is made impersonal through the use of a teaching machine. Educators are afraid that teaching machines tend to put learning on an assembly line. Creativity and originality are lost as pupils work continually with programs that are too cut and dried. A machine cannot inspire students in the same way that a creative teacher can.
6. Students are able to work alone in a review or advanced program of study.	6. Teachers still find it desirable to check on pupil progress through checking machine tapes or by checking pages from a programmed text.
7. Programmed instruction is a time-saver to the teacher: a learning sequence is prepared for her; she does not have to make up as many tests or assignments or correct as many papers.	7. Teachers find it time-consuming to change programs and difficult if they are not mechanically minded.
8. While some students are doing purposeful drill, the teacher is free to give instruction to other pupils.	8. Some educators fear that some of the success with teaching machines may be attributed to the novelty effect. If they become commonplace, some of the stimulation may be lost.

In the hands of competent teachers the teaching machine or programmed textbook can be used to foster pupil growth (1) in areas where students have known weaknesses or (2) in new and advanced learning levels. Programmed instruction has possibilities for individualizing instruction, but it may require considerable time and effort before teachers and pupils can realize the full benefits from teaching machines or programmed texts. The field is wide open for experimentation at all learning levels, but the conclusions that educators draw will still be tempered by their *philosophy of education or the educational goals which they believe must be realized* by given individuals at different stages of their development.

Television As a Form of Programmed Learning. Promoters of teaching machines stress the need to individualize the teaching process; therefore, educators may put them in a separate category from television. But actually, teaching machines and TV have one common attribute in that they depend on packaged materials which standardize teaching for all who use them. Television may bring the outside world into the classroom, but the information or skills relayed to the learner are standardized in such a way that the *individual's stage of readiness* is ignored. It is impossible to make allowances for the pupil who needs additional background or for the one who finds nothing new in the presentation due to his wide reading and background of experiences. One argument in defense of educational television is that programs are prepared by authorities in the field who have the time and ability to present materials more effectively than the average classroom teacher. One cannot deny that this may be true, but the end result is a standardization of the curriculum. This may eliminate any opportunity of the teacher to be creative or to present material in the light of pupil needs or the needs of a given community. Some of the arguments against television may be minimized with a form of closed-circuit television in which programs can be prepared for local consumption or for a limited number of schools in a given area.

One of the problems of teaching with motion pictures has been that of getting large groups to a central viewing center. With closed-circuit television the teacher and the pupils can remain in their classroom and view an interesting program. Closed-circuit television also enables several teachers to view a program of common interest at the same time. A special lesson may be prepared by a master teacher for showing to the children of a particular age or grade grouping. This type of presentation is especially helpful in a school where the teachers of a grade or subject have worked out a plan to capitalize on the strengths of various teachers working within related learning fields. Team teaching can be employed on a formal or informal basis to improve the quality of the teaching within a school or school system.

One of the advantages of closed-circuit television lies in the possibility of utilizing an interschool communication system to relay questions to the instructor putting on the special program. It helps pupils to carry on discussions with the instructor. This enables the instructor to personalize the educational television program in terms of special needs and interests. Weaknesses of a common nature can become the basis for special programs. Also, in some areas where closed-circuit television is used discriminately, special enrichment programs may be put on to meet the special needs or interests of gifted pupils excused to go to a common viewing center according to a prearranged schedule.

Educational television may be supplemented by many commercial television programs if teachers make a special effort to guide children's interests in the programs they select for viewing in nonschool hours. If this is done, many of the reported twenty hours boys and girls spend each week in front of the television screen will not be wasted. Many teachers have found that it helps to talk about television programs in class as a means of analyzing them collectively in terms of content, advertising, and authenticity.

Worthwhile programs can become the basis for homework assignments. Thus, a documentary can lead to a better understanding of social studies, science, and language arts. Similarly, films based upon literary classics can supplement literature or English classes, and new interests in music and art may be stimulated by selected programs. Of course, television can help pupils acquire a better understanding of current events through newscasts and news analysis.

While there are arguments against using television to instruct children, one cannot escape the fact that millions of boys and girls attend schools which have limited facilities and a limited staff. Television offers many of these students a chance to study subjects or courses that otherwise would never be offered to them. Early experiments with educational television have shown that children attending small schools can profitably learn science, foreign languages, typing, mathematics, music, history, and geography through a medium still in its infancy.

In addition to making new courses available to pupils on a mass or selected basis, educational television programs have provided a method of enriching traditional subjects. Classroom teachers have been stimulated to try new methods of teaching after watching a specialist teach some phase of a subject. The end result has been an updating of the teaching by the regular teacher, plus enrichment by the specialist.

USE OF TEACHER AIDES

Every teacher has to contend with school routines which detract from the actual act of teaching. In an effort to free teachers of what they often describe as clerical or nonprofessional responsibilities, some school systems have experimented with the employment of part- or full-time teacher aides. These teacher aides may or may not be college graduates, but this is not an essential if they have a sincere interest in work that actually involves children. Since they are not certified to teach, they are usually prohibited by law from actually introducing new learning skills, but they can often free the teacher so that she can devote her full attention to the individual and group needs. When this occurs, the teacher aide becomes an assistant to the teacher. The teacher aide may work closely with one or more teachers who are working as individuals or as members of a teaching team. In either case, she gives them time to work with boys and girls on a more personal basis.

Teacher aides free classroom teachers for more effective teaching in a number of ways. For example, they may take attendance; record marks and complete office records; distribute supplies; collect lunch money, etc.; correct papers, workbooks, and standardized tests; work with small groups of children who need special practice or drill; set up audiovisual equipment; write assignments on the blackboard; run off duplicated materials; supervise children in the lunchroom, playground, and library; assist on field trips; complete routine chores such as dusting, watering plants, etc.; process new books; write correspondence, file; and arrange for parent-teacher conferences.

It has been estimated that an average teacher can devote an extra seven to fifteen hours a week to the instruction of children if she has a responsible assistant. In addition, she is much more efficient when she works, because she does not have to interrupt a teaching lesson to admonish someone for talking, to repeat a direction or assignment, to answer the telephone, or to excuse pupils who have to leave the room.

In a few communities one may find volunteer teacher aides, but in others they are considered as Board of Education employees who receive monetary compensation. The salary factor can be a deterrent to the widespread use of teacher aides in communities which are resisting the steady increase in school costs, although some communities have justified teacher aide salaries by increasing class sizes. While the evidence still fails to show that small classes are more desirable for academic growth than large classes, good educators find it difficult to justify the use of teacher aides if it means that the teacher will have to work with large numbers of children. The fact that the class enrollment has increased means that there are more bodies in the classroom, with the result that freedom of movement is limited. If the use of teacher aides results in an increase in class size, the number of potential interactions in a given classroom increases to the point that it is almost impossible to release them! Pupils have fewer leadership opportunities, because the program tends to be formal. Even with an assistant, the teacher soon finds it difficult to do much along creative lines with so many pupils in a room that she can scarcely find free corners in which to work.

In all fairness to teachers, one must remember that the majority of our classrooms already have more than thirty pupils. For teachers to know their children and to meet their complete educational needs is an impossibility unless positive steps are taken to *release them* from time- and energy-consuming nonteaching responsibilities! Teaching assistants of a nonprofessional nature may well be the answer.

SPECIAL HELP PERIODS

In an attempt to meet individual pupil needs more effectively, some teachers reserve a period of the day for special help. During this time all the children are busy at assigned tasks that do not require close teacher supervision or instruction. She is thus free to concentrate on boys and girls who require special help. These teachers often use specially prepared materials to diagnose and correct pupil difficulties. In elementary schools where there are special teachers for such subjects as art, music, or physical education, the teacher may use one of these help periods to give special instruction to pupils who require it.

SPECIAL ADJUSTMENT CLASSES

Pupils who are not up to desired standards on standardized achievement tests or up to the expectations of their teachers may be sent to an ungraded special adjustment class for all or part of a day. These are established to give assistance to pupils whose potentiality is far above their academic accomplishment level. Pupils in such adjustment classes may come from the third to the sixth grade, with the expectation that they will be given help in the areas of their greatest need. When these pupils show growth, they will be tested again. If they have made sufficient progress, they are returned to regular classrooms. In a small school that doesn't have a special adjustment class, the intermediate grade teachers may reserve one period a day for special help to such problem pupils.

AREA TEACHING

One can find a number of variations of what may be described as area teaching. In one school system bright children or fast learners are allowed to leave the regular classroom for a part of the day to give the teacher more time to work with slower-learning pupils in such areas as reading and arithmetic. In some schools bright pupils are sent to an enrichment teacher who encourages them in activities which will give them leadership and creative opportunities. Capra [2] describes a program for fifth- and sixth-grade pupils which was set up to help teachers cope with the problem of individual differences. He says:

> The bright children are all good readers and can afford to miss this particular lesson rather than arithmetic, science, social studies, or language arts. During this period children are permitted to work individually or in groups in the areas of their special interests. The projects are usually long term and upon completion written reports are submitted to the teacher and oral reports are given to the class. Many reference materials are available and free movement about the room is permitted in a workshop atmosphere.

Here, the children went to a special teacher outside of the classroom for an hour each day while other pupils were reading. In other schools the more able pupils have been allowed to go to special areas for such "elective" courses as foreign language, current events, creative writing, experimental science, and typing.

Following are some of the requisites of successful area teaching:

Preplanning. A major portion of the teacher's energy will be devoted to teaching and supervising children as they work, individually and in small groups. Problems will have to be identified for each student. Each pupil will have to know his responsibilities and how to carry them out. Pupil leaders are selected for group activity, and reporters are appointed to assist them. Each pupil keeps his own record of assignments and responsibilities so that he will know where he is to go.

Timing. Before a class divides into groups, pupils decide how long they will spend in a given work area. Each group depends upon a timekeeper to inform it when to move on to another area or to return to the teacher for evaluation of what has been done. When time is called, all pupils do not have to return to the teacher, since different groups of students may require more or less time to learn a skill or find the information they need. The teacher plans her day so she can give instruction to pupils who should be working together in specific skill areas.

Evaluation. When the children stop working, either the pupil leader or the teacher reviews what has been done to see if definite objectives have been realized. Recommendations made may become the basis for the next day's work. While some kind of evaluation is going on throughout the day, a few minutes are reserved near the end for everyone to get together as a class or in small groups to review what has been accomplished and what still has to be done.

Creative Planning. Learning centers are set up in various parts of the classroom which will help students find themselves during the day. The rigidity of the classroom is broken when area teaching is introduced. Here, one does not find children sitting for the major part of the day, but instead working in different parts of the room or even outside of it. The teacher can bring the children into the planning phase of the program. They consider the classroom in terms of the types of activities which should engage their time and efforts, studying the size of the room, the furniture, the materials available, and special arrangements for learning activities. This will lead to the rearrangement of the room to form specific learning centers where pupils will have the tools they require for creative learning.

A Rich Supply of Work Materials. Each teaching area should have the books, references, work materials (i.e., paint, wood, paper, crayons, hammer, saw, nails, maps, etc.) required. Area teaching consists of more than desks and textbooks. But since all teachers cannot, or will not, want to buy all commercially made teaching aids, they may need some of the raw ingredients necessary for pupils to make materials of their own. While a number of materials are needed, the actual cost is not so great as it would appear, because pupils will share many of the materials they use.

The creativity of teacher and pupils is usually evident in the way teaching areas are set up. Each area should be attractive and comfortable. Each area should be readily identifiable as a center for a particular subject matter. The science area, for example, should be distinguishable from the social studies area. Since space is always at a premium, the teacher will find that it helps to break with traditional room arrangements and furniture.

FLEXIBLE SCHEDULING

Terms like "classes," "grades," and "groups" have been used repeatedly throughout this book, because educators tend to think in terms of numbers of students instead of individual students. In most instances, children who are brought together for a class tend to find themselves moving through an elementary or junior high school in a block. The excuse is frequently given that it is virtually impossible to schedule them otherwise. Although scheduling can be a problem for any school administrator, educators should not neglect their obligation to place their students in teaching situations where their educational needs can be met most effectively. At times, grade labels will get in the way of the person making a schedule if all classes have to be balanced out in terms of comparable enrollments. This is one of the advantages of the ungraded elementary or the ungraded junior high school. Here, children can be placed in learning centers on the basis of academic need, social maturity, creative ability, natural interests, or leadership potential.

Studies have shown that the success of any type of grouping (homogeneous or heterogeneous) depends upon the amount of flexibility in pupil assignments. The fact that a class is formed on the basis of an apparent homogeneity in reading or intelligence is no guarantee that all the students will hold similar interests or be equally competent when they engage in other academic or non-academic studies. Therefore, the teacher—or group of teachers—must be able to work in terms of a flexible teaching schedule. Often, out of necessity, teachers in small schools have had to take advantage of natural interests or skills in order to form multiple-grade classes, or have had to depend upon subgrouping. Team teaching has possibilities because some large combined classes can free teachers to work with individual pupils or small groups of students. However, if this is done, pupils who fail to take part in the all-group activity must not be penalized if they miss out on some important phase of learning. In some schools, for example, pupils have resisted having to go to special teachers for help or enrichment because regular teachers have insisted on programs which call for common learnings for all.

Upper grade teachers find that when their pupils try to take advanced or elective classes, it is difficult to work out satisfactory schedules. For example, bright eighth-grade students who took Algebra 1 along with regular ninth-grade students had no major problem because they substituted algebra for eighth-grade arithmetic; however, when they came to taking a foreign language, they found that they had

TABLE 1
A Comparison Between Block Scheduling and Flexible Scheduling

Block Scheduling*			Flexible Scheduling†		
PERIOD 40 MIN.	SUBJECT	CLASS LIST (PUPILS)	MODULE 20–30 MIN.	SUBJECT	CLASS LIST (PUPILS)
1	Language arts	Mary Dolan Harry Stevens Janice King Robert Taber	1–3	Language arts	Mary Dolan Tracy Walters Fred Staveley Ellen Finch Susan Holmes Muriel Kabel
2	Mathematics	Mary Dolan Harry Stevens Janice King Robert Taber	4–8	Social studies	Harry Stevens Janice King Sidney Foster
3–4	Social studies	Mary Dolan Harry Stevens Janice King Robert Taber	9–12	Art	Jerome Powell Muriel Kabel Perry Thomas A. Harry Moore
4	Remedial reading	Robert Taber Mary Dolan	12	Remedial reading	Robert Taber Mary Dolan
5	Physical education	Harry Stevens Robert Taber Miles Cooper Fred Staveley	13–14	Physical education	Harry Stevens Robert Taber Miles Cooper Fred Staveley
6	Study	Mary Dolan Harry Stevens Janice King Robert Taber	15–18	Mathematics, science	Mary Dolan Janice King Perry Thomas Roberta Brown Miles Cooper Susan Green Alice Henseley Joseph Riley
7	Music	Mary Dolan Harry Stevens Janice King Robert Taber			

* Pupils tend to stay together for most of the day with block scheduling.

† In a very highly individualized program boys and girls may be assigned to classes on the basis of need, interest, or achievement.

to drop a minor subject along with two periods of English or social studies. Although the bright pupils showed their ability to work at advanced levels by obtaining the highest marks in the new subjects, teachers found it difficult to adjust to having these pupils in academic classes for a fewer number of classes per week than was customary. It takes teachers and pupils time to adjust to such changes, but if individual differences are to be recognized, an effort has to be made to introduce flexibility in both scheduling and programming at all educational levels.

More and more upper grade or junior high schools are modifying their curriculum to allow rapid learners to accelerate by taking accelerated or advanced courses. This type of acceleration enables bright pupils to broaden their background by taking a less restrictive program. Such acceleration is becoming more desirable for upper grade pupils who have been allowed to move through the elementary school in a continuous progress program. When these bright pupils take advanced courses in junior high school, the door is opened to graduating from high school in three years or electing to remain in high school as advanced students taking courses which carry college credit. Socially and chronologically they will not have been accelerated, but academically they will have grown so that they can enter college with fifteen to twenty hours of advanced credit.

Another type of flexible scheduling provides mixed or multiple n odules of time for instruction. In schools that use mixed modules, the school day is divided into time blocks based on the amount of class time required to teach a special subject or group of children. Thus, one group of pupils may attend a class for two 20-minute modules while another group of slower learning pupils may attend a similar class for three 20-minute modules.

Good individualized programs may not require mixed modules of time, but many educators are considering the advantage of a modular time schedule, especially when teachers see the need for large blocks of time.

REFERENCES

1. Richard F. Bruns, "Improvement of Reading Through Ability Level Assignments," *Curriculum Bulletin* 57CBM (Houston, Tex.: Houston Independent School District, February 1957).
2. James Capra, "Individualizing Instruction," *American School Board Journal*, 137 (December 1958), 17–18.
3. David Cram, *Explaining "Teaching Machines and Programming"* (San Francisco: Fearon, 1961).
4. Lee J. Cronbach, "What Research Says About Programmed Instruction," *National Education Association Journal*, 51 (December 1962), 45–47.

5. Harry Dunn, *The School Teacher's Manual Containing Practical Suggestions on Teaching and Popular Education* (Hartford, Conn.: Reed and Barber, 1838).
6. Donald D. Durrell and Viola Palos, "Pupil Study Teams in Reading," *Education,* 76 (May 1956), 552–56.
7. Edward J. Green, *The Learning Process and Programmed Instruction* (New York: Holt, Rinehart & Winston, 1962).
8. Helen Parkhurst, "The Dalton Plan," *Twenty-fourth Yearbook of the National Society for the Study of Education,* Part II, *Adapting the Schools to Individual Differences* (Bloomington, Ill.: Public School Publishing, 1925).
9. Carleton Washburne, "Burke's Individualized System as Developed at Winnetka," *Twenty-fourth Yearbook of the National Society for the Study of Education,* Part II, *Adapting the Schools to Individual Differences* (Bloomington, Ill.: Public School Publishing, 1925).

CHAPTER 3

Setting the Stage
for Effective Learning

Many conflicts within a school or community can be avoided if teachers and school administrators subscribe to common educational goals or objectives. Unfortunately, this does not always happen. All too often, barriers based upon a difference in philosophy on the part of staff members divide a staff and, with it, the parents and the general public. If one is to set the stage for more effective learning and teaching, it is essential that the members of a teaching staff make a concerted effort to eliminate differences which lead to conflict, confusion, frustration, and misunderstandings.

The task of bringing teachers together is not always an easy one due to the differences in their backgrounds and training. A primary teacher, for example, who subscribes to a child developmental point of view may minimize the essential values placed upon the fundamentals to realize social and emotional goals. In contrast, an intermediate or upper grade teacher whose training calls for high-level academic accomplishments may minimize the social values. The differences in these major objectives can create problems for boys and girls struggling to adjust to the teachers' standards and methods. The academically oriented teachers may set standards without considering pupil readiness to live up to them, whereas the nonacademically oriented teachers may fail to challenge pupils to work with new materials or skills commensurate with their abilities or past accomplishments.

While teachers should use different approaches to solve teaching problems, *it is imperative that they subscribe to the same basic educational philosophy*. They need to set their sights upon the realization of common goals—some which may be realized in the span of a few days, weeks, or months, and some which can be realized only after longer periods of time. In some schools teachers may work together to establish a written philosophy which can set a pattern or direction for new and experienced teachers as they work with children, but many teachers need more than a series of written philosophical statements to guide them. They may need a strong principal to help them avoid placing different interpretations upon words, phrases, statements, and principles.

Establishing Goals for More Effective Learning and Teaching

When educators sit down to develop a common philosophy of education, they do not have to create something entirely new, since each individual staff member has been exposed to fragments of educational philosophy dating back to their own school days. Many of them will have been exposed to, if not indoctrinated with, the thinking of such early educators as Pestalozzi, Spencer, Chapman, Dewey, Counts, Kilpatrick, Bode, Herbart, and others. Some teachers may remember the Commission on Reorganization of Secondary School's seven cardinal principles, namely; health, vocation, citizenship, command of the fundamental processes, worthy use of leisure time, and ethical character. But other teachers may have considered them as mere clichés. Some teachers may subscribe to the cardinal principles, but because they are so general, they can do so without actually modifying procedures that may conflict with those of other staff members.

Many modern educators can find a base on which to build a school philosophy in the objectives outlined by the Educational Policies Commission. [3] This will be especially true if they accept the basic premise that:

> The general aim of education in America at the present time is the fullest possible development of the individual within the framework of our present industrial, democratic society. The attainment of the end is to be observed in individual behavior or conduct.

If teachers can accept this aim as a guiding principle, they should be able to develop procedures which will help them meet their basic needs. Subject matter will still be important, but the realization of other essential goals will be given recognition by all teachers of a given grade or series of grade levels.

After reaching agreement on a general educational philosophy, teachers must make an effort to understand each other and have respect for each other's opinions, ideas, and methods as long as they are consistent with the accepted goals. There is a need for a common yardstick when standards are set for and with children. For example, boys and girls may have to make major adjustments when they encounter teachers who do not agree on words like "discipline," "satisfactory progress," "failure," "freedom," "maturity," and "intelligence." Similarly, office records can become meaningless if teachers use terms which have varied meanings.

NEED FOR ESTABLISHED AND WRITTEN POLICIES

Many problems teachers encounter in a new school could be avoided if they could turn to a written record of the school's basic philosophy of education and the type of teaching expected in the classroom. The educational goals depicted should be realistic and attainable. Too, the written document should not stifle initiative nor prevent experimentation. Similarly, it should not restrict teachers who find it necessary to modify their program to meet individual differences.

The need for an established policy or at least for an understanding is essential in schools which introduce a foreign language, a new science program, or a new math program at lower grade levels, to ensure that upper grade teachers will be prepared to accept the students at an advanced level. Otherwise elementary school teachers may find that their attempts at enriching the curriculum or accelerating pupils may come to naught insofar as the pupils are concerned.

Putting These Goals into Effect

NEED FOR CONSISTENCY IN TEACHING PRACTICES

Many intermediate grade teachers will provide slow-progressing pupils with third- or even second-grade readers for reading instruction, yet give the whole class arithmetic, social studies, and science books designated as fifth- or sixth-grade texts. This failure to recognize individual differences in readiness for learning frequently starts at the first-grade level, where teachers make every effort to assign pupils to reading groups on the basis of their readiness for formal reading, yet fail to teach arithmetic or writing on the same terms.

In some cases teachers may place so much stress on the realization of one objective that they overlook other desirable goals. This lack of consistency is often evident when too much stress is placed upon children's academic needs, with the result that social and emotional needs are ignored. This failure to direct a balanced program is a cause of pupil frustration, retarded academic or educational growth. In many instances it may be a prime factor in causing early pupil withdrawal from the school.

OBSTACLES TO STUDENT PROGRESS POSED BY POOR ADMINISTRATIVE PATTERNS

Pupil progress can be held back where no provisions have been made to allow children to move on to higher learning levels. Research has shown that students can master a grade's reading or arithmetic skills in six, seven, or eight months instead of the prescribed ten-month program, but administrative barriers may prevent teachers from allowing such pupils to move on to higher learning levels. For example, teachers will frequently assign pupils to lower grade level materials, but seldom will one find these teachers assigning fast learners to materials of higher grade levels. They are usually afraid to encroach upon the next teacher's curriculum. What would they do if their predecessors had allowed good students to study skills and materials prescribed for *their* grades? Once the pupils had been exposed to advanced books, would the administrators make provisions for new and different ones to avoid duplicated effort and hence boredom?

Good administrative leadership is an essential if teachers are going to make adequate provisions for both the slow and the fast learners. The organizational pattern must allow for flexibility in the use of materials and in the assignment of students to teachers who can cope with problems based upon varying rates of learning. The principal and his teachers can mutually agree on a policy which accepts and encourages the teachers to take all pupils where they find them. If this is done, more teachers will stop holding back fast-learning pupils because of the uncertainty as to what would actually happen to such pupils if they entered higher grades with a background of skill or proficiency beyond that normally expected for pupils entering such new classrooms.

TEACHER ADJUSTMENT TO A GROUP APPROACH WITHIN THE CLASSROOM

Teachers who have taught all pupils from a single text and through an all-class approach may require time to accustom themselves to a pattern of teaching which calls for more than one level of group activity in a subject. They will have to get used to the new conditions under which children learn and teachers teach; for example:

The teacher has to accept the idea that she does not have to be the center of attention for all the pupils in a given class.

The teacher may have to accept more pupil activity than she has been accustomed to allowing, and even some confusion. Yet she has to help pupils establish rules of conduct and self-discipline.

The teacher should feel secure when children are engaged in small-group activity while she works with other pupils, setting the tempo for learning.

Children have to be taught to work for prolonged periods without close teacher supervision.

Children must be taught to move about with consideration for others.

Some basic guidelines may be helpful to the teacher attempting the group approach: Relax while teaching; learn to work in a world of activity; learn that activity is not synonymous with confusion; be prepared to abandon your desk; make directions clear; let children feel their work is important; be prepared to work with individual students and learn their needs and study habits; vary composition of learning groups according to the purposes and to prevent cliques; set an example for students which leads to their trying to emulate you; work with pupils in group and self-evaluation.

TEACHER RESPONSIBILITY TOWARD CHILDREN WHO LACK CONFIDENCE IN THEMSELVES

Parents often see intellectual growth and mental stimulation as prime reasons for sending children to school, without realizing that there is more to education than their introduction to the mysteries of reading, writing and arithmetic. The fact that a boy has an IQ of 125 may be accepted as evidence that he will be ready for reading instruction before his peer who has an IQ of 95; however, this apparent intellectual readiness will not lead to success if the pupil lacks confidence in himself. What the pupil thinks of himself can determine how fast and how far he will go educationally. Under teacher pressures some children go through the process of learning basic skills, but their hearts are never in their work. They perform because they know that it is expected of them, but fear may control many of their reactions to teacher demands, with a resultant low success level.

Teachers have a responsibility to identify children lacking confidence in themselves. Unfortunately, many of these children who need help go unrecognized throughout their school lives, for example, the apparently extroverted pupil who is loud and obnoxious. On the other hand, some of the pupils who need help are quiet, timid, and withdrawn. Too often, the teacher accepts this docility without realizing that the pupil needs attention and sympathy and understanding.

TEACHER RESPONSIBILITY TOWARD THE
EMOTIONALLY DISTURBED CHILD

Every child who lacks self-confidence may not be emotionally disturbed, but most emotionally disturbed children do lack self-confidence. Teachers often find that children who are overly emotional are tense in new or strange situations and need a bit of teacher help in adjusting to the new situation. Teachers must be ready to accept nonconformity due to emotional tensions and must remember that many of these pupils are groping for answers. With sympathetic teachers these pupils often can relax and attain the success that leads to self-confidence and a freedom from tension or insecurity.

THE TEACHER'S JOB—NEVER FINISHED

While the teacher helps boys and girls reach new stages of growth or maturity, she must accept the fact that her job is really never done. Someone must help them on to newer and higher levels, but skills or work-study patterns once mastered may not suffice to help them face the new challenges. Many children will also require review, reteaching, and practice to maintain a foundation for success at higher levels.

As the pupils near adolescence, their needs multiply, but conflicts arise as youngsters seek independence in a world which continues to place new barriers before them. The teacher can help pupils find the independence they seek by studying their growth patterns and helping them to reorient themselves to the problems of today's world. Some of the boys and girls will achieve their goals with a minimum of teacher help, but others tax every bit of patience that she has. There will even be times when the teacher reaches an impasse and finds she cannot help a particular pupil over an academic or nonacademic hurdle. In this case the teacher should not let her pride get in the way of going to the principal or other staff member for assistance; teaching can call for complex skills requiring the teamwork of many people. But she must occasionally accept defeat with more maladjusted children in order to be free to assist the rest of the class.

An interesting lesson with a group of students should not be accepted as evidence that the teaching was successful or that any real learning took place. Children can enjoy being entertained, but teaching is more than entertaining. The teacher has to consider what she did to help the pupils attain desired goals. This can be accomplished only when the teacher is prepared to evaluate and re-evaluate what has been done for and with the children. The evaluation must be considered in the light of effecting changes in the way boys and girls think as well as what they may have learned. If her work is to be effective, the teacher must be prepared to take some time out each day to review what she has done in the light of her original objectives. Thus, she may ask:

Did the class understand the original objectives?

Did the pupils accomplish what they set out to do?

Was the lesson effective and purposeful?

If the group went off on a tangent, was the result worth the time and effort spent on the new activity?

Successful teachers frequently make plans for activities months ahead of time, even to the ordering of new materials: textbooks, supplementary references, library books, manipulative materials, science equipment, films, recordings, etc. Yet changes will have to be made where the teacher finds the pupils in one class have different needs and interests from those of previous classes or groups. However, long-range goals and objectives are less likely to change than the short-term day-to-day objectives. Replanning and retiming are prerequisites if the teacher is to cope with the individual differences of her children and the detours which result from her attempt to realize the educational needs of all the children in her classroom.

MAKING THE TEXTBOOK MORE EFFECTIVE

Since children cannot learn everything through first-hand experience, the teacher must direct them to the best secondary sources available. She may expose them to recordings, tapes, films, slides, speakers, and field trips, but ultimately she must fall back on the written word. Master teachers may prepare their own materials to minimize an overdependency upon textbooks, but many of them have learned to their sorrow that their homemade teaching materials seldom come up to selected commercially made textbooks. In contrast, many average and less-than-average teachers become overly dependent upon textbooks and workbooks. Actually, the problem is one of *technique*. Used properly, the textbook is an instrument of more effective teaching, but it should not dictate the entire learning process.

In many schools the teacher's program is structured by the quantity and quality of the available textbooks. This can be unfortunate, because the amount of money spent for textbooks continues to be small in proportion to the total spent on education. The lack of sufficient books may force the teacher to become overly dependent upon a single text, with resulting pupil-teacher frustration.

But lack of funds is not always the reason for an inadequate textbook supply. The authors have repeatedly seen money allocated for texts returned or diverted to other uses. Frequently teachers or principals fail to order supplementary materials. In some instances, textbook money is not wisely spent. A teacher can have many books on her shelves, but too many copies of the wrong book. In many school systems teachers and principals need to take a look at the books they have, then redistribute them or put them into a central room where everyone can have access to them. In other schools the answer may lie in better requisitioning and in helping teachers and principals select more appropriate books.

In this chapter the term "textbook teacher" is used critically. Actually, it should not be assumed that every teacher relying heavily on textbooks is to be classified as a poor teacher, because the opposite is true. *Good teachers need more books, not less.* They find strength in a large supply of varied and useful textbooks.

The Role of the Textbook in the Educative Process. The way some teachers use a good text has led some to label the book an "assistant teacher." Actually the word "assistant" can be dropped in some classrooms where the whole program is *dominated* by the textbook. The role of the teacher in the teaching process is explained thus by a textbook publisher: [1]

> With all they have to do, there is no reason for them to plan the organization of the course in detail. The author of the textbook can do that for them. There is no need for them to think up all the precise language required for the teaching of mathematics, science, or English. Nor should they have to rely entirely on their own resources for the planning of class discussions, practice materials, projects, activities, further reading. The author of the textbook can do these things for them and probably better than the ablest teacher can.

While some teachers may resent having the textbook writer take over so many of their responsibilities, one cannot escape the fact that good textbook authors develop their books around a recommended teaching method. It may be so well described in the teaching guide or manual that teaching is simplified for both experienced and inexperienced teachers. Unfortunately, some teachers order textbooks without considering how the author intended the book to be used. If the teacher continues to teach according to past patterns, the value of the textbook can be lost. This often happens in arithmetic, with the result that a good book is relegated to the closet shelf because it does not contain enough practice material to suit the teacher's concept of teaching. Before rejecting such a book, the teacher should consider the author's philosophy in light of her own. She should ask: What was the basis for the methods she (the teacher) used? Were they based upon the same concept of teaching and learning expressed by the author? If not, should she modify her approach to the teaching process or should she turn to a book which is in line with her background? With all the new approaches to arithmetic, many teachers find that they have to study arithmetic all over again if they are to teach the new mathematics successfully.

Many publishers employ consultants to ensure that a given book is used properly. Some companies even lend out sets of books for a trial basis under the direction of a trained company supervisor. Actually, the true test is the way a book meets children's needs. The vocabulary load, the organization of the material, the interest level, the use of references, and other aspects of a book will determine its suitability for a given class.

Essentially, the teacher should know the value of the books available to her class. As a professional she must continue to examine new textbooks and other teaching aids to know the tools of her trade. When asked to recommend a book or series of books, she should base her recommendation on more than a pretty new book cover design and a few new illustrations.

Overemphasis on Mastery of Subject Matter by Textbook Teacher. Time is the textbook teacher's greatest enemy, since she generally feels obligated to take children from the first page of a given text to the last. Due to individual differences in the learning needs of children, many intermediate grade teachers resort to oral reading with the entire class listening and following the content line by line and page by page. Frequent interruptions for interpretation or skill development upset the time schedule. Here, the emphasis upon subject matter memorization is often placed upon a higher level than understanding of what has been read.

All too often the mastery of subject matter becomes a fetish on the part of the teacher and the general public. Drill and more drill is recommended to attain success, which is recognized as the ability to pass oral or written examinations. Unfortunately, the standards are usually beyond the slow learner's ability or too low to challenge the fast learner. If there is a question of interpretation, the teacher handles it. There is little, if any, opportunity for creative thinking, research, or sharing of experiences and ideas.

The Value of Knowing Books Other Than Those Used in the Classroom. Books are the tools of a teacher's trade. This means that teachers have an obligation to their pupils and to themselves to get acquainted with the textbooks and library books related to the grade and subjects they teach. It isn't enough just to master a basic text. If a teacher wants to provide boys and girls with a variety of experiences, she should be prepared to raise their sights as they work in selected fields. They should be exposed to supplementary textbooks and references, but this is not easy for a teacher who does not have a wide acquaintance with books.

Many teachers find book exhibits at teachers' conventions help to keep in touch with materials that are available. Other teachers find a visit to a curriculum laboratory at a nearby college stimulating. Many large school systems have developed their own curriculum library so teachers can have easy access to new textbooks. This is especially valuable for a review of current courses of study. Publishers are usually more than ready to supply a limited number of sample copies. As a result, a wide collection of trade books is often accessible to teachers if they will take the pains to look for them. In many schools the principal makes new textbooks and other new materials available to his staff by bringing in special displays of trade books for their examination and review. The true test of the success of this is usually reflected in a steady increase of teacher requests for more and better textbooks, library books, and other teaching aids that have been brought to the faculty's attention.

Multiple Textbook Teaching. Teachers can be less formal about their teaching if they have access to multiple textbooks. They can often help pupils reach higher goals than the single textbook teacher, because many different books can be adapted to meet individual pupil needs. Teachers can divide pupils into different work groups. Assignments can be made on the basis of stages of readiness without having to individualize them. Mass assignments can still be made, but the teacher is less likely to do this. Instead of giving out page-by-page assignments, she encourages the pupils to find information for themselves.

Although it may be more difficult to teach with multiple textbooks than with a single text, teachers have reported greater enjoyment in being free of the restrictions of a single textbook. They report that teaching becomes more challenging and less monotonous.

When using multiple textbooks, the teacher must be alert to the varying demands of all types of pupils. This can lead to extra teacher effort as she familiarizes herself with more than one textbook. She has to be prepared to grow as the pupils grow. It is essential that she knows what to do for the brighter pupils who are capable of digging deeper and wider in their search for answers to problem situations. At the same time she must be prepared to help enrich the total background of slower learners to ensure that they find success and understanding in the books they read both independently and collectively. And by using multiple textbooks the teacher does not ignore subject matter: many pupils may master more with them than they can with single textbooks, because the teacher is able to direct them to books written in a language suited to the reading and experience level of her pupils.

Mixed Textbook Teaching. Instead of ordering a set of textbooks, some teachers request mixed sets of books to cope with individual differences. The term "multiple texts" refers to any number of different textbooks from one to thirty, though there may not be enough copies of a given book to allow several pupils to work together with the same text. When referring to mixed sets, one tends to think of the use of two, three, or four different titles instead of one. Thus, a sixth-grade teacher may have ten history books by one publisher, ten from a second, and ten from a third. The books may all deal with the same field of study, but they may not be of equal difficulty or interest. Pupils are free to work with the set which meets their basic needs. No one book may carry the label of basic text for the course.

The teacher may still use multiple texts to supplement the one mixed set of three titles, or she may use the mixed set the way teachers use a single text. If pupils are grouped for instruction, each section may work with a particular textbook, although it is not necessary to group children for social studies the way they may be grouped for reading. In making assignments, the teacher may refer the pupils to common topics or questions which can be answered by referring to any one of the textbooks. Pupils learn to find answers through looking at the index or table of contents since the teacher will not list the pages they need to read in one or more books. The brighter pupils are often advised to read from at least two of the books comprising a set in order to get another author's view or to enrich their background.

Overdependence on Textbook Labels. When elementary school teachers receive a new book, they ask, "What grade level does it represent?" All too often the answer lies in the number of bars, periods, stripes, stars, or other code symbols used to designate a recommended grade. While it helps to know that a book was prepared for a particular stage of learning, the teacher should not allow her choice of a text to be determined by the publisher. The true test of a book should be in the way it meets children's educational needs. A set of readers with a fourth-grade label (code) may be valueless in a fourth grade composed of children from a low socioeconomic level. Due to factors beyond their control or the teacher's, the children may be working on a second- or third-grade level. Similarly, the teacher in a very high socioeconomic level community may find books bearing a fifth-grade label will be far more challenging and desirable.

Essentially, the graded textbook has been constructed for *average learning* boys and girls. The books are generally prepared by leading educators who have made a special study of the fields of reading, social studies, science, arithmetic, or other specialized fields. These specialists try to give teachers a teachable book in terms of modern approaches to the learning process, which means that they dictate what the modern teacher may use or how she teaches. Usually, the specialists tend to be conservative since their continued success depends upon the success of the teachers using their book.

Many publishers would be happier if teachers selected books on the basis of pupil needs instead of on a grade label, but too many teachers seem to want someone else to tell them what book is appropriate for a given grade. Unfortunately, teachers who want to deviate from custom often cannot get parental or administrative approval for assigning books from higher or lower grades than the grade designation on the classroom door.

Lack of Consistency in Assigning Textbooks. Teachers often show inconsistency in the way they assign books to their pupils. This is apparent in elementary schools where teachers use subgrouping in such subjects as arithmetic and reading. Here, the boys and girls are divided into different levels of instruction in reading, yet for the rest of the day no attempt is made to supply them with other reading materials comparable in ease or difficulty with the book used for instruction. All too often pupils work in content fields on an all-class basis, with the result that many are forced to try to master a level of understanding above them. This can frustrate the pupil, because many average and below-average readers are unable to read independently in the so-called graded subject texts.

The Single Textbook Teacher—A Dominant Pattern. A large segment of the nation's teachers are single textbook teachers. They do not make provisions for individual differences since their teaching is based upon a uniform approach to the acquisition of knowledge. All pupils are expected to master the contents of a single textbook, and this is usually based on having them work through the book page by page and chapter by chapter, regardless of whether the material is repetitious to some or frustrating to others. All too often success depends upon the pupil's ability to parrot answers based on one book. Reading a second book may not help the ambitious pupil since his answers may not agree with the teacher's book. The rigidity of some textbook teachers is seen in their refusal to allow two editions of a given title because of variations in content or page numbers. Of course, teaching through a single textbook is easier than using multiple texts.

The single textbook teacher is in conflict with a philosophy of education which emphasizes helping boys and girls solve problems and seek out answers. Pupils can still refer to their texts as sources of information, but they are not expected to limit their search for answers to a single source. The class program should be enriched through more student contributions based on using multiple books, newspapers, magazines, technical reports, and encyclopedias. Unfortunately, the contrast between the two types of classes is not always recognized by a public dominated by the "textbook mastery" concept of education. The single textbook teacher is frequently recognized as an authority capable of pushing pupils through a subject so that they can regurgitate facts and figures to pass a standardized test. By contrast, the modern teacher, who is interested in developing comprehension skills, independent thinking, and leadership qualities, may appear quite ineffective, although studies have shown her pupils can more than hold their own in competition with pupils who mastered their skills and acquired background through the textbook approach.

USING THE WORKBOOK

Teachers who work with arithmetic or reading groups are usually quite concerned about the other children in the class who are supposedly working at their seats. Are they engaging in profitable activities, or are they wasting time? Often the means to successful grouping may be the way children are assigned workbook exercises. In some school systems boys and girls as well as teachers are frustrated by a constant exposure to workbooks. During the course of the average day they may work in six or seven different types of workbooks, with the result that their work becomes repetitive and needlessly monotonous. While workbooks are often misused, they cannot be ignored since they can be the answer to finding materials for children who need practice in certain skills.

In recommending workbooks, it must be remembered that every teacher is not capable of making her own materials. Commercially prepared workbooks, while not perfect, are often much better than homemade imitations. However, the teacher should refrain from using workbooks unless she can select a type that can be adapted to the basic needs of her pupils and can then make individual or group assignments based upon their stages of readiness.

If children can operate freely without constant teacher supervision and direction, they may not have to depend upon workbook activities. But unfortunately, many boys and girls work on a low self-directive level, which means that teachers feel obligated to give them seatwork exercises that will keep them busy and profitably occupied. In addition, some teachers are quite adept at preparing special enrichment or supplementary activities which are less restrictive.

Standards for Selecting Workbooks. In selecting workbooks, teachers should have a yardstick to help them judge the various workbooks before them. For example, Andreen's [2] study of workbooks showed that the two greatest weaknesses in commercially prepared workbooks were the lack of adequate provisions for motivating learning and the lack of materials organized to provide for individual differences. Some time has elapsed since Andreen reported his findings, but the admonition to look for materials which will provide for pupil needs on an individual basis and help motivate them to action is still a wise one to follow.

Educators may find it helpful to look for the following features: exercises that are related to the day-by-day activities of children in purposeful learning situations, clear directions, material that meets local school or class standards, exercises that are diagnostic in nature to locate boys' and girls' strengths and weaknesses, suitable practice material, and exercises that are easily corrected.

REFERENCES

1. American Textbook Publisher Institute, *Textbooks in Education* (Chicago: Lakeside Press, 1949), p. 7.
2. Earl P. Andreen, "A Study of Workbooks in Arithmetic," *Journal of Educational Research,* 32 (October 1958).
3. Educational Policies Commission, *The Purposes of Education in American Democracy* (Washington, D.C.: National Education Association, 1938).
4. Ernest R. Hilgard and David H. Russell, "Motivation in School Learning," *Forty-ninth Yearbook of the National Society for the Study of Education,* Part I, *Learning and Instruction* (Chicago: University of Chicago Press, 1950).
5. Metropolitan School Study Council, "Grouping Within a Classroom," *A Study of Grouping Practices Designed to Improve Individualization of Instruction Based on Experiences of Teachers in Council Schools* (New York: Metropolitan School Study Council, 1952).
6. E. T. McSwain, "Intermediate School Grouping," *Portfolio for Intermediate Teachers,* Leaflet No. 5 (Washington, D.C.: Association for Childhood Education, 1946).
7. Mary Clare Petty, *Intraclass Grouping in the Elementary School* (Austin: University of Texas Press, 1953).
8. Herbert A. Thelen, "Group Dynamics in Instruction, Principle of Least Group Size," *The School Review,* 57 (March 1949), 142.
9. George I. Thomas, "A Study of Reading Achievement in Terms of Mental Ability," *The Elementary School Journal,* 47 (September 1946), 28–33.
10. George I. Thomas, "Formula for Purchasing Basic Readers," *The Nation's Schools* (April 1957), 57–58.

CHAPTER 4

Observing and
Understanding Pupil Behavior

The successful teacher is an artist who has learned to adapt her teaching methods and materials to the maximum development of the children assigned to her. Because she works constantly with children who have different backgrounds, purposes, and drives, along with different physical, emotional, and social needs, the teacher can never guarantee the outcome of her efforts. She may attempt to mold them into prescribed models of the educated boy or girl, but she will find that "end products" defy standardization. At times she will be able to impart knowledge and teach skills based upon common pupil needs, interests, and stages of readiness; but there will be other times when her efforts appear fruitless due to individual differences in the learners that result in different stages of readiness and accomplishment.

Some children will find it easy to succeed with a teacher. Others may try manfully to please her, but success comes so hard that they may be frustrated unless she takes special pains with them. She will find teaching is a challenge to her as she tries to help individual pupils express themselves with different mediums. While she avoids activities which result in continued frustration for individual children, she does not spoon-feed them. Each pupil has to learn how to work for himself when he works in a setting which gives meaning or purpose to his endeavors. Essentially, the teacher's success and progress depends upon her understanding of the basic needs of her children and her readiness to teach in terms of their "stages of readiness" for new and higher levels of learning.

When one finds, for example, pupil scores clustering about a grade norm in a given subject, one can ask questions about the quality of teaching or learning going on. In many instances, it is just another indication that teachers have been teaching toward mediocrity or conformity. This should never occur where boys and girls are encouraged to work close to accomplishment levels commensurate with their real ability. The range of growth or achievement for individual children will reflect the quality of the teaching. The better the teaching, the greater the range of accomplishment! A study of reading and arithmetic achievement test scores will frequently show a narrower range of achievement in arithmetic scores than in reading, since elementary school teachers are less apt to provide for individual differences in the field of arithmetic than they do in the field of reading. The range in reading achievement in some sixth-grade classes will extend from four to six more learning levels than in arithmetic.

Good teaching promotes differences by encouraging children to grow in all subject fields. Reading skill is recognized, but other skills are not ignored. This often occurs in so-called "homogeneous classes," with the result that much of the original homogeneity in achievement will disappear between September and June. At the start of the year the pupils may achieve close to a given norm, but with a good teacher and good learning tools, differences will appear. Actually differences will appear despite the teacher, but the range in actual achievement will not be as great as it is where the teacher continues to make provisions for individual differences.

Teaching Children by Understanding Their Basic Needs As Influenced by Their Background

When the teacher does not know the nature of the children she is working with, she teaches on the *assumption* that all the children have the same basic needs and are at the same stage of readiness for a given lesson. Growth does occur for some children without too much help from the teacher, but for others progress comes slowly even when the teacher takes special pains to help them. All too often the assumption is made that the teacher has been successful if she meets her goal of promotion of the class, but few people know how far these children could have gone if the teacher had directed her attention to *known* needs instead of *assumed* needs. To do this, teachers must know the characteristics of their children and their abilities, interests, needs, and backgrounds.

Teachers will find numerous studies and guides to help them get to know their children. Too often teachers will look at these guides without realizing that there are still children who do not fall into one of these basic patterns.) Other children will exhibit some of the characteristics described, but may show contradictory behavior patterns under different learning conditions. For example, most teachers will find that a cross section of their children will have one or more of the needs set forth in Table 1 (see pages 82–84).

Because children grow at different rates and in varying amounts, all ten-year-olds do not fall into a set pattern.) Some ten-year-olds will resemble eleven- or twelve-year-olds, while others may still show characteristics or needs of seven- or eight-year-olds. A few of the more mature ten-year-old pupils may show characteristics and needs resembling those of twelve- and thirteen-year-olds. Table 1 shows the needs of children who belong to overlapping age levels, such as primary, intermediate, upper grade, and high school. It would help if teachers would think in terms of multiple age-grade groupings instead of traditional grade designations. This means the teacher must realize that her children may not be ready to learn skills prescribed in terms of grade standards. Somewhere in the primary or intermediate grades, children will reach a stage of learning for prescribed skills or bodies of knowledge, with a likelihood that a primary curriculum or an intermediate grade curriculum will be more to the point than a curriculum designated as a first-, second-, and third-grade, or a fourth-, fifth-, and sixth-grade program. This is often apparent in the overlapping of test scores of fourth-, fifth-, and sixth-grade pupils.

The average class will often have some children who are achieving at levels above or below the intermediate grade level, but most pupils will show achievement within a three-year range. How to provide for these fringe children can become a problem even when grades are eliminated in favor of an ungraded school pattern of organization. If the teacher attempts to classify her children in terms of the needs set forth in Table 1, she will find the exceptions pose problems for her because of differences in their maturation levels. (Thus, a mentally mature pupil may have problems because he is socially or emotionally immature.) Similarly, a socially mature pupil may be physically or mentally immature./ Therefore, these pupils may have needs different from those of any one of their peers or of the children in an instructional group. This is what makes homogeneous grouping virtually impossible.) Although sex differences, for example, should make no difference in the ability of boys and girls to learn, the fact remains that one sex or the other will excel in one phase of the curriculum. Again, there will be exceptions. For example, girls are apt to mature physically, socially, and emotionally faster than boys, but one will find immature girls and mature boys in the same age grouping.

TABLE 1

Planning a Program of Education for Intermediate Grade Children Based on Recognition of
Their Needs and Stages of Mental, Physical, Social, and Emotional Development

Characteristics of Stages of Growth and Development of Intermediate Grade Children	How the School Can Help Children Realize Individual and Group Needs (Ages 9, 10, and 11)
Mental Development	
Intense intellectual curiosity	Provide books and materials to satisfy this intellectual curiosity.
Interest in other peoples and cultures	Offer material about the cultures of other peoples.
A good attention span	Provide a flexible program and opportunities for longer blocks of work.
Increasing ability to formulate generalizations	Give opportunities to pupils to work individually and collectively with information from a variety of real and vicarious sources. Offer guidance in making generalizations based upon studies and learning.
Considerable interest in planning their own activities	Provide activities for individual and group planning in which child initiates and carries through the greater part of the chosen activity with guidance.
A tendency toward critical and just evaluations of their own activities	Give opportunities for children to evaluate own work through teacher-pupil, pupil-pupil, and teacher-parent-pupil conferences.
An intense interest in dramatic expression	Provide materials and experiences involving skills of dramatic expression.
Ability to express themselves creatively in a variety of ways	Offer opportunities, space, and materials for creative activity with good teacher guidance and encouragement.
Considerable growth in language skills	Make available materials and situations needed to develop and use oral and written communication to express ideas.
Greater independence in reading to obtain answers or information	Provide good and plentiful materials for reading and research, and opportunities for developing advanced reading skill.

Characteristics	Provisions
A growing awareness of time and space concepts	Offer broadening and meaningful experiences involving time and space concepts and relationships.
Greater facility in the understanding and application of number concepts	Provide opportunities for use of fundamental processes in meaningful situations.

Social-Emotional Growth

Characteristics	Provisions
A strong sense of responsibility	Permit children to assume responsibility with and without adult guidance.
Greater awareness of social standards for group acceptance	Provide situations involving application of standards for successful group activity.
Enjoyment of group activity, preferably with those of the same sex	Give some freedom from adult domination, to form own groups and carry out own activities.
Amenable to suggestions	Provide opportunities to develop an understanding of individual and group rights.
A tendency toward organized play and a beginning of the gang spirit	Understand the necessity for "gang" activities and relationships of constructive type.
Approaching the independent planning and working stage	Provide opportunities for planning, executing and evaluating own activities.
Respect for adults, but greater loyalty to peers	Understand strong loyalty to peers.
Greater emotional stability, but some weakness in self-control	Provide opportunities to act in situations requiring self-control and to recognize the value of such behavior.
Strong likes and dislikes	Understand the degree of these feelings and provide situations to modify their intensity.
Ready response to praise and love	Understand the continued need to be loved and create a genuine warm, friendly atmosphere.
Readiness to share possessions	Encourage sound judgment in sharing.
Little prejudice, except under external influence	Provide experiences which will build understanding and create desirable attitudes.

(Table 1 continued)

Characteristics of Stages of Growth and Development of Intermediate Grade Children	How the School Can Help Children Realize Individual and Group Needs (Ages 9, 10, and 11)
Increasing comprehension of family relationships	Provide opportunities for understanding and appreciation of the responsibilities and privileges of family membership.
A religious consciousness	Recognize the development of a religious consciousness and promote a sympathetic attitude toward all beliefs.
A social consciousness	Provide experiences requiring an awareness of, and participation in, many social situations.
Hero worship	Help pupils get acquainted with a wide variety of personalities.
Physical Growth and Development	
Using large muscles	Frequently change activities with periodic rest.
Rapid muscular growth: considerable small muscle coordination, but poor large muscle control	Set up activities to develop and strengthen both large and small muscles and develop new skills.
Rapid development of bone structure, particularly girls	Adjust furniture to meet growing body needs.
Ravenous appetites with fewer food preferences	Encourage pupils to eat appropriate foods to maintain strength and build bone structure. Provide a good lunch program.
Greater resistance to disease	Give pupils opportunities to learn about their bodies and how to care for them.
Pronounced sex differences faster in girls	Instruct pupils about the body changes which come with puberty. Offer activities involving some members of the opposite sex, such as social dancing.
Sensitivity about body changes	Arrange school activities which protect from needless frustration and embarrassment boys and girls whose body structure is changing and who may need time to adjust to body growth and change.
Need for at least ten or eleven hours of sleep each night	Provide opportunities to learn good health practices as well as body care.
An increased interest in outdoor activities, of a highly competitive nature; interest in games of skill and team activity	Provide a sports program to enable each individual to learn the rules and the skills which go with each seasonal sport.

The teacher can read about the needs of children, but it takes keen observation and skill to identify them when she is working with specific youngsters. In a sense, the listed needs and characteristics can be guides to action, but the actual teaching will have to be refined in terms of what the teacher can discover about the individual needs and interests of given boys and girls.

In considering the individual pupil's readiness for success, it helps if the teacher knows something concrete about other factors such as: the pupil's mental health; his interests in and out of school; his home environment; his economic and social background; his physical health; his work-study patterns; his reading level; his accomplishment level in basic skill subjects; his general intelligence level; his past school experiences. Some of the data a teacher needs will be available in the cumulative records kept by the school. In addition, it will be helpful to talk to the pupil, to his parents, and to other staff members who are working or have worked with him.

EFFECT OF MENTAL HEALTH ON LEARNING

Providing an environment conducive to maximum learning includes recognition of mental as well as physical factors. Actually, the two are so closely related that no sharp line can be drawn between them. Children who have good mental health can adjust more easily to school and school problems than those who have poor mental health. It is difficult for a pupil to find success in school when he is under tension at home or in the classroom. He cannot adjust to new learning situations or withstand the stresses, strains, and conflicts of routine class activities. He may become frustrated easily and openly show his inner feelings by emotional outbursts or other actions which may not appear to be related to the cause.

Children should work hard and learn to exert themselves if they are to grow intellectually. Learning is ultimately personal—only the learner can absorb the learning, and nobody else can do it for him. Sometimes failure has to be accepted as a stage in the learning process. Unfortunately, however, the pupil with poor mental health cannot accept this and may become emotionally upset when small things frustrate him. The teacher has to differentiate between the individual who is *temporarily* upset and the pupil whose emotional unbalance extends over a long period of time. Identifying and helping such pupils is easier at primary grade levels than at intermediate and upper grade levels, where many older boys and girls reject offers of assistance due to barriers which have been built up over a long period of frustrating school experiences.

Teachers recognize the home as having a powerful influence upon the child's success in school. Teachers are critical of parents who neglect children, but they often overlook the dangers of overprotective parents. Table 2 shows how parental actions toward their children can elicit responses that come out in classroom behavior. For example, many school bullies are merely home-rejected pupils who have lost the security that goes with being wanted. The rejected pupil has lost faith in himself. He does not feel competent to achieve, so he backs away from responsibility. Frequently, he adopts the attitude that nobody else has faith in him, so he is unable to accept help and tends to be distrustful of those who show affection or regard for his welfare. Studies have also shown that many overprotective parents have actually long since rejected their children. Their solicitude is generally a "cover" which the child has come to recognize, with the result that he develops a negative personality. Many of these children can be rebellious at home and aggressive when they are with their peers.

TABLE 2
Pupil Reactions to Parents' Behavior

Parent Actions	*Pupil Reactions*
Parents share work and play with the child.	Pupil tends to be cooperative; gets along well with his peermates.
Parents are overattentive and overprotective.	Pupil avoids aggressive play, may cry easily, lacks persistence in completing work in school.
Parents tend to neglect the child.	Pupil tends to show off, may lie to cover up or to obtain attention.
Parents use too firm discipline, are unfair or tempers are at the trigger point.	Pupil is apt to lack self-initiative, be overdependent upon adults, not get along well with other boys and girls.
Parents isolate child, threaten him.	Pupil shows insecurity; may be slow to develop social and emotional stability.

Winning over the rejected pupil can take time and energy. Unfortunately, the teacher often fails to recognize the symptoms of rejection, so she can magnify the pupil's problem through her own actions. The hostile teacher or the impatient teacher will make little headway with the pupil who is literally walking around with a "chip on his shoulder." In the old school these children were frequent targets for a whipping, either physically or verbally. Today, understanding teachers may have to curb their desire to strike back at the hostile child. Instead, they have to retaliate with kindness when the pupil is rude and outspoken. They have to be patient when the pupil refuses to take part in social activities and is antisocial. With time, most teachers who are fair and considerate can win these children over.

SIGNIFICANCE OF DELINQUENT BEHAVIOR

One of the problems educators have to resolve is whether delinquent behavior is the cause of pupil failure in school or is merely the aftermath of repeated failure. Studies of juvenile delinquents have revealed two types. In the first category are boys and girls with limited mental ability who have never mastered academic skills. In the second are boys and girls with high mental ability whose achievement exceeds that of nondelinquents. In the first group, one encounters many children who apparently could not find much challenge or success in the school activities in which they could participate. In the second group, one finds boys and girls who failed to find satisfaction in their academic accomplishments. They, too, needed a challenge, but one of a *different* nature.

Authorities have found corrective or remedial classes help delinquent boys and girls find themselves. This leads one to ask why such help could not have been given before they became troublemakers. Generally, such pupils do not suddenly become delinquents. They usually show some signs which the observant teacher can learn to recognize. Elementary teachers have to look for early signs of frustration and the beginning of antisocial behavior in hopes that an early attack on children's growth and adjustment problems will be the best type of preventive medicine. There is no guarantee that the school and its program will be able to resolve the problems of juvenile delinquency, but it may help to raise the sights or goals of boys and girls who have not been able to find the answer to their problems at home or at school.

The gap between the goals of the teacher and learner slipping into juvenile delinquency is too great for the two to come together. As a result, there is a need for a new look at the sequence of school activities at lower grade levels—to bridge this gap and lead to continued success and the solution of pupil problems before they overwhelm the child who is already carrying more than his share of tension, uncertainty, and frustration.

EFFECT OF ECONOMIC BACKGROUND

Studies have shown that where one lives or the race from which one springs is of less importance than the level of the socioeconomic group to which one belongs. For example, children from the lower socioeconomic levels have the greatest number of adjustments to make when they go to school. The higher the status of the parent, the better the chance that the child will be emotionally stable. In a sense, this may be attributed to the fact that children can find more security in the home of average or better-than-average socioeconomic level, although there will be exceptions. One can find neglected children whose parents are at the top of the economic level, and at the same time one can point with pride to children who live in filth and ignorance and who overcome the obstacles of neglect, lack of adequate food, clothing, and other necessities of life without losing their security, pride, and ambition. However, despite these exceptions and some leveling off of the differences between children from all levels of the society, *the fact remains that children who come from lower cultural levels still have to climb the highest in order to find success.* Teachers who work with such pupils are quite apt to find that they are sensitive individuals. Their emotions may be quite close to the surface; therefore, they may have trouble adjusting to school and the problems of living and working with others in the classroom setting.

Paralleling these emotional differences is the incidence of physical and psychosomatic illnesses. The question of which came first is of no consequence here. The point is merely being made that children from lower economic levels are more likely to be absent from school or, when in school, to be in a poor frame of mind to benefit from educational experiences, because they may be both mentally and physically ill. (The word "mental" here is limited to illnesses of a psychosomatic nature, e.g., tics, eczema, asthma, constipation, enuresis.) The lack of a balanced diet may impair growth, which in turn can create feelings of anxiety and uncertainty.

Teachers and school nurses have not always considered absences as legal unless the individual was *physically* ill. Actually, many boys and girls from low economic areas are ill or not in the proper frame of mind for learning due to emotional problems. If forced to attend school when they have an apparent headache or other hard-to-diagnose ailment, they may merely increase their resentment against teachers and the adult authority which they feel is restricting their freedom. The problem becomes increasingly complex when these children miss an excessive amount of school days when they could be taking part in special activities which have been prepared to help meet their educational needs.

Children from low economic levels tend to have the greatest number of social adjustments to make because of their lack of good socializing experiences, both in and out of school. This is especially true at upper grade and senior high school levels, where interactions between pupils tend to be limited almost exclusively to school activities. Studies have shown that children who come from higher income

A Spanish-speaking child receives special help in conversational English.

Photo by Suzanne Szasz, courtesy of PEA School Volunteers, New York City

families tend to exhibit higher levels of social maturity. Their interests tend to be on a much higher plane and they exhibit a self-confidence often found lacking in their less fortunate peers. This latter group is quite apt to be represented by fewer members in areas calling for leadership roles, and in ordinary classroom discussions many of them will refrain from making contributions unless the teacher uses skill to draw them out.

Success in school tends to be measured in terms of scholastic achievement. It has already been pointed out that many children from low economic levels, handicapped by social, emotional, and physical factors, are often not ready for active participation in school functions. The problem of these individuals, however, actually goes much deeper than readiness in school, since many of them feel the effects of their environment long before they begin school. Cultural deprivation starts during their preschool years. This is illustrated by the fact that children from middle- and upper-income families learn to talk at an earlier age. They form sentences and use much more complex sentences in their daily contacts with those around them. This will be reflected in their readiness for reading and writing activities, which is dependent upon the pupils' prior oral language experiences.

Studies have shown that children from low economic levels have a smaller oral vocabulary and may speak with poorer articulation throughout their school careers. Some teachers have argued that this is not true because some of these children grow up in large families where they have many opportunities to speak, whereas many upper-class children are virtually isolated from other child contacts. But talking with other children in a large family is not sufficient background for the advanced levels of communication in the classroom. In upper-class families the child has more contact with adults, and it is this association with grownups which stimulates the increased vocabulary and more mature sentence structure. Similarly, children who mature rapidly—physically and mentally—play with older children and thus acquire a richer vocabulary than children who play with younger children and thus fail to develop mature speech patterns.

Then too, children coming from homes where learning is not held in high esteem enter school with a decided handicap. Not only do they fail to develop a good oral language and an acquaintanceship with rich reading materials, but they lack an adequate *attitude* for learning. Many children stop working in school when the "going begins to get rough" because they fail to see a reason for exerting themselves at tasks which have little meaning to them. Giving such individuals a purpose in life is a problem for teachers when the parents offer no incentive to the children to work for a sustained period at increasingly harder learning levels. Again, the lack of enriching experiences at home results in a lack of readiness for many school activities.

The problems of these pupils start at the first-grade level, where their more fortunate peers forge ahead at a rapid pace because they need to spend less time on readiness activities. Then, as these late starters go through school, their lack of maturity holds them back in social studies, science, and other areas calling for language facilities. Their progress continues to be slow because of their lack of ability to express themselves or to abstract ideas from what they read and hear. To rid themselves of this "millstone," they must work harder and longer than those children who were able to start at higher readiness stages of learning. Again, achievement is related to their attitude toward school. Some of these pupils may not show outward manifestations of their negative attitude toward school and learning, but it is there. Many of these children fail to achieve at high levels because they cannot see the value in working for an "A" when a "C" will suffice to get by. They may even resist the teacher who tries to assist them. In the face of such conditions the teacher must be ready to vary the nature of her instruction. In order to reach these children, she may have to remove them from the large group situation, where the lack of confidence or security is an obstacle. She may offer greater participation in the class activity by children from less favored homes. These children can respond to teachers who are warm and sincere and who try to assist them by placing them in learning situations where their differences from more fortunate children are not going to be accentuated.

Many teachers are influenced in their evaluation of a pupil by group intelligence test results. Unfortunately, IQs often work to the disadvantage of children from low socioeconomic levels, because there is some indication that such tests fail to show the true potential of these children. As a result, the teacher often *underestimates* their ability and places them in a false learning situation. Some of these children who have been tagged as "slow" or "average" learners are capable of achieving at higher expectation levels when the school makes a more concerted effort to do something positive about their lack of rich experiences. A number of studies have shown that pupils who live in slum areas can show a rise in intelligence levels after exposure to good books, plays, music, interesting people, museums, and other similar experiences. In such situations, teachers have to be prepared to accelerate learning by stimulating boys and girls to explore new areas of thinking, living, and acting; but they must also be prepared to go down to the level of the children's understanding and work upward.

EDUCATIONAL GROWTH AND TOTAL GROWTH

Although the authors have repeatedly sponsored an early entrance policy based on individual testing and careful study of the prospective kindergarten child, there is evidence that some children are better off if schooling is deferred even though they may be quite precocious and appear socially and physically mature. Some children who have high IQs may lack interest and drive, others may need to work with teachers who will help build up their sense of security. Because the pressures on educators can be quite troublesome, many refuse to compromise with parents who ask special consideration for early school admission for children who miss an age deadline by a few days, weeks, or even months. At times hard and fast rules and regulations can be harmful to some boys and girls; therefore, a flexible entrance policy is recommended with consideration being given to each pupil's physical, mental, emotional, and social maturation, and to any other factors which may affect his progress in school. In many instances where it is evident that the child may be immature in some phase of growth, the parents should be brought in for a good talk and a presentation of all the evidence.

In addition, all aspects of a child's growth pattern should be considered in the light of the capacities of other children in the class he would attend if admitted. It may not be easy to convince antagonistic parents that a bright child will not be bored with kindergarten or first-grade activities. However, this challenge can be met by teachers who offer a rich program of activities based on purposeful or realistic goals. Sometimes the parents can visit the class or, as a last resort, the child may be entered on a trial basis.

All attempts to accelerate the educational growth of children as they go through the elementary grades must depend upon the total growth pattern of each individual. That a child is six years old chronologically does not mean that he is as mature as many of his peers in a number of growth areas. For example, a study of the ossification of his wrist bones may show that a given child's physical growth is proceeding at a slower rate than may be considered normal. Similarly, consideration can be given to his height, weight, eruption of teeth, and his social and emotional growth. These indexes will help teachers anticipate the probable progress of individual children since they give a picture of the general maturity level of a child.

Because of individual differences in total growth patterns, the teacher will seldom, if ever, be able to elicit uniform responses using the same materials and procedures with all children. Outwardly, many of them will try to give desired responses in terms of pencil-and-paper activities, but inwardly some of them may be at odds with the teacher or the activity. Thus a seemingly slow-learning child may be unable to progress along some lines of endeavor because of slow physical growth that may be in conflict with a more advanced intellect. He may resist anything associated with close muscular coordination even though he is able to work at advanced levels in other areas. His slowness may be due to an inner resistance to pressures which place him in frustrating experiences and may not have anything to do with his actual intellectual learning capacity.

The term "late bloomer," may have its origin in this concept of learning. Growth at early stages tends to proceed at relatively slow rates of speed due to an over-all immaturity, but as the individual matures, he is able to proceed at faster rates and at higher levels until he is making better-than-normal progress. Unfortunately, many parents place an excessive amount of hope on a possibility that their slow-learning child will suddenly blossom forth and surprise everyone with his leadership and achievement. While it can happen, the teacher and parent who study the total growth curves of individual children should be able to face reality when it becomes evident that a child's slow intellectual growth is not paralleling his normal physical growth. The boy whose bone ossification, history of teeth eruption, and height and weight curves are normal is not likely to show suddenly that he is a "late bloomer." Unfortunately, most teachers are not familiar with this type of data. Used properly by educators, the organic age can be used to determine whether an academic deficiency is related to a general growth pattern. This refined measure is more reliable than single age units. It is an average age unit obtained when various measures of growth such as height, ossification of bones, dentition, mental age, strength, coordination, plus reading and arithmetic achievement ages are charted for individual children in terms of their growth patterns. For example, a pupil may appear retarded in terms of his mental age, but a study of his carpal age, his dental age, his height age, his weight age, and his chronological age will show how his mental age compares with the other units of measure. Plateaus in his chart could show a slow growth of the total organism, which might indicate that the pupil's academic retardation is merely following the pattern of physical growth.

Modern attempts to chart individual growth patterns have been facilitated by the keeping of more exact records by school personnel and family physicians. From their records it is possible to see how individuals have grown over a period of years and it is possible to predict how they may grow in the future. Tables for translating physical measurements into age limits have been prepared, but they are still based upon a number of variables which could affect the nature of one's conclusions. However, more study and some experimentation may help show where a pupil has been going in the way of physical growth, which may account for his failure to show desired academic growth.

EFFECT OF PHYSICAL HEALTH ON LEARNING

Modern educators place considerable emphasis upon the condition of each child's physical health, because school success can be positively related to the way children feel. Some children with poor health appear to overcome their handicap—but they are exceptions to the rule. They may succeed due to persistence, fear, ambition, interest, and a better background of experiences than others in their class. This raises the question of how far these pupils could have gone had they not been handicapped by poor health. In contrast, teachers often encounter boys and girls who fail to catch up with their peers after frequent absences due to poor health. They just lack the strength necessary for the physical and mental exertions required by school studies.

When children show they are making a poor adjustment to established school routines, the teacher cannot overlook the possible impact of poor general health. She should readily notice the symptoms which go with good health and should be prepared to help those children who do not exhibit them. For example, she would note that:

1. Healthy children enjoy life. They are naturally active and gladly take part in activities within their range of interest and capability.

2. Physical growth tends to be fairly continuous. It may not be uniform in rate for all boys and girls, but growth should be evident over a period of time. An abnormal interruption in physical growth may be a cause for alarm and investigation.

3. Healthy children tend to have good appetites. Children who fail to eat up to established patterns may be in need of special consideration or help.

4. Healthy children are able to take part in normal school activities without becoming unduly tired. They have a power of endurance and recuperate rapidly with a change of pace or change of activity.

5. Healthy children tend to be cheerful. They may have problems, but they can laugh at themselves or at others at the appropriate time. They can see the bright side of life as well as the gloomy side.

6. Healthy children tend to have fairly good control over their emotions. If a child becomes upset at little things, it may indicate that he is not in good health.

Children who fail to conform to normal growth patterns may have other problems, but the teacher has to look at each pupil individually in considering what is normal for him. The tall boy may be thin and the short boy may be a bit on the heavy side, but both boys can still be healthy in terms of their particular growth patterns.

It has been estimated that only one-third of all elementary school children are really physically healthy. Surprisingly enough, one obstacle to health in our country is that of malnutrition, from which at least 25 per cent of our elementary school children suffer. This does not mean that they do not have enough to eat as much as it refers to how and what they eat. Getting such children to work on a high plane for sustained periods is a problem since they fatigue easily and lack interest in school activities. Some physical factors other than diet may contribute to improper nutrition, such as infected tonsils, poor teeth, or insomnia. Similarly, children with defective vision or hearing can become maladjusted individuals unless something constructive can be done for them. While the extent of poor health or low physical fitness has been emphasized by both educators and noneducators, it is still often overlooked as a primary reason for low achievement or lack of interest in academic pursuits. Teachers and the general public are conditioned to accept seemingly satisfactory progress by children, because they meet artificial grade standards, when in reality they could do much better if they were not handicapped by some physical defect.

Responsibility of Teacher in Maintaining Good Health. Each teacher is concerned with establishing an environment which will foster good physical and mental health. Therefore, she should pay attention to the following: health records of children; adequate lighting; proper seating; symptoms of poor health or physical defects; a balanced program of activities; consultation with principal, nurse, parent, or other agencies regarding poor health of pupils; adjustments for children who have defects or who have been absent.

Attention Required by Visual Deficiencies. Studies have shown that from one-fourth to one-third of all children have at least one type of eye deficiency, with some pupils having more than one visual defect. It has often been assumed that these visual defects are the basic cause of pupil failure, but this has not always been true. Reading specialists who have carefully examined the eyes of poor readers and successful readers have found that both classifications of pupils have a large number of eye defects. [1] This does not mean that we can eliminate visual deficiencies as a cause of failure, because there is sufficient evidence that eye defects can be a contributing factor in the failure of some pupils to make desired progress.

At this point it is not necessary to dwell upon the many kinds of visual defects which children may have, yet the teacher or school nurse should be prepared to detect their symptoms. Since the average person uses his eyes to secure about 75 per cent of his learning, a wise precaution is an entrance requirement which calls for an eye examination by an eye specialist before the pupil begins school. Then, after school has started, there should be frequent eye screenings by competent school personnel. Actually these screenings are not carried out by eye specialists. Usually, a teacher or school nurse uses the Snellen or E Chart to detect possible visual deficiencies. Other schools supplement such testing with the American Medical Association Rating Reading Chart. In a number of schools the nurse may use the Massachusetts Vision Test or the Keystone Visual Survey Telebinocular. Other tests which may be used are the Eames Eye Test or the Ortho-Rater. In using such instruments to screen children, the examiner must remember that poor visual acuity does not mean that the child's achievement is actually affected by the findings. For example, one school nurse would get very excited about children who had a form of astigmatism, yet this defect does not have too much bearing upon a pupil's reading disability.

A pupil may be succeeding in school, but he may be very uncomfortable in the process. Due to the eye defect, the learner may have to strain himself to complete a task. He may acquire a bad headache, or he may not concentrate on his work because of general discomfort or physical fatigue. His eyes may get blurry, he may get dizzy, and he may even suffer nausea. A number of pupils may unconsciously conceal the nature of their defect by moving closer to the blackboard or by holding their books closer to their eyes. If the teacher is observant she will notice some of the symptoms of pupil discomfort due to visual defects. This is especially true where the teacher works closely with her pupils in a small group situation. If she observes at least two to four of the following symptoms, the teacher should refer the pupil to the nurse for further screening:

Excessive rubbing of eyes.

Deliberate attempts to avoid visual work.

A general tenseness when required to do visual work.

Evidence of slow or unsatisfactory progress when required to read or write.

Excessive facial contortions or frowning when called upon to use his eyes.

Holding books too close.

Inability to distinguish colors.

Moving the head incessantly when trying to read.

Frequent loss of place while reading and errors in reading simple materials when the light is good and the print is clear.

Tilting the head forward when looking at the board or at a distant chart.

Complaints of headaches, nausea, dizziness, and blurred vision.

Squinting, excessive winking, shutting or covering one eye when looking at distant objects, and bloodshot eyes.

Undue sensitivity to light.

Frequent stumbling or tripping over small objects.

A tendency to cry very easily or to become irritated when required to read or write.

The presence of crusts on the eyelids, reddened eyelids, sties, and watery eyes.

Moving about the classroom to see what is on the blackboard.

If the nurse substantiates the teacher's suspicions of eye trouble, the parents should be notified.

Attention Required by Hearing Deficiencies. Vision and hearing are generally normal in the average child when he begins school, and may continue to improve as he grows older. Yet, it is estimated than an average of 15 per cent of all elementary school children have hearing deficiencies which may have existed at the start of school or have developed afterward. In some schools the teacher may have as many as one out of six or one out of seven pupils who has some form of hearing impairment which can affect educational progress.

The seriousness of a deficiency in the senses may not be apparent in some classrooms because of the way the teacher teaches. For example, a pupil with a visual defect will show signs of eye trouble if the teacher introduces a new skill entirely through a visual approach. The same pupil will, of course, not betray this deficiency if the teacher introduces him to the skill through an auditory approach. Often the pupil seeks a cue through some other sense to compensate for his deficiency if he is going to progress. In one first-grade class a pupil concealed his hearing deficiency for months by learning to read the teacher's lips. Other pupils who could not hear teacher directions have been able to get by through their skill at observing what other pupils were doing.

Since most teachers can recognize the totally deaf pupil, the emphasis here should be placed upon the necessity of providing a more adequate program of identification and instruction to pupils who have a slight or partial hearing loss. While pupils with a slight hearing loss may not be suffering from their handicap, attention to such defects should be made early since medical care or treatment may prevent a more serious loss later.

Due to difficulties in identifying pupils with defective hearing, parents and teachers may classify such a pupil as a slow learner. His carelessness, indifference, and general lack of respect or politeness may be accepted as an indication of poor training by the home or by preceding teachers. Failure of a pupil to respond to questions may be interpreted as an indication that he does not know the answer when actually, he may not have heard the question. The problem is complicated by the fact that pupils with hearing deficiencies may be able to hear some voices or sounds better than others. The voice or pitch of the speaker may make a difference in the pupil's response. With such variations in auditory stimulation, one can expect inconsistencies in the pupil responses. Adults who misinterpret silence or partial answers may begin to ignore the pupil. Then the pupil may begin to feel rejected and withdraw further and further from his family or group in school.

A hard-of-hearing pupil may have social problems. He may be excluded from group activities because he does not understand directions or, not hearing his peermates, he may be considered standoffish, indifferent, or too independent to associate with them.

Recognizing the signals of hearing loss is not as easy as recognizing visual deficiencies, but some of the following signs may help:

Lack of attention.
Greater awareness of movements than of sounds.
Turning of one ear toward the source of the sound.
Frowning or a strained expression when listening.
Poor articulation.
A blank expression when the teacher is talking.

Cupping one hand behind his ear.

Complaint of a buzzing or ringing in one ear.

Need for having the radio or phonograph turned up unusually loud.

Frequently asking the teacher to repeat statements.

Frequently misunderstanding the simplest directions.

The pupil's inability to hear fully or accurately may be a reason for failure, but other factors may enter into the picture, since academic failure is not usually due to single factors. For example, an emotionally immature pupil may be making slow progress in class. Here, a loss of hearing may be a contributing factor, but the actual low emotional maturity level may be due to other causes; similarly, an individual may have poor speech patterns which have their origin in an early hearing loss. In many instances teachers will not be able to determine positively the role a loss of hearing will play in the pupil's low achievement, ineffective speech, or emotional instability. If the teacher notices a pattern of behavior that may be due to a loss of hearing, she should refer the pupils to the nurse for a special hearing test. Such tests are, however, only screening measures which may point up the need for an examination by hearing specialists—they do not substitute for a doctor's evaluation.

Health policies in many schools call for hearing tests every year or on an alternate year schedule. Usually, the screening is done with an instrument known as the audiometer. The three most widely used are models produced by Western Electric, Sonotone, and Maico. The instruments are easy to operate and can be used to screen up to 40 pupils at a sitting, although fewer pupils are recommended when one is working with primary grade children. If they can write numbers, they can be tested.

Generally, each pupil is given paper, pencil, and earphones and is asked to record numbers transmitted through the audiometer. Numbers are spoken at gradually diminishing degrees of loudness, with the pupil writing the numbers until he is unable to hear them. The test is administered to the right ear and then to the left ear, with recordings being given by a woman's voice followed by a man's. By checking the pupil's performance on four tests, it is possible to identify pupils who have a hearing loss. These pupils are then referred to specialists for study or help.

Attention Required by Speech Deficiencies. While hearing deficiencies can contribute to ineffective speech patterns, other factors, such as physical defects or psychological causes, may be responsible for poor or faulty speech. Because speech is one of the chief means of communication, it is imperative that attention be given to pupils who have correctible speech patterns. Unfortunately, there has been a reluctance on the part of the public to face the problem of speech correction. Parents who may have speech defects or who associate with others who have them have a tendency to overlook the child's speech defect or its significance in his growth pattern. Unless the defect is pronounced, there is a tendency to consider it as a phase that the child will outgrow. In some cases teachers have contributed to this "So what?" attitude because they fail to recognize many speech defects as handicaps to learning.

Studies of the extent of speech deficiencies in the average classroom indicate 5 to 10 per cent of the children have a significant speech problem. To meet the needs of these children, Wendell Johnson [6] recommends the employment of one speech correctionist for 4,000 pupils, if half of the problems are going to be handled by the regular teacher. He estimates there will be about 200 pupils with speech defects in every group of 4,000, but recommends that the speech correctionist's load be limited to 75 to 100 pupils. In view of this recommendation, it is apparent that the teacher cannot ignore her responsibility to pupils who have speech defects of a general nature. In many schools it has helped to have a speech survey made by competent speech experts who can assist teachers in the identification of problem children and in the types of speech help needed.

Educators do not agree on the relationship of faulty speech and reading retardation, but there is some evidence that faulty articulation may contribute to reading disabilities. Thus, the inability of pupils to sound words may result in poor word recognition and poor reading comprehension. Again, pupils may have trouble reading orally, although emotional factors due to speech imperfection may be more the source of the trouble than the actual speech impairment. Teachers must recognize the impact of speech defects upon children's emotional and social maturity. For example, the pupil with faulty speech may not be able to converse intelligently with his peers, and he may be jeered at and ridiculed. Other pupils become self-conscious when they attempt to read orally or speak in an audience situation. Such a boy or girl will draw back and refuse to take part in group activities. Another pupil may exhibit an outburst of temper, anger, or aggressive behavior if he thinks that others are making fun of him. In some instances the pupil's antagonism to the teacher or class may be based upon an imagined reaction by those around him, but the fact remains that he is suspicious and resentful and is therefore apt to be antagonistic to normal school activities.

Young children have a number of faulty speech patterns which are outgrown as they mature. Other children eliminate their problems as they work with the teacher in activities which have as their objectives improvement of speech patterns for all boys and girls, but some special attention may have to be given to pupils who have more serious speech defects. The teacher may assist such individuals by some of the following means:

Starting with the class as a whole and then working with smaller groups to help each pupil see the importance of good speech patterns.

Taking a speech inventory of the children in the class so that pupils who have common problems may be brought together for special work.

Appealing to the children to try to understand and accept the child who has a speech problem.

Trying to establish a rapport with the pupil who has a speech problem even if it is so severe that she feels that she cannot do much to help him overcome his deficiency.

Avoiding placing the pupil in situations where he may become self-conscious. For example, she may minimize having him read orally or speak before the group or class, and she may work with him individually until he is able to join a small group of children who have shown their readiness to accept and help him.

Helping the pupil with a defect to develop self-confidence through engaging in activities in which he achieves higher levels of success than in others.

Introducing special speech games and activities that are interesting and easy.

Informing the parents about the pupil's problem and seeking their cooperation, or referring the case to a speech specialist.

If no specialist is available, studying on her own to plan some specific speech correction activities. (The seriousness of this problem is evident in a report of the U.S. Office of Education, [7] which states that only one-fifth of the pupils who need remedial speech help are receiving such assistance.)

UNDERSTANDING CHILDREN THROUGH USE
OF THE SOCIOGRAM

Some educators will not want to discuss teaching in terms of social factors, but they are ignoring the evidence found in studies which show that children *can* accomplish more when personal relationships are considered. The problem of the modern educator is one of getting other teachers and parents to see that educational success is linked to how the pupil feels about school and school activities. In an attempt to do more for their children by getting to know them better, some teachers have supplemented their studies of pupil records by the use of the sociogram.

Any teacher can make a sociogram without any special equipment or materials. Actually, a completed sociogram is nothing more than a highly refined seating chart based upon recognizing pupil preferences for seatmates, working partners on a committee, or other subdivision of the class. Basically, the teacher asks children to answer such questions as the following:

What three classmates would you like to work with on a special committee?

What three classmates would you most enjoy having as companions at camp?

Who are your three best friends in this class?

Who are the three members of this class you would like to sit beside?

Other educators use a negative question approach, such as:

Who are the three members of the class that you would not like to sit beside?

Who are the three members of the class that you would leave off your committee if you were free to do so?

Who are the three members of the class you would probably have the least amount of fun with if they sat next to you?

Some teachers try to set up a screen to prevent pupils from knowing what they are attempting to do. The pupils can generally see through a teacher's words, so the teacher may as well be frank with the pupils. She needs their cooperation, so if they see the reasons for the questions, their answers may be more reliable since they are honest answers. If she finds that her sociometric grouping is not satisfactory, new sociometric tests can be given throughout the year. This may be done whenever a new unit is started or a new work group is being formed.

A few teachers merely have each pupil put his name on a paper with a listing of his likes or dislikes in preferential order. Other teachers have found it saves time to have the pupils list their preferences on separate pieces of paper to facilitate tabulation of choices. The teacher may make a master listing of pupil choices to identify the most popular and least popular individuals. This becomes the basis for her sociogram. Figures 1 and 2 show a sociogram based upon the teacher's use of circles for girls and triangles for boys. The pupil's name or initials are written in the appropriate symbol. The teacher shows pupil likes or dislikes by connecting the symbols with lines or arrows.

It is apparent that some pupils have a mutual liking for each other since there are girls like Nancy and Gail, Margaret and Cecelia, and Laurel and Donna who reacted to each other in the questions. Sandy's arrows go out to several people, but nobody picks her to serve on a committee. If the teacher does not know why Sandy stands out as an apparent isolate, she should look into the reasons for the girl's apparent rejection by the other pupils. The complete sociogram shows that some of the girls are interested in working with boys. Here, the teacher had to distinguish between the girls who picked on boys because they had crushes on them, and the girls (such as those who picked Michael) who picked a boy as their favorite coworker because he was a good student and an excellent person to work with on special projects or assignments which called for skill and leadership qualities.

The sociogram can be a helpful tool to the teacher when she can secure an honest expression of interests and likes or dislikes. Yet, some teachers still believe in divide-and-conquer techniques of working with children. They are afraid of cliques and go out of their way to divide them. Teachers can actually make use of these natural groupings by helping the pupils see the composition of work groups. When a teacher works with a sociogram for the first time, she may have to face the fact that the sociogram identifies the cliques. The pupils will have selected other students to work with because they are interested in having a good time instead of a desire to do a good job. Here, the teacher can accept the pupil choices to some extent and base her groupings on apparent interest, knowing full well that some of the cliques will produce little in the way of tangible academic results. If this should be the case, she may need to ignore some pupil preferences in order to give her manageable groups. In many instances the teacher will find that the results will be completely different if the pupils are given another opportunity to make a new choice of partners a few weeks later. Often teachers will find that it is wrong to try to separate close friends. With guidance and an understanding of their objectives they can work together at high levels of success without having to make adjustments to each other in the process.

When the teacher decides to use a sociometric device to improve her teaching, she should consider a number of the following factors:

> The sociogram is a useful instrument, but it should *not* be used alone. Teacher observations, consultation with other teachers, parents, and school specialists may be desirable if she is to interpret and build on the findings to help individual pupils.

> The sociogram should be the basis for some class action. If children cannot see that anything has been done with their responses, they may suspect the teacher of having ulterior motives.

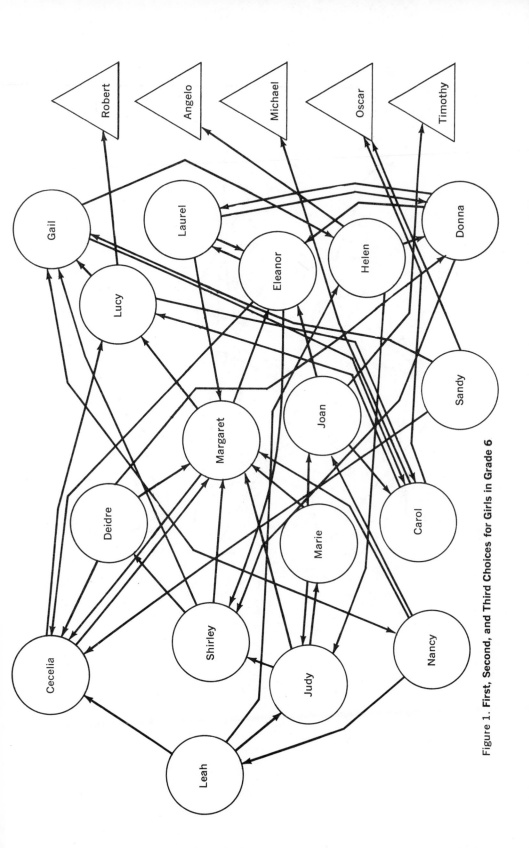

Figure 1. First, Second, and Third Choices for Girls in Grade 6

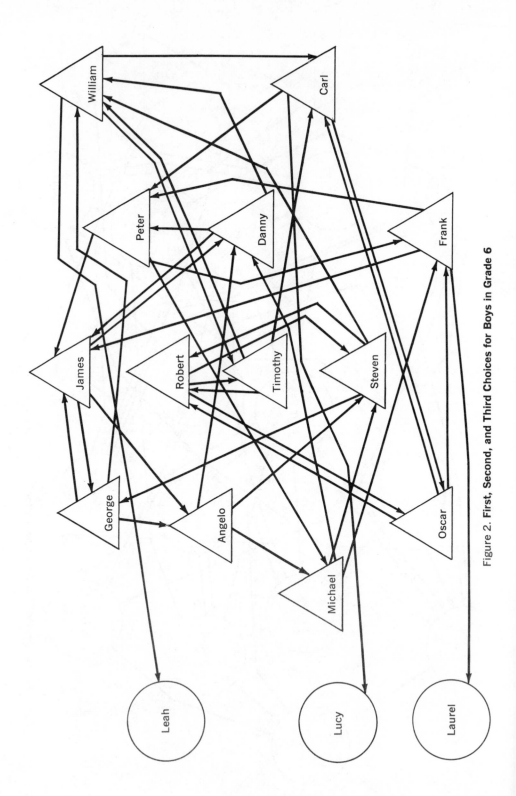

Figure 2. First, Second, and Third Choices for Boys in Grade 6

At various ages children will react differently to such questions as those asked in making a sociogram. Young children may not hesitate to list the names of those they like or dislike. Adolescents may feel that the teacher is invading their privacy by asking them this.

Students should be informed in advance that they may not be assigned to work with all of the pupils they list as desirable work-mates. However, the teacher should form groups so each pupil is with at least one of his choices.

The "isolate" may be the teacher's biggest problem. When possible, the teacher should try to find the reason for the apparent rejection of selected students. Sometimes the teacher will find that the so-called "isolate" is still wanted if the students are asked to indicate fourth and fifth choices. Should he still remain "unwanted," the teacher should try to assign him to one of his first choices. If, however, the "isolate" is among the unliked or "unwanted" by the students of his choice, the teacher should strive to assign the pupil to another group where he has indicated an interest in working with a particular student.

The conditions in a classroom may change over a period of time, so the factors which led pupils to select certain classmates as friends or workmates may no longer exist. From her own observations, the teacher may find it desirable to make adjustments in her group-ings.

Mere regrouping may not be enough. Basic to the improvement of instruction and the growth of the pupils in a class will be the nature of the subject matter studied. Class or group objectives must be clearly understood by both the teacher and the pupils.

A teacher may find that her students do not work well together because of cleavages within the class. Sometimes the barriers are easy to discern, but at other times the barriers are known to exist and cannot be identified. Barriers may not exist at the primary level, but at the intermediate and upper grade levels, children may be conscious of their economic status. Race and religion can divide a class. Strong feelings may exist between pupils of different national origins. Differ-ences in innate ability and academic accomplishment can create teach-ing problems.

The sociogram can show the teacher the nature of some of the cleavages in her class. Certain racial groups, for example, may become isolated by a large segment of the class. Through use of the sociogram the teacher may discover prejudices which need to be eliminated for the good of the class, school, and society. By identifying the cleavages and regrouping the children from time to time, teachers have been able to bring together children who were former antagonists. When the teacher finds a number of pupils are isolated because of barriers, she can elect to keep them together as a group or she can find ways to bring them together in situations which will lead to cooperative learning.

REFERENCES

1. P. A. Fendrick, "Visual Characteristics of Poor Readers," *Teachers College Record,* 37 (February 1936), 452–53.
2. Arnold Gesell and Frances L. Ilg, *The Infant and Child in the Culture of Today* (New York: Harper & Bros., 1943).
3. Arnold Gesell and Frances L. Ilg, *The Child from Five to Ten* (New York: Harper & Bros., 1946).
4. Arnold Gesell, Frances L. Ilg, and Louise B. Ames, *Youth, the Years from Ten to Sixteen* (New York: Harper & Bros., 1956).
5. W. W. Greulich, "Rationale of Assessing the Developmental Status of Children from Roentgenograms of the Hand and Wrist," *Child Development,* 21 (March 1950), 33–44.
6. Wendell Johnson, "Speech Handicaps," *Forty-ninth Yearbook of the National Society for the Study of Education,* Part II, *The Education of Exceptional Children* (Chicago: University of Chicago Press, 1950).
7. Romaine P. Mackie and Wendell Johnson, *Speech Correctionists: The Competencies They Need for the Work They Do,* Office of Education, U.S. Department of Health, Education, and Welfare, Bulletin No. 19, OE-35010 (Washington, D.C.: Government Printing Office, 1957 and 1960).
8. Louise Mohr and others, *Winnetka Child Development Summary* (Winnetka, Ill.: Winnetka Public Schools, 1960).
9. T. P. F. Nally, "The Relationship Between Achieved Growth in Height and the Beginning of Growth in Reading," *Journal of Educational Research,* 49 (October 1955), 153–54.
10. The National Association for Mental Health, *Mental Health Is 1, 2, 3* (New York: The National Association for Mental Health, 1951).
11. New York State Department of Education, *Child Development Guides* (Albany, N.Y.: Department of Education, 1955).
12. New York State Department of Education, *The Elementary School Curriculum Development, An Overview* (Albany, N.Y.: Department of Education, 1954).

CHAPTER **5**

Interpreting
Standardized Test Results

The average teacher is not well versed in techniques of testing and measurement, so she is not always prepared to analyze tests and test results from the same viewpoint as the research statistician. But teachers who have taken a course in statistics should have sufficient background to analyze data and interpret test findings in terms of the educational needs of individual children in their classrooms. They may find it helpful to work with some test problems, under the direction of a principal or teacher who has learned to apply her knowledge in practical school situations. The reader will find some references to statistical terms in the following chapter and in the chapter on reading, but most teachers will not need to go beyond the following section for the statistical background required to understand their children and their problems. They have little need to get involved with correlations and standard deviations; therefore, these are omitted in the following discussions.

Educational Statistics Used by Teachers in Getting to Know Their Children

Chronological Age. The CA, or chronological age, refers to the number of years and months since a child's birth. The chronological age of a boy who is ten years and nine months old at the time a test is given may be expressed as 10-9.

Intelligence Quotient. The IQ, or intelligence quotient, tells us the rate of an individual's mental growth. Through group and individual intelligence tests, one can measure the child's level of mental development. From the statistics obtained from such a test, it is possible to predict the child's rate of future growth. The test results show where a given pupil is in relation to the hypothetical child commonly referred to as the average child.

The IQ is simply an index used to measure a rate of mental progress in relation to chronological age. It may be determined from statistical tables if the teacher has a standardized test manual, but it may be computed if the teacher knows the pupil's mental age and chronological age. Thus:

$$\text{Intelligence quotient} = \frac{\text{Mental age}}{\text{Chronological age}} \times 100$$

$$\text{IQ} = \frac{\text{MA}}{\text{CA}} \times 100$$

ILLUSTRATIONS:

A pupil with a mental age of eight (8-0) and a chronological age of eight (8-0) will have an IQ of 100. One would say that the pupil has an average IQ.

A pupil who has a mental age of eight years and four months (8-4) (or 100 months) and a chronological age of ten years and five months (10-5) (or 125 months) will have an IQ of 80. In comparison to the first pupil, the second child is below average intellectually.

A third pupil has a mental age of eight years and nine months (8-9) (or 105 months) and a chronological age of six years and seven months (6-7) (or 79 months). From the data given it is apparent that he has an IQ of 133, and may be classified as having superior intelligence.

A Normal Distribution. Educators tend to think of test scores in terms of a normal distribution, falling into a pattern considered as a normal curve. Here most of the scores fall midway between two extremes, with fewer and fewer cases falling at the extreme ends. The normal curve is a symmetrical curve having a bell-like shape.

ILLUSTRATION:

If one makes a study of a large number of individual IQ scores and then plots them on a graph, the curve tends to follow a normal distribution or assumes the shape of a bell-shaped curve. In working with thousands of cases from a cross-section of the nation, one finds that the median or middle IQ will be 100, but this will not be true if one is working with a smaller number of test scores. In fact, some communities which have a low or a high socioeconomic level will have distributions of test scores which deviate from the normal curve. Teachers who find the intelligence quotient scores curved to the right will have many high IQ children in their classes, but if the curve is skewed toward the left, the teachers will have many pupils with low IQs in their classes. Grouping plans and teaching plans will be affected by the nature of the IQ distribution in a given class, grade, or school. In a school where the average IQ is 85, the standard set for children will be much different than it is where the average IQ is 100 or 115. Variations such as these are responsible for the failure of the grade standard philosophy to have meanings which are comparable.

A Descriptive Classification of IQs. The descriptive classification which is frequently used to describe IQs in a normal curve distribution of scores follows. The reader must remember that there are no sharp divisions or types of individuals in the normal curve distribution. Pupils who have IQs which border on one of the classifications, or which are two or three points above or below a given cut-off point, cannot be described as falling into a given category with any assurance that they will perform any different from those pupils who have IQs which are just on the other side of the cut-off point. For this reason, teachers are cautioned about giving parents the exact IQ score taken from a single intelligence test. Because of the possibility of score variations, from

TABLE 1
A Descriptive Classification of Intelligence Quotients

IQ Range	Description of Classification of Pupils Possessing IQ	Approximate Per Cent Found in a Normal Distribution of Scores
Above 140	Genius, near genius, or gifted	0.5 to 1%
130 or above	Very superior	4
115 to 129	Superior	13
100 to 114	Average to high average	32
85 to 99	Low average to average	32
70 to 85	Educable to borderline, sometimes called inferior or mentally retarded	13
Below 70	Feeble-minded to educable (the mentally retarded)	4
Below 50	From trainable to institutionalized	0.5 to 1

time to time and from one type of test to another, it is much safer to talk of IQs in terms of *test score ranges* or in terms of approximate IQs.

The Constancy of the IQ. Educators will often disagree on the issue of the constancy of the IQ, and teachers themselves will be perplexed at the variations they will find when they look at several test scores for given individuals. However, teachers must bear in mind that many variables can affect the score of a given pupil. In some cases, teachers will find the test scores from different tests give different IQs. She must then keep in mind the fact that all tests do not measure the same traits; therefore, it is not fair to generalize when two different yardsticks are used to measure intelligence. Again, variations in test findings may be affected by: (1) the health of the pupil, (2) his attitudes, (3) his interests, (4) the way the teacher administered the test, (5) the way directions were given, (6) the way the test was scored, (7) the health of the teacher, and (8) the conditions under which the test was taken (light, noise, and interruptions). Another important element for a teacher to consider is in the *test* itself. The standard deviation of the test will allow pupils to make scores within a range. As a rule, the average child's IQ should not vary more than 5 points above or below his true score. Most authorities consider the pupil's IQ as being approximately constant throughout his life. Thorndike and Hagen [4] state, "For normal children in a typical environment, a Stanford-Binet at age 8 or 9 appears to provide almost as accurate a forecast of ability near the end of high school as would the same test given several years later."

Teachers who are working with test scores from two or more group intelligence tests must remember that all intelligence tests do not measure the same primary mental abilities. In other words, intelligence is determined according to the combination of such factors as the ability to visualize objects in space; word fluency, or the ability to use words according to directions; the ability to use words on the basis of understanding, verbal comprehension; and the ability to recognize numerical concepts and relationships. How these ingredients are measured may determine the rating an individual receives on a given test. For example, the equivalent IQs for children in the 130 IQ range of one test showed the following patterns on five other tests: 130, 134, 130, 132, and 139. The nine-point difference between the first score and the last one *could* make a difference in how a pupil would be classified in some schools. Thus, pupils taking the first test would be barred from a school for gifted children which required an IQ of 135 for admission, whereas they would have been admitted had they been given the last test. Group intelligence tests tend to give comparable ratings for children falling in the average category, but the better group tests will show differences when they measure the intelligence of children at the extreme ends of the normal distribution. Generally, however, the intelligence rating given for those in the low intelligence range may be more accurate than that given for children at the upper intelligence range.

Tests given to crippled children may not give the true ability of the pupils due to problems of physical coordination, such as inability to write, inability to put pegs into the right holes, inability to manipulate blocks. Similarly, a deaf child may be under a handicap because he has not been able to build up the skills associated with oral or written language. This lack of early vocabulary experience, which is acquired by normal children through listening and speaking long before they begin to acquire a reading and writing vocabulary, becomes a barrier. Because of the many variables that can affect the measurement of intelligence, teachers must be prepared to question the results of a single group test. In many instances, a more reliable index can be obtained by the administering of an individual test such as a Stanford-Binet or a Wechsler by a competent examiner under controlled conditions.

The Mental Age Factor. Many teachers refer to pupil capacity in terms of IQ without considering the fact that IQs lack significance unless the age factor is recognized. For example, one may presume that two third-grade children with the same IQ have the same capacity for learning, but a study of the two pupils reveals that pupil A is chronologically older than pupil B. His CA of 9-2 gives him a mental age of 8-7, whereas pupil B's chronological age of 8-4 gives him a mental age of only 7-9. Here both boys have an IQ of 93, but are at different learning levels.

If the teacher understands the significance of the two mental ages, it will be evident that pupil A has reached a stage of mental maturation where he should be ready for most third-grade work, while pupil B is still working at a level where second-grade work may still be giving him trouble. More and more teachers are asked to think in terms of mental ages instead of IQs when they consider the potential of their pupils.

The MA, or mental age, refers to the pupil's performance level. His mental maturity is expressed in years and months on the basis of a raw score representing the performance or ability of average pupils of various chronological ages. In other words, a nine-year-old who is given a mental age rating of 10-6 is conceivably able to perform at the same rate or level as typical pupils in the original test sampling who achieved at the same level or who had mental ages of 10-6. Conceivably, all had the same chronological age, but in reality their chronological ages may not have been the same, since their performances represented the median performance of all children who were ten years and six months old.

The mental age of a pupil can be used as a very accurate indicator of the individual's ability to succeed in most academic subjects. It is based upon factors which measure one's abstract intelligence; therefore, it does not indicate how the individual will learn in situations calling for a different type of intelligence such as social intelligence, mechanical ability, musical ability, or artistic ability. The mental age of the individual will increase from year to year along with chronological age commensurate with the pupil's intelligence.

Teachers can anticipate the capacity of average children much more accurately than they can measure the potential of children at the upper and lower extremes of the intelligence scale. In working with test results for children having a high mental age for their chronological age, the teacher must remember that potential does not mean performance, since pupils who have not had instruction and experience are not likely to achieve at capacity levels. Thus, a fourth-grade pupil who has the capacity to do eighth-grade arithmetic is not likely to achieve much above the average for his grade in this subject unless he has had arithmetic instruction and experiences with numbers beyond normal fourth-grade levels. On the other hand, the pupil may be reading on an eighth-grade level because he has been able to do a great deal of reading on his own.

The teacher can determine the pupil's readiness for a particular level of intellectual activity by studying his mental age. The mental age will tell her whether the pupil is ready for an activity or not, since a given mental age refers to the pupil's ability in terms of a performance level for children of a given chronological age. As a guide to teachers, one starts with the assumption that children with a mental age of 6-2 to 6-6 have a good chance of succeeding with normal reading activities when they start first grade. Then, assuming that average children will

TABLE 2
Grade Level Expectancy for Given Mental Ages

Mental Age Range	Grade Expectancy at Start of School Year	Mental Age Range	Grade Expectancy at the Beginning of Second Semester (Middle of year)
6-2 to 6-6	1st grade	6-7 to 6-11	1st grade
7-2 to 7-6	2nd grade	7-7 to 7-11	2nd grade
8-2 to 8-6	3rd grade	8-7 to 8-11	3rd grade
9-2 to 9-6	4th grade	9-7 to 9-11	4th grade
10-2 to 10-6	5th grade	10-7 to 10-11	5th grade
11-2 to 11-6	6th grade	11-7 to 11-11	6th grade
12-2 to 12-6	7th grade	12-7 to 12-11	7th grade
13-2 to 13-6	8th grade	13-7 to 13-11	8th grade

show a year's mental growth with each year's chronological age, these children should have a mental age ranging from 7-2 to 7-6 at the start of the second grade, and so on. This means that a teacher can make a quick and rough estimate of a pupil's potential through comparing a refined mental age with the data given in Table 2.

ILLUSTRATIONS:

Jerry is a fifth-grade pupil who is only reading on the low fourth-grade level. His parents have made aspersions about the teacher's ability to teach. If she had done her job, Jerry would be reading on the fifth-grade level. The principal admitted that the boy had a 98 IQ, but he demonstrated, through a look at the chronological ages of the children in the class, the fact that Jerry was the youngest child in the class. His CA of 9-10 and mental age of 9-8 showed a grade expectancy of about the middle of the fourth grade; therefore, Jerry was not actually retarded in terms of his potential.

Alice is an alert fifth grader who is in the top reading section. Her reading achievement scores on the Iowa Every-Pupil Test show that she could probably read on an eighth-grade level. Her reading comprehension score of 8.4 is three years above the fifth-grade norm for tests given in December. A look at her mental age shows that she has an MA of 14-9 and may therefore be expected to work up to a ninth-grade level. This means that she can still read higher than the test shows, yet the teacher is still keeping her in fifth-grade reading books.

The average teacher is not a statistician; therefore, an expectancy table such as the one in Table 2 will allow teachers to convert mental ages into expectancy levels. It will allow teachers to make a very good prediction of the potential of all children who do not deviate markedly from the average in ability. See Table 3 for more refined measures if an accurate picture of the potential or expected achievement of gifted pupils is desired. If a teacher is in a hurry and is looking only for a rough index of the pupil's grade expectancy level for a given mental age, she can simply subtract five from the mental age to obtain a rough anticipated grade level performance. Thus, five from a mental age of 11-8 shows a pupil who may have a sixth-grade potential.

Since intelligence tests are not generally administered every year, teachers should be prepared to bring mental ages up to date. Since mental ages of average children will tend to increase with chronological age until mid-adolescence, teachers may adjust some MAs in terms of their chronological age growth. Another, simple procedure calls for the multiplication of the latest chronological age and the intelligence quotient, thus: CA times IQ equals approximate new mental age.

If children have not been given a new intelligence test in three or four years, it is recommended that another group intelligence test be given in order to obtain a more refined picture of the children's ability.

If the teacher notes a wide discrepancy between actual classroom performance and anticipated performance for a given mental age, the teacher may want to have a pupil take a Binet (Stanford-Binet Intelligence Scale) or "Wisc" (Wechsler Intelligence Scale) test. Should the results of this test substantiate earlier group test findings, she must be prepared to diagnose her own teaching in terms of the pupil's apparent educational needs.

Standardized Achievement and Intelligence Tests. Teachers at most grade levels sooner or later come in contact with achievement tests which measure pupil progress in reading, arithmetic, language, and spelling. The teacher usually converts the raw score into a *grade equivalent* to show the pupil's achievement in terms of a standard norm for the grade.

Grade equivalents are based on raw scores representing the pupil's accomplishment shown in years and months by the use of tables found in test manuals. The number or numbers to the left of a period refer to a grade accomplishment level, while the numbers to the right of the period refer to the months of the year. Average pupils are expected to show a ten-month growth over the course of the year, each month being represented by a unit. A grade equivalent of 5.0 represents the average achievement expected of fifth graders at the start of the school year. A grade equivalent of 5.1 represents achievement expected of average fifth graders after a month of schooling or at the start of the second month. A grade equivalent of 5.9 represents achievement expected for average fifth graders by the time they are in the last month of the school year.

Grade norms are expressed in terms of grade equivalents. For example, the grade norm of fifth-grade children tested in December would be 5.3. Pupils obtaining grade equivalents below the stated grade norm are frequently considered as not achieving up to grade expectations, while pupils obtaining higher grade equivalents are usually considered as making better-than-average or satisfactory progress.

Frequently, parents and teachers assume that pupils scoring three or four grades above a stated grade norm are ready to do (and should be doing) work at the grade level indicated by their test score. For example, a sixth-grade pupil receiving a grade equivalent of 10.8 in English shows an apparent accomplishment which is four years and five months above the average for his grade. While this pupil's accomplishment is superior, the 10.8 does not mean, as the parent presumed, that the boy is actually doing tenth-grade work. In the first place, the high score does not represent an actual tenth-grade level of accomplishment, since the scores at the upper level of the elementary battery are extrapolated or assumed scores. It is an artificial score showing a probable accomplishment level presumably reached on the basis of the accomplishment pattern or the measurable parts of the English test. In the second place, the assumption is made that 10.8 represents accomplishment in English which is equivalent to the work that is being done by actual tenth-grade pupils who are working up to grade. Actually, it is doubtful that the superior sixth-grade pupil would have learned the English skills taught in normal seventh-, eighth-, ninth-, and tenth-grade classes without direct instruction.

As a rule, grade equivalents should not be extended beyond the eighth-grade level in special skill subjects, because most pupils do not receive much, if any, actual instruction in lower grade subject skills after they leave the elementary and junior high grades. English is the only possible exception. The 10.8 grade equivalent shows that the sixth-grade pupil had mastered a larger proportion of the skills taught than most pupils in his grade. Most sixth-grade pupils are expected to make a number of errors on the test; if he does not make them, he is automatically given a higher rating even if many of the test items he completed correctly are actually on a sixth-grade level. If the teacher refers to the percentile scale, she will see that the 10.8 grade score is comparable to work done by sixth-grade pupils in the 90 to 99 percentile.

The percentile is a point on a distribution of test scores below which fall a specific percentage of the scores. Usually test scores are reported in terms of a range of scores, thus one obtains a percentile range rating. Most test manuals report test results in terms of grade percentile norms so a teacher can readily see where an individual ranks in relation to the grade norm or in relation to accomplishment by other children in the school or in other schools.

Thus, a pupil whose raw score falls into a range designated as the 74th percentile is said to have a percentile rank of 74. This means that 74 per cent of all pupils taking the test made the same score or one lower than he did. In working with below-average or above-average pupils, the teacher may find it desirable to have percentiles which are not based upon a median IQ of 100. If this is done, slow learners will be compared with other slow learners and fast learners, or gifted pupils, will be compared with children of like ability.

Grade equivalents are of interest to teachers since they show where pupils are in relation to where other pupils in a class or grade are working. If profiles are made for each pupil on a yearly basis, one can observe the individual growth pattern of the pupil from year to year. Similarly, a class or grade profile may show areas of apparent strength or weaknesses for the whole group.

ILLUSTRATION:

In one school a study of the median grade scores for all classes from the fourth to the eighth grades was made to determine whether there were grade or subject weaknesses in need of correction. The reading and arithmetic subtest grade norms tended to be at or about their respective grade norms, but in every instance the median for the language skill subtests were way above grade norms. In contrast, the subtests for work-study skills were way below the established grade norms at each grade level. The teachers began to look at their work-study skills program and began to place new emphasis on such aspects as dictionary skills, the reading of maps and graphs, etc. It took three years of concentrated work in the work-study skill areas before the general pattern for the school showed these medians were at or above grade norms for these areas.

If bright pupils tend to make very high scores on an achievement test, it may be best to try them on a higher level form of the same test in order to obtain more reliable results. Similarly, slow learners may try working with a lower form of a standardized test if one is really interested in seeing what they know or can do.

Instead of the grade equivalent, raw scores representing pupil accomplishment on a standardized test may be translated into *age equivalents*. The age equivalents represent the chronological age of the pupils in the original test sampling whose median score was identical with that of the pupil obtaining the score.

Age equivalents are given in terms of years and months, with the year and month separated by a hyphen (-). It should be noted that grade equivalents are stated in terms of units of ten, but age equivalents are expressed in terms of twelfths, extending from zero to eleven, thus 7-0 to 7-11.

Age equivalents are often used in conjunction with chronological age to see how a pupil is progressing. It is assumed that the pupil is making average progress if the age equivalent obtained for a given subject is the same as the pupil's chronological age. If the pupil's AE is below his CA, progress is considered below average. If it is above his CA, the pupil's progress is considered above average.

When one tries to refine the comparison of the age equivalent and the chronological age, the *educational quotient* (EQ) is the result. If one is using the average of several tests, the results of an age equivalent divided by the chronological age multiplied by 100 gives an educational quotient. If a single subject is the basis for the age equivalent, the result is called a subject matter quotient, i.e., reading quotient, arithmetic quotient, etc.

The formula for educational quotient is:

$$\frac{\text{EA (educational age)}}{\text{CA (chronological age)}} \times 100 = \text{EQ (educational quotient)}$$

The formula for reading quotient is:

$$\frac{\text{RA (reading age equivalent)}}{\text{CA (chronological age)}} \times 100 = \text{RQ (reading quotient)}$$

ILLUSTRATION:

Mary is a fourth-grade pupil who reads well. This is substantiated by her test results. Her reading score is equal to an age equivalent of 11-10, while her chronological age is only 9-8. Mary does not like arithmetic, so it was no surprise to the teacher when she saw that Mary's arithmetic score was only equal to an age equivalent of 8-4. Thus:

$$RQ = \frac{11\text{-}10 \text{ (RA)}}{9\text{-}8 \text{ (CA)}} \times 100$$

or
$$\frac{142 \text{ months}}{116 \text{ months}} \times 100 = 122$$

$$AQ = \frac{8\text{-}4 \text{ (arithmetic age)}}{9\text{-}8 \text{ (chronological age)}} \times 100$$

or
$$\frac{100 \text{ months}}{116 \text{ months}} \times 100 = 86$$

The quotients would indicate that Mary is making better than 1.2 years' progress in reading, while she is making less than a year's progress in arithmetic. Educators usually consider an educational quotient of less than 80 as an indication that the pupil is having *serious* trouble in a subject and should be given special attention and remedial instruction. Since Mary's arithmetic quotient shows only 86 per cent of an average year's growth, she may be considered as being beyond special help; however, her high rating in reading may be interpreted as a sign that she has better-than-average intelligence. This makes her slow arithmetic progress more serious; so systematic study and help for Mary in arithmetic should be considered an essential.

An educational or subject quotient above 100 is considered good, while one below 100 is considered as evidence that less than normal progress has been made. Pupils obtaining quotients lower than 80 may be considered retarded enough to warrant immediate special attention or remedial instruction. Over-aged and under-aged children are considered as having more than or less than the average amount of experience in school possessed by the typical pupil; therefore, the age norms used for average children may not be appropriate for such individuals.

Determining Expected Achievement Level Through Test Results. Good teachers know that teaching can be ineffective if they ignore their children's potential. If pupils are working up to accepted standards for their capacities, progress will be slow, but if they are working far below expectancy levels for their capacity, progress can be accelerated at a rapid rate if special attention is directed to areas of weakness. Teachers can make their own estimates of the capacity of pupils and the quality of the work they do in relation to their ability, but teacher judgments often tend to be unreliable, although experienced teachers may develop their own measuring instruments to substantiate their judgments. In attempting to determine pupil expectancy levels, teachers should realize that studies show a correlation of about .80 between intelligence tests and standardized tests as compared to a correlation of between .40 and .50 between teacher marks and intelligence. A more refined index is the *achievement quotient.*

Many educators object to the use of the educational quotient and the subject quotient since they are based upon a comparison of an individual's accomplishment with his chronological age. A more refined measure is the *achievement quotient,* which is derived by dividing the subject or educational quotient by the IQ or MA. It recognizes capacity. The formula for determining the achievement quotient is:

$$\text{AQ (achievement quotient)} = \frac{\text{EA (educational age)}}{\text{MA (mental age)}} \times 100$$

If pupils are working close to capacity, one may expect an achievement quotient close to 100. As a rule, one should not obtain quotients above 100; however, it is possible due to a number of uncontrollable variables. Slow learners, for example, may appear to be working above capacity, while bright pupils will tend to work below expectation levels. If the slow learner is older, his worldly experiences may enable him to achieve higher than expected. Again, such factors as interest, earnestness, and motivation may affect the test results.

ILLUSTRATION:

Jerry is a fifth grader who tends to do very well in arithmetic, but the teachers have never rated him as having more than average intelligence. His teacher thought that his class work had been better than the test showed. A special intelligence test gave him an IQ of 124, but the teacher refused to believe it in spite of the fact that the individual test gave substantially the same rating that he had previously received on two group tests. His mental age was 12-7. His chronological age of 10-2 was less than his arithmetic age of 10-9. In order to show what Jerry was doing in terms of his ability, the principal computed Jerry's achievement quotient thus:

$$\text{AQ (achievement quotient)} = \frac{\text{ArA (arithmetic age)}}{\text{MA (mental age)}} \times 100$$

or
$$\text{AQ} = \frac{\text{10-9 (arithmetic age)}}{\text{12-7 (mental age)}} \times 100$$

or
$$\frac{129 \text{ months}}{151 \text{ months}} \times 100 = 85$$

Since Jerry is apparently working above the grade norm in arithmetic for average pupils, the teacher could be satisfied with his arithmetic achievement, but the formula shows that Jerry could work at even higher levels if he had adequate motivation and higher-level instruction by the teacher.

Objections have been raised against using the achievement quotient for determining the expected achievement of gifted children. These have been based on the feeling that it is not fair to expect primary-grade children to work at a sixth- or seventh-grade level merely to hold their own with an AQ of 100. In other words, the pupil with a very high IQ should not be expected to achieve at levels far above what he has had a chance to achieve through formal reading or arithmetic instruction in his short life span. In an attempt to give a more realistic expectancy level for achievement based upon high intellectual capacity, these two formulas have been developed.

The formula for determining expected reading levels for children with high IQs is based on an assumption that there is a correlation of .67 between reading test scores and the results of the intelligence test. It is as follows:

Ex. RA (expected reading achievement) =

$$\frac{(2 \times MA) \text{ (mental age)} + (1 \times CA) \text{ (chronological age)}}{3}$$

ILLUSTRATION:

Marty is a very bright second-grade pupil who has a reported IQ of 148. His mental age is 11-4 and his chronological age is 7-8. When Marty took the California achievement tests, he was given the upper primary test which is recommended for grades 3 and 4. He had a grade placement score of 3.2 in arithmetic or an arithmetic age of 8-6, but his reading grade placement score was 4.4 and his reading age was 9-8. The achievement quotient was used to determine his expected reading level. He received a reading achievement quotient of 85, which meant that he would have had to obtain a reading grade placement score of 6.0 to show mere average achievement for his potential. The refined measure

$$\text{Ex. RA} = \frac{(2 \times 11\text{-}4) + (1 \times 7\text{-}8)}{3}$$

or
$$\frac{(2 \times 136) + (1 \times 92)}{3} = 10\text{-}1$$

shows that one may assume that Marty's expected reading achievement is approximately 10-1 years or the equivalent of a grade placement score of 4.7 in the conversion table. In other words, Marty's achievement based on the refined formula is within three months of his expected achievement in the field of reading for his IQ. 10-1 less 9-8 = 3 months difference.

The formula for determining expected arithmetic level for children with high IQs is based on a correlation of .50 between results of the intelligence test and the arithmetic achievement test. It follows:

Ex. AA (expected arithmetic achievement) =

$$\frac{\text{Mental age} + \text{chronological age}}{2}$$

ILLUSTRATION:

Marty's arithmetic grade equivalent of 3.2 was used to obtain an arithmetic achievement quotient of 75. This meant that he would have had to obtain a grade equivalent score of 6.0 to show average performance for his potential under the formula for average children. Using the refined measurement formula it becomes evident that Marty would be expected to obtain an arithmetic grade placement score of 4.2 for the arithmetic age of 9-6 years.

$$\text{Ex. AA} = \frac{11\text{-}4 + 7\text{-}8}{2}$$

or
$$\frac{136 + 92 \text{ (months)}}{2} = 9\text{-}6 \text{ years}$$

In other words, Marty's arithmetic achievement is a year below expectancy levels even with the refined formula. This is acceptable since he has received little, if any, advanced arithmetic instruction.

Many factors can influence children's accomplishment; therefore, any attempt to anticipate what they will do in the future is problematic. A chart (Table 3) has been made to guide teachers in checking the actual achievement of gifted children in terms of anticipated reading achievement for their potential under the refined formula. It should not be necessary to work out the formula for average children since their actual performance will normally approximate the grade equivalent for their mental ages. In working with below-average children, the teacher will find the mental age conversion table (Table 4) is a good guide to follow if pupil IQs have been fairly well established.

ILLUSTRATION:

The beginning first grader starts coming to school when he is approximately 6-2 chronologically. Mentally he is not ready for formal instruction until he has a mental age of about 6-2 to 6-6. A pupil with a 70 IQ has a mental age of 4-3 when he starts school. He should have a mental age approximating 6-0 to 6-2 when he is eight-and-one-half years old. The conversion table shows that the pupil may just about be able to obtain a

TABLE 3

Reading Ages and Grade Equivalents for Pupils with Above-average Intellectual Quotients*

Chronological Age	115 IQ			120 IQ			125 IQ			130 IQ			135 IQ			140 IQ		
	MA	RA	R.Eq.	MA	RA	R.Eq.	MA	RA	R.Eq.	MA	RA	R.Eq.	MA	RA	R.Eq.	MA	RA	R.Eq.
6-2	7-1	6-9	1.6	7-4	6-11	1.7	7-8	7-2	2.0	8-0	7-5	2.2	8-4	7-7	2.4	8-7	7-9	2.5
6-7	7-6	7-2	2.0	7-10	7-5	2.2	8-2	7-8	2.5	8-6	7-10	2.6	8-10	8-1	2.8	9-2	8-4	3.1
7-2	8-3	7-7	2.4	8-7	8-1	2.8	8-11	8-4	3.1	9-3	8-7	3.3	9-8	8-10	3.6	10-0	9-1	3.8
7-7	8-8	8-4	3.1	9-1	8-7	3.3	9-5	8-10	3.6	9-10	9-1	3.8	10-2	9-4	4.0	10-7	9-7	4.3
8-2	9-4	8-11	3.6	9-10	9-3	4.0	10-2	9-6	4.2	10-7	9-9	4.4	11-0	10-1	4.7	11-5	10-4	5.0
8-7	9-10	9-5	4.1	10-3	9-8	4.4	10-8	10-0	4.7	11-1	10-3	4.9	11-7	10-7	5.2	12-0	10-10	5.4
9-2	10-6	10-1	4.7	11-0	10-5	5.1	11-5	10-8	5.3	11-11	11-0	5.6	12-4	11-3	5.8	12-10	11-7	6.2
9-7	11-0	10-6	5.2	11-6	10-10	5.4	11-11	11-2	5.8	12-5	11-7	6.2	12-11	11-10	6.4	13-5	12-2	6.7
10-2	11-7	11-1	5.7	12-2	11-6	6.1	12-8	11-10	6.4	13-2	12-2	6.8	13-8	12-6	7.1	14-2	12-10	7.4
10-7	12-2	11-8	6.3	12-8	12-0	6.6	13-2	12-4	6.9	13-9	12-8	7.3	14-3	13-0	7.6	14-9	13-4	8.0
11-2	12-10	12-3	6.8	13-2	12-5	7.0	13-9	12-10	7.4	14-3	13-2	7.8	14-10	13-7	8.2	15-4	13-11	8.6
11-7	13-3	12-8	7.3	13-10	13-1	7.7	14-5	13-6	8.1	15-0	13-10	8.5	15-7	14-3	8.9	16-2	14-8	9.4
12-2	14-0	13-4	8.0	14-7	13-9	8.4	15-2	14-2	8.9	15-9	14-7	9.3	16-5	15-0	9.7	17-0	15-5	10.1
12-7	14-5	13-10	8.5	15-1	14-3	8.9	15-8	14-8	9.4	16-4	15-1	9.8	16-11	15-6	10.2	17-7	15-11	10.6
13-2	15-1	14-5	9.1	15-9	14-11	9.6	16-5	15-4	10.0	17-1	15-9	10.5	17-9	16-3	10.8	18-5	16-8	11.2
13-7	15-7	14-11	9.6	16-3	15-4	10.0	16-11	15-10	10.6	17-7	16-3	10.8	18-4	16-9	11.3	19-0	17-2	11.8
14-2	16-3	15-5	10.1	17-0	16-1	10.7	17-8	16-6	11.0	18-5	17-0	11.6	19-1	17-5	12.0	19-10	17-11	12.7

* Reading ages (RA) and reading grade equivalents (R.Eq.) estimated for given IQs and mental ages (MA).

(Table 3 continued)

| Chrono-logical Age | MA | RA | R.Eq. | MA | RA | R.Eq. | MA | RA | R.Eq. | MA | RA | R.Eq. | MA | RA | R.Eq. | MA | RA | R.Eq. |
	145 IQ			150 IQ			155 IQ			160 IQ			165 IQ			170 IQ		
6-2	8-11	8-0	2.8	9-3	8-3	3.0	9-6	8-5	3.1	9-10	8-7	3.3	10-2	8-10	3.6	10-5	9-0	3.7
6-7	9-6	8-6	3.2	9-10	8-11	3.6	10-2	9-0	3.7	10-6	9-2	3.9	10-10	9-5	4.1	11-2	9-8	4.4
7-2	10-4	9-3	4.0	10-9	9-7	4.3	11-1	9-9	4.4	11-5	10-0	4.7	11-10	10-3	4.9	12-2	10-6	5.2
7-7	11-0	9-10	4.5	11-4	10-1	4.7	11-9	10-4	5.0	12-1	10-7	5.2	12-6	10-10	5.4	12-10	11-1	5.7
8-2	11-10	10-7	5.2	12-3	10-11	5.5	12-8	11-2	5.8	13-1	11-5	6.0	13-6	11-9	6.3	13-11	12-0	6.6
8-7	12-5	11-2	5.8	12-10	11-5	6.0	13-2	11-8	6.3	13-9	12-0	6.6	14-2	12-4	6.9	14-7	12-7	7.2
9-2	13-3	11-11	6.5	13-9	12-3	6.8	14-2	12-6	7.1	14-8	12-10	7.4	15-1	13-1	7.7	15-7	13-5	8.0
9-7	13-11	12-6	7.1	14-4	12-9	7.3	14-10	13-1	7.7	15-4	13-5	8.0	15-10	13-9	8.4	16-3	14-0	8.7
10-2	14-9	13-3	7.9	15-3	13-7	8.2	15-9	13-11	8.6	16-3	14-3	8.9	16-9	14-7	9.3	17-3	14-11	9.6
10-7	15-4	13-9	8.4	15-10	14-1	8.8	16-5	14-6	9.2	16-11	14-10	9.5	17-5	15-2	9.9	18-0	15-6	10.2
11-2	16-2	14-6	9.2	16-9	14-11	9.6	17-4	15-3	9.9	17-10	15-7	10.3	18-5	16-0	10.7	19-0	16-5	10.9
11-7	16-9	15-0	9.7	17-4	15-2	9.9	17-11	15-10	10.6	18-6	16-2	10.8	19-1	16-7	11.1	19-8	17-0	11.6
12-2	17-7	15-9	10.5	18-3	16-3	10.8	18-10	16-7	11.1	19-5	17-0	11.6	20-1	17-5	12.0	20-8	17-10	12.6
12-7	18-3	16-4	10.9	18-10	16-9	11.3	19-6	17-2	11.8	20-1	17-7	12.1	20-9	18-0	12.8	21-4	18-5	13.1
13-2	19-1	17-1	11.7	19-9	17-7	12.1	20-5	18-0	12.8	21-1	18-5	13.1	21-8	18-10	13.5	22-4	19-3	14.0
13-7	19-8	17-8	12.2	20-4	17-9	12.6	21-0	18-6	13.2	21-8	19-0	13.7	22-5	19-6	14.3	23-1	19-11	14.8
14-2	20-6	18-5	13.1	21-3	18-11	13.6	21-11	19-4	14.1	22-8	19-10	14.7	23-4	20-3	15.2	24-1	20-9	15.8

Note: Based on expectation formula: Ex. $RA = (2 \times MA) + (1 \times CA) \div 3$.

grade equivalent of 1.0. If one used the formula, the pupil would obtain a grade equivalent of 1.7. Actually maturation and some school experience may enable him to score even higher, although his comprehension is still at a zero level. Such a pupil has no business being exposed to formal tests until he has had appropriate instruction and experience at his low stage of readiness.

In contrast one finds that the pupil with the 130 IQ starts school with a mental age of 8-0. Since many pupils with this level of intelligence are already reading when they enter kindergarten, a beginning first grader could take an achievement test in reading shortly after school started and obtain a reading score equal to, if not higher than, the grade equivalent of 2.2 indicated as possible by the formula. This score or grade equivalent does not mean that it will be the pupil's instructional level since teachers should be working with them at least one-half year to a year below the test score. This means that many bright pupils can work in high-level first-grade reading materials while many average pupils are working at the end of readiness materials or are beginning to work with pre-primers.

TABLE 4
Mental Age–Grade Conversion Table for Children with Average Potential

Mental Age	Reading Grade*	Mental Age	Reading Grade	Mental Age	Reading Grade	Mental Age	Reading Grade
		10-0	4.7	14-0	8.7	18-0	12.8
		10-1	4.7	14-1	8.8	18-1	12.8
6-2	1.0	10-2	4.8	14-2	8.9	18-2	12.9
6-3	1.1	10-3	4.9	14-3	8.9	18-3	13.0
6-4	1.2	10-4	5.0	14-4	9.0	18-4	13.0
6-5	1.3	10-5	5.1	14-5	9.1	18-5	13.1
6-6	1.3	10-6	5.2	14-6	9.2	18-6	13.2
6-7	1.4	10-7	5.2	14-7	9.3	18-7	13.2
6-8	1.5	10.8	5.3	14-8	9.4	18-8	13.3
6-9	1.6	10-9	5.3	14-9	9.4	18-9	13.4
6-10	1.7	10-10	5.4	14-10	9.5	18-10	13.5
6-11	1.7	10-11	5.5	14-11	9.6	18-11	13.6
7-0	1.8	11-0	5.6	15-0	9.7	19-0	13.7
7-1	1.9	11-1	5.7	15-1	9.8	19-1	13.8
7-2	2.0	11-2	5.8	15-2	9.9	19-2	13.9
7-3	2.0	11-3	5.8	15-3	9.9	19-3	14.0
7-4	2.1	11-4	5.9	15-4	10.0	19-4	14.1
7-5	2.2	11-5	6.0	15-5	10.1	19-5	14.2
7-6	2.3	11-6	6.1	15-6	10.2	19-6	14.3
7-7	2.4	11-7	6.2	15-7	10.3	19-7	14.4
7-8	2.5	11-8	6.3	15-8	10.4	19-8	14.5
7-9	2.5	11-9	6.3	15-9	10.5	19-9	14.6
7-10	2.6	11-10	6.4	15-10	10.6	19-10	14.7
7-11	2.7	11-11	6.5	15-11	10.6	19-11	14.8

(Table 4 continued)

Mental Age	Reading Grade*	Mental Age	Reading Grade	Mental Age	Reading Grade	Mental Age	Reading Grade
8-0	2.8	12-0	6.6	16-0	10.7	20-0	14.9
8-1	2.8	12-1	6.7	16-1	10.7	20-1	15.0
8-2	2.9	12-2	6.8	16-2	10.8	20-2	15.1
8-3	3.0	12-3	6.8	16-3	10.8	20-3	15.2
8-4	3.1	12-4	6.9	16-4	10.9	20-4	15.3
8-5	3.1	12-5	7.0	16-5	10.9	20-5	15.4
8-6	3.2	12-6	7.1	16-6	11.0	20-6	15.5
8-7	3.3	12-7	7.2	16-7	11.1	20-7	15.6
8-8	3.4	12-8	7.3	16-8	11.2	20-8	15.7
8-9	3.5	12-9	7.3	16-9	11.3	20-9	15.8
8-10	3.6	12-10	7.4	16-10	11.4	20-10	15.9
8-11	3.6	12-11	7.5	16-11	11.5	20-11	16.1
9-0	3.7	13-0	7.6	17-0	11.6	21-0	16.2
9-1	3.8	13-1	7.7	17-1	11.7	21-1	16.3
9-2	3.9	13-2	7.8	17-2	11.8	21-2	16.4
9-3	4.0	13-3	7.9	17-3	11.8		
9-4	4.0	13-4	8.0	17-4	11.8		
9-5	4.1	13-5	8.0	17-5	12.0		
9-6	4.2	13-6	8.1	17-6	12.1		
9-7	4.3	13-7	8.2	17-7	12.1		
9-8	4.4	13-8	8.3	17-8	12.2		
9-9	4.4	13-9	8.4	17-9	12.6		
9-10	4.5	13-10	8.5	17-10	12.6		
9-11	4.6	13-11	8.6	17-11	12.7		

* Can be used to show reading, arithmetic, language grade equivalent for mental age.

SOURCES: Based on averages computed from norms of Stanford-Binet Achievement Test, Iowa Every-Pupil Test, California Test of Mental Maturity—Primary Series, California Capacity Questionnaire, Gates Primary Reading Test, and Gates Reading Survey for Grades 3 to 10.

The fact that bright children start school with an expectancy level comparable to the second grade makes it imperative that the teacher determine her pupils' readiness for reading (see Table 5). One group of bright pupils may need little, if any, work with readiness materials, because they have managed to reach a reading stage without teacher help, but other bright children may start school without having had the exposure necessary for reading success. This latter group cannot show accomplishment up to expectation levels in any field until they receive direct instruction or have experiences which will enable them to begin their academic growth. Some bright children will need to work in the regular readiness and pre-primer program which goes with a basic reader series, but they should not have to work as long or as hard as average children. Once started, they should be able to rapidly narrow the gap between actual achievement and expected achievement for

TABLE 5

Estimating Reading Expectancy Level Based Upon Refined Measure*

No. of Years Pupil Attended School	Estimated Reading Grade Equivalent Expected for Designated IQ Score and Years in School																				
	70	75	80	85	90	95	100	105	110	115	120	125	130	135	140	145	150	155	160	165	170
½	1.3	1.3	1.4	1.4	1.5	1.5	1.5	1.5	1.6	1.6	1.6	1.6	1.7	1.7	1.7	1.7	1.8	1.8	1.8	1.8	1.9
1	1.7	1.8	1.8	1.9	1.9	2.0	2.0	2.1	2.1	2.2	2.2	2.3	2.3	2.4	2.4	2.5	2.5	2.6	2.6	2.7	2.7
1½	2.0	2.1	2.2	2.2	2.4	2.4	2.5	2.6	2.6	2.7	2.8	2.9	3.0	3.0	3.1	3.2	3.3	3.3	3.4	3.5	3.6
2	2.4	2.5	2.6	2.7	2.8	2.9	3.0	3.1	3.2	3.3	3.4	3.5	3.6	3.7	3.8	3.9	4.0	4.1	4.2	4.3	4.4
2½	2.7	2.9	3.0	3.1	3.1	3.4	3.5	3.6	3.8	3.9	4.0	4.2	4.3	4.4	4.5	4.6	4.8	4.9	5.0	5.1	5.3
3	3.1	3.3	3.4	3.6	3.7	3.9	4.0	4.2	4.3	4.5	4.6	4.8	4.9	5.1	5.2	5.4	5.5	5.7	5.8	6.0	6.1
3½	3.5	3.6	3.8	4.0	4.2	4.3	4.5	4.7	4.9	5.0	5.2	5.4	5.6	5.7	5.9	6.1	6.3	6.4	6.6	6.8	7.0
4	3.8	4.0	4.2	4.4	4.6	4.8	5.0	5.2	5.4	5.6	5.8	6.0	6.2	6.4	6.6	6.8	7.0	7.2	7.4	7.6	7.8
4½	4.2	4.4	4.6	4.8	5.1	5.3	5.5	5.7	6.0	6.2	6.4	6.6	6.9	7.1	7.3	7.5	7.8	8.0	8.2	8.4	8.7
5	4.5	4.8	5.0	5.3	5.5	5.8	6.0	6.3	6.5	6.8	7.0	7.3	7.5	7.8	8.0	8.3	8.5	8.8	9.0	9.3	9.5
5½	4.9	5.1	5.4	5.7	6.0	6.2	6.5	6.8	7.1	7.3	7.6	7.9	8.2	8.4	8.7	9.0	9.3	9.5	9.8	10.1	10.4
6	5.2	5.5	5.8	6.1	6.4	6.7	7.0	7.3	7.6	7.9	8.2	8.5	8.8	9.1	9.4	9.7	10.0	10.3	10.6	10.9	11.2
6½	5.6	5.9	6.2	6.5	6.9	7.2	7.5	7.8	8.2	8.5	8.8	9.1	9.5	9.8	10.1	10.4	10.8	11.1	11.4	11.7	12.1
7	5.9	6.3	6.6	7.0	7.3	7.7	8.0	8.4	8.7	9.1	9.4	9.8	10.1	10.5	10.8	11.2	11.5	11.9	12.2	12.6	12.9
7½	6.3	6.6	7.0	7.4	7.8	8.1	8.5	8.9	9.3	9.6	10.0	10.4	10.8	11.1	11.5	11.9	12.3	12.6	13.0	13.4	13.8
8	6.6	7.0	7.4	7.8	8.2	8.6	9.0	9.4	9.8	10.2	10.6	11.0	11.4	11.8	12.2	12.6	13.0	13.4	13.8	14.2	14.6

* Formula: Years in school × IQ + 1.0.

their mental ability. Unfortunately, many bright children do not narrow the range, with the result that they reach intermediate and upper grade levels without having to stretch themselves to attain levels of success which would be good for pupils with average intelligence, but which are far from satisfactory for bright pupils.

The Use of Standardized Tests to Ascertain Instructional Levels

Frequently, teachers look at a list of standardized test results and exclaim, "This test is off. I know that the boys and girls are not doing arithmetic or are not reading as well as this test shows. Take a boy like Jerry, for instance. He made a reading score of 5.3, yet he is still working in a fourth-grade reader. No, the test is just too easy." Further support comes from last year's teacher. She says, "I know Jerry from last year. I am sure that he could not read on a fifth-grade level this early in the new year (October). To get a score like this he had to get outside help. He must have copied from someone or he was just lucky in his guessing."

Such rationalizing is unfair to the pupil who really tried to do his best on the test. The problem does not lie in the fact that the test is easy, but in the teachers who do not know that a test score does not mean that a pupil should be working at the level represented by the grade equivalent given.

Standardized Tests as a Measure of Pupil Capacity. Most pupils try to do the best they can when they take a standardized test. They work rapidly with few pauses due to time limitations and they work under pressures which are nonexistent in their regular class activities. As a result, they often obtain test ratings which represent achievement close to capacity or frustration levels. Ordinarily they work at what one would call a "good cruising speed." With motivation, they can achieve higher for a short time, but they cannot keep up the pace. Many teachers do not see this. All too often they assume that pupils are capable of working in class activities or activities based upon predetermined grade standards because student scores were just above or below the norm for the grade. In some classes, for example, teachers are likely to group children for instruction on the basis of a given test score. While this may bring together pupils who are working at a comparable level in some phases, the instructional level may be too high for individual pupils.

Actual Instructional Activities vs. Ideal Test Score. A car is capable of going 120 miles an hour, or a fifth-grade pupil is capable of achieving on a sixth-grade level. The speedometer says it for the car, the test for the pupil, but in both instances the performance is a pressure level which cannot be sustained for long periods of time without something happening. Some part of the car can break down under the strain, and the pupil may crack under the continued pressure. One may obtain a replacement part for the car, but such parts are not easily found for the pupil. If the pupil has done his best on the test, he worked close to frustration levels and should not be exposed to a day-by-day program at that level. Many teachers do not realize this. They tend to think of the test score as an achievement level upon which they can plan new instructional programs within a grade curriculum.

Teachers are less inclined to offer bright pupils a program in terms of their high academic achievement, but they are apt to push slow or average learners. For example, it is not fair to place a sixth grader in a sixth-grade basic reader merely because his September or October test rating gives him a 5.9 reading comprehension and a 6.1 reading vocabulary. Frequently, this pupil will need reading instruction on a fifth-grade level or even on a high fourth-grade level reading skills program. In working with pupils testing near the norm, the teacher may find it necessary to take an individual reading inventory to ascertain the pupil's actual reading needs and level. She may even find it desirable to retest him to correct for the standard error in standardized tests. In recommending the lowering of the instructional level by one year, the assumption is made that (1) the pupil was working at a high performance level when he took the test; and (2) the teacher will not depend solely on a single test score, but will consider such factors as pupil interest, mentality, emotional stability, physical strength, and her own day-by-day observations of work and study habits.

For example, one reading teacher found that the average pupil who was sent to her for reading help was unable to make continued progress unless she worked with him in basic readers from one to one-and-a-half years below the normally accepted reading level for the grade. Other reading specialists have set the instructional program from one-and-a-half to two years below the reading test score.

In working with average children, the teacher should set her own limits for instruction, based upon her ability to recognize the educational needs of individual children, but allowing for a year's leeway between the test score and the instructional level in most basic subject fields is a good rule of thumb. If the teacher fails to do so, the pupil may make some growth in a particular subject field, but it will not be at the level where it should be if the teacher actually took the pupil where he needed instruction.

Independent Reading Level vs. Test Rating. A young child may work successfully with the teacher on materials written on a grade level below his test score, but he may be less successful if he has to work with it independently. A pupil gets a great deal of help from the teacher and from other pupils that is unobtainable when he is on his own. Unless there is someone to give him clues, to reinterpret, to help with new words, or to merely talk the problem through to a possible solution, the pupil may be lost. His instructional materials must be easier than his test score, but his independent reading level calls for still easier materials for independent reading and study. If teachers observe the reading habits of children, they will note that boys and girls usually select books for enjoyment or independent reading which are easier than their instructional materials. Usually, teachers can feel safe in assigning pupils to work with materials which are approximately two years below the pupils' reading test scores. This recommendation is in line with the fact that the frustration level may be at or just above the pupil's capacity level, so the independent reading or working level will generally be about two years below the pupil's capacity or frustration level.

This relationship is often forgotten or not completely understood when homework is assigned. The poor pupil is expected to complete assignments independently in books which are based on a grade standard and which may have no relationship to his reading level. As a result, one finds many pupils who cannot read problems or understand the meaning of the words and sentences in arithmetic, social studies, and science assignments. Many excuses are given for the failure of pupils to complete homework, but seldom is the fact recognized that homework can be frustrating because pupils are *not ready* to study the materials independently. This is one reason why children should not undertake completely new studies without teacher preparation for the study. Frequently, the failure of a pupil is not due only to poor study habits, but to inability to work independently with materials written on or above his reading instructional level. The problem of homework is complicated by the fact that most graded textbooks in content areas are more difficult than the ordinary basic reader for a selected grade. Here again, the problem is complicated by the fact that many teachers tend to place pupils in basic readers before they are ready for them. This is illustrated by the fact that many teachers find it hard to accept average children as reading anything but grade level materials. For example, the new fourth-grade teacher wants to place all her pupils into a fourth-grade reader in the fall if they are supposed to be ready for the grade. Actually, the average pupil may be reading up to grade if he is reading in a 3-2 level reader at the start of the year. (Average children may be reading up to grade when they read in a book one-half year below the grade designated in the code. This is at the beginning or end of the school year.)

Use of Anticipation Achievement Charts. The standardized achievement test can be used to measure pupil progress from year to year, but this is only a beginning. If they care to do so, teachers can work out achievement quotients or they can refer to an expectancy table to estimate what a pupil should be scoring on a test. In working with such tests as the California Achievement Test, they have access to anticipation achievement charts which will help them predict achievement in relation to ability as they work in such areas as reading comprehension, reading vocabulary, arithmetic fundamentals, arithmetic reasoning, mechanics of English, and spelling.

In using these charts, the teacher can compare the actual achievement of individual students, or she can compare class median scores with expectation levels based upon ability. This is done through the use of an intellectual status index which is obtained from a table calling for grade and mental ages as of the date of the achievement test. Once the ISI has been obtained, the teacher refers to an anticipated achievement grade placement chart to determine the anticipated achievement of a pupil or class.

Adjusting the Instructional Level to the Anticipated Achievement Level. When using anticipated achievement scores, the teacher may see that pupils who are apparently up to grade in a subject are still not working up to their potential. The teacher can adjust her instruction to help these pupils work at higher levels, but she may have to make allowances for the possibility of error when working with individuals or small groups of children.

If the teacher is comparing the median anticipated achievement of a group of 250 to 300 pupils, her instructional level for the median student will approximate the median anticipated achievement of the group. Working with a smaller group of 150 pupils, she will have to adjust the instructional level to a point comparable to a one- to two-point differential between the two medians, achievement and anticipated achievement. If the teacher ascertains the median of her class, which may range from 25 to 35 pupils, she will have to allow for a difference of at least 3 points (months) between the anticipated achievement and the instructional level for her median pupils. If she ignores comparative medians and simply compares the anticipated achievement of a single pupil with his actual achievement, she may have to allow for a difference of at least one year between the pupil's instructional level and his anticipated achievement level. This means that the teacher may have to instruct a pupil whose anticipated arithmetic reasoning level is 6.0 on a low fifth-grade level.

Teachers should not take the preceding statement as final, because other factors should be considered, but it should suffice to warn them that anticipated achievement and instructional level for individual students is not the same. Allowing a year's leeway is a good rule of thumb.

Translating Test Norms in Terms of the Group's Level of Ability. Many teachers overlook the fact that test norms are based upon the achievement levels of average children. This means that the teacher who has a "slow" class will have to expect lower achievement norms for her class than the national norm; therefore, a class with a median IQ of 92 may be expected to achieve from 4 to 6 months lower than a class with an average IQ of 100. Similarly, a class with an average IQ of 108 should be achieving from 4 to 6 months above the national norm. Or, put this way, if the median IQ of a sixth-grade class is 92, the median achievement of the class should approximate 5.6 instead of the norm of 6.1. On the other hand, if the median IQ of a second sixth-grade class is 108, the median achievement for the class should approximate 6.7 instead of the norm of 6.1.

All too often, teachers ignore the factor of ability and apply pressure to the pupils in an attempt to raise the class median to the level of the national norm. When this is done with slow groups, the possibility of attaining the stated goal is nil. On the other hand, many teachers and school administrators accept a class or grade median for a "bright" or "fast" moving group which is three points above the norm as evidence that the school, the teacher, and the pupils are doing excellent work. Actually, the "fast" class may be merely coasting in terms of what the children are capable of doing. All praise or criticism may not be deserved unless the ability factor is recognized.

Danger of Accepting Single Test Score. Achievement scores should not be accepted as final since too many variables can enter the testing situation. In addition, teachers must remember that standardized tests are not perfect measures of ability or achievement. While test manuals offer information about test reliability, teachers frequently ignore this section since they do not understand terms like "correlation" and "standard deviation." However, if the teachers will look at the statistics, they will see that a single test score is not necessarily a true index of a pupil's ability or achievement. Teachers may, for example, use the standard error of measurement to establish a potential range of achievement or ability for a pupil or a class. Again, referring to the California Achievement Tests, one finds an eighth-grade manual lists the standard error of measurement as 0.6 for an arithmetic test. This means that the odds are 2 to 1 that a pupil's true achievement will lie within 0.6 points of the score he makes on the test. In other words, the odds are 2 to 1 that the pupil who scores 8.4 will not have a true arithmetic score below 7.8 or above 9.0. If the teacher wants a more exact range, she can certify that the odds are 19 to 1 that the pupil's true grade placement in the area tested will not be more than 9.6 or less than 7.2 (two times the standard error of measurement). Actually, most teachers merely need to be aware of the fact that one cannot generalize from single test scores. A single test result cannot be considered as final. In a retest shortly after the original testing date, pupil scores can deviate above or below the original test scores, so that all gains cannot be interpreted as evidence of rapid growth and all losses cannot be interpreted as signs of regression.

Use of Standardized Tests to Diagnose Difficulties and Modify Instruction. Instead of merely filing away the corrected tests, the teacher should be prepared to use them as diagnostic instruments in an attempt to discover strengths and weaknesses of individuals or of the class. Sometimes, a mere review of a pupil's work patterns on a test will indicate the nature of his problem. In other cases, a casual inspection of the test or test results will not suffice. It may be appropriate to make an item analysis of the errors made on one or more parts of the test to show where a pupil or group of pupils made the greatest number of errors. Such study can be time-consuming and may not be necessary for all pupils, but if the teacher has time, the results may be most revealing.

Some teachers have simplified the job of test analysis by calling on the pupils for help. Names are cut off the tests or answer sheets, and code numbers are used so that the data can be used by the teacher later. With the aid of pupil assistants to help with the counting, the teacher quickly goes through the test items to see how many pupils missed each question. The manual informs her what skill a question attempted to measure, so the teacher is in a position to plan a program around the areas where most of the pupils have trouble. The Iowa Basic Skills Test manual is helpful if teachers want to study pupil needs and plan a program for and with the pupils in terms of these needs.

Standardized Tests as a Measure of Pupil, Not Teacher, Strengths and Weaknesses. The standardized test, properly administered, is a valuable teaching tool in the hands of competent teachers, guidance personnel, and administrators. It is an instrument that can help teachers identify pupil strengths and weaknesses as a means of improving teaching, yet the test should not become the basis for all teaching. The test is used diagnostically, but it does not replace the curriculum. Unfortunately, in some communities tests are used to evaluate the effectiveness of the teacher's teaching. When used this way, teachers and students do not have a pleasant educational experience. All too often the efforts of the teacher are directed toward teaching for the test. While such teaching can achieve the desired results, namely, to get children to pass the tests, other values found in good educational activities are lost. For example, comprehension or understanding become meaningless when the teacher's success lies in her ability to show growth through activities calling for memorization and passivity in place of application and independent thinking.

For example, one superintendent of schools makes it a practice to develop elaborate grade or subject norms for classes taught by individual teachers for tests administered from September to June. The teachers are rated on the basis of the amount of growth evidenced between September and June. Here the standardized test becomes a club rather than a teaching aid. In such a community where funds are limited, there is no need for testing so often. There will be no perceptible pupil growth over the vacation period, so the June tests could be used for diagnostic purposes in the fall without another test at that time.

In another community where teacher success depends upon pupil growth, the teachers have insisted on a third testing period. Here the pupils are given a standardized test in January so that the teachers can make certain that they are getting through to their children, but one can question the values in such frequent testing since the tests are not accurate enough to reveal actual growth in such short periods of time, and the teachers will not have time to do much other work in teaching if they are paying so much attention to what the pupils do on the standardized tests.

In some school systems, teachers administer the tests and then never see them again. Here the administrators may use the test results to show growth of classes within the system without any attempt being made to rate the teachers. In such school systems it is essential that teachers do not have to go on the defensive about the accomplishment of their children. Teachers should be able to see how their children compare with other children in a school or system, but this can be done through using code numbers or letters in any reports which are released for staff or public consumption.

REFERENCES

1. California Test Bureau, *Manual—California Short-Form Test of Mental Maturity, Elementary, Grades 4–8,* S-Form (Los Angeles: California Test Bureau, 1957).
2. Robert L. Ebel, *Measuring Educational Achievement* (Englewood Cliffs, N.J.: Prentice-Hall, 1965).
3. Carter V. Good, *Introduction to Educational Research,* 2nd ed. (New York: Appleton-Century-Crofts, 1962).
4. Robert L. Thorndike and Elizabeth Hagen, *Measurement and Evaluation in Psychology and Education* (New York: John Wiley, 1961).
5. Paul West, "A Study of Ability Grouping in the Elementary School in Terms of Variability of Achievement," *Contributions to Education,* No. 588, *The Teaching Problem and Pupil Adjustment* (New York: Bureau of Publications, Teachers College, Columbia University).

CHAPTER 6

Improving Evaluation and
Reporting of Pupil Progress
and Promotion

Many teachers can evaluate the work or accomplishment of their children, but the problem is how to report their findings in an acceptable language to parents, other educators, and to the pupils themselves. Finding the right words or the right form to communicate to others is a problem for many teachers. If they could just eliminate the "mystery man of the report card," life would be so much easier for teacher and learner. However, this is not possible since other educators, parents, and employers want to know what individual pupils have done *in terms of grade standards or in terms of actual pupil potential.* Evaluation and reporting in terms of rigid grade standards can be easy if one ignores factors of ability, previous background, interest, and the availability of suitable teaching materials. If this is all that is wanted, some first-grade teachers can predict the kind of marks some of their children will obtain several years from now. However, parents and teachers find it helps to know more than mere achievement in terms of a set standard.

If a new school administrator wants to stir up excitement in his community, one of the easiest approaches is to suddenly try to change reporting procedures. No matter what method of evaluation and reporting is used, one will always find *someone* objecting to it. Many administrators have lost their positions when they attempted to introduce a radical improvement in reporting procedures. While compromises are frequently made, many educators continue to dream about the perfect report card, one which will be simple to make out, easy to interpret, and which will tell everyone, including the pupil, where the student is or has been in terms of multiple standards of achievement or accomplishment.

Developing Effective Measures

In various communities, reporting practices vary from a planned parent-teacher conference to a written or anecdotal report, along with one of a varied assortment of printed report cards. These may show progress via letters, numbers, descriptive pictures, and descriptive words and phrases. The majority of the report forms will tell the parent one thing, namely, how Johnny or Mary seems to be working in pre-scribed subject areas. Usually, procedure calls for a report of pupil progress in terms of so-called *achievement level* or *standard*, al-though teachers' interpretations of what that standard is will vary in terms of their own interests, abilities, and backgrounds.

The code for marking pupil progress or achievement may be simple or complex, but over a period of time pressures will be exerted to either give additional information or simplify the reporting procedure. Many parents are not satisfied with newer types of report cards, but by the same token they are not satisfied with a simple S and U report or the traditional A, B, C, D, and F. Some want to know if a B is a high B or a low B. Is the mark of D actually a low D or a high D? Does it mean that he is almost failing, or is he almost doing satisfactory work? Again, does the B mean that the pupil is just better than average, or is he almost superior? If the school is marking pupils in terms of ability, parents may want to know if the B means that a pupil is working almost up to capacity, but then if the answer is "Yes," they want to know where the pupil ranks in terms of other pupils in his class or in terms of national standards. Is his work as good as or better than the average work done in the class, grade, or school? If better, how much better?

REPORT CARDS BASED ON GRADE STANDARDS
STILL POPULAR

Most parents understand report cards which indicate pupil progress through the use of a five-point scale, so many of them resist a change in reporting procedures. Generally, they want to see a reporting system which tells how their son or daughter is working in terms of the *accomplishments of other children.* This creates a conflict since many parents are also interested in seeing an individual's growth in terms of *his own ability* or in terms of past accomplishment. Therefore, one can find some dual progress reports in use, but these tend to be complex evaluating instruments difficult to make out and to interpret. The average parent tends to think in terms of grade standards and wants a progress report which indicates growth or progress in terms of these grade standards. If a pupil receives a mark of B, many parents think he is making pretty good progress. With a bit of effort, special help, or even luck, this pupil may climb to the top of the educational ladder. A mark of A or its equivalent will stand for quality or perfection. The recipient of such a mark will be considered superior to pupils receiving lower level marks. This can be very flattering to the ego of the parents who delight in telling their neighbors, "Mary received an A in *arithmetic*." Actually, they may be saying indirectly, "Look at what we created. We have a young genius in the family." In contrast, a poor report card can be a blow to parental pride. The parents of many a bright pupil often favor the *grade standard* report because it almost guarantees them high marks for their children, whereas a report card based upon *ability* may show that the individual is not working up to levels commensurate with his potential.

Since many parents derive personal satisfaction in seeing a pupil's progress in terms of grade standards, it is not easy to dispense with the formal type of reporting. However, one can find educators resorting to a variety of approaches to tell parents what they want to know. A popular method of reporting calls for the replacement of letter grades with numbers or percentages, but this poses problems because so much of a teacher's evaluation is subjective that it is difficult to see differences in marks like 78, 79, 80, and 81. Such marking results in many inconsistencies on the part of teachers and between teachers due to the lack of objective instruments upon which to *base* a grade. Some parents favor this type of marking, but many teachers are unhappy when they have to give children grades which they do not understand or perhaps cannot do anything about. This is particularly true where children are subjected to strong home pressures because neighboring children or a sibling received higher marks. Some communities use word symbols to tell the same story, with the teacher or the office maintaining a numerical grade for the given symbol or word description.

The emphasis upon grade standard marks helps educators to segregate slower learning pupils from average or above-average students before they reach high school, so they are not usually placed in classes considered college preparatory; however, many of the students who have a long history of poor marks due to lack of effort or ability find it difficult to get satisfaction from their school work. And after years of wearing the label of "slow learner" or "failing student," it is hard to convince them that they cannot do better in the outside world. While marks are not the basic cause for all early dropouts, the competitiveness in our schools has helped create situations that have led to unhappiness with schools and schooling.

Teachers are considered "softies" because they give some slow children higher marks than they deserve under the grade standard concept, but teachers who live closely with and for their children all day long see intangibles, other than mere achievement, which influence their actions. It is often difficult to fail the slow-learning child who sits there trying to please the teacher or to do something which will result in parental approval. He has no time for free reading, drawing, or free conversation, because his work occupies his attention hour after hour. Giving such pupils a passing or acceptable mark on the basis of effort expended is quite different from rewarding pupils who make no effort to achieve on a satisfactory plane.

MARKS BASED UPON ABILITY GROWING IN FAVOR

Teachers frequently oppose the practice of giving grade standard marks, because the marks penalize the slow learner who is working at capacity levels. Moreover, the practice encourages the awarding of high grades to bright pupils who do not have to exert themselves to obtain them. As a result, some schools substitute a form of ability marking for grade standard marks. Theoretically, ability marking has its place, but one can find dissatisfaction with such marking because of the absence of a standard unit of comparison. Normally, children compete to obtain marks, but the competitive element is lost with ability marking. Parents object when they cannot discover how a pupil ranks in his class, because a slow learner who works steadily and is reportedly trying hard receives an A for achieving less than the bright pupil who receives a C because he did not really exert himself. In theory, this can happen for the brilliant student who merely does what he is asked to do. In terms of grade standard assignments he can do the same work as slow learners and average learners do, but without working as long or as hard. In many instances, his work may be more accurate and may show better understanding, but he is ineligible for a higher grade unless he extends himself by doing more than the minimum. Actually, in practice, few teachers give low or failure marks to their best students even when they are not working up to their capacity. Parents and teachers still find it difficult to label pupils who are doing the best work at elementary grade levels with any kind of tag which may be considered degrading even though the students may not struggle as hard to complete assignments as slower learning pupils. In some schools, teachers agree that no pupil in a top section or honors class will receive marks lower than a B equivalent.

TABLE 1
Sample Marking Codes Used on Report Cards

Sample 1

E   Excellent progress
S   Satisfactory progress
SA Satisfactory progress at ability level
N   Needs improvement
U   Unsatisfactory progress

Sample 2

Needs much improvement
Shows marked development
Shows satisfactory growth

Sample 3

E   Outstanding growth, pupil doing strong work
S   Usual growth and satisfactory work at grade level
N   Improvement needed to attain grade level
√   Extra work and effort desirable
X   Oral explanation to the parent desirable
SP Satisfactory growth or progress— see teacher comment

Sample 4

A+	Excellent	96 to 100
A	Fine	91 to 95
B+	Good	86 to 90
B		82 to 85
C+	Fair	77 to 81
C		73 to 76
D	Unsatisfactory	70 to 72
E	Very poor	60 to 69
F	Failure	below 60
Passing grade		70

Sample 5

Rapid progress
Good progress
Satisfactory progress
Slow progress
Unsatisfactory progress (failing)

Sample 6

E   Outstanding achievement
S   Above average achievement
M   Average achievement
T   Trying but below grade standard
U   Unsatisfactory achievement (Consistently unsatisfactory achievement may be regarded as failure.)

Sample 7

S   Satisfactory progress
U   Unsatisfactory progress

Sample 8

Note: Three times a year the pupil receives a report indicating how well he is working up to his ability. Twice a year he is given a report based on standards of achievement for his grade.
(Ratings on report of progress)
1   Progress up to ability
2   Has ability to do better
3   Progress much below ability

(Ratings on report of achievement)
A   Much above average
B   Above average
C   Average
D   Below average
E   Much below average

Sample 9

Capable of doing better
Finds work difficult
Shows satisfactory progress
Shows high quality work

Sample 10

Shows improvement
Satisfactory progress
Needs improvement

Ability marking has come to the foreground because teachers have been resisting the practice of giving the slow-learning pupil low or failing marks throughout his school career regardless of how he tries! No matter how such pupils work or try to comply with teacher requests, it is virtually impossible to reward them with a good or even passable mark if grade standards dictate the nature of a pupil's rating. Each year thousands of boys and girls give up or have the inclination to do so, because they are unable to live up to parent or teacher expectations. In class after class they begin assignments with other children, but they are still working at them when others have finished, or they find that they are not able to give the teacher the answers she expects. They repeatedly fail to meet prescribed educational goals because of their backgrounds. Many of these children begin to find frustration at the lowest grade levels, and by the time they reach the intermediate grade level, schooling no longer appeals to them. By junior high school some of them are already waiting for the day when they can join the ranks of the early dropouts.

Evaluations Based on Ability Hard to Defend. Regardless of whether a school is evaluating children in terms of ability or of a grade standard, one will find teachers stating or implying that a given pupil is not working up to his ability. Thousands of teachers have been guilty of the cliché, "Charles could do much better." While these teachers may be correct in making such an assumption, many of them would be hard pressed to defend it. Some teachers may have evidence to support their statements, but others are skating on thin ice when they refer to a child's potential. Studies have shown that many teachers do not know the true potential of given children! Teachers will frequently make reference to a *single* intelligence test score, in itself hardly sufficient evidence of a pupil's true potential. (It has been pointed out that the standard error of measure alone may throw a pupil into different classifications of learners when a second test is given.) When referring to ability, the teacher must consider a pupil's social and economic background, because studies show that pupils from low socioeconomic backgrounds have to overcome obstacles to learning that children from more favorable home environments never face. Ability (in such instances) is not easy to determine, and if actually measured, is no guarantee that the individual can work to capacity unless the school provides a rich and broadening program to compensate for what he misses at home.

It is often difficult to determine the basis for ability marks or comments which may be made to parents concerning a given pupil's potential since teacher evaluations are influenced by many factors. Carter, [2] for example, reports several studies which indicate that girls are inclined to receive higher marks than boys. Studies of class rank in most schools will show that the number of boys in the top 10 per cent of a given class is smaller than girls in spite of comparable ability. One reason for the disparity in the teacher ratings of boys and girls who do comparable work is because boys tend to be nonconformists in many ways. As a result, they are not regarded favorably by many teachers. Other studies have revealed a tendency by women teachers to give higher marks than men teachers, even in a school system where ability marking is the practice. Boys and girls may not like to be labeled as "teacher's pet," but it does pay off. Teachers tend to give higher marks to pupils they *favor* than to pupils they do not like, despite the fact that the latter pupils may be achieving on a higher plane than the pupils who are in the good graces of the teacher.

It is often difficult to compare teacher ratings of the same individual since they may not use the same evidence to substantiate their evaluation. It is almost impossible to explain teachers' thinking processes. This subjectiveness is often tempered at different grade levels by the difference in emphasis placed on pupil marks. For example, primary grade teachers tend to place less emphasis upon marks than upper grade and secondary school teachers. Thus a difference in educational philosophy, as well as in training and experience, may influence the nature of a pupil's rating as he goes from teacher to teacher. Often, due to emotional barriers, the necessary rapport is never established between the teacher and given students, and this leads the teacher to underestimate what these pupils can do or have accomplished.

Many teachers make the mistake of using the intelligence quotient (IQ) to classify children. Actually, they should be using the mental age (MA), since two children with the same intelligence quotient may not be at the same learning level. Teachers should also remember that chronological age (CA) can affect performance. If one pupil is young and the other overaged, their rates of growth or accomplishment will not be the same even though they have the same intelligence. Thus, a boy who is 7-10 chronologically may have a mental age of 8-3, whereas the boy with a mental age of 9-3 may be 8-10 chronologically, yet both pupils have an IQ of approximately 105. One can expect more of the pupil with a mental age of 9 years and 3 months than one can expect of the pupil with a mental age of 8 years and 3 months. Translated into terms of expectancy levels, the younger pupil may be capable of doing high-level second-grade or low-level third-grade work, while the older pupil may be capable of doing high-level third-grade work or low-level fourth-grade work.

It should be emphasized that reliance on an IQ test is based on the assumption that the test was administered properly and scored correctly. In addition, it must be assumed that the two pupils were in top form when they took the test, that they understood the directions, and actually tried to do their best. It must also be assumed that the tests actually measured intelligence and not reading ability or prior experience.

One may ask why a pupil is still in the second grade when he is old enough to be in the third grade, particularly since he has the potential that calls for success with third-grade work. Conceivably, such a pupil may have a long history of illness or a social or an emotional background that makes it essential that he remain with younger children because they give him a greater feeling of security. Again, if the pupil's class performance is low, it may be advisable to recheck his intelligence, since gross discrepancies between potential and achievement can point to future trouble. A second test may indicate a lower actual potential. Should this be true, the teacher who marks upon ability may find it desirable to reevaluate the ratings given earlier and then readjust them in terms of the new estimate of the pupil's intelligence (ability).

Reporting pupil progress in terms of ability is sometimes based upon a bit of subterfuge. In some communities, parents receive ratings based upon *apparent* ability, but the office records require grades showing pupil rank in class based upon grade standards.

Parental Dissatisfaction with Ability Marking of Superior Students. Parents of slow-learning children find satisfaction in ability marks since their children are not as conspicuously identified. Here, the ego of both parent and pupil is uplifted by the marking system. Accomplishment, no matter how slight, is recognized by the teacher, and the learner does not have to dread termination of a marking period. While average pupils stand to benefit from ability marking, ambitious parents soon begin to show their dissatisfaction. Traxler [8] reports that parents tend to be critical of marks based on ability alone. They want to see how their children rank in class!

Other educators have also found this true, so they have tried to develop a reporting system which would not be competitive, but which, instead, would recognize ability and effort and yet appease the parents. They have found that such comments as "Satisfactory" or "Is making fine progress for his ability" are not specific enough. Parents want to know more. A typical parental comment will be, "I know that Jane is working to capacity, but what does it mean? Has she learned to read as well as her friends? Does an A or Good Progress mean that she is an excellent student academically, or does it mean that she is an average student academically who has learned to conform?" Another parent will ask, "Can Oliver get into high school or college with these marks? Is he really an A or B student in terms of academic accomplishment? He does not do very satisfactory work at home, so we cannot see how he can rate so high unless the school is failing to challenge children."

Ambitious parents want to know whether their children are doing better than other boys and girls in a given class, grade, or subject. A rating of B or C becomes meaningless to the parent when he discovers that the favorite son ranks at the bottom of the reading, arithmetic, or social studies classes in terms of *actual* achievement.

USE OF DUAL MARKING SYSTEMS

Some educators have tried to meet teacher and parent interests in pupil evaluation by the development of a new, but complex, dual marking system. The new report card attempts to tell parents where a pupil stands in relation both to his own ability and to other pupils in the class. In evaluating pupil progress, the teacher attempts to give the pupil two ratings. Here, a typical report card calls for a set of marks in a column set aside for an evaluation based upon the *individual's ability* or *potential*. A second column or coding provides for a rating based upon *actual achievement in terms of established standards*. Although the authors favor this system of reporting, the fact remains that it does create problems because (1) it is too complex for many parents to read accurately and with understanding; and (2) it is too difficult for many teachers to complete with a high degree of consistency and reliability.

So many factors have to be considered in the evaluation process that, after the outstanding pupils and the poorest pupils have been graded, it is most difficult to grade the middle group of children in a class without feeling that some factor has been overlooked. A dual marking system merely compounds the teacher's problems because she now has to be consistent in what she *says* regarding ability and achievement in various subjects and from one marking period to another. If she uses a coding or descriptive words, she has to make every effort to ensure that it says what she wants to say.

To ensure that teachers and parents understand each other, some school administrators have teacher-parent meetings to explain the philosophy underlying the dual marking system and the terms used. Written directions or explanations are often developed to guide teachers in the evaluation of children and to help parents interpret the dual coding that is used to inform them about the ability and achievement of their children. Actually, this type of reporting can be most fruitful if parent-teacher conferences are held to review the report card ratings, but if this is done, the educators may consider the advisability of substituting a planned series of parent conferences in place of the formal report card.

Identifying Under- and Overachievers with Dual Marking System. When the *underachievers* and the so-called *overachievers* have been discovered, the teacher is in a position to take a more positive approach as she plans new activities based upon her observations and knowledge about individual children. If she finds individual pupils who are not working anywhere near expectation levels, she may revamp her approach for these children in hopes that she can identify the reasons for their low achievement. She may have to retest some pupils to verify reported intelligence or achievement levels. In other cases, she may find that interest and cultural factors help account for discrepancies between pupil performance and actual accomplishment in class.

The dual marking system may result in a diminishing of the pressures upon average and less-than-average children, but at the same time bright children may find that they have to exert themselves if they are to meet teacher and parent expectations in terms of their potential. However, these bright children must be exposed to a program that allows them to progress at their own rates of speed. A teacher cannot fairly rate a bright pupil *low* in arithmetic achievement if he does all that he is asked to do but is never introduced to higher level arithmetic skills and concepts. She has to place him in a learning situation which will allow him to work at advanced levels if he is to work close to expectation levels for his high intellectual ability.

Reports show that the dual marking system has been a boon to school administrators because teacher marks tend to be more consistent, since teachers have to study the principles of evaluating children in greater detail if they are to work effectively with the more complex and more professional approach in marking or grading the progress of individual children.

ILLUSTRATIONS:

Teachers in one school system use a standard report card with two columns for the rating of children at the end of each marking period. Each pupil is rated twice for each subject. In the first column the pupil is rated in terms of grade standards. He is rated again with the same letters or code symbols in the second column, but this time his progress is evaluated in terms of his actual expected performance for his mental age.

Teachers in another school evaluate each pupil's relative achievement in subject matter in terms of his ability through a combination of letter and number grades. At the start of the school year the teacher, through observation and study of the pupil's test records, classifies him in terms of expected and/or permissible alternate performance levels for his IQ. The IQ, or ratio of mental age (MA) to average chronological age (CA) for the grade level, gives the pupil's ability for the work in basic subject fields.

In one school the pupil's ability rating is listed on the report card in a conspicuous place so the parent knows that the child falls into a given ability range. All marks or codes are based upon this designated classification of the pupil's potential.

Generally, if a pupil does work appropriate for his *ability* level, he receives a mark of S followed by a 1-2-3-4 which designates the *performance* level. If the pupil *fails* to work up to his ability level, he receives a mark of U followed by a 1-2-3-4 to show his actual performance level. In other words, a bright pupil who fails to make a sufficient effort would receive the paradoxical-seeming mark of U-3 or U-4. Teachers base their ratings upon a guide sheet that sets forth definitions for various performance levels.

TABLE 2
Establishing Ability Levels for Pupils

Indicated Ability (For fundamental subjects)	Intelligence Quotient or Ratio of MA to Average CA for Grade Level	Performance Ranges or Expectation Levels	
		PROBABLE	ACCEPTABLE OR OCCASIONAL ALTERNATE*
A	140 and above	1	2
B	139–128	2	1
	127–110	2	3
C	109–97	3	2
	96–85	3	4
D	84 or below	4	3

* Dependent upon circumstances, i.e., instructional facilities, special pupil aptitude or interest, etc.

Note: Teachers may use a few points higher or lower in determining expected performance levels if in their judgment the ratings are too high or too low.

Performance Ranges or Expectation Levels. The following is a detailed guide to the code system used in Table 2.

1—Generally fast working speed. For 11- to 14-year-olds, ranging approximately more than two years above average grade level in fundamental school work accomplishment (doing about as well as many children who are more than two years older would do on the same or similar subject material). For the 9- to 10-year-olds, the range of performance would be two or more years above. For the 6- to 8-year-olds, this range would be more than one year advanced. In some subject areas and in some classes there would be no youngsters working at this level. In other classes there might be two or four youngsters who would maintain performance at this level in certain subject areas.

2—Medium to medium-fast working speed. For 11- to 14-year-olds, ranging from approximate grade level to one and two years above average age-grade levels for the subject (doing about as well as many children of the same age, and often as well as those who are one or even two years older would do on the same or similar subject material). For the 9- to 10-year-olds, performance would range from average to above-average. Twelve to fifteen youngsters in a class of thirty pupils can be expected to perform at this level in a subject.

3—Medium to slow working speed. For 11- to 14-year-olds, ranging from approximate grade level down to one or two years below average age-grade level accomplishment in the subject (doing about as well as many children one or even two years younger would do on the same or similar subject material). For the 9- to 10-year-olds, the performance would range from average down to one or occasionally to two years below average. Approximately fourteen to twenty youngsters would maintain performance in a subject at this level.

4—Slow working speed. For the 11- to 14-year-olds, ranging from more than two years below average age-grade level accomplishment for the subject (doing about as well as many children would do who are two or more years younger). For the 9- to 10-year-olds, the performance would range two or more years below. For the 6- to 8-year-olds, the performance would range more than one year below. Approximately four to ten pupils would maintain performance at this level.

Under this system of marking, instruction is essentially instruction of groups within each classroom. The teachers are not expected to bring all children up to a fixed grade standard. Provisions are made to teach each pupil at the level where he can achieve the greatest amount of growth in terms of his potential.

Evaluating Children Assigned to Homogeneous or Honors Classes. A dual progress marking system lends itself to the evaluation of children in homogeneous or "honors" classes. However, where ability is not used in the evaluative process, teachers may have problems when they mark papers or report cards. Should children in low class sections receive marks extending from the highest possible to the lowest possible mark? Should children in the top class section receive anything but high marks, or do their marks range from the highest to the lowest possible mark? If so, does one try to distinguish between an A given to children in the top class section from an A given to children in the low class section? Questions such as these may appear ridiculous to some lay citizens, but they pose problems if they remain unanswered.

Teachers, parents, and pupils want to know what marks mean. If the pupil receives an A or its equivalent for work which is inferior to that of the lowest pupil in the next highest homogeneous section who receives a D or F, what incentive is there for pupils to try to get into higher sections? Some bright pupils have been able to see through such a marking system, with the result that they have refused to exert themselves enough to warrant being placed in an honors section of a grade. To exert themselves thus would mean that they would have to work hard merely to hold their own in competition with other bright children. By letting themselves get assigned to average sections, they are able to secure top grades and are ranked as the best pupils in their classes without too much effort. This has been particularly true where all pupils tend to do the same work regardless of class or section classification. Second and third graders have discovered they could be considered the best students in an average or low reading section with less effort than if they were placed in the top reading group, with the result that they have deliberately engaged in a "slow down" to avoid placement in the highest reading section. Students at the high school level have refused assignments to honors classes where they would not be guaranteed high marks because the possibility of a low mark would endanger their chances of being accepted in the college of their choice. To meet such challenges, educators have:

Attempted to distinguish between the marks given children in different ability sections. Thus, a pupil in the average section might receive a report showing letter grades followed by a 2; for example, A-2, B-2, C-2. Similarly, pupils in the low section would receive marks followed by a 3; for example, A-3, B-3, C-3, D-3, etc.

Restricted the range of marks given to children in different level sections. Thus, pupils in the highest learning sections could receive the equivalent of A's, B's, and C's, but they would not receive lower marks. Similarly, pupils in the lowest learning sections would receive marks of C, D, or F, but they would not be eligible for marks equivalent to an A or B. Some teachers have objected to such restrictions on the theory that pupils in top sections would not produce quality work because they know that they cannot be given a mark lower than a B.

Based the range of marks that are given to children on the basis of intelligence. Thus in one school, all marks of an A equivalency are reserved for pupils with an IQ over 130. Since pupil achievement is not always commensurate with the potential for a given IQ, some teachers are advised to consider achievement in the fields of reading and English. The addition of these new factors complicates the marking unless the teachers have some leeway in adjusting marks in terms of their own observations concerning pupil ability or potential.

Set standards of achievement for pupils in terms of designated intelligence ranges. Thus, to obtain an A, children with superior intelligence are expected to show achievement comparable to what other children with similar intelligence have done. Some of these bright pupils may receive a B or even a C if it becomes apparent that they are not working above the average category.

IMPORTANCE OF PARENT CONFERENCES

Research studies have repeatedly demonstrated the lack of value of standard report cards because teacher marks have been unreliable and often lack consistency. In addition, it is often impossible to tell the parents what one wants to say through letter grades or short descriptive words. Nothing is so effective as a face-to-face talk between parent and teacher. In some schools, parent conferences replace the traditional report card, but in others they merely supplement it. Planned conferences can be extremely helpful to parents and teachers who sincerely want to help children to overcome handicaps and to work to maximum learning levels. Such meetings enable the teacher and parent to discuss intelligently the aspects of a child's growth which cannot be reported in a formal reporting system, i.e., achievement can be reported on in writing, but at a conference the teacher can supplement her statements with actual samples of a pupil's work and compare it with the work of other children.

Recently, there has been an increased interest on the part of parents and teachers in patterns of behavior and character. What pupils do as social individuals, how they go about their work, and the nature of their attitudes and interests are all a part of the story teachers can tell in the parent conference. The teacher may also get an insight into many aspects of a pupil's background which are not revealed in the classroom. To be most effective, the conference should be held when neither parent nor teacher has the feeling that she has to rush. Privacy is imperative. Establishing a rapport is essential for a mutual sharing and understanding of the child's problems both at home and at school.

Unfortunately, some very excellent classroom teachers cannot express themselves clearly in a parent conference. They may have many things to say, but they have trouble communicating. Some will say too much, and others will not say enough. Other teachers may confuse the parents by educational jargon. One may find a teacher who assumes the role of a psychologist by trying to solve the mother's or father's problems as well as the child's. *Some parents frighten teachers, but more often teachers frighten parents!* Parents should leave a conference with the feeling that they had a fruitful meeting. They should learn how their child is growing academically, socially, emotionally, intellectually, and physically. They should have a feeling that their child is in competent hands. After the conference, the teacher should make a few notes outlining any recommendations or special points covered in the conference. These notes should be helpful as the teacher works with the pupil and may be extremely valuable when other conferences are held with the same parent.

Many schools hold very effective parent conferences during school time by using substitute teachers or special teachers to cover their classes during the scheduled conference period. In other systems children are released early for a number of days in order to allow teachers to meet parents individually. The authors favor incorporating regular conference days in the school calendar, but others favor half-day sessions which will count toward the minimum number of required days.

THE VALUE OF THE WRITTEN REPORT

With many parents working and with teachers commuting long distances to schools, numerous parent conferences can become a scheduling problem. Consequently, some school systems have adopted the practice of sending home long written reports in place of the typical report card. Theoretically, the written report eliminates many of the objections to the report card. Words and sentences replace cold symbols, letters, or numerals. The teacher is free to express her feelings, findings, and observations in terms of the individual child. She can expound freely on points which need explanation. She can tell parents where a child is in terms of his ability or in comparison with other children in the class.

Although the written report has many advantages, educators find some disadvantages in this type of reporting. For example, written reports require considerable time if they are to be meaningful. Many times, teachers are unable to say what they want to say on paper since composition is not their forte. Poor handwriting or sentences with grammatical, spelling, or punctuation errors do not help teachers make a very effective impression upon the parents.

Some schools use the written report as only one of several types of reporting procedures. One school system sends home three formal report cards plus one detailed written report. Another school system has the teachers meeting with parents for two formal conferences alternating with two written reports. In either case, neither a short note about a special problem nor a chance meeting with a parent in a grocery store is accepted as meeting a reporting standard. A good report, whether written or oral, is based upon careful consideration of all phases of a pupil's growth and progress. This takes time and thought.

A Guide to Writing Letter Reports to Parents. To help teachers write better reports, administrators often develop a file of the better letters (minus identifying names) which come to their attention. Some schools have teacher-teams evaluate the letters which are sent home, again collecting samples to illustrate good and poor writing form. In addition, the teachers may be given an outline or guide to assist them as they write. The following are points that may be included in such a guide:

All written letter reports should be written in *nontechnical*, easily understood terms.

The letter should be *informative* about what the child has been doing in school and, in some instances, what he will be doing in the future in designated areas or subjects. This is true if help is desired.

The written report should be *brief* (one to two pages), *direct*, and *personal*.

The written report should assume a *positive tone*, even when a critical statement is made.

The teacher should avoid making *generalizations* or statements that can apply to everyone.

The teacher should be able to support any statement she makes with evidence if called upon.

Each teacher should strive to write *complete sentences* which are grammatically correct. (Parents may judge the teacher on the quality of her writing.)

The teacher should indicate what provisions have been or will be made to meet *special needs* of the pupil.

Teachers should point out *ways parents can help* where desired.

Specifically, the written letter report *may include* some or all of the following comments about the pupil:

1. His *work-study pattern.* Is he cooperative? Does he show interest, originality, or creativity? Is he careless or indifferent?

2. His *social adjustment* to other pupils, the teacher, and the day-by-day pattern of school activities.

3. His *specific traits,* such as cooperativeness, reliability, courteousness, sportsmanship, determination, attention span, appearance, leadership qualities, initiative, behavior, accuracy, attentiveness, etc.

4. His *physical growth and development* in comparison with other boys and girls in his age-grade group.

5. His *emotional stability* and the nature of any pronounced emotional problems.

6. His *achievement* in major academic or subject fields, for example: progress in terms of his own potential and in terms of the growth and progress of comparable children; reading level and interests; test results in general terms; and areas in which special help is needed.

7. His *mental maturity level* and *attitude* toward school and life in general.

A teacher's letter to a parent will frequently depend upon the rapport she has established with the parent. If a parent understands the nature of a learner's problem, the teacher does not have to go into as much detail as she does when she is introducing the parent to a new problem. Some teachers have so much that they want to say that they themselves have developed a checklist which includes many small details which cannot be included in a formal report card and which would necessitate a very long, detailed letter. There is some merit to the checklists, but they should supplement and not replace the letter report, which should be a form of personal communication between the home and the school. In any case, the final report which goes home should make it clear to the parent that the school and its teachers are truly interested in the welfare of individual children. The report should be a well-thought-out evaluation of the work or progress of an identifiable child, and it should be a report which tells parents what they want to know about the nature of the learner and his problems.

ADJUSTING REPORTING PRACTICES TO THE LOCAL SITUATION

One of the difficulties one encounters when teachers talk about evaluation is that of determining what terms mean. Although national standards are satisfactory guides in some communities, they are not for others. Thus, while a mark of C may be considered as a mark for average children living in an average community, it is possible to find schools in depressed economic areas where few, if any, pupils would be eligible for such a mark. Similarly, the mark would be considered far from satisfactory in some wealthy suburban communities where the average IQ is 120 or higher. For example, one may ask how to assign marks to children where the average IQ is only 80; here, the fifth-grade or ten-year-old pupil who reads on a high second-grade reading level is among the best readers in his class. In terms of a national standard, the pupils in his reading section are two to three years retarded in reading, yet they are reading close to expectation levels for their mental ages. Without some consideration of the ability factor, these students would never receive anything except failing marks.

Every teacher in a given school should understand the grading system which has been adopted, and then make an effort to evaluate her pupils in the light of established policy. It is essential that all staff members "speak the same language" as they work with each other and with children and parents. From time to time new staff members will need to be oriented to the school's philosophy and general pattern of operation. If changes are made, all staff members must accept them if there is to be continuity in what the teachers do with children from grade to grade or from subject to subject. Since evaluation involves judgments, there will always be some subjectiveness in what teachers do when they grade papers or rate individual children; however, teachers in a given school can establish guidelines which will help them remain fairly close as they evaluate children in their day-by-day, month-by-month, and year-by-year progress through a given school or school system.

SUPERIORITY OF NEWER TYPES OF REPORT CARDS

Modern parents want to know more about a child's progress in school than ever before. The written report, the parent conference, and many new report cards are steps toward keeping parents fully informed. Many of these report cards include a number of personalized statements which indicate areas of strength or weakness in addition to a standard mark. Some schools use a combination of letters and other symbols to designate progress in a particular skill area.

Educators have found that they have to be selective in the learning characteristics they include in a report card. They should include statements or skills which will interest parents and which can be rated *objectively*. One can study a wide variety of the newer types of report cards in circulation without ever seeing a traditional grade, although the office may still require teachers to submit a mark which can be used on cumulative reports for future reference (see Figure 1).

These report cards tell what the learner is doing and how he is progressing in specific subjects. They are quite different from the traditional report card, which tends to indicate how much subject matter has been learned. All phases of pupil growth may be included in the newer report cards—physical, social, emotional, and academic. Many school systems will report progress in terms of individual capacity instead of in terms of grade standards. Many of the newer report cards use descriptive statements which may be checked or marked according to a prescribed code to show areas of strength or weakness. In a report using a code such as the one on page 152, teachers can tell parents what a given child is doing by means of a dual code which can be translated in terms of statements describing how the pupil works and his rate of progress.

Like many other report cards, this card has space for special comments by teacher and parent. Other report cards have sections devoted to social attitudes, health habits, cooperativeness, and creativity. Not all of them call for a dual marking or code, but there is a trend in this direction. Some of them merely have a space for the teacher to check areas which need attention. While many parents find the modern report cards give them a better picture of what a pupil is doing in class, occasional parents frankly state, "It takes me too long to find out

Figure 1. **Areas Included in a Modern Report Card Designed to Show Basic Skills Taught**

Subject and Work Skills	Academic Achievement	Work-Study Pattern
LANGUAGE ARTS		
Reads with understanding....................		
Is able to use library resources independently.....		
Reads well to others.........................		
Is able to read content materials independently...		
Shows growth in the development of reading vocabulary.		
Expresses himself effectively and correctly in situations requiring oral language proficiency......		
Expresses himself effectively and correctly in situations requiring written language proficiency...		
Understands and uses proper grammatical forms..		
Shows originality in his writing................		
Speaks clearly and distinctly.................		
Spells correctly in all of his written work........		
Writes legibly and with good speed............		
SOCIAL STUDIES		
Is able to interpret events and their subsequent effect upon the lives of people...............		
Shows ability to understand what he reads that relates to both past and current happenings....		
Is able to interpret maps, graphs, and charts.....		
Contributes intelligently to group discussions.....		
Is able to assume responsibilities requiring leadership ability...............................		
Shows ability to use reference materials.........		
Shows understanding of time and space relations.		
ARITHMETIC		
Shows mastery of fundamental processes........		
Is accurate in computations..................		
Can solve problems independently and correctly...		
Works with reasonable speed.................		
Shows a good understanding of numbers and number relationships.........................		
SCIENCE		
Shows an interest in science and scientific procedures.		
Shows ability to understand science principles....		
Is able to apply science knowledge acquired to explain natural phenomenon..................		
Makes contributions to science classes from his readings and observations..................		
ART		
Shows respect for art and its materials..........		
Shows ability to use various media creatively.....		

Achievement Code	*Work-Study or Citizenship Code*
A Is making exceptionally good progress.	1 Pupil works with a minimum of supervision, begins promptly, recognizes responsibilities, cooperates with others, shows courtesy.
B Is making better than average progress.	
C Is making what may be considered as satisfactory progress.	2 Works effectively if given specific directions, meets obligations, generally can be depended upon to observe class rules regarding work and behavior.
D Is making progress slowly; needs considerable extra help and attention.	
E Is not making very much progress; may be considered as failing to meet expectation or achievement levels established for his age and grade.	3 Requires constant supervision, lets others do his share in group activities, does no more than is expected, takes no added responsibilities, loses interest quickly, has to be reminded about the need to observe class rules.
	4 Wastes time, works poorly, must be constantly reminded about his obligations, habitually offers excuses, interferes with work and progress of others in class.

whether or not my boy is passing," or "I just cannot understand what all the checks, asterisks, and squares mean." Other parents report that they can often give help to a pupil when the report card lists subtopics such as the following under a major subject, thus:

Language Arts

READING	LANGUAGE
Understands what he reads.	Expresses ideas well in oral speech.
Is able to attack new words readily.	Speaks distinctly.
Can read well orally.	Can write complete simple sentences.
Can read well silently.	Can use words as tools to develop creative expression.
Understands sequence of a story.	
Is reading library books independently.	Is acquiring a good vocabulary which he can use in his written work.
Finishes workbook assignments on time.	Uses word book or picture dictionary as a tool for writing.

BASIC PRINCIPLES FOR SETTING UP A REPORTING SYSTEM

1. Many kinds of reporting practices are in use, but each school system should adopt the one which best reflects its own philosophy, objectives, and curriculum for a grade, series of grades, or school division, i.e., primary or intermediate grades. Research studies show

that teacher marks tend to be unreliable and invalid indexes of pupil growth and achievement, but they cannot be dispensed with easily, since they are the basis for many rewards: promotion, the college of one's choice, the field of business of one's choice. Therefore, all staff members should subscribe to common principles of evaluating children within a school or series of grade levels, and the symbols used should carry a definition uniformly understood or agreed on.

2. The method of reporting should show how successfully the school is meeting its broad and specific objectives. Most standard reporting systems show pupil progress in fundamental skill areas. Growth in other areas is not usually recorded, because such growth may not always be evident or may be difficult to evaluate. So new kinds of reports may be needed to show growth in social relationships, leadership, creativity, work-study skills, and so on.

3. The reporting system should serve many purposes: It must enable teachers to satisfy the parents' desire to know where the child has been going or where he is with regard to (a) standard achievement and (b) ability. The system should indicate areas of special accomplishment as well as areas where assistance is desired. The reporting system should be diagnostic in that it points up areas which may become the basis for present and future programs of instruction.

4. Standardized test results alone cannot be used to show pupil growth and progress. The national norms are seldom based upon the same instructional goals or objectives as in a given classroom. However, a teacher may compare her own observations with the results of a standardized test to substantiate her own marks or to review pupil needs. If used wisely with teacher-made tests, the teacher's observations and discussions with other teachers who have worked with individual children will often help toward a more reliable or dependable evaluation than just using a single index.

5. Teachers should be prepared to examine their own biases or prejudices before attempting to evaluate the progress of their children. Studies have repeatedly shown that pupils who conform tend to obtain higher marks. Furthermore, many teachers have a direct or indirect bias when it comes to marking pupils who come from different homes or environments. Boys tend to receive fewer high marks than girls, just as children from low economic and social levels may have to work harder to secure the same mark given to more fortunate pupils.

6. Teacher marks should recognize individual differences in growth patterns or readiness for learning. Marks should be based upon recognizing real pupil growth. Mere achievement in terms of prescribed grade standards is no guarantee that a given pupil has made substantial growth.

7. Teacher evaluations which recognize pupil ability have value,

but teachers must understand what they mean by *ability*. A single intelligence test may be a very unreliable instrument upon which to base a pupil's report of progress; it may be more desirable to establish expectancy levels upon a range of intelligence. Teachers should avoid the use of such general comments as, "The pupil is working up to his ability," unless they are prepared to substantiate them.

8. Teachers should consider whether it is desirable to ask or expect pupils to work continuously at capacity levels, in the face of the physical and emotional strain this can cause.

9. Teachers must evaluate pupil progress continuously. Instruction should not be based on a hit-or-miss type of teaching. Constant evaluation is an essential for effective instruction, and a cumulative record should be developed and used.

10. Evaluation is a multiple responsibility, and the teacher should work closely with parents and coworkers.

Understanding Promotional Policies

The promotional policy of a school may or may not be consistent with what teachers do with and for children throughout the school year. Research studies have shown that the act of retaining children has little value for most pupils. These conclusions are correct for schools or classes where teachers fail to group children in terms of their instructional levels, but they may not be true where teachers attempt to work with pupils at their appropriate learning levels.

In the former case, the common practice calls for the repetition of a class or grade by pupils who fail to attain *desired* goals of achievement. Nonpromotion in such cases has little value to the pupil, because here the teacher merely reexposes the student to skills or subject matter without trying to bridge the gap between his actual learning level and the instructional level.

In the latter case, nonpromotion is quite likely to mean something different for the pupil, since his teacher should not be reexposing him to the same skills he worked with during the past year. If the teacher takes this pupil from where he was academically the previous year, the grade he is actually in will have little real meaning to him, although socially he may face problems. Further studies of the effects of nonpromotion are needed to see what happens to boys and girls who remain behind in classes where boys and girls continue to work at their learning levels and not at a grade standard.

Under the old concepts of nonpromotion, it was customary to hold back from one-fourth to one-third of a first grade, with the pupils repeating what they had been exposed to the prior year *regardless* of their readiness for the learning activities on the second or even third go-around. These children were frustrated early and many of them never overcame this frustration.

In contrast, one finds modern children learning at their own pace in many ungraded primaries without this frustration. Anderson [1] reports that many pupils who made slow progress in the ungraded primary during their first year were able to catch up with their chronological-aged peers by the time they were ready to leave the primary grade unit. Here, the school serves as a leveling agent for many boys and girls who began school with a poor foundation for learning. The growth acceleration seems to come with maturity as the teachers continue to work with slow-progressing pupils at the children's rates of learning. This does not mean that *all* slow-learning pupils catch up, but enough do to make one ask why educators were so long in seeing the futility of pushing children into activities before they were ready for them.

CONTINUOUS PROMOTION NOT ALWAYS CONTINUOUS PROGRESS

Dissatisfaction with early nonpromotional policies has resulted in a trend toward continuous promotion. In many communities this refers to a policy of keeping children together on the basis of chronological age instead of on the basis of achievement. Here, promotion is automatic for all, regardless of whether a pupil has completed the work of a designated grade or deserves the right to move into the next higher grade with his classmates. One can build a case for a policy of continuous promotion on the basis of the futility of holding children back under traditional teaching methods and philosophies of education, but one cannot escape the fact that promotion or nonpromotion is an *individual matter*. A blanket policy or a 100 per cent promotional policy can still be harmful to the individual child regardless of how he is taught in school.

In many schools one can find boys and girls who are totally unprepared for formal learning activities. Pushing these immature children on merely because they are chronologically ready to enter the next grade can hurt them. They need a chance to catch up, sometimes academically, but in many instances they need time to develop along social, emotional, and physical lines. Because of their immaturity, they do not fit into higher learning situations. As a result, automatic promotion can lead to just as much frustration, if not more, as holding other children back. Many such children will welcome the opportunity to remain with a teacher they know and love if parents will refrain from placing them under extreme pressure. The authors are not advocating a policy of nonpromotion so much as they advocate a policy which is based upon the understanding of the needs of individual students.

If the parent and teacher have been working closely together over the course of the year, the issue should not be so much one of continuous promotion as one of continuous growth. They should be able to see whether a given action will result in a continuation of the child's social, emotional, and academic growth. Will it be easier for the child to work with younger and less mature children for a time where he can hold his own with a minimum of frustration, or will it be easier for him to continue with his chronological-aged peers who are working at such advanced levels that he is constantly frustrated in his attempt to keep up with them? The answer to such a question will depend to some extent upon the way the school is organized and how children are grouped for instruction.

If the teacher takes her children where she finds them, in order to help them progress normally, the issue of promotion or nonpromotion should not exist. On the other hand, if the pupil is in a school where teachers recognize neither individual differences nor a stage of growth for learning, the promotional policy of a school can have serious consequences to the pupil. In such schools there is little to be gained by having pupils repeat a grade, regardless of their needs, but by the same token the pupils will not make much progress in the advanced grade with a teacher who is not prepared to work with them at their learning level. Here, continuous promotion may not mean continuous progress for individual pupils until someone is ready to plan an instructional program for them in terms of their needs.

THE UNGRADED SCHOOL AS A SOLUTION TO THE PROBLEM OF CONTINUOUS PROGRESS

While many educators have been able to resolve the problem of continuous progress without changing the nature of their school organization, the easiest solution for others may lie in some form of ungraded school pattern of organization. In 1967 approximately 17 per cent of the nation's 87,000 public elementary schools were operating gradeless school programs at the primary levels. This represents a doubling of the number of such school organization plans in a five-year period. Unfortunately, some school systems have adopted the name "ungraded" without making any significant change in the way children are grouped, taught, evaluated, or promoted. In such schools, children still have to contend with restrictions which go with the formal graded school, which means that continuous progress is still a form of hypothetical rationalization.

Educators are finding that the ungraded school has a promise for children that is often missing in many graded schools. Essentially, it is only a new method of 'organizing the school, because teachers will continue to use the same teaching tools and materials in working with the children, but within a framework of a different teaching philosophy and approach to learning. Traditional grade standards tend to disappear as teachers adopt an approach to teaching that is based upon continuous progress in selected areas, especially in the field of reading. This is true where parents and teachers accept the fact that traditional grade requirements or offerings often fail to give adequate challenge to better-than-average children, but that at the same time they result in frustration for pupils who are less gifted intellectually, socially, emotionally, and physically.

The ungraded school attempts to free teachers from grade restrictions. Standards are still maintained, but boys and girls attain them at their own rates of learning. Their progress, however, will still depend upon the readiness of the classroom teacher to plan in terms of children's needs. Unless the teachers are prepared to do so, continuous progress may never become a reality, since it is not the organization pattern that counts so much as what teachers do within the classroom with boys and girls. The new setting has possibilities, as will be seen in another chapter.

ELIMINATION OF ACADEMIC ACHIEVEMENT AS BASIS FOR PROMOTION AND NONPROMOTION

Adults are prone to think of promotion or nonpromotion in terms of academic achievement, and thus they tend to ignore other factors that affect the child's welfare. Placement of a child in a particular learning situation should depend upon his *total stage of development*. While a pupil may be retarded academically, he may still be maturing socially, emotionally, and physically. Most adults have seen evidence of this fact when normal thirteen-year-olds find themselves in eighth-grade classes with sixteen-year-olds who cannot compete academically but are far more worldly-wise than their younger classmates. If there is concern for any of the children in such classes, it is likely to be for the *average* children, who may learn something nonacademic from the older pupils.

Adults often show an unwillingness to consider as "handicapping factors" the social and emotional immaturity of pupils who show an intellectual maturity with an accompanying success in their academic activities. However, some of these children will, on occasion, be much happier if left to work with children who are younger chronologically, socially, and emotionally. Thus, one may find a physically immature boy who is miserable and unsure of himself because his small stature does not allow him to take an active part in the rough-and-tumble activities of the bigger fellows who are his own age. His interests may not be on a par with his chronological-aged peers, so it is no pleasure to associate with them. If left to himself, he will play with younger boys from the preceding grade. Also, one can find some very unhappy sixth-, seventh-, eighth-, and ninth-grade pupils who find themselves left out of activities because certain normal, physical changes are slow in making an appearance. Their interest in and readiness for activities involving members of the opposite sex just is not there. The problems of such children can be accentuated if they happen to be pupils who have been accelerated academically.

Orlo L. Derby [3] makes the point that few children ever benefit in their total growth pattern as a result of retardation or nonpromotion. He says, "The one legitimate reason why a child should not go on is probably that he is immature socially, emotionally, and mentally." Actually, academic retardation may result from one or more of these factors, but true causal factors may be hard to discover. Children who come from culturally deprived homes may not be ready to learn to read, write, and speak on a par with average children. Some of them may have the mentality, but they lack the incentive or purpose that is an essential for success. Their sense of values may not be the same as that of the teachers, which leads to conflict and a lack of under-standing.

When educators are seriously considering what is best for a certain boy or girl, they have to contend with "emotionalism" on the part of the teacher or of the parents. This may make it difficult to decide what is best for an individual pupil. Some adults will argue that a pupil should not be held back because of what it will do to his personality. Here again, one must consider the nature of the school setting that the pupil will have to face if he goes on with his chronological-aged peers. Will the frustrations that go with continued academic failure in the next grade be greater than the so-called "feeling of inferiority" which it is claimed he may develop if he is left behind his friends? In the past, educators have made an issue about this point. Heffernan [5] says:

> Non-promotion is devastating to the personality of children. It deadens initiative, paralyzes the will to achieve, destroys the sense of security and acceptance in the family circle, and promotes truancy and delinquency.

The authors are willing to yield to Helen Heffernan if the child is merely going to repeat the same experiences which he was exposed to formerly, *but the arguments will not hold true for many children who remain in a learning situation where every effort is made to assist the pupil in overcoming the obstacles which are holding him back.* Parents and educators have overemphasized the concept of grade and grade placement. The ungraded school is evidence that the pupil's grade placement is inconsequential as long as the pupil is able to make continuous progress. Also, one finds multigrade and multiage classes where boys and girls work successfully on their own learning levels. Children can be very happy in a classroom setting which allows them to succeed continuously as they work. This should be the criterion which determines where given children are placed. This does not mean that one ignores chronological, social, physical, emotional, and mental factors, because they are important aspects of the learning process. However, with teachers who recognize individual differences through grouping and individualizing instruction, children are not exposed to personality-thwarting activities in the classroom.

In some cases, parents have a right to worry about what happens to a pupil's personality, but in other cases the parent arguments are insincere and are prejudiced on the basis of emotions rather than on what is best for the child. Family pride can be the biggest threat to a pupil's personality. Educators have rested safely and securely behind a 100 per cent promotional policy because it was easier to do so than to try to argue with belligerent parents. However, democratic administration should not allow the rights of individual children to be lost in the face of blind emotionalism. If the method of reporting has been of high quality, the teacher and other staff members should have been working with the parents over many months to determine what would be best for the pupil in the future. All too often, parents are not prepared to accept that a son or daughter may require more time to reach a designated learning level than it took a sibling, and they let their emotions rule what they say and do. This is where a sound method of reporting will set the stage for questions regarding promotion and placement.

Remember, a pupil has to live at home as well as at school. He has to find a measure of acceptance in the home; therefore, when he fails to progress at levels deemed satisfactory to the parents, the equilibrium of the home may be upset. Family pride, for example, can be so important that some parents will go to any extent to preserve what may be called a family image. Sometimes, in order to save face, the best offensive is an attack on the teacher or school. Frequently, a charge of incompetency or discrimination helps to win a point. Or some parents, when faced with the disgrace of having a failure in the family, threaten to move or transfer the boy or girl in question to a better school. In some cases, they not only transfer the pupil to a private school, but move to a completely new neighborhood. In view of such personal objections to nonpromotion, educators have to consider seriously the impact of their recommendation upon a pupil in terms of his day-by-day home relations.

As in all phases of education, educators should decide each child's future in relation to promotion or nonpromotion in terms of what is best for the individual. Helping parents see differences in behavior and achievement is an important part of dealing with this whole question.

REFERENCES

1. Robert H. Anderson, "Ungraded Primary Classes—An Administrative Contribution to Mental Health," *Understanding the Child*, 24 (June 1955), 66–72.
2. Robert S. Carter, "How Invalid Are Marks Assigned by Teachers?" *Journal of Educational Psychology*, 43 (1952), 218–28.
3. Orlo L. Derby, "Towards a Rational View of Promotion," *Understanding the Child*, 23 (April 1954), 43–45.
4. Robert L. Ebel, *Measuring Educational Achievement* (Englewood Cliffs, N.J.: Prentice-Hall, 1965).
5. Helen Heffernan, "Grouping Pupils for Well-rounded Growth and Development," *California Journal of Elementary Education*, 21 (August 1952), 42–50.
6. Kenneth A. McDonnell, "A Dual Mark for Reporting Pupil Subject Accomplishment," *American School Board Journal*, 131 (August 1955), 19–20.
7. Robert L. Thorndike and Elizabeth Hagan, *Measurement and Evaluation in Psychology and Education* (New York: John Wiley, 1961).
8. Arthur E. Traxler, *Techniques of Guidance* (New York: Harper & Row, 1957).

CHAPTER 7

Recognizing the Need for Creativity

Creativity Is the Teacher's Responsibility

The teacher *has* to set the stage for children before they can express creativeness. A pupil who has talent cannot reveal it unless there is an opportunity for him to express himself where others can see his accomplishments. Many children do not know what they can do until they have worked with a variety of mediums and under different circumstances. But some teachers have to learn that "all children can be creative to some extent." They find it difficult to accept creativity unless it comes up to a standard, yet the poorest student in a class may be creative when he writes a few simple words to describe his feelings. His writings or his picture may be inferior to the work done by brighter children, but it will tell how or what he felt at a given moment in the light of his prior experiences and training.

Teachers are prone to confuse the word "creative" with the word "talented." Children can be creative at times without having real talent, but the talented individual must demonstrate that he is more than creative—that he can do something on a superior plane. The teacher must look at the talented pupil as one who shows outstanding creative ability in a given field and who, if encouraged and given advanced-level instruction, could probably make a career in his field of interest and skill. Unfortunately, teachers forget that talent often represents an acquired skill which may make a pupil excel for a time, and that the individual may still not be truly creative if what he expresses does not originate from within. A girl may paint what appears to be a very good picture, but it is only a copy. A boy may play wonderful music on his violin, but every selection is from a known composer. This boy is a skilled musician, but his skill is based upon hours of practice under good teachers. Though talented, is he creative?

DEFINING CREATIVITY

Creativity must be considered as a stage of sensitivity which depends upon the experiences of the learner. The teacher may look at creativity as an end product, but she has to go beyond to see creativity as a process. What did it take out of the learner? Was the creation something new? Did it give the pupil a chance to express himself through a new medium with unusual effectiveness, that is, unusual effectiveness for *him*? If the act of creating was effective, it must have had an effect upon the creator. This is what the teacher has to look for, because this is where the pupil shows that he is both creating and growing.

Creativeness may become evident in the work of boys and girls at every grade level and in any subject field, and when it does, it should be given sufficient recognition to make the individual want to continue to create. Unfortunately, some creative work is never recognized, so that the incentive to work at high creative levels is lost. Perhaps this is due to a feeling on the part of teachers that creativity is that which is unique to the fine arts. They fail to see that class work in language arts, social studies, science, and mathematics can be enriched through the application of creative skills by individual children. These individuals can often solve problems which defy less creative students. Consequently, teachers in all subject fields can be on the lookout for the attributes which Lowenfeld [3] says differentiate the significantly creative person from the noncreative person. Lowenfeld's attributes are as follows:

> *The creative person is sensitive to problems* and can identify himself with problems.
> *The creative person is flexible.*
> *The creative person has a fluency of ideas.*
> *The creative person is original.*
> *The creative person has the ability to redefine or rearrange* and can see new uses for an object or gives it new meaning.
> *The creative person is capable of both analysis and synthesis.* He is capable of taking the whole down to basic elements or of combining elements to form a new whole.
> *The creative person appreciates a coherence of organization.*

DEVELOPMENT OF CREATIVITY IN THE CLASSROOM

Many of Lowenfeld's attributes of creativity are often associated with very bright or gifted children, yet teachers frequently find brilliant children who fail to demonstrate any special talent or creativity in their work. When this happens, one must ask whether the individual has ever actually had a chance to express himself in an original manner. For example, the child who has not been anywhere, has not seen anything, or has not read very extensively may be perplexed when the teacher says, "Everyone will draw a picture to illustrate a place he visited during vacation." Such an assignment may not necessarily be easy for all those who have traveled and difficult for all those who have stayed at home: Some of those who have traveled may have gained nothing from their experiences, whereas a child who has not been anywhere except to the grocery store may be just aching to describe the funny little fat man who works at the register. Will the teacher accept such a portrayal even though it does not exactly fulfill the assignment?

When the pupil expresses himself, he may be drawing upon something close and personal. How he feels about things and people may be easy to reveal when he is in the lower grades, but as he gets older, his sensitivity to what others think can hold him back unless he has had many experiences which give him confidence that he can say or do things which others will accept. For example, children who have had only few experiences with poetry-reading or poetry-writing at the intermediate grade level will not be ready to express themselves through poetry as they go through junior or senior high school. The pupil who has the ability to do so or who wants to do so may find the lack of prior experience too much for him. He does not trust himself to say what he wants to say or do what he wants to do. If someone is crude enough to snicker, laugh, or openly criticize a pupil's first attempt at creative expression, it may be his last honest activity of that nature.

Because creative expression comes from within, the teacher has to help by being receptive herself and by helping children to see individuality as something to be encouraged instead of ridiculed. If the other pupils have not reached this level of maturation, she may have to establish a one-to-one relationship until children with other common bonds can be brought together in a learning activity where they can share their inner feelings and desires.

Too, curiosity, the desire to know the *what* or *why*, need not be stifled in school. Given encouragement, many boys and girls will be able to demonstrate that "creativity is an outgrowth of early curiosities." Children who want to know *why* are stepping out of the world of the known to that of the unknown. They are often willing and anxious to explore, experiment, test, take apart, question, tell how they feel. If in school the individual finds his questions are ignored, ridiculed, or treated as unimportant, he may soon stop asking them. Here again, the teacher must be receptive and able to adapt herself to the needs of her pupils.

Because the curious pupil *wants* the satisfaction that comes with discovery, he may spend long hours of concentrated activity to attain a desired answer. He may be so highly motivated that he expends greater amounts of energy than is considered normal when teachers talk about the attention span of growing boys and girls. When the teacher observes an individual or a group of children deep in thought or concentrating intently on their work, she should be ready to modify her time schedule so as not to terminate too abruptly the study under way.

It is evident, then, that free-thinking and creative men or women do not grow in a vacuum, but in an environment that fosters the development of creativity. A school can place so much stress upon the academic phases of education that boys and girls are exposed to a very narrow set of experiences, with the result that their potential for creativeness remains a resource which is never discovered. One of our problems in our modern schools is that of protecting *all* children, not just the gifted, from internal and external pressures that curtail freedom of expression. Those who advocate a return to the good old days, to the good old basics, to the elimination of the frills of art, music, and creative writing courses, are forgetting that placing boys and girls in classrooms which thwart the opportunity for free expression is depriving them of the one basic element so essential if we are going to *encourage* and not *inhibit* creativity.

Educators sometimes become confused or swayed by pressures for a one-sided curriculum, especially for children known to have a high intelligence or an apparent talent. There is a tendency to ignore the exploratory values of education for *all* children in a world which places so much emphasis upon specialization. But bright pupils can have gaps in their backgrounds or growth patterns that can restrict what they do when they reach adulthood—one has only to look at the thousands of college students who, after years of education, are still trying to find themselves. Studies show that most college students have trouble deciding what they are going to do until they are midway through college, and even then some of them do not stay with career choices they make. In view of this, it is hard to justify early specialization by boys and girls whose experiences have been limited. Rather, all children need to live in a school environment which will allow them to be exposed to a multitude of experiences, where they can work with many kinds of mediums, where they can explore new fields of study, where they can experience both success and failure as they work with challenging situations.

Developing a Stage of Readiness for Creative Activity in the Classroom. One of the fallacies about education lies in an assumption that boys and girls can be given so-called "creative assignments" to complete on the spur of the moment, with the expectation that the finished product will be expressive in terms of content, grammatically correct, free of punctuation mistakes, and well written in terms of penmanship. Children who can turn out such creative productions under the pressures of the classroom must be commended, because they are doing things professional writers and artists seldom do. Actually, teachers have to help boys and girls develop a stage of readiness for what they call creative activity. To do this, the following suggestions might be helpful:

1. *Give children practice with long-range assignments.* They need time for planning, thinking, exploring, and evaluation. They need to learn how to budget time and to rework materials until they can show a finished product that they can be proud of. Long-term projects or assignments should begin in the intermediate grades and continue through high school.

2. *Be sure the children clearly understand the nature of the assignment.* The first stage is the assignment, which may be teacher-directed or which may originate with the individual student on the basis of a personal interest. For many children, the big problem is one of getting started. They are not certain that they know what to do or how to begin. Objectives must be clearly stated and directions should be clearly given or assigned if more than one pupil is involved.

3. *Give help in finding ideas or problems to those children who need it.* Children who have learned to work at highly creative levels are usually full of ideas for creative activities. Other pupils may have minds utterly devoid of ideas unless something is done to stimulate them. Basically, children have to see that a problem exists. They must sense it and see that a solution is necessary. The teacher may have to help slower-thinking pupils see the implications in a problem or project.

4. *Many children need a practice or warm-up period.* Practice activities of a warm-up nature after a long weekend or vacation get pupils back into the thinking and action stage so that they can do a better job when they begin their major project. In some classrooms where writing is stressed, the children are given a sheet or two of paper at the start of the day, with fifteen or twenty minutes to write about anything that may be of interest to them.

5. *Encourage children to be original.* Boys and girls should be encouraged to be as original as possible. The teacher may have to stress the importance of stating their own reactions to an idea or situation. She is not interested in their giving her something copied

from a book or picture. If they must use materials or facts compiled by others, they should give their sources of information.

6. *Encourage children to look for the unusual or uncommon.* There is often a "sameness" in what children do for teachers. This can become quite boring to teacher and learner unless the pupils can be encouraged to see the unusual, the unexpected, and the hidden. In reading, they may learn to look for little details. On a science field trip, they may seek unusual specimens of plants, insects, or birds. The idea of anticipating what may happen or what may have happened can be stimulated by playing the role of detective with current events stories.

7. *Help children get acquainted with school and community resources.* Children who do not have all the answers they need to solve problems may require some extra help if they are to use school or community resources which are new to them. Additional data or material may be needed to acquire the special skills necessary to complete a creative project.

8. *Set reasonable time limits.* Teachers who expect good results should try to avoid rushing children with their work. It should be made clear that quality is to be preferred to quantity. A short paragraph well written can be a more effective preparatory step to vivid expression than a long story lacking interest, content, or structure.

9. *Encourage children to use the medium or technique that will be most effective in terms of their objectives.* For example, in one class pupils held the interest of the group with their original cartoons. In another, role play was used to solve a problem.

10. *Make constructive evaluations.* The point has been made that children should not work for marks; however, anything that takes time and effort should be looked at in terms of some form of evaluation. Before turning in a report, story, or picture, the creator should make his own evaluation. He should feel that he is meeting his own standards as well as those of the teacher. The pupil may share his unfinished project with the teacher, assuming that a relationship has been established that will allow him to feel at ease when she hears or sees what he has done. Her reactions to what he has accomplished should be positive to prevent discouragement or the dropping of an incomplete project. What he has done should be evaluated in terms of his work in the past rather than in terms of an artificial standard established by or for others. Group projects may be evaluated by other members of the class as well as by the teacher, but criticisms or suggestions should be kept on a constructive plane.

The Effects of Criticism. Children react differently to criticism. Some can take it without showing any ill effects, whereas others are so sensitive that a negative reaction to what they have done will result in a lack of desire to repeat an experience or go on to new phases of an activity. Sensitive children may bask in a teacher's praise, but they may not be able to take her criticism even when it is deserved.

Whenever a pupil attempts to use a new medium, he needs to achieve a feeling that he has been *successful*. Because he may be afraid that someone will not accept his first picture, he may tear it up rather than face the fact that it does not look the way it was meant to look. Standards are important, but they do not have to be too rigid when one is beginning. Teachers should remember the way they fumbled the first time they tried to dance, to make a dress, to paint a picture, to write a poem, to sing a solo, or to address a roomful of strangers. In the right setting and in the right situation, children will see the need to improve techniques without being sensitive to constructive criticism. They will learn to appreciate suggestions and help.

The Classroom Setting Should Encourage Creative Activities. Children can learn to adjust to many types of learning situations, but it is easier if they can work in a classroom that lends itself to creative activity. For example, the teacher should make effective use of the modern movable classroom furniture that has replaced the bolted desks of years ago by rearranging it in patterns appropriate for a particular learning activity as often as necessary. Many teachers have found it helpful to establish learning centers such as a science corner, a library corner, a corner for storing unfinished projects, or a corner for private conferences or small-group activity.

Creative teachers place a high value on books, but the secret of their success may lie in how the books are used. Teachers also use a great variety of materials to supplement the textbook, and in creating a new environment for learning, they often find that they have new solutions to the problem of keeping children physically and intellectually busy. A classroom where one finds other teaching aids to supplement the standard textbook does not have to be the dull, dead, stultifying place of yesterday. Children can look forward to attending a class where there are new experiences waiting and where there are things to do that satisfy their desire for knowledge and success.

Stimulating Creativity in the Classroom.   Many children start their academic careers with a pattern or coloring book. As a result they begin to work with raw materials that help destroy the creative spirit which they have within them but which they cannot release. Many elementary school teachers continue this inhibiting of creativity by giving mass seatwork lessons based upon coloring or drawing within the confines of a series of lines, circles or outlined objects. Form becomes too important as the child tries to make a reasonable facsimile of the real thing in terms of adult eyes or standards. Only little hand and finger muscles are called into action, which leads to frustration and tension without achieving any significant objective.

In contrast to this type of teaching, one will find teachers who eliminate the counting and coloring of balloons by telling stories involving the use of several objects. The story appeals to the children's natural desire to express themselves, with the result that they may act out the story and then draw their own pictures to illustrate what they heard and learned. The teacher does not have to tell them how many objects to draw. If they have followed the story as told and acted out, they will often depict the number of objects in their drawings. In addition, each pupil will be able to express himself freely in terms of his own feelings or reactions to the activity.

One of the worst threats to the development of creativity of any form lies in the continued emphasis on marks. Before children start attending school, they know what marks mean. Someone is going to decide whether they measure up to satisfactory standards, so when they begin formal work in school, many of them commence to think in terms of grades or marks. Therefore, the teacher is urged to minimize or even forget marks when children engage in new or creative activities. She has to let them find themselves, to acquire confidence in a new medium, and then if assistance is needed, must be ready to give help without destroying their feeling of accomplishment.

Training in self-evaluation and in self-discipline is an essential factor in the development of creativity. Each individual must be able to see relationships between standards and the need to master special techniques or skills if he is going to express himself on an acceptable plane; therefore, many teachers do not mark pupils in new expressive activities. Some art and music teachers refuse to give their pupils marks so that the children can feel free to express themselves without feeling that the teacher's dissatisfaction with their work in these fields will be transmitted to parents. Similarly, a science consultant refuses to give marks to his intermediate grade pupils, and when asked why, he says, "We should build up a feeling for science in our classes. Children learn science and want to do things within the field of science because they are curious and they find enjoyment in what they do. They would not work harder than they do, and many of them, under the pressure of marks, would no longer volunteer when I ask someone to show me how principles work." This kind of teaching is not the easiest kind of teaching, because it deprives some teachers of a "club" which they feel that they should have in order to get boys and girls to exert themselves. Some teachers ask how they can tell parents or other teachers how the children are progressing when marks are eliminated or merely minimized.

A lack of marks means that the teacher has to depend upon creating a natural environment for learning. Boys and girls have to learn to work for the teacher because they see themselves growing as they work with and for her. In turn, the teacher sees growth as she works with them individually and collectively. She does not always have to administer formal tests to see that they are learning. If she is doing a successful job it will be apparent in the quality of the work that the children produce.

Helping Pupils Find Themselves. The development of creativity should not be left to chance. While some individuals may find themselves without any apparent help, the fact remains that the school can do more to help them develop creativity than any other community agency can. The school is the *only* place where the child can express himself freely and creatively. Here, he may come in contact with one or more teachers who will encourage him to express himself freely as he works in class, but this in itself is not enough. Each school should have as its goal the early identification and encouragement of pupils who have latent potentialities of creativity. It will help if at least one teacher is free to help pupils express themselves freely. If that is not possible, all the teachers in the school should at least try to help pupils discover themselves through self-expression. The teachers should realize that they do not have to be artists along some special line of endeavor. The important thing is to know that boys and girls are not to be mere copyists. Success lies in the teachers' ability to stimulate boys and girls to express themselves in a style of their own.

Boys May Be More Creative Than Girls. Studies of the academic achievement of elementary school children would lead one to believe that girls tend to be far superior to boys in academic areas. Yet, other studies seem to point to a possible superiority on the part of boys when it comes to creativity. Reading authorities have known that boys are quite likely to be poorer readers than girls, at least in the primary grades. As a result, some girls are apt to get an academic start on the boys which takes years to overcome. This ability to read earlier may be the reason why girls excel in other communication skills such as writing and composition. They read widely, acquire a good vocabulary, and thus have a background which enables them to express themselves easily, both verbally and in writing. Boys tend to be more active physically; therefore, they seem to have a shorter attention span when it comes to sedentary tasks such as reading and writing. However, these same boys will spend hours working on special projects which intrigue them. This ability helps them when it comes to creativity.

Studies of both sexes show that boys are superior to girls when it comes to their ability to think independently, constructively, and creatively. As boys go from the first to the third grade, their ability to think creatively increases faster than the girls' ability does. At this point boys and girls begin to approach a common level. Fourth-grade girls begin to catch up with boys when it comes to the ability to be creative, but they seem to be less radical in what they do. At times, girls seem to have an ability to be less expressive about their creative thoughts. They are less impelled to action; yet, when they are, they can get away with things which boys cannot. Boys seem impelled by internal tensions to want to express their creative thoughts. Boys do things which make them appear to be nonconformists. This leads to their rejection by the teacher and sometimes by their peers. Boys tend to explore and experiment more than girls, although this may be only an outward symptom since social pressures tend to restrict girls more than they do boys.

Creative Children May Have to Discipline Themselves. When other children are out having a good time, the creative individual may have to discipline himself to do the work necessary to master essential skills to express himself more fluently. He may have to read widely in order to acquire background. If musically inclined, he may have to practice playing on an instrument for many hours before he can express himself vividly and exactly the way he wants to when he has a specific goal. Similarly, if he is artistic, he may have to sketch many people, objects, animals, and places before he finds that he has the ability to express what he thinks and sees in the world about him. These practice periods can be most tiring to the pupil who has a conflict of interests. At times, adults may have to intervene to make certain that he does not falter and give up. Practice or drill may be the only way he can acquire the facility he needs to have with pen, paint, brush, or violin bow.

Good work-study patterns are therefore a help if one is going to engage in creative activities. In some instances, the hardest work may be the rewriting, correcting, and revising of an original draft. A boy may work for several hours perfecting a model; another pupil may work for hours memorizing and trying to dramatize a role in a play; still another may spend many hours doing research before he begins to write a scholarly report or term paper. Pupils who have not acquired them will find it most difficult to engage in activities that call for prolonged periods of concentration and physical or mental activity. The ability to note details, to pick out the chief characteristics, to see many little things in an action, picture, scene, or story may be a *must* to creative people like artists, writers, painters, and scientists. Like them, creative children have to discipline themselves to seeing things as a whole, to seeing things quickly which are not noticed by average people. They have to develop an awareness of their environment and the changes which they see in it from day to day. In order to express themselves effectively, they should get used to looking for the unusual or uncommon. At the same time, it is important for them to see relationships if they are going to translate what they see and hear in terms of feelings which can be transmitted to others who have not seen or heard them.

CREATIVE CHILDREN AND TESTING PATTERNS

Studies of standardized test results of both creative and noncreative children have repeatedly shown that creative children can score higher than average or noncreative children, yet their school grades often fail to come up to the level of their less imaginative peers. Here again, one has to cope with the problem of conformists and nonconformists. Since creative children are not always conformists, they often have to work harder to please teachers than nonconformists do. Studies have repeatedly shown a tendency on the part of teachers to give higher grades to pupils who "toe the line" or show a willingness to refrain from nonconformist actions. In many instances, the creative pupil may not be delinquent in his behavior. He may have merely antagonized his teachers by doing things differently. For example, he may have been guilty of merely obtaining correct answers without following procedures outlined in the textbook. This ability to think out answers before the teacher is ready for them by working with shortcuts or new techniques can upset a teacher. And some teachers are confused by pupils who can use their high ability or imagination to work out solutions to problems faster or more easily than they can. Teachers can often anticipate the actions of most children, but this is not always possible when dealing with a truly creative child.

Creative children have shown that they have less native ability than pupils who scored lower on achievement tests. The fact that creative children may have less than genius ability can be very disturbing to educators, because of the widespread tendency to recognize pupils with superior intellectual ability. As a result, the creative pupil who needs recognition is overlooked and may be ignored. Teachers frequently make the mistake of assuming that creative people are always intellectual. They think in terms of homogeneous grouping or build great plans for developing greater creativity by improving the curricular offerings for gifted boys and girls. Such endeavors may help some gifted pupils become more creative (since many bright children are creative), but educators cannot ignore the need to make creative people more creative though they are not intellectually gifted. Torrance [7] points this out when he says:

> If we were to identify children as gifted on the basis of intelligence tests, we would eliminate from consideration approximately 70 per cent of the most creative.

Educators must learn to use some other yardstick if they are going to measure creativity in children. The intelligence test is not reliable for this purpose, and current tests of creativity have not been developed to the point of real reliability. Consequently, we have creative children in our schools who do not receive the assistance or recognition necessary for a fuller development of their creative faculties.

The term "gifted" is more often associated with high intelligence and with high academic achievement than it is with creativity, but educators tend to be slow in seeing the necessity of refining the term to include the creative child. The National Merit Scholarship Corporation has evidenced some concern over the failure of high schools to recognize creative pupils. Many creative pupils, whose scholastic records show that they have not been able to obtain high grades from their teachers, have shown an ability to make high scores on the National Merit Examinations. The fact that these individuals have acquired the background which will enable them to outscore boys and girls who have a long history of high academic performance is disconcerting. It leads one to ask why they have not been recognized in the classroom as having ability. In one of the reports he has made for the National Merit Foundation, J. L. Holland [2] says:

. . . for samples of students of superior aptitude, creative performance is generally unrelated to scholastic achievement and scholastic aptitude.

As a result of such statements, colleges have been asked to accept students whose high school records may not come up to desired levels. The world of business and industry, as well as the colleges and other fields including the various arts and sciences, need these creative people, and all teachers must do more to help identify them and to help them work at higher levels of creativity as they go through school.

Children's Need for Opportunities to Share Creative Efforts

WRITING ACTIVITIES

Children of all ages can get a great deal of satisfaction from work they can share with other pupils, in the classroom and in other grades, and with parents. The school newspaper or even the school magazine helps higher grade students express themselves through mediums which will be read by others. These pupils will devote long hours to the task of writing and preparing the paper for the printer. One may find less pretentious jobs being done at the intermediate and primary grade levels. Here the pupils may select the best stories of their classmates for duplication by an office machine. The teacher should guide their efforts, but the work should not be hers even if it is to be shared by children in other classes. Sometimes the best stories are put aside for a booklet that can be sent home to parents. If a typewriter is available, some primary grade children can even type their stories for the room newspaper. The quality of the work that goes into a room or class newspaper will vary according to the age and experience of the children. With encouragement, creative writing can start in the first, second, and third grades, long before the pupils have been exposed to formal grammar. One second grader who enjoyed working on a class booklet for parents and for the pupils in the next class wrote:

Mysterious Blue Fingers

Our class did 30 stencils for our planet reports. We all came home with blue fingers. Miss Parsons (The Office Secretary) worked like anything. Every time stencils came from the office all finished, Mrs. Klein screamed. We wrote a thank you letter to Miss Parsons.

BY Nancy C.

A seventh-grade teacher said, "I have a few boys and girls who should go back to the second grade to learn how to write short, simple sentences," but another teacher said, "That is not children's work. The teacher told them what to write." Actually, this was not true. The boys and girls had lived together and had worked closely together sharing their experiences. There were some pupils who collaborated in the writing of stories or articles. They chose words wisely, but often had to look them up in the big picture or beginning dictionaries. They had learned where to place some commas and periods, so most of their work was completely original.

Boys and girls at various grade levels have contributed the following:

Magnets

Our rooms have been studying magnets. Magnets will attract things that are made of iron and steel, but they won't attract copper and other metals. Magnets can go through paper, water, glass. Magnets have magnetic fields. If you take iron dust, paper, and a magnet, you can make a picture of the magnetic field. You put the iron dust on the paper and the magnet under it and tap it. You will see lines shaping the magnet.

Magnetic field

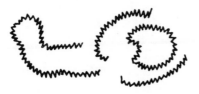

BY Daniel B. GRADE 2

Cloth

In our class we do many things in art. Now we are working on beautiful weaving. We made looms out of cardboard and put our warp thread on them. We will weave the weft threads on these looms. Some people are doing tapestry work. They draw a shape and cut it out of material. This will be sewn on burlap. They will end up with a beautiful tapestry. An earlier project was drawing forms in action. The figures we drew were from living models. This was a very interesting project, and fun, too.

BY Pris H. GRADE 4

Science a la Carte

The Alfred Vail students learn science in a very interesting way. They have organized room Science Clubs. The students have voted for a president, a vice-president, a secretary, and a committee chairman. Instead of the teacher showing and explaining an experiment, the pupils pick out, learn, and explain their own experiments. An example of one of the interesting experiments was made by our science teacher, Mr. Gionti. He found a very old vacuum cleaner, which he brought to show us. An attachment to the cleaner let out a great force of air pressure. Mr. Gionti let us figure out how objects are pushed into the air, and why they work as they do. So we found out the forces that get an airplane off the ground and keep it in the air.

BY Linda M. GRADE 5

These samples of children's writings illustrate what boys and girls can do when they have experiences to write about. They show that boys and girls at various levels can write effectively and in an interesting manner. *The fact that they are writing at all grade levels is the all-important issue.* More upper grade teachers would have less reason to complain about the caliber of writing done by their pupils if these same students had been exposed to experiences calling for some form of creative writing at lower grade levels, especially writing experiences that they could have *shared.*

Although there may be a special incentive for writing for a class or school newspaper, many children write because they have something to say. They find satisfaction in the actual writing and then they acquire added satisfaction from sharing what they have written in class. In some rooms pupils save their best writing for a class exchange period. Here children pass their papers from one to the other for quiet reading. In other rooms the best papers are read by their authors before small groups, and then the papers judged best are read before the whole class or to children in other classrooms.

Techniques to Encourage Children to Write. Teachers at all grade levels work at the task of getting boys and girls to express themselves more effectively on paper, but they use a variety of teaching techniques to attain their goals. Some teachers refuse to admit that children can write until they have first developed a mastery of basic and correct grammar, sentence structure, punctuation skills, and the parts of speech. Some believe that outlining or even diagramming must be taught to fifth graders before these children can begin to write; other teachers refuse to see that creative writing can begin at the primary level without such preliminary writing activity. Still other teachers insist on the study of long lists of descriptive words as a preliminary activity to writing.

While boys and girls do have to master some of these skills, research does not substantiate the view that children cannot write successfully until they have taken part in formal grammar exercises. If children do not write, it is not because they have not taken the time to study writing techniques as much as it is because they have *nothing they want to say nor any reason for saying it*. Frequently, students will surprise adults with what they can write if they are reminded that "Writing is merely talk that has been written down. Try to write the way you would say it." To prove the point, some teachers have written down what the pupils say when they describe an interesting experience. (This can be made dramatic through using the tape recorder.)

One technique calls for compiling lists of problem situations for other boys and girls to write about. Here, the pupils enjoy creating problem situations and sharing the solutions written by various children. The problems can range from the commonplace to the unreal and fanciful. One teacher brings in art pictures to stimulate conversation and, ultimately, writing; another teacher projects colored slides which become the basis for oral and written stories. A second-grade teacher has found tremendous success with illustrations from such magazines as the *Saturday Evening Post*. She shows the cover picture and asks the children to tell what they see or feel as they look at it. The results have been the basis for further discussion and art activity.

As a rule, children learn to write by writing. In the lower grades, boys and girls often have something that they want to say long before they can spell the words they use. Instead of making a fuss about poor spelling, the teacher can give the children a list of basic words which can be kept in notebooks or on a chart in the front of the room. Some teachers merely write new or unusual words for them as they request help. In addition, the children are taught to use the dictionary at an early stage in their training. Ultimately, the children are expected to learn the most frequently used words. If teachers want to teach correct spelling, rules of simple grammar, and rules for punctuation, the teacher may give all-class, small-group, or individual instruction when the children need help, or she may give help in a special instruction period when they are not in the act of writing.

Photo by Dorothy Overmeir, courtesy of Duval County Schools, Florida

A child absorbed in a creative project.

Courtesy of Campus Elementary School, State University at New Paltz, New York

Another young child absorbed in self-expression.

Creative Children Often Reveal Inner Feelings in Their Creative Efforts. Many children write or draw as though they were mere on-lookers. They include all the important details, but there is nothing *personal* in what they produce. As a result, some teachers stress putting more feeling into their pictures or stories. They want children to make an honest effort to react to things which they have experienced or which are going on around them. Some children never get to this stage, but the work of many creative children often reveals inner feelings which are not suspected in ordinary conversations with them. A boy may be crying out for a chance to be independent, another is telling the world that he is lonely, a third child may be trying to show his fears and general insecurity, while a fourth child is just happy and wants to let the whole world know it. Inhibitions are often lost when some children work in a medium they have learned to use successfully. They may not know why, but the act of *creating* helps solve personal problems and gives them a new outlook on life.

ART ACTIVITIES

Art activities are often used to help boys and girls work off tensions or feelings of strong emotion. Unfortunately, many bright students build up a resistance to them, because they have not been encouraged to take part in activities that tend to conflict with academic interests or pressures to concentrate on areas calling for greater intellectual challenge. As a result, one can find many bright junior high or senior high school pupils whose sensitivity to their environment results in frustration when they try to use their hands to create objects or pictures of what they see and feel. They tend to be quite sensitive to their environment, yet cannot reproduce what they feel because of their lack of satisfying experiences with art mediums. They may try writing poetry or short stories or even music; but they still need to explore other mediums to find the release for inner feelings that they have about life and the world around them.

Art is a field which appeals to many individuals because it gives them a chance to be different. However, this is possible only where the teacher tries to build an environment in which boys and girls feel free to express themselves in a variety of mediums. On the other hand, the urge to create can be destroyed by art teachers who are more concerned with perfection and form than with *individuality*. A strongly teacher-dominated class can frustrate boys and girls who enjoy the feeling of creating something on their own. There is nothing more disturbing to creative-minded students than to have the teacher pick up his brush to touch up a tree, house, or sunset. Years later a very bright girl would still get angry at the thought of an early art instructor who spoiled her winter scene by putting that touch of blue in her ice. Blue ice may have been real and important to the art teacher, but his action destroyed the beautiful picture in the eyes of the pupil. She was trying to create a picture that she could say was "all hers."

Many low-average and average children are willing to let others do their thinking for them, so they often find "pattern art" a satisfying type of experience. Tracing and cutting out pattern designs gives them a measure of success without too much exertion on their part, but boys and girls who have the ability to think, along with a desire to demonstrate their initiative, find such art work distasteful. They frequently have to overcome the pressure of the conformity art thrust upon them from the moment they can begin to make marks with a crayon. Long before school starts, fond parents are giving young children coloring books and cutout books to keep them busy or entertained. Many teachers work hard to overcome this concept of art based upon the use of commercially prepared copy- or tracing-books which find their way into the school in workbooks and other types of teaching aids. These teachers want children to express themselves in a number of mediums, so they are appalled at the thought of conformity art. They want children to select their own ideas and subject matter, and the medium which is most suitable for the feelings they want to express.

Conformity Art. This type of art activity calls for little initiative on the part of teacher or learner. All too often, teachers who are not creative themselves find it easy to direct art lessons which consist of one of the following types of activities:

Pattern art. Children are given patterns or designs to color or cut out that are the exact duplicate of every other pupil's.

Outline art. Children are given a workbook or prepared sheet showing the outline of a picture or object, perhaps even with the colors specified.

Copy work. Each pupil is asked to reproduce the picture of an object. The pupil who makes the best reproduction is rewarded for his art ability.

Dictation art. Pupils are given specific directions which will enable each one to reproduce an object made by the teacher.

Art of this type can be overdone at all grade levels. Although it may appeal to young children, it can be most frustrating to those whose small muscles are not ready for the confined and restricting movements necessary as they work with crayon, pencil, and scissors. If they run over the line, they destroy the perfection demanded by parent or teacher. Having too many experiences with conformity art can cause boys and girls to turn away from art as a medium that could help them express their individuality and feelings. This expression is often evident when young children are given large sheets of paper and are allowed to draw what they see and feel—without having to worry if their pictures lack a form which is easily recognized in terms of real objects or real people.

Relationship of Art Activities to Students' Interests and Needs. The easiest kind of art instruction is that which is aimed at the whole class. Like textbook teaching, it fails to meet the basic needs of individual boys and girls. Previous art experience or interests or native talent have little place in such classes, yet it is the only kind of art instruction that most children have in the elementary schools. It will take time to educate classroom teachers, and the art specialists who work with these teachers, to restructure and replan the art curriculum for boys and girls in terms of basic needs and interests. There are art teachers who have shown that they can carry on a well-balanced art program which allows for individualism and creativity.

Creativity calls for originality and is the result of individual initiative and performance. To achieve this ideal, the instructor has to be ready and able to guide boys and girls into new channels of activity, but channels where they will be able to plan and think for themselves. Each student must be able to see art problems and work out solutions for himself. If an answer does not come readily, the pupil should be free to try other mediums, or at least to modify the medium he started with. Art is a subject that children of all ages should learn to enjoy. Early interest in art must be protected, encouraged, and built upon instead of destroyed.

The aim of art education is not to develop young artists in school as much as it is *to make art a part of their daily lives.* When children engage in art activities in school, there will be some common enriching experiences, such as trips to art museums or the viewing of a special art film or a slide collection, but much of the work with art mediums should be of such a nature that the act of creating involves the whole child. He should learn how to use all of his senses to acquire new insights into the world about him. The product of his activity is not as important as the fact that he puts himself into the act of creating.

The role of the art teacher will vary from class to class and from grade to grade. If the students are highly creative, they will resent too much teacher domination and control over their artistic endeavors; but if they have had limited art experiences and are not too creative, they may literally beg for attention both individually and collectively. The more creative-minded art student can often work on a fairly independent level while the art instructor makes herself available for encouragement and motivation of the noncreative students who lack confidence in their ability to be creative. These latter children may have so many questions about their work that the teacher wants to quit working with them. She will make an assignment, give a direction, or show a pupil how to proceed, only to find him back a few minutes later with the same kind of question he asked earlier. A teacher may find this pupil's lack of confidence in himself is so real that, instead of relying upon his own intuition and feelings for guidance, he will cling to the teacher and to others about him because they have ideas he can use. Formal art or pattern art activities often appeal to him as long as art is compulsory, but unless he can find inner satisfactions in his art activities which give him a feeling of repeated success, much of his art interest, if he has any, will be transitory. If the art teacher is to be successful, she should strive to make art a subject which is interesting enough and appealing enough to the various students in her classes to make them want to continue their art experiences even when art is no longer required.

Art Ability and Intelligence Tests. One may find an artist who is a genius, but all artists are not intellectually gifted. In other words, talent and high intelligence are not positively related. It would be an asset to the educator if he could use intelligence test findings to identify the potential artist, but present tests do not lend themselves to this type of classification. The average intelligence test is not a valid instrument to measure art ability since it tends to place too-high values upon verbal and numerical abilities, whereas art ability is largely nonverbal in nature. However, art ability and intelligence reportedly have a positive relationship until children reach the age of approximately ten.

Art scales have been developed which measure intelligence through a study of children's drawings. Lowenfeld's [4] scale helps teachers ascertain a pupil's intelligence, but he warns them that the scales merely indicate where a child is and not where he may be in the future. These drawings tend to show that gifted children can develop their conceptual ability up to their mental ages. Because gifted children are able to see relationships or develop concepts at an early age, they may begin to scribble earlier than pupils with less intelligence. Frequently, these gifted students will show an awareness of form two years earlier than average children. However, poor or slow muscular development can be a limiting factor when they try to engage in higher-level art activities.

By studying the characteristics of children's drawings, the teacher can discover areas which indicate specific levels of art maturity or a lack of art maturity. A low rating in one characteristic may not be significant, but a study of the student's emotional, esthetic, physical, perceptual, and intellectual growth patterns can be most informative. Creative growth is one indication of the child's total maturity. The mature creative individual has been described as one who is independent in his early scribbling. He does not depend upon outsiders to stimulate him to action, nor does he imitate. Also, the well-adjusted creative pupil will be one of the first to give a name to his pictures and will develop stories about them without teacher assistance.

MUSIC ACTIVITIES

Educators are often urged to do something different for musically gifted pupils, such as placing them in special classes, giving them special instruction, or accelerating them through school so they can concentrate at an early age on their music. While some schools attempt to do these things, there is a general feeling that the musically talented still need to be a part of the same program that is offered to other talented or intellectually gifted children. But the program must attempt to meet their special needs. Some of the musically talented who have high intelligence will find themselves in special full- or part-time classes for gifted children, but many of them will be placed in programs that call for a broad program of enrichment activities. Some of these musically talented pupils will be at a disadvantage since they will most likely have to find time to continue to take an active part in vocal or instrumental music activities as well as to continue with non-school-sponsored music lessons. Because these music activities are time consuming, the students may have to work out special schedules or work patterns that will enable them to complete regular and special assignments without being penalized.

Musical talent may be hidden due to lack of cultural opportunities, a lack of stimulation by the home or school at early levels, or a lack of adequate financial support. The broad and enriching curriculum may give some culturally deprived children new insights and opportunities. And here is where individual differences can take over. For example, one pupil may want to express his feelings in the field of art, another may want to write, a third may turn to science, while a fourth turns to music. As these pupils work in these fields, they may find new interests or develop new goals.

Determining Exceptional Musical Talent. Since music has an appeal for many children, parents frequently misconstrue as talent a child's experimentation with this new facet of his environment. Should the child's interest in music be sustained, the parents can provide him with a variety of experiences which allow him to explore the field of music, maintain his interest, and develop skills without actually forcing him into such a narrow educational pattern that other interests or talents are neglected.

Parents must remember that while there have been some childhood prodigies, the fact remains that some of the world's finest musicians did not begin to reveal their superior talents until they reached adulthood. Some of these individuals had already become successful in other fields of endeavor. Martin Luther, for example, was a very gifted musician and composer, although he is not always remembered for his musical ability. One of the problems of intellectually gifted children lies in the fact that they have wide interests and may have several talents, one of which may be music. As they go through high school and college, they have difficulty in making career choices because of the conflict of interests.

Educators have used various tests such as the Seashore Measures of Musical Talent in an attempt to make early identification of musically gifted children. The reliability of such tests has been questioned, since they may actually measure achievement based upon early training or exposure to music. Educators can make fairly reliable predictions about a child's possible success in music only when test results are studied in relation to general observations by teachers and musicians who have worked with the pupil.

The results of achievement tests and intelligence tests, along with actual musical performance, interest in music, physical coordination, persistence, and tonal memory are factors that go into the evaluative process. Music training in given musical fields may be given to pupils who have high ratings, but the exact nature of their musical giftedness may not appear until they reach late adolescence. Some of these children begin to reveal specific strengths and weaknesses as they go through junior and senior high school. Furthermore, latent talents may appear to overshadow other talents. A promising musician may show skill as an artist, writer, or scientist, or a promising artist may show skill as a musician, and so on. This was illustrated by Wagner and Schumann, both of whom showed high literary interests and ability which could have led to their being recognized as great writers instead of as musicians. The authors are not discounting the fact that child prodigies will not be discovered. Artists like Rubinstein, Mozart, Levitsky, Shelling, Heifetz, Kindler, and Stravinsky revealed their musical giftedness at an early age, yet men like Wagner, Berlioz, and Tchaikovsky did not show their musical talent until they were beyond their adolescent years.

Thousands of boys and girls who have studied music at home and in school find it is difficult to continue early music interests in the face of adolescent pressures. Homework, for example, often takes so much time at the secondary level that budding musicians have to forego essential practice periods. Also, interests in companions, sports, a car, a job, or another field of endeavor may result in the termination of music lessons. On the other hand, the junior or senior high school band and orchestra become proving grounds for many youngsters. A girl may have a chance to sing a solo, a boy may play an instrumental accompaniment to the singer, and another student finds that his musical composition is accepted by his peers. Thus, in the right school environment the musically talented may demonstrate for the first time that they have more than average ability. With guidance and encouragement the musically talented pupil may find it advantageous to continue with further study and training.

CREATIVE DRAMATICS

Modern children grow up in a world of movies and television where they see actors and actresses dramatizing life in a way with which the school apparently cannot compete. In most cases the child is a spectator, but if the school wants to put new life in some phases of the curriculum, it has an advantage over television in that it can, through creative play, cast the boy or girl in a role where he becomes the actor. This does not become a new course, nor does it mean that the school is going to start training boys and girls for a life on the stage. Actually, creative drama starts long before boys and girls go to school. Preschool children may play school with older brothers and sisters. As they grow up, they play house, cops and robbers, cowboys and Indians, or spacemen.

One may find creative play goes on in the kindergarten or first grade where teachers have a simple make-up box or a trunk containing old dress-up clothes. The children require very few directions as they depict life at home or in an imaginary world. Usually, such play is undirected and is the result of spontaneous by-play between two or more individual children, but teachers who so desire can direct such activity into meaningful and purposeful creative dramatics. Thus, a kindergarten teacher can read a story and assign roles to individual children to reenact or to pantomime.

As children get older, they still have the desire to engage in similar, but more mature, forms of dramatic play. Unfortunately, many of them do not have enough opportunities to express themselves. Some children may take part in special assembly programs or special holiday pageants, but this type of performance may be too time-consuming and involved for many teachers who are not creative themselves. However, the basic needs of many boys and girls can still be met through dramatic play without costumes and other props which many teachers believe detract from regular teaching. Dramatic play can be highly creative and may be used by every teacher with any pupil age group, with the result that every subject can be made realistic and alive through creative presentations by the children. Creative dramatics is a form of communication, and through experimentation, the teacher can discover creative children.

Value of Dramatics in the Class. With careful planning, creative dramatics can become a tool to help develop the whole child. Although every child may not be aided in the same way, many boys and girls will find that creative dramatics is a powerful force in helping them develop various facets of their minds, bodies, and personalities. Creative dramatics frequently helps this development in the following ways:

1. By building interest in a curricular offering when children are able to dramatize parts of it or see it dramatized.

2. By fostering the use of imagination to solve problems.

3. By fostering sensitivity to problems of living.

4. By releasing emotional tensions by helping children identify with other people and their problems.

5. By helping children develop leadership qualities by planning a program, writing a script, assuming the identity of a character other than themselves, creating scenery, working out novel sound effects, or directing the actions of others.

6. By emphasizing the values in teamwork.

7. By developing physical coordination. Here, it is not easy to separate creative dancing from creative dramatics, for body movements may be quite graceful as the actors depict a scene or a story without words. The word "dance" is not necessarily associated with a formal, set pattern of steps. In order to use body movements to express ideas or feelings, a pupil may have to skip, hop, run, crawl, or jump, gracefully.

8. By developing new communication skills.

REFERENCES

1. Frank Barron, "Creativity, What Research Says About It," *National Education Association Journal*, 50 (March 1961), 17–19.
2. J. L. Holland, "Creative and Academic Performance Among Talented Adolescents," Paper presented at the Annual Meeting of American Educational Research Association, Chicago, February 24, 1961.
3. Viktor Lowenfeld, "Current Research on Creativity," *National Education Association Journal*, 47 (November 1958), 538–40.
4. Viktor Lowenfeld, *Creative and Mental Growth* (New York: Macmillan, 1952).
5. Carl R. Rogers, "Toward a Theory of Creativity," in M. Barkan and R. L. Mooney, eds., *Conference on Creativity: A Report to the Rockefeller Foundation* (Columbus: Ohio State University Press, 1953).
6. Abraham Shumsky, *Creative Teaching in the Elementary School* (New York: Appleton-Century-Crofts, 1965).
7. Paul Torrance, "The Creatively Gifted Are Cause for Concern," *The Gifted Child Quarterly*, 5 (August 1961).
8. Robert C. Wilson, "Creativity," Chapter VI, *Fifty-seventh Yearbook of the National Society for the Study of Education*, Part II, in Nelson B. Henry, ed., *Education for the Gifted* (Chicago: University of Chicago Press, 1958).

PART two

CHAPTER 8

Developing More Effective
Work-Study Skill Patterns

Many traditional academicians will protest about the waste of intellect with the emphasis on readiness activities today, but the fact remains that few pupils suffer from deferring the introduction of higher levels of learning until they are completely ready for them. This means the pupil must be socially, physically, and emotionally, as well as mentally, mature enough to work independently and cooperatively with high-level materials and ideas. Thus, as each individual goes on to higher grade levels, it becomes imperative that someone consider his stage of readiness for each new stage of learning. Readiness is not merely reading readiness, but rather readiness for fifth-grade science, for sixth-grade arithmetic, for seventh-grade grammar, or for eighth-grade history.

All too often teacher indifference to the readiness factors has led to incidental teaching or partial learning. The fact that many pupils have been able to survive and even show signs of high-level accomplishment from traditional teaching methods and materials should not be accepted as evidence that these old methods are good methods for the 1960s and '70s.

New Responsibilities for the Modern Teacher

The modern teacher has to teach *more* in less time, yet she cannot force learning too soon. There are times when a given method may be the best approach to a problem, but every teacher has to be flexible in her choice of teaching procedures. Teaching cannot be structured in terms of a single formula. The ingredients lack stability; teacher and learning combinations are seldom uniform. This fact must be recognized if education is to become meaningful to boys and girls who have yet to find satisfaction in school activities. Since pupils do not fit into a particular mold or pattern, it may be necessary to use a variety of approaches to challenge them as they progress through school.

Children who have not found enjoyment in reading during their elementary school years will not do the reading required for high-level success at upper educational levels. By the same token, children who have not learned how to work and study will not find much success when they are given responsibilities calling for information and skill in areas where there is no teacher to give them page numbers and directions. Helping boys and girls surmount these two obstacles is not easy, but it cannot be transferred to the shoulders of growing boys and girls; they need a great deal of help along the way, and it must come early. By the time the pupil reaches the sixth grade, the task of retraining or reeducating him becomes a time-consuming and, often, thankless task. It is difficult to change poor attitudes or work-study patterns if such training is delayed too long. Reteaching and relearning are much more difficult when children have acquired faulty learning patterns and have begun to build up a negative attitude toward sound teaching and/or learning techniques.

Each teacher has an obligation to help pupils reach higher learning stages by the development of better attitudes toward the educative process and by the development of better work-study patterns. *How* pupils study is more important than *what* they study. This does not mean that teachers will ignore content or subject matter, because it is an essential ingredient in the learning process. In the past, too much attention was placed upon the "what" aspect of teaching and not enough time and thought were given to the "how" aspect of the learning process.

Most classroom teachers use only a few teaching methods. Methods that apply to one subject will generally apply to others; therefore, the teaching methods and learning activities described in the following pages are not categorized in terms of any one subject field. Teachers are urged to take a new look at how boys and girls go about the task of learning new skills or acquiring additional knowledge. Do they waste time, or do they merely go through the motions of study because they do not know how to do better? If so, whose fault is it? Unless someone takes them where they are and helps them at their learning levels, growth can be only haphazard. This is not good education. The teacher will find that she wants to help the learner, but the pupil may be resistant when he finds that the learning process is far from easy. She may have to be ready to counter pressures which tend to draw some pupils away from her. She has to be prepared to work with the reluctant learner as well as the willing one, and must help each individual find challenge and enrichment in a program which is aimed at helping the boy or girl achieve success in the educative process.

DELEGATING RESPONSIBILITY

Children mature slowly if the teacher continues to tell them what to do. If children are going to learn to assume responsibilities, they need opportunities to demonstrate that although they will continue to expect leadership from the teacher, she has to help them become more self-sufficient. In many classrooms some pupils show their early maturation and readiness to initiate and carry out activities on their own. They are the ones who can help plan an activity and will work with little teacher direction or urging to realize their objectives. These pupils will usually be prompt in turning in assignments; they will not have to be reminded constantly that they have work to complete. Having finished one assignment, they are not content to sit around as if they had nothing else to do. Without waiting to be told, they will proceed to the next activity or will find something constructive to do on their own. If they make a mistake, they will proceed to try to find the correct solution or will ask for help. In many instances, they can resolve their own problems if the teacher will allow them to discuss their problems with their peers. Some pupils can accomplish a great deal through a team approach.

With guidance, more elementary school children can learn to assume responsibilities of a constructive nature. This is often evident in the first grade, where youngsters readily learn the meaning of self-direction once the teacher sets the stage for them. She gives them directions they can understand, and there are interesting activities they can undertake when a directed activity is complete. Some pupils will quietly finish a set of questions and will proceed to the library table; others will go to the easel; some will proceed to work at the science table, while still others will turn to special work which is not yet completed from prior activities.

At higher grade levels the more mature pupils will readily go from a teacher-directed activity to a pupil-initiated activity without having to be told. They will demonstrate their ability to persevere on various problems and projects which interest them. Even when the work is difficult and frustrating, they will show their maturity by the way they organize their thought processes and work materials. Some will look for shortcuts and will try to apply past knowledge or previously learned skills to the solution of difficult problems. They will accept criticisms and, at the same time, will be self-critical, because they recognize the value of criticism as an aid to progress. Because they are acquiring maturity, they seek an ever-increasing amount of independence and will find that the school does not meet some of their basic needs when everyone has to conform to a common work and behavior pattern. When this occurs, some mature individuals who are ready for responsibility will begin to rebel—inwardly, if not outwardly.

BEGINNING GROUP OR COMMITTEE WORK

When children have had little experience with small group activity or with a form of committee activity, the teacher may have to move gradually to avoid losing control over the class. A sudden release from a continued experience with activities dominated by the teacher can result in some pupils literally going "haywire." Many children do not know how to act when they move from a teacher-dominated class to a teacher-guided class. They still expect the teacher to tell them what to do, and when she does not assume a commanding role, they need time to get acclimated to the idea of pupil leadership.

When committees are formed for the first time, poor chairmen may be selected. It may take time to discover that the popular girl or boy may not be the best person to lead a research assignment. Here, the teacher will have to help the pupils see the qualities of leadership needed for particular types of activity. Intermediate grade children may find it helpful to work ahead of time on a study of committee organization and operational techniques. If pupils are not ready to select good long-term leaders, they may use rotating chairmanships. Under such a plan the pupils get to see how their classmates operate under pressures normally not encountered in the classroom.

Mistakes, however, will be made, and the teacher may have to hide her frustrations when a poor student leader is selected. She may have to work closely with the new leader to help him get started or recommend a co-chairman.

Duration of Initial Group Activities. As the teacher watches her pupils at work in a group or committee setup, she has to assess the value of the activities going on. If there is a lack of good student leadership, if resources are inadequate or are not used properly, if pupils fail to take their new responsibilities seriously and too much time is being wasted, or if there is too much fooling around, the teacher will have to decide whether to bring the activities to a rapid halt or to allow them to proceed to a logical end.

Many new group activities have to be of short duration until the pupils get used to the new plans, because they are faced with an entirely different type of grouping from what they may have experienced before. Those who worked in reading groups at the primary level remember working in a teacher-dominated situation or working independently at their seats. For the first time now, the teacher may change her role from that of a director of pupil activity to that of a supervisor and coworker. This transition must be a gradual one. Discipline will have to be maintained, and pupils who need special direction and help must continue to receive it. Brighter pupils should be ready to work in subgroups much faster than others. If grouping is new to the children, the teacher will start off with her top pupils since they can readily carry out many activities without too much teacher direction. As these bright pupils work together on a committee, the teacher works with the remaining two-thirds of the class. She observes the two class divisions and tries to identify pupils who can assume leadership roles. When she is ready to divide the class into several committees or subgroups, she may move several potential leaders into key committee responsibilities by either direct or indirect means. Such teacher leadership may be frowned on by some educators as being too autocratic, but the teacher has to set the stage. If leaders are to be made, she has a responsibility to help identify them and place them in positions where they can assume responsibility.

Left entirely to chance and without teacher guidance, the first committee experiences of the students can be disheartening, whereas they should be pleasurable and satisfying. To protect herself and the class, it may be best to limit the first group activities to a short period of time. If the teacher then finds that she can control her class and still have the group experiences meeting definite objectives, she can sponsor projects calling for a longer period of activity. If the class shows that it is lacking in readiness for group activity, she may have to sponsor exercises which will lead them to what is termed "group readiness." In other words, they learn the meaning of the word "freedom" when it is given to them. If they show that they can follow directions and accept responsibilities for group and individual actions, they can proceed to work on group activities of a higher level and for longer time intervals.

Need for Careful Supervision. Teachers who plan to work with children in committees or in subgroups must still remember their responsibilities as teachers to *both* the children and the parents when they select student chairmen or pupil leaders. In other words, self-discipline is a worthy aim, but the courts are likely to favor the pupil should he be injured in an activity not properly supervised by a certified teacher. As long as the teacher is responsible for the welfare and safety of the children entrusted to her, she must continue to supervise their activities regardless of whether she is working with them directly or indirectly. From a legal standpoint, a teacher can be held accountable for what happens when she frees a group of students to work in the library or any other part of the building without supervision; but she also has a professional responsibility to ensure that the children will engage in educational activities commensurate with their abilities, interests, and academic needs. She has to help them plan activities and locate materials; evaluate their progress; answer their questions; and help them learn new skills or techniques necessary to continue with a technical phase of an assignment. If a group goes off on a tangent, the teacher has to be ready to bring it back to the right path. Committee work does not mean "trial and error" learning. All of this calls for continued supervision of individual and group activities.

A teacher literally has to have "eyes in the back of her head" when three or four groups are working on a project, but she does not have to play the role of a policeman. She does not foster pupil growth by staying behind her desk. She has to be continually alert to what is going on in the classroom and must be able and ready to give help to individual students or groups of students. She has to stop monitoring and must become a participant. She works with the children and helps them to evaluate their own work. Upon her shoulders falls the responsibility of keeping records of activities which are under way in the classroom. If progress is slow, she has to help the pupils find new ways of operating so that growth can be continuous and rapid. If another group is apparently moving too fast, she has to check to see that pupils are not missing important details or essential skills. If they are, she may have to use her skill to slow the group down. Group work is not easy for the teacher, but it can be enjoyable and rewarding.

Outlining Group Members' Responsibilities. If children are to succeed and show continuous growth, each pupil has to know what is expected of him before he starts an activity. Some teachers set the stage by carefully writing directions on the blackboard, by giving the pupils printed guide sheets, or by having regular planning sessions. What she does with the children depends upon the make-up of the class. With fast learners, directions can be brief and to the point; but with average or below-average work groups, the teacher's directions may have to be detailed and so specific that there is no question about the group's objectives. The teacher must, however, avoid the extremes of too specific or too vague directions; for example, directives should not be so vague that the children go home with a report that they did not have any work in school because the teacher did not tell them what to do. A middle-of-the-road position may call for the pupils to keep notebooks so that they can review what a group set out to do; thus, the teacher would not have to repeat questions or assignments for particular children. They need to learn how to find answers for themselves;

therefore, her role as a teacher may be one of guiding, rather than telling, so that the students will be able to think some problems out for themselves.

Many pupils fail to see what is expected of them because they do not see a reason for their activity. They have a right to know their ultimate goal or objectives; if they do not understand the "why" of an activity or skill, they may not accomplish very much. Teachers must remember that although goals appear very clear to them, they may be very vague and unrealistic to fourth, fifth, or sixth graders. Regardless of whether the pupils are working in a single textbook or in a form of group activity, the teacher will find it helpful to review both the short- and long-range goals. If a committee approach is used, it may suffice to review the goals with the leaders who will, in turn, review them with the members of their committee.

Goals or directives may be discussed in one or more planning sessions before the children break into work groups. From time to time they may come together to make reports of progress or to review their goals. Sometimes this planning session may be a discussion period; at other times, it may be a teacher telling or explaining session. If the activity has been motivated by pupil interest or pupil questions, the objectives may be self-evident. However, even here misunderstandings can develop. As the children begin to work on their own, the teacher can circulate among them to see that they know what is expected. By listening and by watching them as they work, the teacher can locate individual pupils who do not know exactly what they are trying to accomplish.

TEACHING CHILDREN HOW TO STUDY AS THEY STUDY

More and more educators are beginning to recognize that success in school and life depends upon the individual's ability to study. All too often it has been assumed that children who have learned to read are able to study effectively, but this is not necessarily true. A girl who read widely and talked freely headed her class in high school, but she encountered trouble in college because she was unable to collect and organize her thoughts and ideas easily on paper. In contrast, one wonders how a young man went on to receive a doctorate since he could not read 100 words a minute. In the latter case, persistence and long nights of painstaking effort to read a few more pages helped him overcome his reading handicap, because he could retain what he read and was able to organize his facts easily when he had to write a report.

Actually, studying is an art which is not easy to evaluate. Knowing only how to read and to write will not do the trick unless other ingredients are present. For example, many children never seem to find the ingredient to success which may be called *drive*. They need a motivating force to spur them on. Interests or desires may become important factors in determining what some pupils will do when the road to learning begins to become difficult. On the other hand, some pupils never realize their desires, because they are unable to work for the sustained period necessary for success. Attempts to measure ability to study will fail when such an intangible as *drive* or *interest* has to be considered.

However, one can measure some of the other necessary skills which make success possible for the individual who wants it. For example, the Work Study Skills section of the Iowa Every-Pupil Tests of Basic Skills will reveal weaknesses in the area of map study skills and the use of references. It may show that pupils do not know how to use an index or lack dictionary skill. Follow-up studies on pupils who had taken this test have repeatedly shown that those who did not score high in these areas had not been engaging in activities which could be considered as promoting better work-study skills patterns. In such communities, teachers have found that the test picture can be reversed when they teach boys and girls how to read a graph or chart, or teach them to use the index to find topics instead of giving them page-by-page assignments. Similarly, children who learn to use the dictionary as a matter of course have no trouble on a test measuring dictionary skill.

Studies have shown that good work-study skills are based upon teaching and practice in designated areas. The teacher cannot assume that children learn how to study unless there have been constant directions in the *how* and *why* phases. Then the quality of pupil work may be the only evidence that the teaching has been successful. Children will not refer to the index or table of contents for direction if the teacher continues to refer them to designated pages for study. On the other hand, children have no choice but to look at the index if the teacher makes it a practice to list assignments according to themes or topics. If children are using multiple textbooks as a regular day-by-day occurrence, they soon learn how to locate information on their own. Similarly, if children are expected to read charts and maps in social studies and arithmetic classes, the practice and skill obtained over a period of time in using such materials gets the individual over the "What do I do now?" stage. It takes good teaching and practice before a number of boys and girls get over the feeling that reading maps and charts is the equivalent of learning a new language.

Teacher observation is a most effective tool if it is used analytically and followed by corrective teaching. If children are given assignments which call for organization skill and research, the teacher who is observant can soon detect the students who depend upon others for help or who waste a great deal of time and effort through meaningless trial-and-error approaches to the problem.

Some educators advocate the teaching of work-study skills as an isolated subject. This may be desirable at the secondary school level when it is evident that the pupils do not have the training needed for success in academic subjects, but not at the elementary school level. Many of the ingredients for success are a basic part of the elementary language arts and social studies programs. Skills like outlining, reading for information, note taking, summarizing, map reading, learning to listen, or learning to discuss problems openly and intelligently must be taught as children study many subjects, and then must be repeatedly used in daily class work.

As a rule, every pupil who leaves the sixth grade should have acquired good study habits, and essential skills should have been introduced which, with reemphasis in the seventh and eighth grades, will lead to higher achievement without reteaching.

One of the responsibilities of the teacher is to see that boys and girls can read for information, can interpret new types of materials, or can summarize their findings either in an oral or written presentation without copying verbatim what they have read or heard. Good teaching is evident when children can use a variety of written materials with understanding. If the children are given specific study help when they are called upon to study independently, they will not need to take a special course in learning how to study. Attention to the following areas at the elementary school level are prerequisites for success:

1. *All pupils should be taught to study with a purpose.* Children need to know what they are looking for when they study. They must understand what they are trying to do and why. Without purpose and understanding, most teacher assignments are meaningless.

2. *All intermediate grade children must learn to read with comprehension.* The emphasis in a good reading program must call for skill in reading intelligently and independently many types of reading materials.

3. *Children must learn to vary their rate of speed when they read different types of written materials.* Elementary school children are not usually concerned with speed reading; generally, they will not read nonfiction materials at the same rate they read fiction. But pupils must learn to adjust their reading pace to the purpose which underlies the activity. If they have to read for detail, they will have to read slowly. If they have to locate isolated facts, they may be able to skim over irrelevant material and concentrate their attention

on the important facts. When reading for mere entertainment or enjoyment, they may read rapidly without taking time to read lengthy descriptions that detract from the story or plot.

4. *Children should be taught to use many types of reference sources.* From the third grade on, boys and girls can begin to learn to use many kinds of reference materials. In the fifth and sixth grades they should be taught how to use an index file, an encyclopedia, the world almanac, an atlas, and a standard dictionary.

5. *Children should be taught to locate the most significant points.* Children must be taught to listen for them in a speaker's talk. Most speeches have only a few main ideas, so the students who can readily identify the objectives or theme can follow the talk more easily and remember it longer.

6. *Children should try to secure a "whole view" of a selection.* Before children begin a long assignment, they should try to discover what it is all about. It helps to look through the table of contents and to glance through the pages of the book in order to get familiar with the topic or the nature of the reading materials.

7. *Pupils must be trained to judge sources of information.* Whether children write reports or engage in discussions, they need to give serious consideration to the reliability and recentness of their sources of information. Children should learn to ask themselves: Do we have all the facts? Is our source of information up to date? Is the author biased in any way?

8. *Children must be taught to think for themselves.* Gone are the days when employers could say, "We do not care if children learn to think in school. We are better off if we can employ men and women who do not think too much when they work." This point of view was expressed by the supervisor of an assembly line in a large, new electronics plant. He was frank enough to admit that good thinkers were not too productive workers on the assembly line. However, the main office in this plant was worried because competitors were ahead of them in the race for "brains." Scouts were constantly on the alert to identify top-flight engineering students who could be induced to join their organization. Today, selfish interests cannot afford to stand in the way of an educational program that has as its prime purpose the development of a thinking citizenry. More than ever before, the schools must concentrate on the realization of this objective. Alert teachers realize that education has to be more than a passive acquisition of knowledge and skills. More than ever before, the educated person needs a rich background of information; but, at the same time, he must be able to use this material as an aid to thinking.

9. *Children should be actively involved in the learning situation.* The most brilliant mathematician can fail as a teacher unless he can get down to the level of the pupils. If he does not involve the students in the learning process, his wealth of mathematical knowledge will not be transmitted.

10. *Children should work with problems they can relate to their daily living.* Studies have shown that children will learn more when they study personal problems or problems which can be related to their daily lives. Therefore, teachers who are interested in teaching better study habits do not have to work with artificial problems. In fact, young people can benefit from formulating and expressing their own problems.

11. *Children learn more effectively when they can associate personal experiences with the new activity.* Children build on past experience; therefore, the pupil who has limited experiences may be handicapped when it comes to acquiring new experiences because he has so little to build on. Also his chances for success will be enhanced if the past experience was a pleasant and successful one.

12. *Teachers should vary the length of assignments.* Teachers must recognize the differences in pupil attention span. Pupils with a short attention span will not be too successful when they have assignments which call for prolonged activity. They will be less frustrated with several short work periods than with one or two long ones. Other pupils can take long assignments without showing any signs of fatigue or loss of interest in the activity.

13. *Children may respond more effectively to some methods than to others.* This may be due to differences in pupil backgrounds and their stage of readiness for a particular skill or body of knowledge, or these differences may be due merely to habit. Pupils who have learned to study in one particular way may not see the necessity to change to a new approach, even when an old pattern of study is poor and ineffective. It may take considerable reteaching to effect a change in study patterns. Only continued teacher observation of pupils at work will show which pupils need to modify their study habits.

14. *Children must overlearn some important facts and skills.* One of the dangers of teaching in a nonstructured program lies in the ease with which teachers and pupils assume that a skill has been learned or that facts are known. Everything can seem so clear on the first presentation that any additional expenditure of time and effort seems wasteful. Actually, little may be retained unless there is a follow-up activity to ensure that the learning will be permanent. Should there be a time lapse between activities of a related nature,

Students learn research techniques.

A fifth-grade pupil checks books in the school library.

the teacher will find that some pupils have trouble recalling what is expected of them unless there has been some overlearning.

15. *Children must see that there are many ways to solve some problems.* The slow learner may have trouble learning a single approach to a problem, but average and better-than-average students are able to master a skill and then find other approaches or short cuts to a solution. Alert teachers will promote activities which will enable boys and girls to see that there are several ways to solve many problems and that the course of action should be determined on the basis of reason.

Types of Work-Study Skill Activities

USE OF THE LIBRARY AND ITS FACILITIES

During the course of a child's schooling he should have several exploratory experiences in the use of a library and its resources. For example, young children may go to the library to meet the librarian, to hear someone read stories, and to borrow interesting books. This is the beginning of the development of library consciousness and an awareness of the rich resources available to children with wide interests in reading. These young children can quickly learn to visit the library on their own.

Older children should continue to use the library for good reading materials, but they need to be given instruction in finding information to help them solve problems. They may begin by getting acquainted with special shelves containing technical or reference books related to topics of special interest to them individually or to areas studied in the classroom. Mature fifth- and sixth-grade pupils can learn to use the card index to find resources on their own. Some of them may begin to learn to find materials through the Dewey Decimal System, although this library skill may not be taught until children reach the seventh grade. The time to begin technical library instruction should depend on the maturity of the pupil and the need for these skills. Many teachers take it for granted that boys and girls know how to use a library. In actuality, many pupils who go to schools in small towns never see a good library until they go to high school or until they are old enough to travel to the nearest city to borrow books from a large city library. Many small town libraries lack an adequate reference file or card catalogs, and essential reference books are often lacking because they are too expensive or because no one guided the librarian in book selection.

Intermediate and upper grade teachers can and should try to assess the nature of the library skills which their children possess. Should they be found lacking in these skills, the teacher may directly teach them some needed library skills, or they may work with a regular librarian who can help them do so more effectively. After the boys and girls have been given the instruction or orientation they need for independent activity, the teacher must give them assignments which call for the use of the library facilities; then, as the children work on assignments or projects, the teacher must continue to assess the effectiveness of their work. With proper orientation, the average and above-average pupils should be able to select materials from a variety of sources other than a set of encyclopedias. Older pupils and bright pupils should be familiar with the *Reader's Guide, Who's Who in America,* the *World Almanac,* and the *Statesman's Yearbook.* They should be familiar with the use of an atlas and numerous special reference collections relating to particular fields of study such as social studies and science.

LEARNING THE PARTS OF A BOOK

All children should learn at an early age that titles and book jackets can be most deceiving to the unwary. The fifth-grade boy who took pride in the fact that he had never started a book he did not finish went through some dry and meaningless books before he learned the meaning of selectivity when searching for a book. Children learn with help how to judge books which will meet their needs and interests. The first-grade teacher can help them by introducing them to the title page and the contents page. They may readily see that the stories in a first reader center around such topics as the farm, pets, friends, or the circus. They can learn to locate their favorite story by turning to the contents to find where it starts, although the less mature reader may not see the connection between the listed titles and the page reference —he is more likely to thumb through, looking for the picture that goes with the story.

As children grow older, the teacher helps them discover the makeup of the books they use by studying the contents. Basically, all children should learn that the contents is located in the front of the book; tells the pupil what topics or subjects are treated in the book; and shows the order in which topics are listed and the pages where information about a topic can be found. Once they have become familiar with the contents, the children should have practice in locating materials by referring to it instead of having the teacher give them page references.

To use the index effectively, children need to know the alphabet and should have had sufficient alphabetizing exercises. Primary grade children can learn to locate the index, but they may not use it effectively until they can alphabetize correctly; alphabetize beyond the first letter of any given word; and recognize prefixes and root words. As they study a topic, they must learn to look for key words and then find them in the index in order to locate additional information in one or more special reference books.

Teachers have many opportunities to teach children the parts of the books they use. Lessons can begin with an introduction to the books the teacher has given out. Together, teacher and pupils look at the book or books and talk about their observations. They may look at pictures, or an interesting selection may be read aloud. They may look at the contents, with the teacher asking questions to see if the children can anticipate what lies ahead. Intermediate grade teachers will often find sections in their English books which are helpful in instructing pupils in the use of the index. Spelling books may help give pupils alphabetizing practice.

Before turning pupils loose in the library, the teacher may find it most helpful to borrow an encyclopedia, or a set or two, if they are available, for a careful look at their composition. Special instructions are frequently available to upper-grade students from the representative who acts as the agent for a particular set of encyclopedias. Children should also be instructed in the use of a glossary. Older children will find it helpful if the teacher will go over with them the makeup of a newspaper or popular magazine.

How far each teacher should go in the introduction of books, magazines, and papers will depend upon the maturity of the children, the nature of their past experiences with such materials, and the use expected by the boys and girls of the knowledge or skills taught. Children who have had considerable experience in the library, where research skills were essential for success, will not need to spend much time with the teacher getting acquainted with books and references; but if they are just beginning to have these experiences, the teacher cannot afford to neglect her responsibility to teach them how to use reference tools readily.

VALUE OF SYSTEMATIC TRAINING IN DICTIONARY USE

Lazy children will often avoid using a dictionary, but children with curiosity and good work habits will find that they cannot do quality work without making frequent use of this reference tool. While formal dictionary training is not usually introduced until children reach the fourth grade, all first- and second-grade children can begin to get the dictionary habit through the use of picture dictionaries. More mature first-, second-, and third-grade pupils will find pleasure in looking up new words in a beginning dictionary, or in compiling their own, using the adult dictionary as a guide. Children can learn to use the dictionary as an interesting tool in many phases of communication, but they must learn to use it efficiently and with a minimum of effort. For example, many pupils waste time when they refer to the dictionary simply because the teacher failed to impress upon them the significance of guide words. Other pupils have trouble using the dictionary because they have not learned how to alphabetize beyond the first letter. Efficient dictionary use calls for practice. At times the teacher may have to teach some dictionary skills to the whole class, but many of the basic skills are taught as a part of the reading or the spelling program; therefore, the actual use of the dictionary is often taught to small groups on an individual basis. Teachers may assign pupils exercises from commercially prepared workbooks, or they may make up their own to ensure that pupils have individually or collectively learned the following dictionary skills:

1. Alphabetizing words automatically and in serial order by their second, third, and fourth letters

2. Using guide words to see how vowels and consonants are pronounced

3. Understanding accent marks and diacritical marks

4. Dividing words into syllables

5. Finding appropriate word meanings and spellings as an aid to writing

6. Determining abbreviations and finding synonyms, homonyms, and antonyms

7. Forming plurals and using prefixes and suffixes

Each intermediate grade pupil should have a copy of a dictionary which he can use freely at his desk, and from time to time he should be able to refer to a copy of a more advanced dictionary. The more able and upper grade pupils should learn to use the large unabridged dictionary often found in the library or in special upper grade classrooms.

TEACHING CHILDREN TO OUTLINE FOR THEMSELVES

Teaching children how to outline can be a waste of time unless pupils see an outline as the way to organize thoughts, ideas, and information. Although primary grade children can begin to work with simple outlines, their efforts are more in the way of *listing* things they see, do, or read. Here, form is inconsequential; but as the children mature, they find that listing is not sufficient. They have to concentrate on the separation of topics and ideas to bring together those which are related—as either major headings or topics, or as subtopics under a major heading.

When boys and girls are ready to study a new topic, or to begin a study unit, it may help them to list the things which they feel most need consideration. For example: name of the topic or theme, gist of each paragraph, secondary topics or ideas (for fifth- or sixth-graders).

The children should see the outline as a simple way to organize their ideas or findings. Later, they may refer to the outline to give a talk or summary on what they have studied. The quality of the pupil's work will often be revealed in the kind of outline he makes. Children whose reading comprehension is at a high level will readily select the main ideas, but those who rate low in reading comprehension will frequently miss the central theme of a paragraph. As a result, these pupils may be listing words that have no meaning or relationship to each other.

TEACHING CHILDREN TO MAKE MORE EFFECTIVE REPORTS

Help in preparing reports must be systematic and should start at the third- and fourth-grade levels with pupils who have learned how to express themselves by mastering the mechanics of writing and reading. The reports may be either oral or written and must be based on some independent or group studies. As pupils reach the junior high school level, their teachers must avoid overloading them with nonessential or busy work to give pupils time to prepare reports based upon careful study and quality work. At this level a single pupil report can meet the educational standards and objectives of at least two teachers, such as the social studies and the English teachers. In teaching the writing of reports, teachers should aim for the following goals:

1. Children should be taught how to organize materials to make an oral presentation clearly understood, giving the facts simply and correctly.

2. Boys and girls should learn to use notes and outlines and not merely read or recite from memory long reports not in their own words.

3. Pupils should be encouraged to use visual aids—including the blackboard—to illustrate some of their points.

4. Pupils giving reports should be so well versed in their topics that they are able to answer questions that go beyond the initial report.

WORKING TO IMPROVE DISCUSSION TECHNIQUES

The word "discuss" is overused in many classes. Day after day, pupils hear teachers say, "Let us discuss what we have read," but the activities which follow are not really discussions. All too often a few children talk as they answer questions and parrot back what they know the teacher wants. Seldom do they talk about a topic in a deliberate fashion with varying opinions offered constructively and amicably to settle an issue or decide a course of action. The teacher should be ready to intervene to help pupils see that discussions should involve the ability to reason without the loss of tempers or outbursts based upon emotions. They must also see that discussion is more than mere talk. It means using words discriminately to present several sides to an issue or to analyze problems on the basis of the evidence given in order to draw conclusions they can justify.

When one talks of improving discussion techniques, it is necessary to consider how the teacher can encourage children to consider the pro and con of issues based on intelligent thinking. When they give answers or make contributions to a discussion, they should have had sufficient experience to talk sensibly and intelligently. If called upon to substantiate a statement, they should be able to do so. Children have to be taught that discussions center around a problem, with each individual having the responsibility to give consideration to every logical and possible solution. Each pupil should look at a discussion as an exercise in cooperative class thinking. They have to see that discussion is not like mere conversation, that one discusses with a definite purpose in mind. This purpose should be clearly understood at the beginning, and what is said should be related to that purpose. Once the objective has been realized, the discussion does not have to be prolonged unnecessarily; therefore, the practice of artificially trying to keep a discussion going to give everyone a chance to talk is educationally unsound. If all the children are not getting a chance to talk about problems, the size of the discussion group should be reduced to permit greater participation. Through the formation of one or more other discussion groups, the pupils can carry on independent discussions of the same problems.

Discussion and Classroom Recitation. Teachers and pupils must see that the terms "recitation" and "discussion" are not synonymous. In the traditional classroom, recitation consisted of having pupils parrot back answers based upon what they had read or heard. Many pupils knew what the teacher wanted and they tried to give her the answers she expected. This is not possible if the discussion is real, because the answer or solution may not come out the way the teacher expected it would. In the discussion, pupils can show their individuality and, sometimes, their independence. They do not always have to conform to a set pattern. In a good discussion, the minority opinion should be respected if it is based on sound reasoning, even when it does not agree with the thinking of the majority.

The recitation generally consists of an exchange between the teacher and two or three individuals. When she asks a question, she expects an answer from the first pupil she calls upon, but if he cannot satisfy her, another pupil is called upon. When the teacher's question has been answered, every other pupil can breathe a sigh of relief— "That's another hurdle passed." The teacher is satisfied that everyone else knows the answer to the question, so she goes on to another topic or to another question, forgetting that many of the children did not react to the question even though they may have heard the answer. Some of them did not understand the question which preceded the answer, so it had no meaning to them, either.

The discussion may center around a problem that interested the students as they studied a phase of social studies or science, but it may also not be subject-centered. It may arise from some aspect of group living in the classroom, school, or community. Personal problems make good discussion subjects, but they are not teacher-centered. Sometimes problems arise in a class spontaneously, but often the teacher may have to set the stage for the discussion. In this case the teacher asks questions which are more thought-provoking than those asked when the students are called upon to recite. If the teacher wants to promote discussion, she tries to ask questions that do not call for just a single answer. A good question may have several possible answers. When children attempt to answer these questions, the fact that one response will not suffice can lead to the discussion in which various individuals try to bring together different facts to substantiate different points of view. The children are called upon to weigh the various answers and to select the best one.

When the teacher calls upon individual children to recite, the pupils are not always stimulated to think clearly. If they know their subject matter, they can give satisfying answers; but if there are several possible answers, the children must be given opportunities to think a problem through. They have to weigh the facts and try to analyze them to reach a logical answer or make a reasonable decision. In a discussion, the pupils exchange information and stimulate each other. There is interaction among pupils as well as between pupil and teacher. In the formal recitation the reaction is generally limited to the teacher and the pupil, a reaction that is merely repeated until the answer is obtained. The teacher may ultimately call upon a dozen or more children to get her answer, but this is *co*-action rather than *inter*-action.

In the recitation period the slow learner is at a disadvantage since the teacher expects him to know all the answers. His individuality or lack of readiness does not matter. He is part of the class and should be able to respond when called upon. But in the discussion period the slow learner can make his contribution even though it may be only a minor one. The essential factor here is that each individual's contribution, no matter how small, will be weighed before a final conclusion is made. Since the pupil is reacting to other children, there is a good possibility that he can be stimulated by the remarks of others. Then again, the pupils may understand their peermates in a discussion better than they understand the teacher.

Teaching Children to Evaluate What They See and Hear. When some fifth graders began arguing about a population figure in a textbook, the teacher had to help them see that the apparent discrepancy in their findings was due to the fact that one figure had been taken from a much later revision of a standard textbook. This is something some of the brighter pupils would have discovered for themselves, but other pupils had to learn that because the mere circumstances of time intervenes, one does not accept every statement or figure in a book. The ability to find the publication date of a book can be learned quickly if children see the necessity for doing so. They have to learn to examine materials they use, in terms of recency and accuracy, if they are to understand and interpret current problems.

Children need considerable help in forming judgments or conclusions on the basis of what they read, see, or hear. This is not an easy task, because of the tendency of many individuals to accept everything which is written or spoken as being true and accurate. If pupils have not been taught to be critical, they may not detect errors—or even actual attempts to influence their thinking—through the withholding of important data or the slanting of details to infer something other than what actually happened. As children mature, they have to learn to look for motives. They may have to learn to ask: *Is this really what happened? Does the author have the true facts? Is he trying to infer something which is not so? Do other writers agree? If not, how can I find more information which will let me make my own judgment as to what is right or wrong?*

The teacher has to help individual pupils distinguish between relevant and irrelevant data. When pupils discuss problems in class, it will be up to the class and the teacher to insist that speakers refrain from always talking in generalities. Children have to learn to distinguish between factual evidence and that which is based upon opinion or inconclusive evidence.

Importance of the Pupil Leader. Some children can assume the role of a leader with little apparent effort and training, but other children have only the potential for leadership. They may have had a rich background of experiences, but they have always let the natural leaders take over. If the teacher is to help both types of individuals, she has to give each a chance to serve as leader. Giving the latter pupils this responsibility can be the making of them. There is a temptation to elect or appoint the so-called "natural leader" to direct a committee or lead a discussion. When this is done repeatedly, there is little opportunity for the pupil with potential to show that he can assume leadership responsibilities.

When the teacher breaks her class into several discussion groups, there is an opportunity for many potential leaders to acquire the practice they need in leading small groups. Also, by rotating the leadership role, more pupils can test themselves. They may find that they lack the background to keep a good discussion moving, perhaps owing to social and emotional immaturity. The pupil in charge of the discussion must understand the importance of his role. With poor leadership, the activity can be meaningless; with good leadership, the discussion can be a stimulating learning activity. On the other hand, each pupil taking part in the discussion must understand that the leader does not work alone. Each pupil must be willing and ready to make worthwhile contributions and must be prepared to support the leader; this is particularly true where the leader is new to his position.

The discussion leader must be ready to act independently when decisions are necessary. He will be a member of a team, but his responsibilities will vary according to the pupils working with him. If everyone is alert and prepared for the discussion, his job may be an easy one; but if his coworkers are not prepared, his task can be difficult. To do a competent job he should be able to:

1. Keep the discussion going. When a point has been definitely made clear, he knows that it is time to move on to another aspect of a problem.

2. Secure contributions from everyone. He encourages the shy, reticent pupil and holds in check those pupils who would monopolize the discussion.

3. Analyze the situation, sensing when the discussion is going well or when someone has led the discussion off the track. He tries to encourage intelligent discussion and to secure statements based on fact rather than conjecture.

4. Sense when the discussants have lost contact with their listeners. His team may have to be stimulated with a key question or it may be best to stop.

5. Keep track of time in order to allow each member of the group to make his contribution and to allow the speakers time to cover all phases of a problem.

6. Help individual speakers find a way to express themselves in an audience situation without being too conspicuous.

7. Summarize what has been said, or lead others to do so. Help draw conclusions as to the effectiveness of group activity, as well as a conclusion regarding the high point or findings of the discussants.

The Panel Discussion. While the panel discussion and the round table can serve the same purpose, the panel discussion has some advantages over the round table. In the round table discussion the discussants do not come prepared in the same way they do for a panel presentation. Because the latter is more formal, panelists prepare themselves for their talks by studying one or more aspects of a problem. Since each panelist will make a formal presentation to the audience, notes are not out of order. In fact, some pupils will feel a greater security in the panel discussion, because they can prepare and even memorize what they have to say before the moderator directs a question at them.

After the panelists have made their presentation, the moderator may open the discussion to the whole group. Now everyone has an opportunity to express himself on questions other than the one discussed originally. Panelists may not agree with what other speakers say, so the moderator may have to exert himself to prevent them from becoming embroiled in an argument. When the audience has a chance to participate, the moderator may have to interpret questions and direct them to panelists who may be best prepared to give the questioner a satisfactory answer.

The Buzz Session. Teachers can use the buzz session technique with either small or large groups of children, because every pupil takes part in the activity. The discussion is highly informal and requires no special preparation. The classroom teacher will introduce the children to a problem, then will tell them to group their chairs together so that five or six of them will be able to sit together to talk about the problem. There is no denying the fact that the teacher will have to contend with an increase in the volume of sound, but it will be purposeful and constructive noise. All children find satisfaction in the activity, particularly if the topics for discussion are related to things they can understand. During the buzz session, four to six clusters of children will talk informally with no predesignated moderator or leader. Some students who are more proficient speakers may take over a buzz session group, but for the most part the composition of such a group will not be the same from one session to the next.

If the teacher wants answers to specific questions, the children in each buzz session group will select someone who will take notes or present a summary of the main points covered by the participants. How long the children "buzz" may depend upon the nature of the problem discussed and their interest in it. New problems or topics for study may result from the notes or summaries, or the pupils may return to a study of the first problem with a greater intensity of effort and interest. During the actual buzz session, pupils have an opportunity to share their thoughts and experiences about topics of importance and, free of teacher domination, the pupils may surprise her with the variety and quality of their informal remarks. For some pupils it may mean a release from tensions (e.g., for shy pupils who would not speak out before the whole class).

HOMEWORK—SETTING A POLICY

Friction and misunderstanding about homework can often be avoided by the development of a sound homework policy clearly understood by teachers, parents, and pupils. Such a policy can often eliminate some pressures on the teacher and the pupil. For example, a policy which states that there will be no formal homework in the primary grades will help the teacher who is besieged by parents to send home more arithmetic homework. In addition to having an official policy about homework in the lower grades, the school may issue a supplementary leaflet telling parents what they can do if they want to assist their children with less formal activities. For example, it could recommend a type of homework which calls for wide reading at home for at least thirty minutes a day. Such homework does not have to be teacher-administered once parents understand that they are sharing in the education of their children by helping to build an interest in reading. This, they should understand, is one of the best preparatory steps which can be taken to meet the challenge of the academic curriculums of the secondary schools and college. Free reading activities may not appeal to the mental-discipline minded parents, but the school can help them to see that most children need this extra reading time to fix skills taught in school and to develop new and wider reading interests.

Homework which is given at the intermediate and upper grade levels may be more formal, but the time required for homework and the type of homework will still be quite different from that required for high school classes. Homework at the middle grade level will not necessarily be regular or fixed in amount; since there is a greater chance for teachers to know their pupils and their needs, homework can often be individualized. The homework policy may recommend that long-range projects or assignments be given, with parent and teacher guiding the pupil in planning his time and use of materials. This policy may help teachers see that homework is really a "side issue." It should be an outgrowth of what is done in the classroom. This attitude toward homework is important, because some teachers devote too much time to making out assignments, correcting papers, reviewing children's work, and chastising pupils, so that there is little actual teaching time left. This is especially true in many departmentalized upper grades.

Parents and teachers have to see homework as more than busywork, which usually results only in continued pupil, teacher, and parent frustration. Where this is occurring, something is wrong, and attempts should be made to study the elements leading to the frustration. Homework problems do not suddenly develop at the ninth-grade level. Long before this time, observant parents and teachers can detect danger signs in the boy or girl who has not learned the basic work-study skills introduced at lower or middle grade levels. Unfortunately, the interests and needs of individual pupils have often been ignored by teachers who continue with mass homework assignments that ignore readiness factors. As a result, the authors are tempted to rule out arbitrarily all homework below the seventh grade and then to establish restrictions on the amount or kind of assignments which could be given at upper grade levels, but, again, individual differences intervene. Some boys and girls actually enjoy the challenge in homework which recognizes their interests and needs. Also, where assignments are based upon a recognition of their basic needs, some children find that homework does help them resolve school adjustment problems. Therefore, elementary school teachers may consider homework as desirable for some pupils when assignments enable pupils to make up work lost through prolonged absence; help pupils to overcome specific difficulties; encourage research activities; give pupils the time and stimulation necessary for good creative activity; help pupils develop self-direction and independent thinking; help pupils learn to budget their time realistically; give pupils opportunities to test principles taught in class; and help pupils learn to work independently as well as cooperatively.

Teacher Responsibilities Concerning Homework. The ultimate nature of the homework the teacher gives to children depends upon her concept of her role as a teacher. If she takes children where she finds them during the day, it will be inconsistent for her to make mass homework assignments. In making out assignments, the teacher should be able to ask herself: Will this assignment do for Tommy? Mary? Susan? Will Jerry or Billy or Lily be able to find the resources needed for the completion of the assignments in their cluttered, impoverished homes? What values will it have for Nancy and Oliver, who are always working with advanced materials?

Homework is related to individual work-study patterns taught in school, but some pupils cannot work at home because there are no reference resources available or because there is no privacy. Recognizing the difficulty some pupils have in applying good work-study skills to tasks assigned for nonschool hours, some teachers set aside a portion of a school period for independent study. Through a better program of supervised study, some of the objectives for homework can be realized. With good planning, many elementary teachers can give pupils the time needed to do independent work while the teacher is available to assist them when and where they need special materials or help.

Actually, homework tends to be less of a problem in the elementary schools of today than it is in the junior high school and upper grades where, because of departmentalization, it is much more difficult to know children and to individualize pupil assignments. The responsibility of the teachers at these grade levels will vary according to the nature of the subject and the age and grade level of the children.

Pupil Responsibilities Concerning Homework. For success at upper grade levels where homework is usually an essential part of the program, pupils must constantly make use of work-study skills taught in the lower grades. Here the pupil should see homework assignments as an extension of the day-by-day activities of the school. They should help him develop skill in working out problems for himself and in the development of work-study patterns which call for a minimum expenditure of time and energy to complete quality work. Homework can be much more meaningful if pupils observe the following principles:

1. Homework assignments should be clearly understood before the pupils leave school.

2. All work assignments must be completed by the individual alone.

3. All assignments should be turned in on time unless circumstances arise which prevent this; then permission should be obtained for late completion.

4. Pupils should understand the reasons underlying an assignment and should try to evaluate their efforts in terms of them.

5. Each pupil should take home the materials he needs to complete regular homework assignments.

6. Pupils should learn to work on long-range assignments in terms of a planned schedule.

The Role of the Parent in Homework. Overanxious parents frequently insist on homework for children even when it interferes with normal growth patterns. At the opposite extreme are parents who act as though they had no responsibility in the development of work-study patterns that will lead to success. Both kinds of parents can hurt the children unless they can adjust to a balanced point of view. All parents should show an interest in school and school activities, especially in those activities which result in homework. Parents must protect children from unnecessary exploitation, but at the same time they must be prepared to give them guidance and help, both in planning their time and in the wisest use of their potentialities. If children have to cope with homework problems, parents can help boys and girls solve these problems in a number of ways.

First of all, the parents can be sympathetic when the child has a pile of homework, but they should not attempt to do the work for the child. Should the work load be excessive, the parents should try to discover what the school's homework policy is or find out why their child is devoting so much time to it. A parent can also help a child to find an answer if he is frustrated, but if this happens too often, the parent should consult the teacher to determine the reasons for it.

Second, parents can evaluate the work children complete at home in terms of quality: They can check to see whether the written work is neatly done and complete, and from time to time they can ask questions to see whether the child knows what he is doing or has done.

Of course, parents should try to provide their children with a proper place to study and work. And they should help pupils budget time so that they can work with a minimum of interruptions and have adequate free time to pursue activities of their own choosing, as well as those sponsored by parents and teachers.

REFERENCES

1. George Beauchamp, *The Curriculum of the Elementary School* (Boston: Allyn and Bacon, 1964).
2. William H. Burton, *The Guidance of Learning Activities,* 3rd ed. (New York: Appleton-Century-Crofts, 1952).
3. Donald F. Cay, *Curriculum: Design for Learning* (Indianapolis: Bobbs-Merrill, 1966).
4. Martha Dallmann, "Homework," *Grade Teacher,* 79 (November 1961), 36, 114–15.
5. Ronald Doll, *Curriculum Improvement* (Boston: Allyn and Bacon, 1964).
6. Grand Rapids Public School Teachers, *Growing by Doing* (Grand Rapids, Mich.: Board of Education, September 1951).
7. Maurice Hillson, *Change and Innovation in Elementary School Organization* (New York: Holt, Rinehart & Winston, 1965).
8. Duane Manning, *The Qualitative Elementary School* (New York: Harper & Row, 1963).
9. Paul Mok, *Pushbutton Parents and the Schools* (New York: Delta Books, 1965).
10. Waldemar Olson, "Homework: Friend or Foe to Children?" *Instructor,* 71 (January 1962), 6, 76, 82.

CHAPTER 9

Meeting Individual
and Group Needs in the
Field of Reading

F ormal education for most children begins when they are introduced to their first reading books. While many intellectually
gifted children can master the reading skills taught in primary grades
with little, if any, adult instruction, most boys and girls depend upon
classroom teachers for guidance and direction. These children often
start school with a desire to read, but find that reading is not easy.
Before they can learn to read independently, it is essential that they
achieve a stage of *maturity* which will lead to success and a form of
security when they are placed in a reading situation. Frequently,
teachers will try to help children avoid early frustrations by a series
of preparatory activities called "readiness" activities, which may be
shortened or prolonged according to the needs of the individual child.

Although there are some first-grade teachers who teach reading to
all pupils in a class at the same time, most will spend the major portion
of their time working with subdivisions of the class, especially as
individual differences become more pronounced between groups of
children.

An Overview of Reading Instruction

There is no one best way to teach reading. Teachers and school
principals do not like to admit that some children do not learn to read
at levels commensurate with their innate ability. But there isn't a

school system in the country that does not have some children with reading problems. Because reading skills are not acquired at the same rate by boys and girls who are chronologically the same age, there is a tendency on the part of some educators and pseudo-educators to criticize the plans of instruction found in various schools. In many communities these critics would substitute a phonetic program, new teaching methods, or just another set of books. Claims are often made for particular reading programs which are in reality not complete—and which in many cases may even be harmful for a certain group of children.

An effective reading program is a composite of several methods of teaching. As the director of the reading activities in the classroom, the teacher is the key individual in the school. The principal may give her textbooks, but the teacher ultimately has to decide on the time and procedures to be followed. For some children visual activities may be given extra attention, whereas other children may need auditory help. A few pupils may find success with a tactile approach combined with visual and auditory activities. In a modern elementary school classroom, the master teacher will lead the children through many reading activities in a single reading lesson. She readily notes where help is needed and plans new lessons which will provide the practice necessary for a successful reading activity the next time she meets the children. She provides phonetic instruction when it is needed, and she stresses comprehension skill development when it becomes apparent that the pupils are merely reading words.

THE APPROACH TO READING THROUGH
BASIC READING SERIES

McGuffey is often credited with fathering the idea of a basic reading series, but he would certainly not recognize most basic readers in current use. To many adults, the introductory preprimers often appear ludicrous, but they forget that exposure to such books is only one step in a complicated learning process. Modern children usually have their first formal reading experiences in work materials and beginning readers that have been carefully prepared by highly competent reading specialists. The books are colorful and the illustrations appeal to children. Attempts are made to control the vocabulary to minimize frustration and give sufficient practice for mastery of a basic reading vocabulary. For a time new teachers were advised to avoid the use of teacher guides, but today the inexperienced teacher is advised to work with the teaching manual prepared for a particular basic reader. (Few teachers will, of course, need every activity described in the average manual.) The basic reader actually is a key to learning, but children are advised to extend their reading experiences by reading in many different kinds of books, and this is where the teacher can help direct boys and girls.

The authors of basic reading series attempt to provide a sequential pattern of learning activities through the use of several books. Children are expected to move from one learning level to another and from one book in a series to another. In theory this is excellent, but in practice, teachers will find that some students do not need one type of activity, whereas other pupils may need to keep repeating the same type of activity from one year to the next before they master a principle or skill.

Reading Skills Found in a Typical Reading Series. As children progress from one learning level to another, teachers have to help them maintain and extend reading skills. This means that repetition is often necessary; therefore, skills introduced in the first and second grades may still receive attention in the sixth grade. Some critics have criticized modern teachers for using a "see and say" method of teaching. While attention is given to this method, good teachers know that children must learn *both* phonetic and word analysis skills.

When teachers work with a basal reader, the authors take some of the chance element out of teaching. Varied skills are introduced with sufficient repetition to help foster growth even with the most inept teacher. Some teachers maintain a checklist of the reading skills introduced in different level readers. By observing pupil progress in relation to specific skill areas, a teacher can modify her instruction if pupils show that they have not mastered a designated reading skill or if it is apparent that review or practice would help in the retention of a learning skill.

Reading skills such as these will not all be learned in a year or two, but over the span of the primary and intermediate grades all pupils should be exposed to them. Some of the skills will be easy to teach, others will have to be presented over and over again. No one teacher can be held responsible for the development of all the skills, but each teacher must be prepared to evaluate pupil achievement and progress in order to modify instruction to review or enlarge upon learning skills introduced at earlier levels. No upper grade teacher can obtain the best results from her students by assuming that lower grade teachers have completed the task of teaching children how to read. Readiness for new learning activities is not limited to the first grade; each teacher must ascertain where pupils are before going into higher learning activities or areas calling for new skills.

Children need exposure to several types of reading before they are truly proficient. Should an area be neglected, gaps will appear in the background of the pupil that can ultimately lead to difficulty.

TABLE 1

Reading Skills Taught in a Sound Developmental
Reading Program

Ability to note picture details.

Ability to associate sound and meaning with printed words, phrases, and sentences.

Ability to interpret and organize main ideas.

Ability to recognize emotional reactions and motives of characters.

Ability to make inferences or interpret ideas not directly stated.

Ability to generalize on the basis of training and experience.

Ability to extend new meanings to familiar words.

Ability to perceive cause-and-effect relationships and context clues.

Ability to apply structural analysis to unlock new words.

Ability to use phonetic analysis to unlock new words.

Ability to use dictionaries to discover associated meanings.

Ability to perceive relationships:

Association through use	Time
General–specific	Place or space
Part–whole	Analogous
Class	Size and quantity
Sequence	Cause and effect

Ability to form and react to sensory images: visual, auditory, kinesthetic.

Ability to read silently and rapidly with a high level of comprehension.

Ability to associate and substitute consonant sounds and symbols.

Ability to extend reading interests through independent reading activities.

Ability to strengthen memory based upon observation, association, visual imagery, auditory imagery, and logical relationships.

Ability to interpret figurative, idiomatic, or picturesque language.

Ability to identify and evaluate character traits.

Ability to identify and react to the mood or tone of a passage, story, or poem.

Ability to project the idea, mood, or tone of a selection in oral interpretation.

Ability to interpret the author's purpose or point of view and to evaluate and react to ideas in the light of current problems.

Ability to apply skills learned in class to their personal reading, including stories, books, magazines, newspaper articles, reference materials.

THE COMPONENTS OF A BASAL READING SERIES

The authors of one noted basal series have divided their reading program as follows:

1. The developmental reading program
2. The functional reading program
3. The recreational reading program
4. The enrichment reading program

In this section, we shall consider aspects of this kind of reading program and of the facets of reading pictured by Dr. George Bond, reading specialist at the State University of New York at New Paltz, as a reading tree (see Figure 1). Dr. Bond visualizes the complete reading program as a tree of knowledge resting comfortably on a sound readiness for reading, as evidenced by a healthy root system which consists of separate and interrelated stages of readiness. Teachers who ignore one of these primary indications of the child's readiness for formal reading are weakening the reading tree from the very start. Children who have been brought through the intensive reading readiness programs are ready for the formal reading program represented by the tree and its related parts, the branches.

The Developmental Phase of the Reading Program. The heart of the reading program rests in the trunk of the reading tree and consists of what is usually described as the developmental or basal reading program. Children receive systematic instruction daily on an individual or small-group basis in a graded reader appropriate for their stage of development. They work hard to acquire a basic vocabulary as a foundation and then learn to read through a mastery of structural and phonetic analysis skills. The new readers learn to associate word meaning with new words and are given experiences which help them develop comprehension skills in the light of their previous understanding and experiences. As the children get older, they learn to concentrate on the perfection of reading skills, learning to read rhythmically, smoothly, and with expression. At the upper grade levels they learn how to increase reading speed and how to vary it with various types of materials.

The Recreational Phase of the Reading Program. Good home, school, and public libraries are essential if the recreational branches of the reading tree are to be fully developed. In many schools the reading program falls down because teachers and parents fail to realize that only through recreational reading can children apply the skills acquired in the developmental reading stage. Children who limit their reading experiences to a daily 20- to 30-minute instructional period with a teacher cannot begin to keep up with peers who are reading independently during the day and are taking library books home to read at night. Many of the better readers in a school will frequently read a book a day without adult assistance. They soon find that children's literature gives them many pleasures and answers many of their questions. Here they find compensation for their effort in reaching an independent reading level. Most poor readers are children who have not acquired a recreational reading habit. They need the practice which comes from reading more than a single text with a teacher. Without it, they find it becomes increasingly difficult to retain skills introduced by the teacher.

The Corrective or Remedial Phase of the Reading Program. Children who have been taken step by step through a sound reading program should be able to avoid having to spend time on the correc-

Figure 1. THE READING TREE

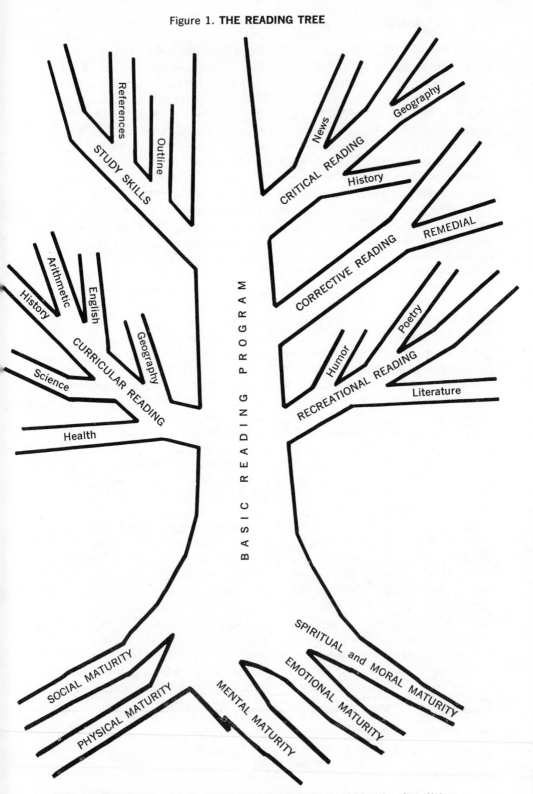

SOURCE: Reproduced by permission of Dr. George Bond, Professor of Education, State University of New York at New Paltz, and the New York State English Council.

tive or remedial branch of the reading tree. However, children who have missed preliminary steps or failed to master basic skills should be given corrective help. Minor deficiencies can be corrected in the regular day-by-day activities of a reading group, but pupils who show extreme retardation for their ability will require special assistance.

It is a mistake for the regular class teacher to stop working with those pupils who are assigned to work with a special reading teacher for corrective help. These pupils must continue working in the developmental program and in other phases of reading even as they work in the corrective phase. Through the development of a sound reading program, teachers should be able to anticipate trouble and take steps to correct problems before they reach the stage where remedial help is essential.

The Study Skills Phase of the Reading Program. Success in the intermediate and upper grades will depend upon how well specific work-study skills have been mastered. For example, research in any subject field depends upon the pupil's ability to apply his training in reading to acquire knowledge and understanding in areas other than the reading text. This means he should be able to outline, take notes, budget time, find and use other references without adult help, read for ideas, and retain what he has studied. He should be able to take examinations more effectively, because he will have acquired background and training needed to prepare for them. The study skills phase of reading is intertwined with the functional or curricular reading branches and can seldom be isolated from them.

The Curricular Reading Phase of the Reading Program. The true test of the pupil's progress in climbing the reading tree depends upon how steady he is when he gets out on the subject-centered branches of the big limb called curricular reading. For example, fifth-grade pupils who are making slow progress in the fifth-grade reader will have trouble reading geography, history, English, science, or arithmetic books bearing a fifth-grade label. They must be able to put their reading skills to work if they are to abstract ideas, knowledge, or special skills from these graded textbooks. They must be able to read new words and give them meaning in terms of their use in special subject fields. This is where they use such study skills as reading maps, charts, tables, diagrams, and figures. Statistics must have meaning as a pupil reads them, not merely when the teacher explains them. The curricular branch and its offshoots do not stand alone. Branches from the recreational limb enrich the subject, branches from the study skills limb aid them in finding materials and understanding them, and the critical reading branches enable them to evaluate what is read.

When children read in a special subject field, the role of the teacher is still that of a reading teacher. She must recognize that children will not achieve desired goals unless they can apply their reading skills to the new body of knowledge or to special skills associated with the subject. This will be especially true where the new material is loaded with new words, special terms or phrases, and new concepts. Thus it becomes the teacher's responsibility to help pupils read more effectively in the subject of the moment.

The Critical Reading Phase of the Reading Program. Critical reading is "thinking reading." Children who cannot rest their weight on this set of branches are only partially educated. This is the key stage of the reading process for life in a democracy. In America the ability to think, as one works in any content area, is an asset for a fuller life.

Classroom teachers will find this phase of reading is most difficult to teach. It calls for a type of teaching that many traditional teachers are not prepared to carry out. Getting boys and girls to evaluate what they have read is a skill that calls for more than mere regurgitation of the facts and figures found in a text. We often encounter bright students who can memorize easily but are lost when asked to give their own interpretation of what they have read. They cannot evaluate ideas or facts in the light of research and then use their knowledge to solve real problems in the everyday world about them. Too many pupils assume that if it appears in print, it is true. They need to learn to read from a variety of sources, to compare, and then to make their own generalizations. Pupils who have not learned to read critically and think creatively are vulnerable targets for propaganda specialists. Here, every teacher has a prime responsibility to help children read for more than mere information or skill.

Problems Created for Teachers by Basic Readers. Boys and girls do not usually master *all* of the reading skills taught, and many may learn a rule or skill only to lose it with the passing of time. Reading experts recognize this and may introduce skills two or three years before children are expected to master them, relying on review of these skills, as well as on sequential development. As a guide to teachers, some basic readers are usually cover-coded by the use of dots, stars, lines, or figures. Thus a "3-2" indicates a book that is normally recommended for the second half of the third grade. With the acceptance of graded basic readers has come pressure to categorize pupils in terms of the books completed by the end of the school year. This frequently leads teachers to push boys and girls through a book in order to meet an arbitrary grade standard. By the same token, teachers may have pupils in their top groups coast in order to preserve the next level reader for a subsequent grade. As a result:

Many bright pupils who read very well and who could master the reading skills ordinarily introduced one, two, or three grades above the one they are in are held to activities that lack challenge.

Two young children receive special help in reading; in background, other children work at another level.

Many pupils with average reading ability will finish books assigned to a grade; some of these will be able to proceed with the book designated for the next grade when school resumes in the fall, but others will regress over the summer and need to review basic skills.

Slow progressing pupils may complete only a portion of the reading books recommended for a grade. Each year they fall further and further behind, with the result that they are unable to find success in normal readers designated for higher grades. School becomes increasingly frustrating as their inability to read in special subject areas is reflected in poor marks and a feeling that they don't belong.

GRADEDNESS VS. CONTINUOUS PROGRESS IN
THE TEACHING OF READING

Grade standards fall down when children from different socioeconomic areas are brought together in the classroom. It is wrong to expect them to progress through the same readers at the same rate of speed. This is where grouping procedures fall down! If teachers take pupils where they find them in September and allow them to progress steadily from one learning skill to the next, they will not end up at the same level of the learning ladder in June. This has led many teachers to support the concept of "continuous progress" in the teaching of reading. Thus boys and girls are assigned to teachers so as to fit into teachable groups. Here they receive instruction in terms of past achievement and readiness to master higher-level skills and concepts. Grade level restrictions are not considered important as long as teacher and pupils work purposefully from one sequential learning activity to the next. Under the concept of continuous progress, pupils may not fail in a second or third grade. They merely begin work in the new school year with materials that were not completed at the close of the preceding year.

Acceptance Levels in Schools Not Recognizing Continuous Progress. In schools where teachers are expected to teach in terms of grade expectation levels, the teachers have to come to an understanding as to what reading levels mean. For example, average achievement for second-grade pupils may range from one second-grade book level below 2-2 to one book level above. Thus, if a boy has finished a 2-1 book by June, his progress may still be considered as normal for the grade. It will mean that subsequent teachers will have to work with books below a designated grade, but this is to be expected. Achievement test scores repeatedly show how futile it is to expect uniform performance. Due to individual differences, a range of five years in reading achievement is not unusual in a fourth grade. This range will be extended for each higher grade level.

One group of teachers eliminated friction among staff members by establishing an acceptance level for pupils that was below normal grade level standards. Of course, establishing acceptance levels for children at designated grade levels will vary with different communities or schools. It is foolish to expect book-deprived children to progress at the same rates of speed as pupils coming from high socioeconomic levels where reading materials are more available. In the former situation, few students will come close to the acceptance levels shown in Table 2 for average learners. In the latter community, the achievement shown for bright pupils could represent low-level performance.

The graded textbook may suit a national average, but many schools are filled with classes that do not conform to a normal curve distribution of ability, experience, or interest. Dissatisfaction with the problem of trying to place children in teachable groups has led to some changes in school organizational plans. For example, "cross-grade" grouping has enabled teachers to work with boys and girls who have a common

TABLE 2

Guidelines for Teachers Who Must Subscribe to
Grade Standard Restrictions

Name of Basic Reader (Ginn Basic Readers)	Achievement Level Desired by June	Acceptable Level for Average Pupils	Possible Levels for Bright Pupils
Grade 1			
Readiness materials			
Preprimers			
Little White House (1-1)			
On Cherry Street (1-2)	1-2	1-1	2-1
Grade 2			
We Are Neighbors (2-1)			
Around the Corner (2-2)	2-2	2-1	3-1
Grade 3			
Finding New Neighbors (3-1)			
Friends Far and Near (3-2)	3-2	3-1	4-1
Grade 4			
Roads to Everywhere	4	Halfway through 4	5 or above
Grade 5			
Trails to Treasure	5	Halfway through 5	6 or above
Grade 6			
Wings to Adventure	6	Halfway through 6	Reading independently

reading need. Here, achievement, interest, or special reading needs may be the basis of pupil assignment. Grade levels as such are no longer considered important. Some duplication of teacher effort is avoided, and teachers are given more time to work with fewer divisions or subdivisions of a grade or set of grades. Some schools preserve grade lines but subscribe to some form of nongradedness for children of a common chronological age range. In a few schools the problem of grouping may be resolved by the introduction of individualized reading programs: each pupil moves through the basic readers or controlled reading activities at his own pace. Some principals have preserved the traditional graded structure but attempted to resolve the number of reading groups and the issue of standards by regrouping the pupils at the very top or very bottom of a class to limit the spread of achievement in a designated section of a grade.

The Problem of Encroachment on Another Teacher's Domain. When all teachers in a school subscribe to true nongradedness, or what may be called continuous progress, the problem of teacher encroachment should not exist. In such schools, activities are prescribed for groups of children on the basis of readiness for new levels of learning. If a fourth-grade teacher finds eight pupils, most of them boys, who cannot read at a third-grade instructional level, she teaches them lower grade-level skills. By the same token, if she has eight pupils, most likely all girls, who show mastery of the basic skills normally taught in the fourth grade, she takes them into higher-level readers or introduces them to poetry, high-level literature, or encourages greater independent reading.

However, a visitor can enter most elementary schools and find teachers working with pupils at levels below standards set for a grade, but seldom, if ever, will he find very many teachers working with books one, two, and even three grade levels higher than the grade itself. Repeatedly, teachers have said, "We know our better children can complete the basic reader early, but we can't put them into books of the next grade. Mrs. Sheffield won't like it." There are many Mrs. Sheffields who believe that they are to teach the books assigned to a grade. If children are allowed to progress at their own rates in lower grades, what will be left to teach? Therefore, woe to the teacher who trespasses on her domain!

Moving Children Through a Controlled Accelerated Reading Program Without Missing Essential Skills. Bright children can avoid frustration with a program of continuous progress since they are allowed to accelerate through a graded series of activities without actually skipping a grade and its related activities. The key to such action will be the teacher and her skill at evaluating progress. Through the use of formal and informal tests she can determine whether or not the children are reading too fast. Have they learned the skills shown in her checklist? How do they measure in areas calling for comprehension skills? This latter area should be the one that receives the *greatest* amount of consideration. High scores on reading tests in word analysis or phonetic analysis have little meaning if the pupils show low comprehension. When this happens, the pupils need to slow down their vertical growth to concentrate their attention in areas that will lead to better understanding.

Planned acceleration may begin with first-grade children who need little in the way of readiness activities. These pupils work together with preprimers long before their slower peers. They may not need to read all the preprimers, or they may finish all those prescribed, but skip the extra practice associated with supplementary ones. Essential reading skills are taught sequentially or as needed, yet the fast readers who are allowed to progress continuously on the basis of reading success or performance may complete all basic first-grade requirements by March. By June they may complete the first stage of a second-grade reading program.

In September, the pupils pick up with the second-grade reading activities dropped in June. This may mean completing or reviewing a 2-1 reader prior to starting a 2-2 reader. By January these children may be ready to start work with the first stages of a third-grade reading program and by June they may have completed the entire third-grade reading curriculum. With freedom to continue to accelerate, these pupils may enter the fifth and sixth grades ready to read one or two grade levels above their average-learning peers. At this stage the level of a reader will become insignificant, because the children should be concentrating on the improvement of work-study skills and research skills to ensure continued success with independent reading activities.

Since reading is an individual activity, the bright pupils may not require daily reading sessions with a teacher. Once they have mastered prescribed skills, they should be encouraged to explore new areas such as drama and poetry. For example, children who have been exposed to poetry reading may find parallel activities in the area of language arts that may be reflected in poetry writing. The reading of plays may lead to simple playwriting and dramatic presentations. These pupils will find many ways to express themselves once they know the basic techniques for successful independent language arts activity.

Extensive Reading Required Before a Child Becomes a Proficient Reader. While some children can accelerate, large segments of the school population continue to fall behind each year. This will be especially true of reading-disadvantaged children. Many of them may be lucky if they can show a five or six months' growth in ten months of schooling. Language deficiencies, lack of motivation, or too few experiences may be important factors in their failure to find success with reading. Many children, however, fail to become proficient readers because they have never read enough satisfying books to acquire the habit of reading.

Reading is like bike riding. It has to be worked at day after day. Talking about reading or listening to others read will not suffice: The individual has to take books which are adequate for his stage of development and peruse them. He may start with picture books or books with a simplified vocabulary, but the essential thing is that he is continually working with reading materials. He will have to build his vocabulary and learn how to extract meaning from new words. With practice his speed increases and he can read without having to turn to the teacher for assistance. Reading has to become automatic.

During a typical day children are exposed to many kinds of written material, much of it even more difficult than that used in their reading groups. A constant diet of such frustration will not suffice. They need to read and read, but they have to have practice with recreational materials—books, for example, that are not as difficult as the basic reader. The constant diet of textbooks must be supplemented by library books and supplementary easy readers. As a rule of thumb, these books should be about a grade below normal class instructional levels, although extremely poor readers may drop their recreational reading level down two or three years unless the teacher guides them in the selection of books which appeal to their special interests and which are within their range of comprehension.

Children who do not acquire the habit of reading whole books before reaching adolescence may never do so. They need to feel secure with the world of books and find enjoyment in them, otherwise the pressures of adolescence, rigid secondary school assignments, and new interests will deter them from starting books other than those assigned for reading.

Elementary school teachers can encourage the habit of reading through the introduction of interesting library books at the lowest grade levels. These books should appeal to the natural interests of children and should be read with at least 90 per cent comprehension. The vocabulary should not be too difficult. As a rule, young children should not encounter more than one difficult word in a hundred running words. To encourage wide reading, the authors recommend the reorganization of the typical elementary school day to provide *at least one free reading period of at least twenty to thirty minutes.* Where this has been done, teachers find that children will acquire some of the practice they need to become familiar with something more than textbooks.

Intensive Reading Needed as Well. While advocating *extensive* reading as a supplement to textbooks, it is essential that teachers continue to give pupils *intensive* reading experiences. She has to be prepared to help them discover new reading techniques, and from time to time they will need to brush up on skills introduced earlier. If the intermediate grade teachers are stressing independent reading activities, it may help to pull even the best readers into a "special needs group" for review or for help with new aspects of reading. For example, the new group may find it helpful to share their reading experiences. The teacher may find that encouraging them to think about their reading experiences helps them grow. For real understanding they must take time to digest what they read. They must be encouraged to speculate about the characters or a situation. Students cannot begin to read creatively until they can begin to infer things from their reading—until they can visualize a setting or a character without having to have every detail labeled by the author.

In teaching creative reading, teachers have to help children see *relationships between and among people and situations.* They have to anticipate what is going to happen. It helps if they can see how a story ends and at the same time can visualize a different ending. The reader may need help in sensing the mood of a story or poem from descriptive words. This may call for activities based on developing the children's power of mental imagery. For example, the teacher may read a selection orally, or, better still, she may play a recording of a story or poem in which a talented actor uses his voice to express emotions that are not revealed in ordinary class readings. In this instance the auditory approach supports the visual stage to the point that the individual student may project himself through the printed page to other lands and other times.

Children must learn to read beneath the surface. They need to ask themselves such questions as, "How?" "Why?" "Is this possible?" "What is the author really trying to tell me?" This kind of reading may take more time and may require more effort. There will be times when the pupil just reads for pleasure, but he has to vary such reading with something that has depth, something that leads him to think, to make comparisons, to ask questions. Such reading is necessary and need not be dull if pupils are encouraged to read in fields of current controversy that are within their range of understanding.

Providing for Individual Differences in Reading Through Subgrouping

Much of the subgrouping done in modern schools centers around reading activities. Primary grade teachers are usually prepared to work with three subgroups. Intermediate grade teachers may plan subgrouping activities, but the wide range in achievement and in reading differences may create frustrating problems. Upper grade teachers may do some group work, but many of these teachers still need help in understanding the basic concepts of subgrouping. Grouping for many of these teachers consists of homogeneity of classes within a grade rather than homogeneous subdivisions of a class. If teachers are going to work constructively to teach essential reading skills appropriate for materials used at different age or grade levels, there should be a consistent pattern of grouping and teaching within an entire school or

Participating in a special project to help improve reading ability and interest, these children hear a story at the same time that they read it in an effort to increase rapid, automatic responses to words in print.

Members of this subgroup receive individual attention for their particular reading difficulties.

school system. Where this does not occur, the efforts of teachers and pupils may result in growth that is far from what could be achieved.

SETTING UP SUBGROUPS IN ELEMENTARY GRADES

One of the first responsibilities a teacher has to her new class is to get acquainted with them through the use of records and observations. In many classes the teacher may need to use informal as well as formal tests to determine strengths and weaknesses. Once this has been done, the teacher can begin to structure her classes in terms of small teachable subgroups. How she groups and what she does with the children in a particular section will vary according to their ages and stages of development. Most elementary school teachers tend to assign pupils to reading groups on the basis of achievement, but intermediate grade teachers will find that *interest* can be the basis for grouping. When the teacher first assigns pupils to a group, she does so on an experimental basis. If some individuals cannot work successfully in a particular book or with a series of special learning activities, they may be reassigned to other work groups. When the nature of the work changes, some of the children may be reassigned to other groups or they may even work in two different learning groups.

Some of the advantages of a reading program based upon subgrouping are:

1. Instruction is personalized when a teacher can work with six to twelve boys and girls who have common reading needs. Children can get to know the teacher, and she can become familiar with their specific stages of growth and development. No pupil is lost in a small group; sooner or later he will have his chance to read or talk. He cannot hide his inability to read or his unwillingness to try, the way he can in an all-class situation.

2. Reading books and work assignments suited to the specific stages of readiness or growth of individual children can be used.

3. Subgrouping allows boys and girls to work at their own rates of speed without feeling pressure that they should be competing with pupils achieving at higher reading levels.

4. Growth in reading is promoted by small group instruction, instruction in new reading skills, and in oral and silent reading activities centering around common problems, interests, and levels of reading achievement.

5. Average and fast learners are not held back by pupils who require much more time to master concepts or lower-level reading skills.

Most primary grade teachers can work successfully with two or three small groups. As pupils become adjusted to school and its requirements, individual differences make themselves apparent to the observant teacher. This has led second- and third-grade teachers to consider the formation of a fourth or even fifth reading group. In some instances a "buddy system" will enable teachers to avoid the necessity of such action, through an interchange of pupils who do not fit into current groups. In other schools the principal may help structure a class by reassigning isolates or deviate children—those at the extreme top or extreme bottom of a class—to other groups, thus enabling the teacher to work with a narrower range of reading needs.

The better the teaching in the primary grade, the greater the spread in achievement in upper grades; therefore, the need to improve grouping practices becomes increasingly important. An intermediate grade teacher cannot expect to work with five or six subgroups on the same basis that primary teachers work with three sections. She does not have enough time to teach multiple groups in all phases of the curriculum, but individual pupil needs are so complex and varied that they cannot always be met with the assignment to semipermanent reading groups. Intermediate grade teachers should therefore be prepared to do some subgroup work in reading. A low reading group may have to meet daily, whereas a fast learning group may meet the teacher only two or three times a week. If she is working with the development of functional reading skills, special needs classes may be formed to help pupils as they work in curricular reading. These special-purpose groups do not have to be permanent. If the teacher is flexible, the composition of such groups can be varied from time to time. The time problem may be partially solved by integrating reading and language arts activities, and then integrating both types of activity, with such special subjects as social studies, science, and mathematics.

One approach to grouping at middle and upper grade levels calls for the departmentalization of reading. All pupils in a given grade are assigned to teachers on the basis of achievement. This same plan can be extended to include pupils from three or four grades, with the result that no teacher has to work with more than two subdivisions on a given day.

In many upper grade classes it is possible to introduce a new skill to the entire class, with subgroups being formed only when it becomes apparent that some students need additional practice. For example, a fourth-grade teacher may introduce the dictionary to the entire class, with subgroups being formed to give some pupils extra help in grasping diacritical marks. Again, everyone may work with alphabetization beyond the first letter. Pupils who show proficiency in this area can work independently, while further instruction on a small-group basis is given to those in need of assistance.

Independent Seat Activities for Pupils. Many kinds of reading activities will be found in teacher manuals and workbooks, ranging from those that require wide reading to those merely calling for the insertion of words in a blank space. Following are some independent reading activities to occupy pupils while the teacher concerns herself with one of the class subgroups.

Reading supplementary readers or library books.

Making and using word dictionaries with magazine pictures with names or descriptive words. Words giving trouble are written down and defined for study.

Writing creative stories, poems, jokes, descriptions, or personal experiences.

Illustrating stories they have read or heard.

Making "get well" cards for classmates or relatives who are ill, or crossword puzzles based on the use of reading or spelling words.

Making outlines based upon their work in special subject areas.

Working with commercially prepared materials developed to measure comprehension or speed (i.e., standardized timed reading tests).

Engaging in activities calling for work analysis skill.

Writing a script to dramatize a story or exciting incident.

Conferring with peermates when they have questions. Here team learning is recognized.

Viewing film strips or other visual aids.

Practicing selections to read to children in lower grades.

What pupils do when they have a choice can be most revealing to the teacher who attempts to evaluate their actions when they are working at their seats. By working with her pupils, she can see where they are challenged and where they have merely been doing busy work.

Unfortunately, teachers seem to feel that pupils have to put something on paper to demonstrate that they have fulfilled their obligations. This is true of classwork and homework. As a result, many children spend hours trying to complete fairly meaningless written activities, when they should be reading instead. When in doubt about what to give pupils for seatwork, teachers should give them more independent reading time. Group sharing periods will help teachers evaluate what the pupils do when they are not supervised.

TABLE 3

Activities of Children in Sixth Grade During Reading Instruction

Group A (Average readers, pupils making steady progress)	Group B (Slow or immature readers making slow progress)	Group C (Mature or rapid readers working well independently)
Pupils in group A go to assigned work area while teacher talks to pupils in group B. She tells these children what to look for in their reading activities at their seats as first group books are passed out and introductory period of silent reading begins. Teacher illustrates point for pupils in low reading group before releasing them.		Pupils in group C have an outline posted on the rear wall indicating areas of study or projects they are working on for science and social studies classes.
Teacher stops silent reading, asks questions to see if pupils know what they have been reading. She reviews number of new and difficult words for meaning and pronunciation, asks questions to see if pupils can tell what is inferred from certain clues or passages. Pupils reread orally selected portion of story, discussing it as they read. At end of lesson teacher passes out guide sheet and tells pupils to try to answer designated questions as they read new assignment at their seats.	Pupils are given books by group chairman. They read quietly in search of descriptive passages which they will be able to read orally to the other pupils. Passages may describe people, places, or dramatic incidents. A pupil from top group is ready to help pupils who seem to be in need of help. (Group is working with fourth-grade book.) Pupils who finish search go to library table for recreational reading book, but most pupils read quietly, making notes of location of passages they consider truly descriptive.	Pupils pair off in groups or work alone on search activities. Pupil chairman rotates to see that every pupil is studying references dealing with appropriate topics. Pupils go to reference shelves or use books in desks to begin a piece of research or continue from where they left off previously. Some pupils quietly take notes, others make charts or illustrations. Chairman may quietly discuss progress of pupils as he circulates room.

Group A (Average readers, pupils making steady progress)	Group B (Slow or immature readers making slow progress)	Group C (Mature or rapid readers working well independently)
Pupils return to seats where they quietly read new assignments in beginning section of sixth-grade basic reader. As they read, they look for answers to questions on guide sheets. When in doubt about a point, teacher permits gathering of no more than three pupils to discuss the reading assignment.	Teacher reviews new words with pupils in group B. They discuss meaning of words, discuss the need for descriptions in books. Pupils take turns reading their descriptive passages. Other pupils try to identify characters, places, or events. Pupils practice reading descriptions for expression of mood or thought. Teacher questions lead to discussion of central character's leadership qualities.	Pupils continue with assignments. Chairman and three pupils move to a corner of room to discuss progress of various pupils in relation to beginning of reports on group activities.
Pupils continue working on new reading assignment. As pupils finish, they turn to study of spelling words or quietly take out recreational readers in preparation for forthcoming book report.	Pupils return to seats to start assignments. Some have sheets with reading activities to help them with certain skills. Some read library book for oral book report. Some write descriptions as they reread story discussed in class.	Individually pupils go to teacher to report on progress, ask questions. Teacher sees that pupils are using references wisely and are taking appropriate type notes. Shows group of three how they should present material in outline form.

LOCATING THE STUDENT'S READING LEVEL
AND SPECIAL READING NEEDS

Before attempting to assign her new pupils to one or more reading groups, the teacher should review the background of each individual. This may involve a study of past achievement test scores, teacher reports of pupil progress in basic readers, report card grades, health records, and any other pertinent data which will help support her own observations as she begins to evaluate their skill and ability when they work with her. Primarily the teacher will want to identify each student's *instructional* level and determine from this the pupil's ultimate *frustration* level as well as his *independent* or *recreational reading* level. Experienced teachers may readily determine where children need special help or instruction, but new teachers may find it difficult to initiate balanced instructional groups. Due to lack of experience or training, considerable time may be wasted on trial-and-error grouping activities.

The following comments illustrate techniques used by different teachers:

> I simply use the promotion list as a guide to placing children into groups in September. It tells me what books individual pupils were reading in and I proceed from there. When I get acquainted with the children, I frequently assign pupils to new learning levels.

> I place children in their respective groups partly by test results, partly by IQ's, and partly by the fluency and comprehension shown when they read to me individually or as part of a tentative group.

> First of all, I make a survey of their oral reading, then I try to measure their silent reading skill through many informal tests. I prefer to depend upon my own judgment, based upon years of teaching, to standardized test results.

> I rely heavily upon standardized test results and I note reports of low pupil progress in areas like spelling. I pay special attention to teacher comments indicating good work study habits. These pupils tend to make the best progress and should be placed in a top group.

The fact that teachers are not consistent in their grouping procedures can lead to mistakes in pupil assignments. This possibility is always present when too much emphasis has been placed on a promotion list or a single teacher report or test score. The subjectiveness of teacher marks may negate the value of marks as a criterion. When using standard test marks, there is always the question of validity plus the fact that the test is a frustration instrument. Thus, instructional levels should be set at about one-half grade or one book (in a two-book series) *below* the grade designation for the text. Teachers must also allow for considerable regression over the summer months. This factor helps account for the fact that several weeks of each new school year must be devoted to review or reteaching of skills taught at a lower grade level. It may also be considered as one reason for regrouping when a teacher begins to work with a new class.

TABLE 4
A Guide for Teachers in Identifying Appropriate Reading Levels

---

Each teacher should be prepared to identify the various reading levels of her students. Reference may be made to a series of teacher-made tests or to a commercially prepared survey test. In many cases a teacher will be able to use informal reading techniques to determine whether or not a pupil is reading material which fits into one of the following categories:

His independent reading level

A pupil should read a book that he can understand and enjoy. He should miss no more than one word out of one hundred running words, with 90 per cent comprehension. In addition he should demonstrate that he has good silent reading habits.

His instructional reading level

This should offer a continual challenge. It will be above the independent reading level and below a frustration level. For success at the instructional reading level the pupil should: (1) miss no more than one word out of twenty running words or five out of one hundred; and (2) understand from 75 to 85 per cent of what he reads.

His frustration reading level

Children need to encounter success after success in their reading endeavors; therefore, when they approach a frustration point, it is time to stop. Failure to reassign pupils to easier reading materials often turns them against anything associated with reading. The teacher may consider pupils working at or close to the frustration level when they: (1) miss one running word out of every ten they read; (2) fail to comprehend at the 50 to 60 per cent level.

Teachers have to acquaint themselves with their students' various reading levels. Some use the guiding principles shown in Table 4 as a frame of reference when they try to classify students in terms of instructional, recreational or independent, and frustration levels of reading. Their ultimate decisions regarding such levels may be based on a combination of factors, such as data from records plus their own informal tests during the first weeks of school.

Growth in reading achievement will show imperceptible gains if children continue to work close to frustration levels. If the pupil is kept at this level, his insecurity may become evident to the observer who may notice mispronunciation of words, word substitution, repetition of words, or simple waiting for someone to tell or pronounce the next word. An individual may be considered as working above his instructional level when the teacher has to literally *push* the pupil through a basic reader.

Informal Reading Inventory to Establish Reading Levels and Areas Where Special Instruction Is Needed. Teachers electing to go beyond the guidelines established by rate of reading and comprehension may use an informal reading inventory to help identify pupil reading levels in areas where special instruction is necessary. They may devise their own testing materials or they may base their survey on commercially prepared materials. Because of the complexity of some of the commercially prepared materials, a teacher may limit her study to those pupils who show the greatest need for help; however, some school systems use teacher aides or substitute teachers to assist the teacher while she is making her survey.

TABLE 5
A Typical Informal Reading Inventory

Selecting the reading materials

The teacher should select a set of graded readers that are new to the children in the first three or four grades. Selections for older pupils should be taken from special areas other than reading. In either case, the teacher should make certain that the survey materials are devoid of technical words or phrases that could confuse the reader.

Selecting the paragraphs to be read

Teachers may have students read designated paragraphs from different level books, or they may provide the pupils with duplicated copies of the selections to be read. These guidelines should be observed:
   1. Selections of 100 to 150 words should be taken from the middle of one or more graded readers.
   2. Two different selections should be taken from both the primer and first readers. Preferably they should come from the beginning and end since vocabulary steps up rapidly at these initial reading levels.

The preparation of evaluative questions for designated selections

In a very informal situation, children are asked questions by the teacher after they have read a selection. A more valid result is obtained when questions are prepared in advance and kept on cards for easy reference. In some cases a single question will suffice to show that a pupil cannot read successfully at a designated level. In other cases, several selections from different parts of a book may be required with appropriate questioning after each trial. In preparing these questions, the teacher should observe the following guides:

1. Mere oral reading will not suffice, so a set of questions should be prepared to go with each silent reading selection. The student should be able to answer at least half of them correctly if he understands what he has read.

2. Two or three questions should be based upon recognition of details.

3. At least one question should be of the inferential type. It should require reasoning with the facts found in the reading selection.

4. At least one question should be concerned with the ability to follow a thought sequence.

5. At least one question should be based upon the identification of the central theme or idea in the selection.

Reading the selection

1. During the first two or three weeks, children read for the teacher either individually or in small groups. She has several selections prepared in terms of the range of reading expected, but she may not have a pupil read more than one selection at a sitting. Each teacher will work out her own timing in terms of class size, the time available, and the interest and response of the children to the informal test situation.

2. Teacher and pupil should hold their own copies of the reading selections.

3. The teacher should note how the pupil holds his book, along with any special mannerisms, "crutches," or other signs of poor reading habits.

4. The pupil should start reading in a fairly easy book and proceed to read increasingly more difficult material until his independent, instructional, and frustration reading levels have been identified.

5. The pupil is asked to read orally several brief samples at sight. (This should not be done in the regular group reading session, but during a period when teacher and pupil can work together relatively alone.) The student should be given a chance to read the selection silently before it is read orally.

Through listening to the pupil read orally, the teacher is able to observe immediately whether the selection is too easy or too difficult. As an observer, she can note faulty oral reading habits. Comprehension is determined by evaluating the individual's response to the questions asked following the oral reading.

6. The pupil may be asked to tell what he has read after being asked to read selections silently. This gives the teacher a check on the student's memory and ability to recall key bits of information. She may find oral rereading desirable to recheck on points missed.

In both the silent and oral reading exercises, commercially prepared materials may show pupil ability in terms of grade equivalents based on the time taken to read and the number of questions answered correctly.

Use of a Checklist. Instruction can be pinpointed if teachers will develop and use a checklist to record mastery of essential reading skills or areas where special reading assistance is desired. Table 6 shows a composite picture of information that can be recorded for each pupil in the class. The data may be abbreviated or expanded depending upon the age-grade range of the pupils assigned to work with a teacher. In one school system a separate card is used for each student to show when and where each separate reading skill is introduced or mastered. Succeeding teachers recheck the pupil's mastery of the silent and oral reading skills and plan small-group instruction for those who have common learning needs. Students identified because they do not have many common reading needs may be given individual instruction, or they may work with children in other classrooms who are coping with similar phases of reading or problem areas.

Determining Reading Achievement and Reading Capacity. One reason for grouping children is to help bring reading achievement closer to reading capacity. Unfortunately, reading achievement is usually evaluated in terms of grade standards and not pupil capacity. This is hardly fair to pupils who have limited mental ability or who come from very low socioeconomic levels. While such children may bear fourth-, fifth-, or sixth-grade labels, they should not be penalized for failing to work successfully with graded materials. All too often classroom teachers are pressured by parents, school administrators, and other teachers to push slow-progressing pupils into reading materials which are *beyond expectation levels* for their capacity. Reading teachers are inclined to place too much emphasis on the intelligence quotient. Since IQ merely refers to a rate of learning, the mental age (MA) may be more helpful. It refers to an individual's *maturity level* at a given time, and can be translated into a reading age to give the teacher the pupil's reading capacity, thus: A reading test score may be given as a grade equivalent or as a reading age. A pupil with a raw score of 30 in reading comprehension could receive a grade equivalent of 4.6 or a reading age of 9-10. The RA indicates that he is reading on the level of average boys and girls who have reached the chronological age of 9 years and 10 months.

It may suffice for the average teacher to stop with the reading age because, by comparing actual achievement in terms of expectancy levels for their mental ages, the teacher can see when pupils are making normal, average, or slow progress in reading.

For example, a fourth-grade teacher can see that a girl who has a reading age of 9-10 and a chronological age of 9-10 is reading on a level comparable with average peers. In contrast, a boy, who is chronologically 11-0 years old has a reading age of 10.4. By simple comparison one can see that he is not reading up to his chronological age. The implication in a traditional school would be that the boy is lazy or is not working up to grade level expectation, but a study of their comparative mental ages will show a different story. The girl actually has a mental age of 10-8, which is equivalent to a reading expectation of 5.4. This would indicate that she is working about eight months below her actual capacity. But the boy's mental age of 10-5 shows a potential capacity of 5.2. This would indicate that he is working just one month below the achievement level for his potential. In this illustration, mental age tells the teacher a story that is not always apparent to the casual observer. Most people would have pressured the boy to work at higher levels, whereas the girl would be lauded for working so well. Actually she could work at a somewhat higher reading level.

Statistically minded teachers may want to work with the index known as the reading quotient since it will show them mathematically how students read in terms of actual mental ages. Thus, the reading quotient (RQ) would be determined by working the following formula:

$$RQ = \frac{\text{Reading age (RA)}}{\text{Mental age (MA)}}$$

A reading age which is the same as the mental age would give a reading quotient of 1.00. If the RA is less than the MA, the RQ will indicate reading retardation in terms of the per cent of capacity. While few classroom teachers are interested in a more refined measure, some reading specialists and principals may want to use a reading index (RI) to show the amount of retardation in reading. They may want to use a weighted formula which gives consideration to chronological age as well as mental age, and if they are working with gifted pupils, they will find it desirable to refer to the formulas showing expected achievement in reading and arithmetic (see Chapter 5). However, for simple computations of average-children expectation levels that are more exact than the one given above, they may want to try the following formula:

$$RQ = \frac{\text{RA}}{2\,\text{MA} + \text{CA} \div 3}$$

Statisticians may include elements other than MA, but to average teachers the foregoing may be more than they will use or understand. If they are satisfied with an approximate estimate of capacity, they may find the simple rule of thumb procedure recommended below will meet their needs.

Easy Ways to Determine Reading Expectation Levels. Since teachers with a limited statistical background seldom become involved

TABLE 6

A Composite List of Oral and Silent Reading Deficiencies

Types of Reading Deficiencies	Pupil Names							
Chronological age								
Mental age								
Reading age								
Actual instructional level								
Reading achievement test—grade equivalent								
Vocabulary achievement								
Comprehension level								
Inefficient reading habits								
Habits of pointing								
Physical habits:								
Vision								
Hearing								
Voice and speech control								
Body movements showing tension								
Position of book, relation to eyes								
Body position								
Fluency of reading								
Word-by-word reading								
Inadequate phrasing								
Habitual repetitions								
Disregard for punctuation								
Attempting to read too fast								
Dawdling over reading material								
Word recognition—word analysis								
Lack of basic sight vocabulary								
Errors on easy words								
Failure to use context clues								
Ineffective visual analysis of words								
Ineffective knowledge of visual, structural, and phonetic elements								
Overanalytical:								
Analyzes known words								
Breaks words into too many parts								
Uses a spelling attack								
Unable to attack common words								
Fails to get word meaning								

Comprehension skills									
Failure to get main idea									
Failure to see important details									
Inability to reproduce thought									
Inability to make inferences									
Inability to skim									
Inability to outline									
Inability to adjust rate to different types of comprehensions									
Inability to discuss reading									
Inability to do elaborate thinking									
Inability to organize topics									
Lack of sense of paragraph organization									
Lack of phrasing ability									
Insufficient sentence sense									
Insufficient experience to understand reading selection									
Inability to use index									
Lack of skill in use of dictionary									
Inability to alphabetize									
Reading attitude									
An aversion toward reading									
Indifference to books (reads only as directed, not on own)									
A short attention span									
Easily distracted									
Extra reading habits									
Unnecessary vocalization									
Overdependence on marker									
Loses place easily									
Lip movements in silent reading									
Unnatural voice									
Irregular eye movements									
Head movements									
Other types of reading deficiencies									
No ear for sound									
Omitting portions of sentences									
Dependency on others to pronounce words									
Poor word recognition of words similar in meaning									
Eye strain, evidenced by frowning, squinting, rubbing eyes									
Poor work study habits									
Inability to express or sense feeling									

Note: Difficulties which are checked should be based on repeated observation of weakness. Infrequent or occasional errors should not be counted.

in refined studies of pupil achievement in terms of expectation levels, they may find that they can determine capacity levels through one of the following procedures:

1. *Using an age-grade table to determine reading expectancy level.* When the teacher administers a group intelligence test, she will find an age-grade table in the manual. It gives her the pupil's mental age and an intelligence grade placement for the mental age. If the intelligence test is given at the same time as the reading test, the teacher can readily compare the pupil's reading achievement with that expected for his mental age. If the pupil's listed mental age is not recent, it may be brought up to date. Thus, for a rough calculation, she may multiply the pupil's IQ by his CA. This will not give an exact mental age in the same sense that a new test would, but it can be used to serve as a working index to estimate potential reading expectancy levels.

2. *Simply subtracting the pupil's reading grade from his mental age.* Mental ages given in the table referred to above have been computed to show reading ages based on computing the norms of several types of achievement and intelligence tests. Simply stated, the mental age may be considered as equivalent to the reading age, so it becomes the expectancy level. Therefore, a teacher can subtract a pupil's reading grade equivalent from the pupil's mental age to see how achievement compares with the individual's expected reading achievement.

3. *Rule of thumb.* Rough estimates of the pupil's reading grade may be made by simply subtracting 5 from the pupil's mental age. This will approximate the pupil's reading grade. Simple comparison with actual reading grade equivalents will show how the pupil's achievement stands in relation to actual potential.

4. *Use of anticipated achievement tables based on multiple norming.* At least one standardized achievement test publisher, the California Test Bureau, has developed tables in its manuals which can be used to compare actual achievement with anticipated achievement. Large anticipated achievement charts are available to help determine whether children are working up to expectation levels. The reading table shows separate achievement levels for reading vocabulary and reading comprehension. The teacher has to convert an up-to-date mental age to what is designated as the intellectual status index. If the teacher has changed the mental ages from years and months to total months, this is quickly done by reading the ISI from a chart for the mental ages given according to grades.

5. *Use of achievement expectancy tables.* Expectancy tables have been computed which will readily tell a teacher approximately what she can expect in the way of reading achievement for a given mental age.

Teachers are reminded that markedly under- or over-aged children will not have the same school and non-school experiences as average children in a given grade. Therefore, standard age-grade norms will be inappropriate. Similarly, expectation levels of culturally deprived children may appear low where mental ages are derived from an intelligence test that has a very high built-in language factor. Where children come from highly concentrated disadvantaged high schools, a culture pre-test may be used in addition to other indexes, one of which may be parental occupation and training plus teacher observation of work-study patterns, talent, etc.

The Nature of the Reading Lesson

The statement is often made that anyone can teach reading in an elementary school. Those who make such statements tend to look superficially at the content of elementary textbooks. To adults who may work with very technical material, the books are very simple. It shouldn't take much brainpower to read such "stuff" with children. What they forget or overlook is the fact that good elementary teachers are not striving to have boys and girls master the content as much as they are trying to teach them the basic reading skills *so essential* for learning in the content subjects and other areas. A good reading lesson consists of more than sitting and listening to children read a simple story.

STRUCTURING EFFECTIVE READING LESSONS
TO MEET CHILDREN'S READING NEEDS

The basic reader is merely the vehicle through which the teacher operates. Knowing what to do and when to do it are essentials for promoting maximum pupil growth in reading. For example, a reading survey may point up specific reading skills which must be taught. One group of children may need help in the use of rhyming words, another group may need help in alphabetizing, while a third group may need help in picking out main ideas. They will have many other reading needs, but it may take some time to realize the short- and long-range objectives that underlie a sound reading program. As the teachers work with different groups of children, they may have to make use of many techniques to achieve desired goals.

The same content may have to be used quite differently with a group of slow-learning students than is necessary when the teacher is helping fast learners to acquire proficiency in a given reading skill. For example: The slow-learner group will take a longer period of time and repeated exposure to an idea or concept before they understand what the teacher is trying to do. She may have to use visual, auditory, and kinesthetic exercises to present the idea and then follow up with numerous drills or practice periods. In contrast, a lesson for the faster learners may require very little in the way of background or explanation. Some pupils will grasp what she is striving for with a mere hint or outline. They can often infer from her opening remarks what is expected of them. With the first group she may have to tell children "how," but seldom "why"—as she does for faster pupils. Children who fall into the average learner classification will require concrete examples, but they will usually be able to move into areas of abstraction with a minimum of explanation and practice. These children will require more directions than the fast learners, but they will often demonstrate their readiness to work with a greater degree of independence than the slow learners.

Good teachers structure their reading lessons in terms of the problems the pupils they are working with face and how they can best learn. Thus a teacher's manual may be *ineffective* as a guide. The fact that lessons are outlined to help pupils form visual images is no reason for teaching them to students who show no weakness in this area.

Preparation for Reading Lesson. A teacher who has a specific objective in mind when she teaches a lesson will often have to set the stage for the activity through a "warm-up" period. This will often be true with a slow-learning group because of their low retention and inability to anticipate what may be coming. Frequently, these pupils will act as though they had never worked with a particular phase of reading until their memories have been jogged.

How the new selection is introduced depends upon the experiences of the students and their level of learning. With young children a teacher may want to begin by having them talk at length about incidents similar to those experienced by the characters. Sometimes this can backfire, because the pupils may be so motivated to talk that the period ends before the lesson can be taught. If a story is a continuation of one started the previous day, little time may be needed to develop the setting, characters, or plot; but when it is new, outside motivation may be needed. This is where the teacher may have to stimulate interest by sharing a personal experience. However, her attempts to motivate the children may not be too successful where children have had limited worldly experiences.

Before starting a new selection, a teacher may review troublesome words. If there are pictures, children may study them to note details or to make inferences concerning what may be coming. The preliminary discussion may lead to the introduction of new words with appropriate exercises to ensure that the pupils understand their meaning. Word drill activities so essential at primary grade levels will be replaced by discussion of key phrases at the intermediate grade levels. Here, guide questions may be used to help students locate main ideas or to assist them in visualizing a place or scene.

Silent Reading Before Oral Reading. Having been introduced to a selection, children should read a portion silently under the guidance of the teacher *if* they are going to be asked to read it orally. This will give them a chance to try their own reading skill. They become familiar with the story and can practice reading words and phrases that could trouble them before an audience. For some children, this can be important. They need to build up their reading confidence in the silent reading period. If they encounter a new word, they can try to break it into syllables or they can try to determine its meaning from the context. Should they still need help, the teacher can provide it. Many teachers make a mental or written note of troublesome words and then find opportunities to review them with the individual students who missed them.

Building Skills by Oral Reading. Children read orally to realize many different objectives. They will read for information or for skill in pronunciation and enunciation. It may be necessary to read for expression, with attention being paid to punctuation and phrasing. Fast learners find that they can obtain the main thought of a paragraph much faster if they read silently. In contrast, the slow oral reader may find that sounding out words helps him to remember. Moreover, the mere act of pronouncing words gives him a feeling of accomplishment!

By the time children reach the intermediate grades, the oral reading lesson can be used to help develop listening skills, especially helpful to poor readers. If they have tried to read the story once silently, they may not need to follow each word read aloud to grasp the thought or idea of a passage. Frequently, the reader may help his listeners through the use of expression, or even mannerisms. How the passages are read becomes increasingly significant when the audience is being trained to think in terms of thought sequences. Can the listeners picture the setting, characters, actions? If facts or ideas are important, the pupils may find they can listen better when they take notes. These can become the basis for discussion after the reading. In many classrooms the oral reading session and the discussion period may be followed by individual activities such as the writing of answers to questions, or the preparation of a word list or of a list of descriptive phrases. They may be asked to summarize a portion of a story or they may be asked to fill in an outline. A good final activity may call for a short dramatization of incidents that lend themselves to such activity. In both oral and silent reading, pupils may be asked to illustrate scenes or characters.

Older pupils who have been asked to read a selection silently with a set of guide questions will frequently be permitted to go on to another selection without an oral rereading if they show that they have acquired the understanding necessary to answer the questions.

Although some teachers overemphasize the importance of oral reading, this activity can be quite satisfying to most students. Many boys and girls find enjoyment in rereading a story after a discussion period. Thus, fast readers may find pleasure in relaying the feeling of a selection to their peers. Those who are untroubled by word recognition skills may enjoy the audience situation and can role play the various character parts. They may need help in expressing emotion or feeling, but this can be acquired with practice. A reading subgroup may be redivided to give oral reading practice to two or more segments of the children. If reading is to be satisfying, every student must be given several opportunities to read during a lesson. Extremely shy children who are reluctant to read orally may find a one-to-one relationship with a teacher will help build the confidence that is needed to read successfully before a larger audience.

One important use for oral reading is to motivate children to engage in newer and higher-level reading activities. Also, the teacher can frequently check on an individual's comprehension through oral reading. This is an important phase of reading and should not be slighted in favor of skill in oral delivery of a message.

ILLUSTRATION:

One teacher had her fifth grade divided into reading teams of six students. They would select materials to read to each other before making a tape of an oral reading presentation. The teacher would then listen to the tape with the students who made the recording. Collectively, they would analyze the reading to see where individual pupils needed help. The group secretary would note areas where a given student needed assistance. Team members would then work with each other to correct their reading faults.

A second-grade teacher would tape the entire reading lesson for later analysis when she could devote her full attention to details such as word omissions, the repetition of words, phrases, and sentences, or the substitution of words. She would then plan special reading activities for those who had a common reading need.

Oral reading is slow and therefore time-consuming. By the time children leave the third grade, they should be ready for a *different type* of reading. They will still want to read orally from time to time, but this will depend upon their personal goals. A poem, play, or interesting passage may be thoroughly enjoyed when it can be read orally to an audience, but this will not be true for much of the content material children work with in the intermediate and upper grades.

Boys and girls need help when they begin to work in content fields such as social studies and science. They have to learn how to get the thought from a page; they must learn to draw conclusions on the basis of the facts presented. Since these formal subjects tend to be loaded with technical words and phrases, they can be frustrating to individuals who cannot read up to established grade norms. It does not help them to try to read orally with such materials, yet more teachers rely upon oral reading of a social studies text than they do upon silent reading. When asked how they justified an all-class approach to social studies with children who normally read in three different level readers, the common answer was, "The slower readers can follow the better readers and they will enjoy the pictures."

A Balanced Reading Program Consists of Many Reading Activities. In essence, reading consists of two basic but related activities, namely, *the recognition of words on the printed page* and *the understanding of the words and word groupings on a given page in terms of the context or intended meaning.* Any reading program which ignores either of these two phases must be incomplete and ineffective. In addition, a third element, *interest,* must be included for any high degree of success. A well-designed reading program should help the student to acquire success in the following reading skills:

1. *Word recognition.* The beginning reader will need to build a basic sight vocabulary before he will have much success with reading materials. The first-grade level will be where teachers start. They introduce children to the names of objects they see and know, until each individual has learned to associate a given combination of letters with a spoken word. A teacher may use experience charts, labels, flash cards, or a tracing technique to help pupils acquire the basic sight vocabulary considered essential for introductory work with formal reading materials. Preprimers will present a limited number of words over and over again. As a rule, boys and girls will readily build a sight vocabulary of words that enable them to picture or see objects which are not actually present. Thus, many poor readers will read the words "automobile" and "airplane," yet miss such simple words as "than," "from," and "when." The latter words are part of a list of structure words which are essential for reading success, but which are often incompletely mastered because they do not lend themselves to visual imagery.

Children are taught to recognize words through a number of approaches. The simplest clue may be word association with a picture. Here the picture leads the individual to expect to see the word referred to in the illustration. Also, many words are recognized as a part of a context which would have no meaning in isolation; for example, children learn to associate prepositions as a part of a phrase, or they may learn an entire group of words such as a phrase or common expression. Boys and girls often depend on word configurations as a clue to a word and its meaning. A capital letter, a word within a word, or double letters may serve as the clue that gives recognition.

2. *Comprehension of phonetics.* While every good reading program may begin with word analysis skill development, it will not end there. Sooner or later the children will be introduced to *phonics*. There are critics of the basic reading approach who decry the delay in the introduction of phonics; however, the real issue is one of timing. *When* to introduce phonics is the question and not, "Will the children learn to attack new words phonetically?" Most reading series combine a sight-and-say approach with phonics, but sounds are usually introduced after the basic sight vocabulary has been developed. Children will be taught to associate letters and letter combinations with the sounds attributed to them. Unfortunately, English is not a phonetic language; therefore, boys and girls may have trouble with phonetic analysis. Letters, for example, may depend upon their position in a word for an appropriate sound. This will be especially true of vowels. Letters are combined to form syllables containing vowel sounds. This can pose problems to the slower learner especially when the prerequisite for a sound combination is mastery of a rule.

Phonics should be taught to children in small groups. Instruction should be provided in terms of the readiness of the individuals for a particular phase of work. Essentially, the work should center around the speaking and writing vocabulary of the individuals since sounding out a word will not help the pupil acquire the meaning so important for reading with comprehension.

3. *Structural analysis.* This is one of the key approaches to reading success. While the ability to sound words is important, the combination of sight and sound is essential. When the teacher introduces children to structural analysis, she helps them analyze words visually in an attempt to locate familiar elements that will give them meaning. Thus, she may help children locate key words or root words which were learned earlier as a part of a sight vocabulary building program. They may see that the addition of a suffix or prefix will give them insight into another word world. They may learn also that word meanings may change through internal changes as well as through inflected word endings.

Boys and girls may learn that some words are often combined to form compound words that have entirely new meanings from their individual meanings. Some of these words may be written as one word, while others may be hyphenated or contracted words. Instruction will take on new meaning if it is based upon reteaching where there is a known need rather than through a mass and generalized approach.

4. *Dictionary skills.* Boys and girls may begin their first work in a dictionary at the first-grade level; their book may be a simple picture dictionary, but it can be an important phase of their reading. In some classes the children may make their own picture dictionaries to assist them in both reading and writing. As the children progress through the grades, they will learn that many new words will not have meaning to them through ordinary phonetic and structural analysis clues. In this case the dictionary habit becomes an important key to the mastery of new material. The dictionary will give the individual a number of meanings that can be associated with the context. Learning how to locate the new words in the dictionary is one of the first skills associated with good reading. Following this, the pupils learn to select the meaning and pronunciation of new words.

A capable reader makes use of word-attack skills with a minimum of teacher assistance. Once he has learned to combine phonetic and structural analysis skills with dictionary skills, he is well on the road to working successfully as an independent student. From time to time he may need review work, but on the whole his success will depend upon repeated practice with a wide variety of interesting and challenging materials.

Children do not need to look up every new word, but the dictionary habit should be so well established that it can be used effectively, especially when other approaches fail to open the door to understanding.

Value of a Record of Children's Reading Needs. Cumulative record cards generally carry a number of test scores, but seldom do they give a picture of the actual reading needs of children. As a result, each teacher may have to take her own inventory and follow the progress of individuals through various learning activities. Some teachers trust to their memory the basic reading needs of their charges, whereas other teachers make notes in a plan book or on file cards. The informal inventory card will be most helpful if it can be referred to from time to time. This may be supplemented by individual progress charts containing lists of basic and supplementary books read plus reading skills that need attention. While teachers can make up their own progress charts, a school may purchase or print individual record cards which merely call for checking skills and/or reading books. These cards become a part of the permanent record of the school.

The publishers of several good basic readers have prepared reading tests to accompany their books. While they are not always standardized in the same light as the more widely used achievement tests, the subtests can be used to identify areas and build a program of reading activities that will foster immediate growth in such areas as: word meaning, word recognition, vowels, structural—compounds and endings, contractions, use of context clues, use of rhyming words, use of initial consonants, use of consonant blends, creative reading skill, ability to draw conclusions, ability to follow directions, ability to pick out a sequence, ability to pick out a main idea, ability to alphabetize, ability to interpret attitudes, ability to interpret feelings, ability to note details, and vocabulary growth.

Although a teacher may group children for instruction in different level basic readers, the common needs of individual students will often overlap. This can lead to the formation of special learning groups comprised of boys and girls who ordinarily work at different reading levels. If special reading help groups are established to work on specific word-attack skills, membership may change from time to time to accommodate the needs of individuals who have different learning needs.

Successful Reading Experiences in Relation to an Individual's Interests. Success in reading for many students depends upon the development of a liking for the act of reading as a method of gaining information about areas of special concern or interest to the individual. Young children and very slow learners may find the process is not worth the effort unless a basic need can be realized.

Many of these children need a purpose before they will exert themselves to work with materials on higher educational levels. How far they go depends on the motivating force used to attain designated goals. At times, they can be pushed and prodded into reading, but ultimate success does not come until they can sit down with a book and realize a personal need. Thus, children will read and make an extra effort when they are exposed to books that appeal to one of their special interests. Differences in interests and backgrounds may require different approaches.

In encouraging wide reading, teachers must remember that the interest level of materials read should be related to the maturity level of the individual. Pupils who are socially and emotionally immature will read low level educational materials. Similarly, slow progressing pupils will seldom try to read materials that threaten their security; they will avoid materials which frustrate them with words and ideas beyond their comprehension levels. These children will not stretch themselves unless the motivation is strong. Reading interests reflect the quality of the culture to which the children have been exposed. They will not read at high levels unless they have reading experiences which they find enjoyable at these levels. When they are free to read independently, they will read about things they understand and which contribute something to their personal growth. To a large extent, children's reading patterns will reflect parental attitudes toward reading as well as those of the teacher and their peers.

Teachers who attempt to discover the nature of children's reading interests will find that these can become powerful motivating forces. Entire reading programs can be built around the specialized interests of selected students. Boys and girls will expend more energy and will work for lengthened periods of time when the motivation comes from within. Frequently, hobbies or interests in animals make a good starting point. When working with children who have had very limited experiences, the teacher may have to develop interests by broadening the children's horizons—for example, by means of a field trip. Classroom teachers will find that children's reading patterns have been affected by technological advances in science so that books read widely a few decades ago no longer have any appeal. A teacher will often find that she can learn a great deal about children's natural interests through listening to them as they talk informally. Indeed, an *interest inventory* may help when working with children. When drawing one up, a teacher should remember the following:

1. Children's interests may change from time to time according to the nature of their problems. Adolescents, for example, who are looking for status and are trying to become adults, will often need materials which will help them discover a vocation. Also, they will try to resolve problems centering around money, personal attractiveness, study habits, personal and moral qualities, and a philosophy of life. Primary grade children will try to identify themselves with people and places they know. As they grow older, they find enjoyment in reading about people who live in distant places. Intermediate grade children often read for information, but they will frequently read to escape reality. Adventure stories will give some of them a chance to identify themselves with heroes or heroines.

2. Many children's interests stem from programs they have seen on television. It is a medium which can be used to cultivate wide reading about people, places, and events.

3. Children learn to appreciate good literature when they have a teacher who appreciates good literature; therefore, her enthusiasm

for books, especially poetry and good literature, can become contagious.

4. Children often see things from a different point of view than adults do. It is therefore important for the adult teacher to project herself into the child's world in an attempt to see what the child views as important, where his interests lie. Outwardly, a student may appear to be an adult, but inwardly he still has a foot in the door leading to the world of boys and girls. Books recommended by parents and teachers must therefore be directed toward *pupil* interests rather than adult interests.

Boys and girls need to read widely before they can acquire the ability to discriminate between good and poor reading materials. They may begin with a simple interest as a motivating force and then go on to read in many other areas as their world expands and their interests multiply. What they read will often depend upon the nature of the experiences encountered in the classroom. It is increasingly important that teachers work to extend the interests of their students into areas where they will find reading materials that stimulate them to go on when they are not reading merely to satisfy an instructor.

Individualizing the Reading Process

Most elementary school teachers use a basic reading series to teach reading. Some of them will attempt to individualize the reading program through the use of independent reading and teaching based upon common needs and interests, but they will continue to depend upon graded texts and graded materials when they meet the children for formal reading instruction in the reading circle. Dissatisfaction with the reading materials and recommended activities has led a number of teachers in different parts of the country to organize their classes around what they call a truly *individualized* reading program.

The authors firmly believe that individualized reading can be a most effective way to approach the problem of individual differences, but teachers cannot drift into this type of teaching. To be effective, the teacher must understand what reading is and what children need to know to develop facility with the many types of reading materials they are going to be exposed to over a span of time.

For the past thirty years, master teachers have demonstrated their ability to teach children to read without resorting to time-tested graded readers. Their dedication to their work plus an experiential background cannot be discounted as having a direct bearing upon the achievements of their children in good individualized reading programs. Although these teachers have had good results, there is no guarantee that the mass of teachers can dispense with present reading programs and still turn out children who can read as well as or better than those confined to a basic reading program based upon group or class reading activities. School administrators should encourage their better teachers to experiment with individualized reading, but they should still insist on controls to ensure that reading skills are taught when needed and not on a hit-or-miss basis.

Dorothy White [13] lists *successful teaching experience* as one of the teacher qualifications which contribute to success in an individualized reading program. The teacher is the key to the success of any reading program, but in the new individualized program her role is even more important. She no longer has the protection of a sequential program of activities carefully developed by the authors of a basic reading series. While she may make use of their books, they are not usually considered as the core of her program. She will be on her own as she guides children in the selection of reading books and sponsors reading skill activities on the basis of her own observations and tests. For maximum success she will have to be a teacher who can recognize the basic reading needs of boys and girls and plan activities for each pupil in the light of his total needs.

ADVANTAGES CLAIMED FOR INDIVIDUALIZED READING

Proponents of an individualized reading program claim some of the following advantages for the programs they want to see extended:

1. Reading is carefully planned around individual needs and abilities.

2. Children are enthusiastic about reading as they are no longer labeled as slow, average, or fast readers.

3. Bright children are not held back by slower-learning individuals. Average readers do not have to keep pace with faster or better readers, nor do they have to wait for slower readers.

4. The instructional period is no longer a period of boredom or frustration since individuals progress from one learning level to another at their own rate of speed and not that of their peers.

5. Children can read in fields of their own interest.

6. More pupils learn to read extensively as they find personal satisfaction in the actual act of reading. Reading becomes an exciting source of information to the pupil.

7. Self-selection helps pupils develop an abiding interest in reading.

8. Children learn to work in an environment that stimulates them

to read. All children receive individual attention from the teacher when help is needed.

9. Teachers report they find a new interest in children's literature.

10. The teacher and the pupil no longer feel the pressure of grade standards. Children obtain the reading practice needed for success in content reading as well as appreciation of reading activities.

Each pupil in an individualized reading program sets his own reading pace. Since he does not belong to a formal reading group, he is not under pressure to keep up with other students. The teacher may have established goals to be realized, but there is no pressure to work up to traditional grade standards of achievement in a designated period of time. The pupil progresses in terms of his own needs and interests and not those of a hypothetical average pupil.

Each pupil in the class can enjoy the feeling that comes when he can say, "Now the teacher is all mine." He does not have to sit in a large reading group and wait for his teacher to ask a question or listen to him read a few lines. When he joins the teacher for a reading session or discussion of his reading activities, he is the center of attention. He may be the only one in the class who has read for his own benefit. Once the common needs have been met, each pupil will again be free to read independently and then once again report alone to the teacher. If the teacher helps guide him in the selection of a book, it is because she knows his basic needs and recognizes his interests. She may be merely helping him find immediate satisfaction with his reading instead of allowing him to waste time in the selection of a book which is either too easy or too difficult for him. The teacher helps him see his own growth so that reading, on a more mature level, becomes a challenge to the pupil. He wants to continue to grow in reading proficiency because he sees himself making progress, and the act of doing so can be contagious. Growth in reading skill leads to a desire to read more, and practice in turn leads to further growth.

SETTING UP AN INDIVIDUALIZED READING PROGRAM

Some teachers work individually with boys and girls in what appears to be a group setting. Actually, each pupil is working independently of the others, but the children favor working together. They may hear each other read when the teacher is busy, or they may ask for permission to sit together when it is time for them to read. While many pupils enjoy working alone with the teacher, some may feel better when they can continue to work in a setting in which they are surrounded by two or three friends. In some classrooms, children may join the reading circle because they have shown an interest in such common areas as horses, dogs, Indians, science, etc. In other classrooms the pupils may take their places in the reading work circle according to where they sit in the class. It helps cut down movement within the classroom if several children leave their seats at the same time to join the reading circle. It also saves the teacher time by having the children who are going to work with her "ready to read" when she finishes with another student. She does not have to interrupt the total class to see who is ready to read next.

In an average classroom the pupil may read with the teacher for a short time each day, or he may meet her three or four times a week depending upon his needs. For the most part he may have her full attention; however, there will be times when he may join four or five other students for a special lesson that is pertinent to all members of the instructional group. In either case he is close enough to the teacher to realize that she is keenly aware of him as an individual. She knows what he can accomplish, and if he has a reading problem, it is difficult to conceal it from her.

Working with pupils individually gives the teacher a chance to observe a pupil's mannerisms or weaknesses. She can watch his lips and note his eye movements. If he shows signs of tension, she can make note of the fact and then try to do something to give him the sense of security he needs. She can help him build up his self-confidence by making him feel important as he works. If a mistake is made, it is not something that will be picked up by other classmates since most of his activities are with the teacher and not with a large reading group. As the only member of a reading group, he cannot escape his responsibility when asked questions. He knows that he is accountable to her for an answer. When he joins a work group, he knows that what is done collectively is aimed at helping him over a hurdle.

Individualized Reading Within Group Instruction. The teacher can listen to individual children read, she can discuss phases of their reading with them, or she can teach a special skill on a one-to-one basis, but many teachers still make use of a group approach to attain desired goals.

1. Boys and girls are naturally gregarious; therefore, they enjoy meeting with the teacher in a small group to exchange ideas and experiences. They may read selections to each other, tell interesting incidents, or dramatize a selection they have read. Children who have read the same books may make a combined report or may give their interpretations of what the characters were like. The individual students or the teacher may lead a discussion of a topic considered of interest or value to the other group members.

2. Children are frequently brought together in a small group when it is apparent that they have a common need for practice with a particular reading skill.

3. Children may meet together to read a book which seems to meet their common interest. Each pupil may read the same story, but at his own pace. The discussion and conference activities, however, can continue to be individual. Frequently, pupils will make individual reports to their peermates that create a demand or waiting list for a given book title or author.

Some children will share their experiences with a small number of their peers, but the same pupils would never make a contribution to the entire class. Also, there are some other children who cannot seem to understand what they are to do if they are left *entirely* alone. They seem to need an opportunity to work within the framework of a small group, with some individualized attention. They may be imitators or followers, but if they need the security of belonging to a work group, they can be encouraged to work in a setting which will foster their maximum growth.

Importance of All-Class Sessions. The individualized reading program does not dispense with an all-class approach. There are many types of all-class sessions. For example, boys and girls have many common needs that can be realized collectively as well as individually. A film may be used to furnish background for a period of history or to introduce a lesson in phonics; a tape recording or record may introduce children to a classic story, play, or poem. Frequently the teacher will make use of a word game to introduce a new skill. The instruction on an all-class basis will depend upon the nature of the lesson and the prior experiences the children have had with the skills being introduced.

Many all-class sessions will be planning sessions merely to bring everyone together to assign jobs or to receive directions. In some classes, the planning sessions are generally teacher-dominated. In others, the pupils may demonstrate their leadership qualities by deciding on the type of activities they would like to take part in during the reading period. Some might decide they would like to spend the period in the library, others would ask for help with problems they have been encountering, and still others might ask to work together on a play. In many planning sessions, both children and teacher develop a work schedule. They decide who is going to read with the teacher and who is going to report to the class or to a subgroup on the reading activities they have completed.

The all-class session may be a terminal activity. Individuals or groups of students may report to the entire class. They may read selections of interest or tell an exciting incident. These sharing and reporting activities may be the prelude to a group discussion or the start of a special teacher lesson. A word drill may stem from a pupil report; a lesson in summarizing may follow a number of overly long reports.

Importance of the Teacher in an Individualized Reading Program. The argument that an individualized reading program is an undirected and unguided program is far from the truth. Too many people have been told, "Individualized reading is easy to teach." As a result, some teachers who have failed to consider the teacher's role have made the mistake of putting aside their basic readers and teacher manuals with the expectation that children will be doing all the work. Some of them discover that the new program calls for more skill and understanding than they possess.

Some school administrators have failed to recognize the fact that the new approach to reading has been successful because a master teacher has set the stage for a good individualized reading program. An inexperienced or poor teacher cannot emulate the work of the master teacher. To be successful, the teacher must be ready to assume a large amount of personal responsibility for the reading program. She must know the basic principles of child growth and development and should be an experienced reading teacher. She should be ready to identify reading needs and difficulties and then must know enough about reading to assist her pupils over their reading hurdles. She should be familiar with the interests of children and the types of literature that appeal to different age groups. Basically, she should be a good organizer, because the individualized reading program needs to be guided and directed. The teacher remains a key person in the program. She structures the pattern of classroom organization that will most effectively permit pupils to reach their maximum levels of growth.

The capable teacher is not misled by childish whim or fancy. Interests are recognized and extended. The teacher keeps a list of the books read and then guides the individual to explore new worlds. If she has been working to help a pupil build a basic word vocabulary, she may keep a detailed record of the words taught or those which give him trouble. The teacher may spend long hours selecting books which will appeal to her students. From time to time she will rotate them in the light of new reading needs or interests. She makes certain that she is familiar with the books in order to discuss them intelligently. Her inventory or record of progress for each of 25 to 30 pupils becomes the basis of reteaching or individualizing pupil assignments.

When a teacher conducts such a program, she has to give a great deal of herself. It requires strength, energy, and time to keep pace with her children. It takes initiative and imagination to be a good teacher, especially in an individualized reading program.

Still Room for Failure in an Individualized Reading Program. Success in reading depends upon many factors; therefore, no one method of teaching can be considered a cure-all for the problem of failure. While an appeal to interest and purpose is a strong inducement, it is not always sufficient motivation to overcome the impact of low intelligence, lack of language experience, emotional tensions, social maladjustments, physical deficiencies, or a poor reading foundation. Studies of children who have gone through an individualized reading program will show both high and low pupil achievement; therefore, it is essential that one take stock of the situation to see wherein the blame may lie.

Given excellent reading teachers, plenty of time, and materials to work with, it is possible to minimize reading failures, but this will be true under *either* the graded basic reader program or the individualized reading program. There is no proof as to which system gives better results, because both groups of teachers will tend to emulate each other when working with children who are making little reading progress.

In studies comparing achievement or reading growth of children under the two methods of teaching, the abilities of children have been equated, but not the abilities of the teachers. Thus teacher competence, experience, interest in children, and skill in diagnosing children's needs are factors that can make a difference. Also, reports of teacher success are subjective. All too often an outstanding teacher reports children are learning more or are reading more because they are in an individualized reading program. This may be true because teachers in such classes have had to make an extra effort themselves to learn reading techniques and get acquainted with children's books. Reportedly, children who have worked with such teachers show an increased interest in reading, are growing in vocabulary development, creative writing, oral expression, and creative thinking. Unfortunately, some of these elements do not lend themselves to ready evaluation.

In a study by Jenkins, [14] a number of second-grade pupils in California schools did show significant gains in reading when standardized reading test results were compared with those of a control group. Thus:

1. The control group averaged 1.14 years in total reading gains, while the experimental group working in an individualized reading program averaged 1.41 years.

2. Twenty-five per cent of the control group had total reading gains of more than 1.6 years, while 46 per cent of the experimental group scored within this range.

3. In vocabulary growth the control group averaged 1.09, compared to 1.96 for those in the experimental program.

4. Fifty per cent of the experimental group gained two years or more in comprehension, while 24 per cent of the control group scored in this range.

While such results appear significant, a number of variables must still be analyzed. This has been evident in other studies stressing higher achievement for the traditional reading program based upon the use of a basic reading series. However, there are indications that better teaching may be going on in classrooms where individualized reading programs have been established under experienced teachers who accept, as well as understand, the individualized reading program.

Need for Recreational Reading in Individualized Program. It may surprise teachers to hear that children in an individualized reading program still need time for recreational reading, since it is generally assumed that all their reading is recreational. Actually the pupils spend a great deal of time on mastery of reading skills and reading for information. In addition, they need time and opportunities to read independently without having to account to anyone for what they read.

Reading, writing, and speaking needs are often combined in related activities. Thus a book read independently may become the basis for a written book report or summary. Also, the discussion or sharing activity may meet the need for oral language or listening experiences. This sharing of ideas and experiences is a part of the reading process; children need to react to what they read. Hence the need for group or class activity as well as for individualized activity.

The Reading Session as a Conference. Most people associate reading with a pupil demonstration of his ability to read. Here the pupil reads and the teacher quizzes him to see whether he knows the meaning of words or has extracted the thought of a paragraph. While this type of activity will be commonplace, many sessions can become conference periods in which teacher and pupil get acquainted with each other. A child may express his desires and hopes. Together, they may work out a program which will help him realize new goals. Another session may become an oral assessment or evaluation period. The pupil may show the teacher work which he has done. Her suggestions may point up new directions that he should take. Together they may examine books in the class library which may satisfy his reading needs or special interests.

Importance of a Good Record System. Since the teacher is not guided by the sequences found in a graded basal reading series, the individualized reading teacher may have to develop her own system of recording pupil achievement, strengths, or weaknesses. While some teachers may be able to trust to memory, it is difficult to teach over a long span of time without having something concrete to refresh one's memory. Some teachers make notes when they work with an individual pupil, others make notes after school. These may range from mere jottings of observations to the checking of a complex record of books and reading skills. A good record system should: (1) show simply and clearly what has been read under teacher direction; (2) tell why it was read; (3) show how much time was spent on the reading activity and what was done to correct reading deficiencies; (4) indicate why a book was not completed; (5) help the teacher diagnose pupil reading problems; (6) facilitate the making of formal reports to parents or other teachers; (7) show a cumulative story of the pupil's reading growth pattern; (8) be understood by other teachers if it is to follow the pupil to higher grade levels and be dated to give one a proper frame of reference; and (9) permit some involvement of children.

Other areas which may be included in a teacher's records, depending on her personal skill or interests, are: a summary of pupil-teacher conferences, notations on the way an individual works with his classmates or on his own, and notations of special help given by such specialists as a reading assistant, speech teacher, psychologist, or social worker.

Some teachers report considerable success with the tape recorder. They depend upon a sampling of their own observations or actual reading sessions. Many pupils may take part in preparing a record of their reading accomplishments in notebooks where they may record books they have read or words they need help with. Records may be kept of work assignments completed or special tests taken. Some teachers keep samples of written activities completed by pupils. For an anecdotal system, the teacher may keep a log or diary, and in some classes the log is assigned to the pupil.

Books and More Books. There is little value in starting an individualized reading program unless the teacher has access to a large collection of books. Actually, such a program need not be as expensive as some school administrators think, since money ordinarily used to purchase several sets of a basic reading series can go a long way toward the acquisition of individual copies of basic readers, library books, and reference books. A teacher working with 25 to 30 pupils should have a minimum of three book titles per child which can be used for instructional purposes exclusive of the library books used for recreational reading. Actually, a minimum of one hundred books is no more than may be found in classrooms where teachers used a two-level basic reader plus supplementary readers. In both reading programs library books should be considered as basic for recreational reading as well as information.

Since pupils are not going to read the same book or books at the same reading level, the supply of books must cover the anticipated range of reading achievement in a given classroom. In a first or second grade, the book collection may extend through the equivalent of four grade levels, but in a fifth or sixth grade the collection may have to extend through six to eight grade levels if it is to provide adequate recreational, instructional, and informational materials for slow, average, and fast learners. If money is an obstacle, teachers may be given a fewer number of books, with the understanding that teachers are to exchange books from their basic collections at designated times during the year. In this case title duplications are kept at a minimum.

The school library and the public library may be used, and book carts can be used for exchanging books with other teachers. Parents and other agencies may help build the basic book supply, but teachers should not have to depend upon the generosity of outsiders. The cost of books is insignificant in terms of the total expenditure for each child's education during the year; therefore, school officials must plan to allocate their funds in terms of the importance given to reading.

Initiating an Individualized Reading Program. Teachers who want to experiment with an individualized reading program should obtain the approval of the principal unless the idea originates with a group of her peers or the administration. It helps to have several teachers working together in such a program to ensure continuity for pupils as they progress from one teacher to another. However, there are schools where the individualized reading program is limited to a single classroom. There can be some variations, thus:

Cautious teachers may want to continue working with a basic reader for all pupils, but with limited group activity in order to promote more and more individual activities in the basic textbook several times a week. Once the basic reader has been completed, children read from other sources on the basis of self-selection. However, this is not considered a true individualized reading program.

Or, some teachers start by eliminating all formal group work in the basic readers for those pupils who have demonstrated their ability to work with a minimum of teacher help. The teacher may continue working with two regular groups, while the remaining third of the class is gradually eased into a new and less restrictive reading program. She may find that her slowest learners are not prepared to work independently for some time, but even these children can gradually find a place in the new program. For example, boys who generally find themselves in the slow reading group are apt to demonstrate a spurt in reading because they are encouraged to read on their own interest levels.

At the beginning of the individualized reading program the teacher may have to spend some time orienting the pupils to the roles they are to play in the new type of class organization. They may, for example, need to know where and how the books are to be kept. At the beginning, some of the better readers may want to substitute quantity for quality on the theory that the pupils who read the most books will receive the highest marks. Similarly, slow readers may seek out difficult books on the theory that teachers will reward them for striving to read beyond their normal instructional levels. If the teacher is patient, pupils will learn to pace their reading to the use of materials suited to their own reading needs or accomplishment levels. The key to success in working with pupils new to the program will be teacher guidance and a bit of patience.

Initial disciplinary problems usually disappear once pupils find the enjoyment which comes from successful reading experiences. Frequently, the removal of group pressure carries with it the elimination of frustrations that often lead to behavior patterns that are not conducive to a climate for learning. Limiting the time she works with individuals or groups of children as well as the number of meetings per week will help the teacher supervise and control the class as the members work individually and collectively with materials that do not call for close teacher direction. Frequent planning and reporting sessions will help her to maintain a close check on pupil progress.

Measuring Pupil Achievement. An individual reading program should be evaluated continuously on the basis of pupil achievement. Progress can be measured each time a teacher has a work session or conference with a student. If informal approaches are not adequate, teacher-made tests and standardized tests may be used to confirm her estimate of a pupil's reading needs. A special reading test may show areas of strength or weakness. This will be especially true where teachers examine the subtests to identify reading skills that are considered important for continued pupil progress. Teachers tend to use a wide variety of reading tests, ranging from those they make up themselves to those usually associated with weekly readers or a formal publisher's graded reader test. The tests may be supplemented by teacher observations, checklists, and special inventories of reading skills, interests, and basic needs.

Theoretically, children should progress from one learning level to another, but this does not always occur in real situations. Some children will not always master skills even when they are taught individually. Often forces beyond the teacher's control may contribute to delays in growth. It may not be easy to determine why pupils remain on a learning plateau, and the classroom teacher may need the assistance of a reading specialist to evaluate the reading program for slow pupils. With extremely slow pupils, the teacher may need the aid of a school psychologist.

Teachers who have to assign pupils marks on the basis of achievement may find that grade standards and traditional grade or course requirements are hurdles to overcome. An experienced teacher can measure achievement in reading on the basis of daily class progress, but the inexperienced teacher's report may be highly subjective in the absence of graded reading materials. Thus, teachers should consider the pupil's enthusiasm for reading activities, the number of books read, his choice of reading materials, the carry-over of reading into content fields, and the contributions made in class evaluation periods. Individually, these informal attempts to evaluate pupil progress may be unscientific, but when they are combined with many kinds of observations and special reading tests, the teacher may be able to satisfy the demands of parents and others for recommendations and marks.

RECOMMENDATIONS FOR AN EFFECTIVE READING PROGRAM

Although strong arguments can be raised for an individualized reading program, every teacher cannot be expected to carry out such programs with the degree of success shown by dedicated and/or master teachers. An effective reading program, however, will include many of the essential features found in the individualized reading program. The teachers will often combine features of a language-experience approach, a linguistic approach, and a phonetic approach in the individualized reading or basal reading programs. Essentially, most teachers will need the security that comes from the use of commercially prepared reading materials and evaluating instruments; however, the problems they may encounter often resolve themselves around the way such materials are used.

If individual pupil needs are to be met, teachers must be prepared to carry out a reading program that can be considered flexible enough to meet the demands of time, large classes, and varying pupil needs. This can still be done with graded materials up to a point, and then it may be desirable to introduce a less restrictive reading program.

In some schools teachers may introduce children to reading through the use of basic reading readiness materials, preprimers, primers, and first-grade readers. Once a reading foundation has been established, they may find the staff can move into a very highly individualized reading program. In other schools the teachers may not feel the need for an individualized reading program until children reach the fourth, fifth, or even the sixth grade. In other schools the individualized reading approach may be considered solely for highly gifted pupils who need to work on their own.

Flexibility in some schools may come with a reorganization of the elementary school to permit cross-grade grouping and some form of subgrouping on a less restrictive basis than is found in classrooms where teachers are struggling to meet the wide range of reading needs of the average intermediate grade. In many schools teachers may consider the introduction of a nongraded reading program as the solution to all their reading problems; however, even this approach will not meet every pupil's needs until there is a guarantee that upper-grade teachers will accept children where they find them and teach in terms of their readiness for higher-level activities.

Reading is so essential to success in the modern world that teachers and school administrators should evaluate the reading activities they sponsor in the light of the basic needs of the community, the school, and the classroom. If the reading program is to be successful, the following recommendations should be considered:

1. The goals of each teacher should be consistent with the broader goals of the school, and inconsistencies in the philosophy of individual teachers should be eliminated where they become barriers to children's continuous progress.

2. Reading should be given priority at all grade levels; every child should be offered a balanced reading program as he moves from grade to grade or teacher to teacher. Formal reading instruction does not end with the fourth, fifth, or sixth grade. Reading skills will often have to be taught and retaught at the junior high or senior high levels. Independent and recreational reading should be encouraged at *all* grade levels, while readiness to read in content fields should be given special emphasis at the intermediate and upper grade levels.

3. Teachers should be prepared to teach reading skills appropriate for the reading achievement levels of their students. Where teachers are not prepared to do this, a special in-service reading instruction program may be considered essential.

4. Reading materials should be available for all phases of a reading program. There is no excuse for a shortage of readers, library books, and reference books in any school or classroom.

5. Teachers should be prepared to meet individual pupil needs through either subgrouping or an individualized reading program. Instruction should be based on readiness for a particular reading skill or stage of development.

6. A teacher's reading program should include recognition of such factors as the pupil's physical health, motor control, and vision and hearing; his mental ability and prior reading achievements; his interests, goals, or purposes in life; his language and social experiences; his emotional health; his attitude and his parents' attitudes toward school and learning; community resources and interest in

educational activities; the suitability of available reading materials to the age, interests, and past reading achievements of the learner.

7. The reading program must offer a complete program. It cannot be limited to basal readers or to a special phonetic program, but must include provisions for wide reading in many fields and from many types of reading materials.

8. One of the prime goals of the reading teacher is that of teaching boys and girls to read various kinds of materials with comprehension. The development of a sight vocabulary or a word attack will not suffice if children are just word callers. They must be able to translate words and sentences into comprehensive wholes. Every reading program should include provision for training in the work-study skills necessary for successful research or content learning.

9. Elementary school children need daily periods of instruction in the basic skills, but they may not always have to work with teachers. Many of these skills can be mastered through team learning, the use of teaching machines, special teaching aids, and individualized work-study programs. Ultimately, however, each individual pupil's efforts should be evaluated by the teacher.

10. Children should understand the reason for a given series of learning activities. Frequently, they can assist in the evaluation process and thereby see their own weaknesses. Also, the reading program should be understood by the parents, who should know where their child fits into a particular reading program; if a pupil has trouble with reading, his parents may be able to supplement or extend the reading activities promoted in the classroom.

A good reading program in one school may be a poor one in another school; therefore, the citywide adoption of a basic reading series may not lend itself to the kind of program that has to be taught in select schools. For example, the cultural mores of children from a low socioeconomic area of the city may be such that instruction with prescribed books will have to be deferred for a year or two. This may create the need for reading materials that have meaning to boys and girls who start school with low-level language and experiential backgrounds.

In recent years, textbook publishers have been under pressure to introduce pictures of children who come from nonwhite homes. Moreover, there has been an increasing demand for work materials that depict people and places that have meaning to children who come from disadvantaged homes. Classroom teachers must see the importance of selecting instructional materials that will not offend racial or religious groups. Many of the teachers are unaware of the problems many disadvantaged children have when they return home from a school that has been entirely middle-class oriented. The boys and girls in such classes find that they are living in two different worlds. How to bridge this gap will be a problem, of course, for all teachers of such children. It is a problem that must be recognized, since frustrations that stem from the home often lead to rejection of the school and all that the teacher in the classroom represents.

REFERENCES

1. Emmet A. Betts, *Second Vocabulary Study, Grade Placement of Words in Eight Recent Spellers* (New York: American Book, 1949).
2. Ben A. Bohnhorst and Sophia N. Sellars, "Individual Reading Instruction vs. Basal Textbooks Instructions," *Elementary English,* 36 (March 1959), 185–90.
3. Morton Botel, *Multi-Level Speller, Grades 3 to 12* (State College, Pa.: Penns Valley Publishers, 1959).
4. Richard F. Bruns, *Improvement of Reading Through Ability Level Assignments, Curriculum Bulletin* 57CBM (Houston, Tex.: Houston Independent School District, February 1957).
5. Donald F. Cay, *Curriculum: Design for Learning* (Indianapolis: Bobbs-Merrill, 1966).
6. Donald D. Durrell and Viola Palos, "Pupil Study Teams in Reading," *Education,* 76 (May 1956), 552–56.
7. P. A. Fendrick, "Visual Characteristics of Poor Readers," *Teachers College Record,* 37 (February 1936), 452–53.
8. John I. Goodlad, "Individual Differences and Vertical Organization of the School," *Sixty-first Yearbook of the National Society for the Study of Education,* Part I, *Individualizing Instruction* (Chicago: University of Chicago Press, 1962).
9. Albert J. Mazurkiewicz, *New Perspectives in Reading Instruction* (New York: Pitman, 1964).
10. T. P. F. Nally, "The Relationship Between Achieved Growth in Height and the Beginning of Growth in Reading," *Journal of Educational Research,* 49 (October 1955), 153–54.
11. Catherine Stern and Toni Gould, *Children Discover Reading* (New York: Random House, 1965).
12. George I. Thomas, "A Study of Reading Achievement in Terms of Mental Ability," *The Elementary School Journal,* 47 (September 1946), 28–33.
13. Dorothy White, "Individualized Reading," *National Education Association Elementary Instructional Service Leaflet* (Washington, D.C.: National Education Association, November 1958).
14. Marion Jenkins, "Selected References on Reading, with Special Emphasis on Self-selection in Reading," *California Journal of Elementary Education,* 27 (February 1959), 188–92.

CHAPTER 10

Developing Handwriting Skills

Handwriting was one of the most important subjects offered in the traditional elementary school. As one of the "3 Rs" of education, instruction was mandatory. If the teacher could not teach children to write, she was not considered much of a teacher. For a long period of time, handwriting instruction was aimed at the development of a precise and beautiful form. Each letter was made with great care. Writing was frequently laborious. Speed was not a prerequisite. At that time there was a place for individuality, but as time went on and more people began to be educated, teachers began to emphasize the need for greater speed and for uniformity in writing style.

With the adoption of one or more handwriting systems aimed at teaching and improving handwriting through mass writing instruction, individuality and beauty of style lost their importance. While many pupils learned to write a good hand by following teacher directions or the writing manual, many children were not so fortunate. In theory, these writing systems should have worked. Directions were simple; illustrations were clear-cut. All it took was practice. Unfortunately, most children practiced during the formal writing lesson and then proceeded to write as they pleased for the remainder of the day. This lack of carry-over (transfer of training), plus the fact that many pupils hated the meaningless hand and arm motions which were often a part of the formal instruction, has helped bring about a new attitude toward handwriting instruction. While form and speed are still important, handwriting is now regarded as something personal. The pupil is permitted to develop his own style, although he is encouraged to maintain certain standards for written papers. This is evidenced by the individuality in teacher handwriting styles where a school system does not insist on conformity to one particular handwriting system.

Setting the Stage for Writing Proficiency

In some schools one will find handwriting methods have not changed in half a century, but in others handwriting is taught in a much more informal manner. Unfortunately, many teachers find it difficult to accept the fact that there is such a thing as *handwriting readiness*. Many of the teachers in today's elementary schools go from an incidental approach in writing to a very formal writing period with mass instruction for all. Many first-grade teachers start every child off with the same form of manuscript writing, and many second- or third-grade teachers introduce all pupils to cursive writing. The fact that a child may have muscular coordination problems involving finger, hand, arm, or eye does not deter many teachers from a mass teaching approach. These teachers still set aside a period in the day for handwriting instruction and then usually fail to hold the children to these standards when writing is required in other subject fields. To some of these teachers the idea of dropping the teaching of handwriting as a separate and formal subject sounds like heresy. Actually, there is a need to look at the way we teach handwriting. In too many schools our teaching has been ineffective and time-consuming. Recent research has shown that there is little value in traditional methods of instruction which stressed drill on push and pull exercises, writing in the air, tracing of letters, and the writing of endless circles.

HANDWRITING TAUGHT AS A FUNCTIONAL PART
OF THE LANGUAGE ARTS PROGRAM

If handwriting is to promote continuity of pupil growth, teachers are urged to look at it as a functional part of the language arts program. Here, handwriting instruction resolves itself into a matter of individualized or small-group instruction based upon pupil needs and readiness for advanced instruction. This approach is recommended as a time and energy saver for both teacher and pupil. When she teaches children to write, the teacher expects them to use their newly acquired skill as a means of self-expression and communication with others. It is not enough to have pupils merely copy prescribed forms. In the past, utility was not considered until children reached the fourth or fifth grade. Today, teachers recognize handwriting as essential to the first-

Special teacher uses an overhead projector to teach reading
and penmanship to a combined
second- and third-grade class.

Courtesy of the Ford Foundation

or second-grade pupil as a means of self-expression. The child is taught to write when he has a *need* for it. Up to this point most handwriting exercises have little value.

Children who see a need for writing need little help in beginning writing. Some bright pupils watch the teacher as she writes. They begin to copy her writing, because they see it as a tool they need for communication. They will readily learn the proper handwriting skills when they are introduced, without frustration, because they find satisfaction in writing. This satisfaction is not present in a class where many pupils are taught to write before they are ready to do so, or where they are taught to write in a meaningless situation through exercises which may be both tiring and valueless.

HANDWRITING READINESS PRECEDES FORMAL INSTRUCTION

A child begins to develop handwriting readiness when he sees writing as a means of communication. Through writing, he sees people expressing themselves. His first writing efforts may be merely imitative. His early scribblings may be meaningless to adults, but have meaning to him. Actually, most children have no real need for handwriting prior to the start of school. If the child does learn to write, it is due to school pressures which create a need for written communication. Outside of learning to write his name, he does little, if any, writing in kindergarten, but once he reaches first grade, he is exposed to many activities calling for the development of writing skill.

Before children are given formal writing instruction, they should show signs of readiness for it. With different children these signs appear at different times and in different ways. Frequently, parents think that a child is ready to write if he picks up a pencil or crayon and goes through the motions of writing. Such children may be merely experimenting and are not truly interested in writing, but they may be led to write their numbers or the letters of the alphabet without being able to use them as a means of free communication. Thus, one finds children who learned to write at home suddenly reaching a "plateau" in school. This is usually due to a lack of real or intense interest or need for writing which is strong enough to make them continue to practice and to use learned skills in activities calling for considerable effort and some emotional strain. Growth may stop for some of these youngsters, and the teachers may have to practically start them off again on beginning writing experiences. In cases where parents used faulty techniques, school instruction becomes a reeducational process.

Basic to handwriting readiness is the ability to see differences in symbol patterns. The teacher can measure the pupil's readiness for writing by studying his approach to problems in reading readiness tests. If the teacher lacks a standardized test, she can test his powers of perception through her own tests. Along with visual perception, he needs to be able to distinguish between such terms as "left," "right," "up," "down," "straight," "round," "crooked," etc. These words should not only leave a visual impression, but should have verbal significance. The child should be able to illustrate them verbally and through the use of his hands.

Readiness to read should precede writing readiness. While this is not always observed in school, it is significant if writing growth is to be continuous. For success in both skill areas, reading and writing, he will have to know how to distinguish between symbols, words, phrases, and even short sentences. His eyes should be able to make necessary eye movements to identify letters or words and be able to sweep from left to right as he looks at a word or line of print. Words must begin to have meaning to him—both orally and in print. A basic sight vocabulary is essential since mere ability to copy words will not be sufficient for the next stage of writing, which is communication. When the pupil copies words, they should have identity. Pupils who go through the motions of writing *without an awareness of what has been written* cannot really be called writers.

Assessing Each Child's Stage of Readiness. Children pass through several writing readiness stages as they go through the grades. Each teacher must take advantage of these stages as the pupil grows if his progress is to be continuous. Pupils can take part in group writing activities, but most growth will be individual. The fact that children grow in many directions at different rates of speed means that children reach a stage of readiness for writing at different times. If instruction is to be on a group basis, the teacher must therefore identify pupils who are approaching the same stages of readiness. To do otherwise can lead to forcing some pupils into frustrating writing experiences.

The child's state of readiness for beginning writing may be dependent upon the nature of his visual experiences. In some homes children have little contact with written materials, while in others children may grow up surrounded by books. The latter child has had innumerable stories read to him, so he associates writing with pleasurable experiences. He has books of his own and has gone through the motions of reading with adults. He has looked at pictures and may be able to retell a story by looking at the picture clues. Such pupils are frequently ready to read earlier than average children, hence they may be ready to write earlier than pupils who have had very limited contact with written materials requiring visual acuity.

Children who have had limited visual experiences need to take part in many activities which will assist in the development of their powers of discrimination. They may take part in games calling for the ability to discriminate between round and square objects, between large and small objects, between objects of different colors, shapes, positions, or contours. They need to be able to see likenesses and differences in symbols. This ability, as well as the lack of this ability, is a good indication of the pupil's readiness to proceed with reading and writing activities of a formal nature.

Children's toys can influence writing readiness. If a child plays with toys calling for manipulative skill or close coordination of hand and eye, his writing progress may be enhanced. Young children who have learned to manipulate beads, complete picture puzzles, pound a nail, use clay or manipulate scissors will have a higher stage of writing readiness than children whose play experiences have been limited to games involving the use of large muscles. Very often boys are handicapped in writing because they have engaged in running and jumping activities, playing with wagons, racing with tricycles, and other games involving large body muscles. They may need more help during early writing stages than girls who have spent long hours playing with their dolls, dressing them and cutting out doll patterns.

In addition to having had visual experiences and close hand and eye coordination activities, the pupil has to have a vocabulary of such visual terms as "small," "short," "round," "square," "circle," "sharp," "big," "little," "fat," "blue," "red," "yellow," "long," "tall," "up," and "down." If they do not know these terms, the teacher will have to help them to learn. She may introduce them to games to show them that things are either different or alike. At first, the student will have to learn how to make gross visual discriminations and then work from that point to the stage where he can make fine discriminations.

In the future, the child's readiness for formal reading or writing may be based upon his experiences with television. Both auditory and visual perception may be developed to a higher degree by the time children start school than was formerly the case.

The Meaning of "Left" and "Right." Before starting to read or write, children need to know the meaning of the terms "left" and "right." As they work, they will repeatedly receive directions which involve the use of these two terms. When they start to read, they learn that we *read* from left to right, just as they will have to learn that we *write* from left to right. Some first graders start school with a clear understanding of the differences between these two terms, but other children have to learn them. Teachers often have to help plan activities which call for the use of a particular hand or foot. As she observes the children, she notes those who have trouble and then gives pointed directions to help them remember which hand or foot is right and which is left.

In the reading readiness program, the teacher helps children develop a left-to-right eye movement by getting them used to starting their picture stories at the extreme left. They learn to move their eyes through a picture sequence from the top to the bottom of a page in a left-to-right progression. Here the teacher may find it necessary to train children through the use of a marker so that they will not let their eyes wander as they attempt to read. The teacher works individually or in a small group with pupils who cannot go from left to right as they begin to read.

Developing Readiness by Writing Stories for Children As They Dictate Them. After a pupil has developed his oral language to such a point that he can tell an interesting story, just telling the story is not sufficient. Proud of his accomplishment, he wants his story preserved. Since he has not mastered writing, the teacher may write it for him as he dictates. When he writes through the teacher, he becomes aware of things which he may not have noticed in first telling the story. For example, he sees his words on paper and may become aware that he has written a *sentence* without being able to define it. When the teacher puts those "little marks" at the end of the sentence, he gets his first introduction to punctuation. At the beginning, he may not see the value of the marks, but they help him to collect his thoughts and plan his next sentence. When the teacher writes the story, she writes more slowly than he can talk. He may be disconcerted by her interruptions, but it may help him to review his thoughts. As a result, he may find his story is not so interesting when the teacher reads it back to him.

Writing a story may be an individual matter, but many stories are written collectively on a "reading" or "experience" chart. The teacher may start writing the story on the chalkboard or on a large sheet of newsprint, then solicit sentence contributions from several children. They see values in this kind of writing as it allows them to record ideas, stories, poetry, events, and plans. Form becomes important to the children. They begin to plan good sentences by thinking ahead. They begin to see the need for the little stop marks called "periods," and they become aware of the need to use large or capital letters at the beginnings of their sentences. When the children ask why they are used, the teacher has a chance to teach a good language lesson, although this may not be her prime objective since she does not want to curb creative thinking by introducing grammatical writing before children are ready for it.

Teachers may write for children as a means of introducing them to writing or reading. The reading chart or experience chart helps children see that reading is "talk that has been written down." They learn that the experience chart is a record of what they have said, that it can be read over and over again. It helps them bridge a gap between oral language and reading and between oral language and written language. The more mature children will gradually begin to locate sentences they have helped write and to recognize words that appear frequently.

Whether a teacher is writing a story for a single pupil, a group of pupils, or the whole class, the chief objective of the teacher is to help children express themselves logically and creatively. At the beginning of the primary grades, ideas are more important than the mechanics of English. Once children have learned to express themselves, they will be ready for instruction in spelling, punctuation, and handwriting. In order to attain the maximum awareness of his creative ability, each pupil must have many opportunities to dictate stories, poems, reports, plans, ideas, and funny incidents. They need to write through the teacher about themselves, their friends, and about the things they do, say, hear, know, and feel.

Mental Age and Writing Readiness. In considering readiness for reading, it has been repeatedly pointed out that a child should have a mental age of at least six and one-half to seven years to read with any degree of success. Since there are a number of *common factors* in both reading and writing, preparation for formal instruction in either area is dependent upon a similarity of readiness experiences and stages of growth.

Before pupils begin formal writing, their mental age should equal the mental age required for reading success. A mental age of 6-6 to 7-0 should be a prerequisite for the introduction of writing skills to children who are free of emotional tensions and who show that they have good motor coordination. The more mature the children are when they learn to write, the less need for drill and practice.

Effect of Anatomy of Children's Hands on Writing Readiness. The nature of the anatomy of children's hands may affect their readiness for writing, since children's hands fall into different morphological types. Some educators are concerned over the lack of proper physical development of children's finger, hand, or wrist muscles. Lack of proper bone development may be a factor. For example, X rays have shown that some six-year-olds have only cartilage in their wrists in place of the bone which will develop later. To subject these children to formal writing experiences before their hands have developed properly could result in later complications. This area is one which needs special study since teachers lack facilities which will tell them when anatomical differences interfere with the learning process.

When the pupil comes to school, he has learned to control his body to a limited degree. Until he is eight, this control is usually limited to the larger body muscles. He uses his arm and leg muscles fairly well when he starts school, but skill in the use of wrist and finger muscles comes slowly. Before the pupil can develop skill in writing, he has to be able to make the finger muscles respond to his wishes. This is one reason for deferring cursive writing to the third grade since it calls for finer muscular coordination than required for the manuscript writing taught in most first grades.

Because of the lack of anatomical development of most children's hands, many schools now provide them with large, thick crayons or chalk for their initial writing experiences. These tools will help children to work in art activities without having to work under pressure. If they paint, they are encouraged to use large, thick brushes and are then directed to make their pictures large. Lined paper is not recommended for beginning children, because they need to practice drawing or writing without line restrictions.

Each year several million children begin school for the first time. Most of them carry pencils or sets of pencils which are not suitable for the type of writing experiences they are to engage in as kindergarten or first-grade pupils. Because their muscles are not fully developed, these children should not be allowed to use the thin pencils they bring from home until they have matured muscularly. In many schools the beginning writer is not permitted to write with anything but special, thick pencils called "beginning" or "primary" pencils. These pencils have a diameter which is at least 13/32 inch and have an extra soft lead of oversized diameter approximating 0.166 inch; with these pencils, the pupils can make marks without having to bear down heavily and without having to cramp their fingers to hold the pencil as they write.

Parents should be encouraged to ask for this type of pencil if they insist on supplying children with pencil boxes, or even one pencil, for their beginning school writing experiences.

As children get older and move into second and third grade, the size of the pencil is decreased and the thickness of the lead is reduced to facilitate the finer writing which comes with the development of increased muscular coordination. In some schools, second graders continue using the same kind of pencil they used in the first grade, but after a few months a 5/16-inch pencil will be substituted for the 7/16-inch or 13/32-inch pencil. At the beginning of the third grade the children may continue to use the 5/16-inch pencil, but by the end of the school year most third graders should be able to write with the standard 4/16-inch pencil. All children should be discouraged from using mechanical pencils in the primary grades.

When first graders and kindergarten children begin to write, they are given large sheets of unlined paper so that they can write large letters without being confined by lines. After a short time, beginning first graders may be given paper with one-inch lines, but because of his poor coordination, the pupil is directed to make letters which are at least two inches high (two full spaces). This large writing is soon reduced so that the first grader is using one full space for lower case letters and two spaces for capital letters. If children are going to write large letters, it is frequently desirable to give them extra long paper with wide lines to permit them to write long names or several short words across the paper.

Many schools provide special writing paper which has one-inch lines, with a faint guideline in between. As children progress through the primary grades, their coordination improves so the width of ruling gradually decreases. Although teachers in different schools have their own standards, the following table lists types of paper in common use for writing activities in the elementary grades.

Need for Chalkboard Writing Experiences. Years ago the average classroom had two or three walls covered with blackboards. In modern schools one finds only a few feet of chalkboard at the front of the room. This presents problems to teachers who need space for their own writing and that of children. Many children *never* have an opportunity to write at the "board," yet this is an experience they need. Chalkboard writing for small children is especially valuable for them, because it gives them an opportunity to use their large muscles to write on a large surface without the restriction they find in writing on paper. The larger handwriting at the chalkboard is easier to diagnose by both teacher and pupils. Mistakes are easily noted and corrected. Letter formations can be written unhampered by lines. Because of the shortage of "board" space and the reluctance of some teachers to allow pupils to

TABLE 1

Paper Standards for Elementary School Children

Kindergarten:	Large unruled paper for general coloring and for initial writing (if any).
Grade 1:	Some children will have to start with unruled newsprint. (Teachers frequently crease this paper to provide guidelines for letter sizes.) Others may start with one-inch-ruled paper, 9 × 12 inches or wider. Or, they may use regular ruled newsprint with one-inch lines, with faint ½-inch lines in between.
Grade 2:	Children may continue to use the one-inch-ruled paper with the faint ½-inch lines; but the teacher gradually brings the children around to: ¾-inch-ruled paper, 9 × 12 inches wide; or newsprint with ¾-inch dark lines, with ⅜-inch faint lines in between.
Grade 3:	Children may continue working with ¾-inch-ruled newsprint paper (9 × 12 inches), but will work toward using: a standard 9 × 12-inch newsprint or manila paper with ½-inch rulings; and a standard white or manila paper 7 × 8½ inches with ½-inch rulings.
Grades 4, 5, and 6:	Use standard newsprint or white, lined paper, with ½-inch rulings, size 7 × 8½ inches or 8 × 10½ inches.

write at the "board," some teachers substitute large sheets of unlined newsprint as a medium for writing with large crayons.

HANDWRITING INSTRUCTION ON AN INDIVIDUALIZED OR SMALL-GROUP BASIS

Individual writing needs can frequently be attended to more effectively if the teacher eliminates the formal all-class instructional period. There are times when she may find it desirable to work with the whole class on a common problem, but most often she will be able to work most effectively if her instruction is based upon meeting individual or small-group needs. Too often the teacher sets aside a writing period for group instruction which has little relation to what is written during the rest of the day. Instead of dividing the teaching day into many 30- or 40-minute segments, the teacher should plan to work with children in large time blocks which will allow for integrated activities involving spelling, writing, composition, and work in a content field. During the long interval the teacher can go to individual pupils if they need help, or groups of children can come to her for review or practice activities.

There is still a place in the modern classroom for drill activities, but it is based on a recognition of the functional needs of the pupils. Writing instruction is more than incidental teaching. The teacher keeps samples of pupil work which can be used to measure growth or progress. By reviewing these papers with the pupils individually or collectively, the teacher can identify writing needs and can recommend writing procedures which will help pupils reach higher writing standards. The drill work which has been individualized as a part of a functional language arts program becomes a meaningful experience for the pupil. Attention may be directed to the improvement of letter formation, uniformity of size and slant, or spacing of letters and words. If letters are too small or too large, an attempt is made to develop a size appropriate to the pupil's maturation level. The beginner is encouraged to write large letters, and then he is taught to reduce the size of his letters as his muscular coordination improves. He receives help in getting correct spacing between letters, words, and sentences. He is taught to see that parts of letters which belong below the line are brought down, and that those which extend above the line are brought up to desired heights. Because pupils are required to maintain legibility in all their written work, writing practice and instruction cannot be limited to a 30-minute period.

Helping Children to Become More Proficient Manuscript and Cursive Writers

When pupils learn to write, they learn a complex process which is more than mere mechanical response to stimulation. The child who can look at a word is not really writing when he traces it or copies it on paper. Writing calls for the development of thought processes which depend upon activity in cortical nerve areas. In response to appropriate stimulation, the learner learns to control eye and hand muscles. He readily learns to associate prescribed hand movements to record images received through his eyes. At first he has to think out the writing process: until writing activities become natural and patterns are fixed in his mind, he isn't really writing. During this period he is unable to concentrate too well on what he is trying to say, but if his message is important, he rapidly learns to disassociate himself from the writing process. It becomes an automatic response, leaving the learner free to concentrate on the "what" of writing instead of on the "how."

This is a reason for delaying the changeover from manuscript to cursive writing. Pupils who have just begun to write freely and independently need to continue manuscript writing until they become secure with both the "what" and "how" aspects of writing. They need time to feel the joy of success in their efforts before starting to develop facility with another type of writing which can be frustrating, because of the time and effort involved in again learning the "how." After a pupil completes the initial stages of writing, he is able to do without a copy every time he writes, because he has developed the power of recall. He can write because he has developed the ability to retain both a visual and a kinesthetic image of letter and word formations. Sometimes he has to look at a model or ask for a correct spelling, but if the pupil writes about things he knows or which are of special interest to him, he readily builds up a writing vocabulary which is easily recalled when needed.

For years, teachers emphasized good arm movement, only to find children reverting to finger motion when they were writing after the close of the penmanship period. Since either exclusive finger or arm movements are fatiguing, a combination of the two is now encouraged in order to stress a relaxed writing position.

The pupil has to learn to relax more than the hand for success. Writing calls for a release of tensions. For example, beginning writers cannot remember all the teacher's directions. A series of staccato directions to the class, "Head up," "Backs straight," "Feet flat on the floor," is more than some pupils can take. Many pupils can follow one direction, but cannot grasp multiple "orders." They may want to comply, but lack ability to do so. The writing experience becomes an emotional one—they tense up and cannot do their best. When children

A successful learning experience reveals itself in the face of this pleased youngster.

Courtesy of PEA School Volunteers, New York City

begin to write, the teacher must help them acquire good writing positions, but she must avoid too much verbalism. Handwriting skills must be learned through practice and maturation. Directions, if needed, must be specific and must have meaning to the writer. The pupil must be able to follow directions without tensions or confusion. The teacher must remember that his writing span is limited to the permanency of the visual image he retains each time he lets his eyes go from his writing paper to the copy. If, at the same time, he has to watch his hand, the paper, the pencil, and to listen to teacher directions, he may not be able to relax.

With chronological growth, the pupil finds himself able to exert greater control over his body and his writing tools. Thus he is ready for new skills as he goes from grade to grade. Instead of giving mass directions, the teacher finds it is easier to walk up to a pupil and quietly ask him to try holding his head up, to put his feet flat on the floor, or to turn his paper to the right or left depending upon his handedness. The quiet direction is individualized and personal, and the pupil does not have to feel self-conscious. The number of directions is limited, so he does not have to worry about whether or not he has missed one. He realizes that each of her directions is specifically related to one of his needs, so he follows it. In a relaxed atmosphere, the teacher helps promote pupil growth in writing legibility and speed, but she does not limit her help to a single writing period. Every writing activity becomes a penmanship lesson, with the teacher insisting that he observe good writing standards for all written work! In a natural situation in which he is free from pressures that create needless tensions, the pupil is made to see writing as a method of communication which calls for attention to specific forms and details.

LEARNING MANUSCRIPT WRITING FIRST

Prior to 1925, many beginning writers had trouble learning to write; but since then more and more children have learned to write more easily by first mastering manuscript writing instead of cursive writing. Manuscript writing had its origin in England as an easier method of teaching and learning the art of writing. It was introduced in the Horace Mann and Lincoln schools in 1925 and within a few years was a part of the curriculum in hundreds of public schools. In the beginning, manuscript writing had to be defended against strong opponents, but with the steady increase in the number of schools using manuscript writing in the primary grades, the teacher no longer has to feel that she is "skating on thin ice" if she introduces her pupils to manuscript writing in first grade.

It must be remembered that manuscript writing is not without its limitations. Teachers will find that *not all* children are successful writers, even with manuscript. And teachers themselves must be familiar with the principles of manuscript writing. If a teacher cannot write in manuscript form, she is hardly prepared to instruct young children. Here is where the elementary school principal or the elementary school supervisor has to take a hand. If manuscript writing is to be taught, it should be taught well. The new teacher has to be given every opportunity to familiarize herself with manuscript writing; her preparation cannot be left to chance.

Parents will frequently ask, "Why do you teach print writing?" Years ago this question was often the basis of an attack on the school and its philosophy. Today the question is often based upon parents' curiosity or desire for information. Therefore, an educator's answer does not have to be defensive in nature. In brief, the primary reason for teaching manuscript writing to young children in place of cursive writing is that *children find it easier to learn.* Manuscript writing can be learned faster and is more legible to teachers and pupils. This is because manuscript writing uses the same type symbols found in beginning reading materials. In addition, it requires less use of fine hand, arm, eye, and body muscles, and is thus less fatiguing. The letter formations are also easily made, being primarily simple strokes based on the use of the circle and straight lines. Manuscript writing is easy to teach, and manuscript writers read faster, spell better, and do better in composition than comparable cursive writers do. Also, left-handed children, slow learners, and children with poor muscular coordination and/or with vision defects learn manuscript forms more easily than they learn cursive writing. (Manuscript calls for fewer eye movements and is often prescribed for sight-saving classes.)

Ease of Letter Formation. When a pupil starts manuscript writing, he is already familiar with print writing as a result of his prior reading experiences. In other words, his *reading* readiness exercises have also been *writing* readiness exercises. They help him to recognize readily letter and word formations basic to beginning writing. The process of writing manuscript letters is simplified, because all the letters consist of straight lines, circles, or semicircles. Most of the letter strokes start at the top. They are easily made, and once a letter is made, it stands out. The pupil does not have to worry about connecting curves between his letters, so there is not the concern, confusion, and fatigue that one finds in beginning cursive writers who must struggle with the problem of joining letters.

Letter formations in manuscript writing have a similarity in form and height. In writing them, the pupil learns to follow a correct directional pattern. This is important, so the pupil should have a copy of the alphabet (see Figure 1) showing the direction his pencil is to take as he makes each stroke. If he learns these at the beginning, he will have little difficulty with his writing.

Increased Writing Speed. Because manuscript writers learn to write more easily and with less fatigue, they can write for longer periods of time, and as a result, they write more. In turn, this leads to an increase in writing speed. Some writing authorities claim that manuscript writers who have not changed over to cursive writing by the time they reach the fifth or sixth grade are able to write faster and more legibly than pupils who have learned cursive writing sometime in their school experience. Other authorities claim that adults who use manuscript are slower writers than those who use cursive writing, but there is general agreement that, in their initial writing stages, the pupils who learn to write manuscript will develop a good writing speed without loss of legibility. Since they can write more easily, these pupils come in contact with more words. This can lead to an improvement in spelling and composition. With increased ability in these two areas, less time is necessary to complete written assignments, so speed can be measured in terms of something more than mere mechanical writing skill.

Ease of Learning for Children With Eye Difficulties. Children who have difficulty in adjusting their eye muscles to the reading process find manuscript writing helpful since fewer eye movements are required to read and write manuscript letters. Similarly, the simplicity of the letter formations and the lack of connecting strokes make manuscript writing easy on the eyes of all young children. This is evident whenever they engage in the act of reading or writing manuscript words and sentences. They do not have to concern themselves with fine lines such as they encounter in cursive writing, and they find manuscript letters easy to read or write because they stand out—separate and distinct.

Suitability for Needs of Slow Learners. Children with limited intellectual ability tend to learn slowly in all subjects. This holds true for writing; however, slow learners tend to develop skill with manuscript writing faster than they do with cursive. Manuscript writing has more meaning to the pupil, because he finds success more quickly and with less effort and sees a relation between his writing and what he is trying to learn in reading activities. Since his writing is more legible, his teacher is more receptive to his work even though it may be low in quality. And because the element of repetition is important to the slow learner, manuscript writing is more appealing—it requires shorter and less frequent drill or practice periods.

While many slow learners make progress with manuscript writing, improvements in legibility and speed may come slowly. Because he may have more difficulty in coordinating hand, finger, and arm muscles with his eye and mind, the slow learner may be the last pupil to make

Figure 1. FORMING MANUSCRIPT LETTERS

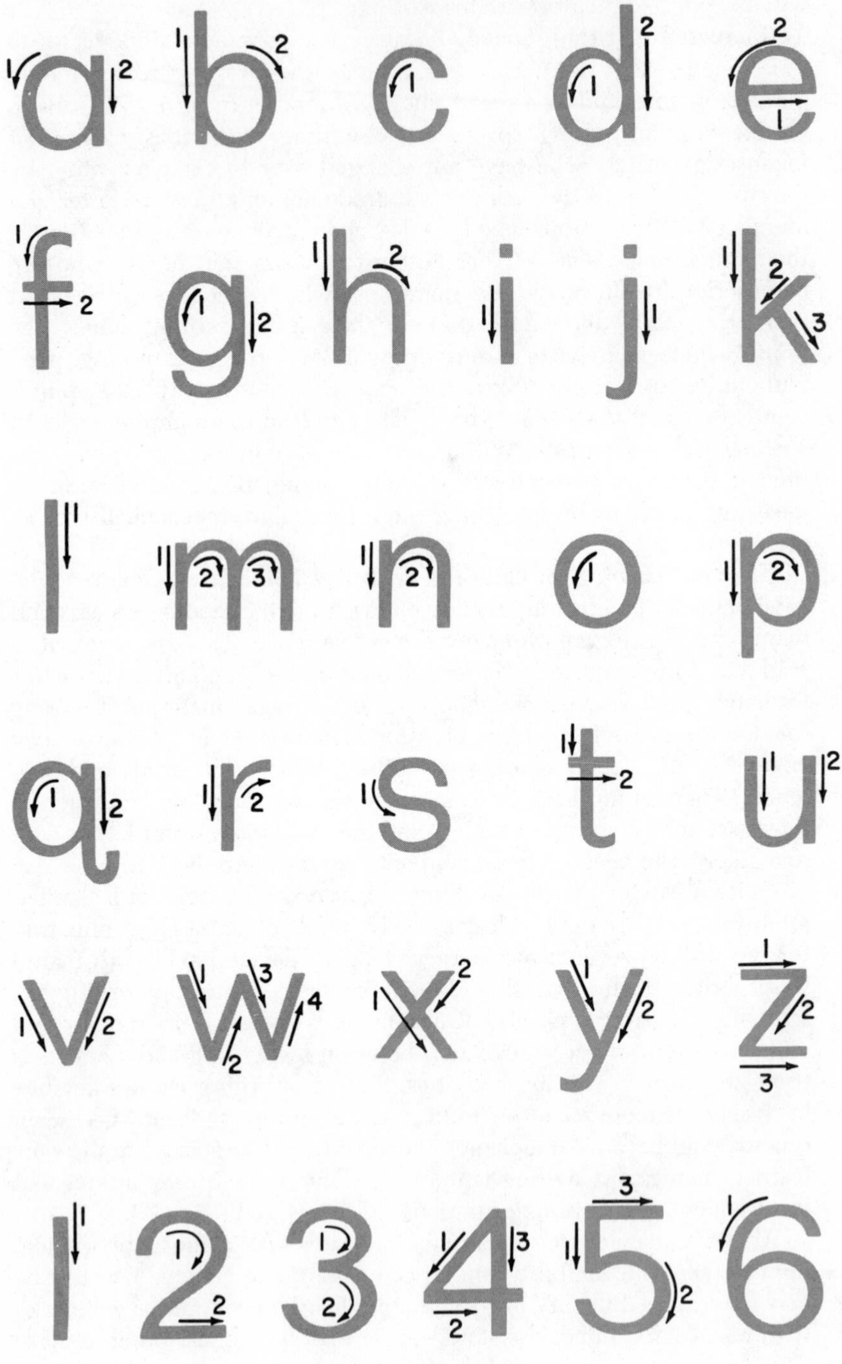

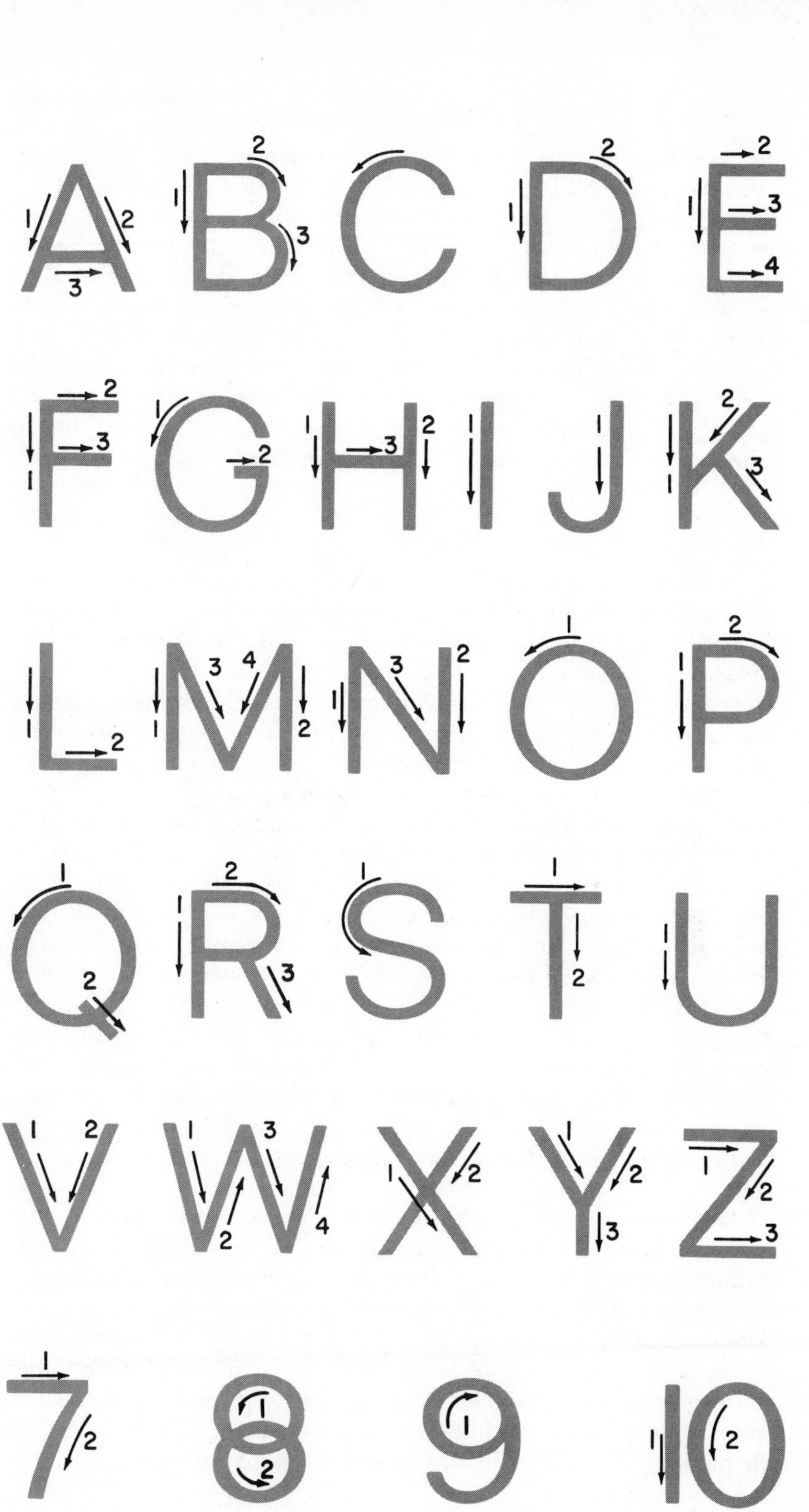

A B C D E
F G H I J K
L M N O P
Q R S T U
V W X Y Z
7 8 9 10

the transition from manuscript writing to cursive writing. Many of the brighter pupils will be ready to make this transition at the end of the second grade or at the beginning of the third grade, but most slow learners will not be ready to do so until they are in the last part of the third grade or the beginning of the fourth grade. With extremely slow learners, it may be much more to the point to accept the pupil's manuscript writing as sufficient for the type of writing that he will most likely do in his nonschool life than to have him try to learn the complexity of a new type of writing. His manuscript writing will readily meet his immediate needs, so he should not be confused by the instruction necessary to teach him cursive writing.

THE MOVE TO CURSIVE WRITING

In some schools it has become common practice to begin cursive writing during the last part of the second grade. However, many school systems have teachers defer the transition to cursive writing until the children reach the third grade. A few schools even delay the change-over until the fourth grade. Arguments have been raised against making the change from manuscript to cursive writing too early because the children are too immature to make changes without encountering serious difficulties. It has been argued that, if the process is delayed, children will need less time to change from manuscript to cursive writing, because they will have better coordination with increased maturity. This means less effort and frustration will have to be faced by the learners. When this argument is given, it becomes evident that the teachers tend to think of the changeover as an all-class activity. If this is so, the authors recommend a general deferment of cursive writing activities until all children start third grade, but in deference to individual differences, teachers can start introducing many children to cursive writing when they show that they are ready for it. This means that teachers who observe principles of grouping based upon readiness, and who do not try to keep all children together for the same kind of instruction, will not hold back their more mature pupils.

Many second-grade pupils are just beginning to feel secure in their manuscript writing. They are just beginning to develop speed and style in their writing. Some have learned to write freely and automatically and have just begun to write about things without having to concentrate on the writing process. They need this period of feeling secure in one aspect of their school work, because so many of their other learning experiences may be creating emotional tensions. The introduction of cursive writing in the second grade can come at a time when the pupils need a chance to write about things, to write creatively, and to enjoy the pleasures which come with success. Although the authors are promoting the idea that children can learn to write manuscript and cursive writing without wasteful all-class instruction, many schools are *not ready* for this writing approach. They are afraid of what they consider an "incidental approach," although that is not what is advocated. In such schools the authors recommend the deferment of cursive writing instruction until *all* pupils reach the third grade, with the understanding that each fourth-grade teacher will have to be ready to give special writing assistance to those slow learners who found cursive writing difficult in the third grade.

Readiness for Cursive Writing. Chronological age or grade placement is not a reliable index of pupil readiness for cursive writing, since other factors contribute to success with the more complex type of writing:

Pupils should show adequate physical development of the body so that there is a good coordination of the arm, hand, and fingers.

Pupils should show a strong desire to write in cursive style.

Pupils should be able to write all manuscript letters from memory.

Pupils should have the ability to read simple sentences that the teacher has written in cursive writing on the chalkboard.

Since children arrive at this stage of advanced writing readiness at varying times, the teacher has to be ready to adapt her instruction in terms of individual pupil growth patterns if she is teaching in a school where teachers are free to take pupils where they find them. If this is possible, the teacher will bring together for instruction the pupils who show signs of readiness for cursive writing. If the teacher has an advanced class, her whole class may be ready for cursive writing several months before a slow-moving class. With a very heterogeneous class, the number of pupils who have reached the stages of readiness indicated above may be limited. In this case it may be best for the pupils if cursive writing instruction is deferred for everyone, unless there is some understanding that the next grade teacher will allow those pupils who have been accelerated into the advanced writing stage to continue working apart from the pupils who may just be starting their cursive instruction with her.

Instruction in cursive writing does not have to be defined in terms of ages or grades if each teacher in the second, third, fourth, or higher grade recognizes that handwriting instruction is a responsibility shared jointly by different grade teachers. Each teacher must be able to evaluate the various stages of writing which children have when they come to her, and she must proceed accordingly. She should accept the principle that writing instruction should not be forced, but rather, should be given when the pupil is best able to take that instruction and make progress with a minimum of difficulty. She must be prepared to give close supervision to the work of the children when they start cursive writing.

What the pupil writes at the start has much less significance than how he goes about it. If his body is tense and his writing is forced, the teacher may work at trying to get the pupil to relax. She needs to help each pupil analyze his own writing by providing him with adequate specimens of good handwriting. Through guidance in detecting writing errors and in directing practice in desired activities to perfect writing skills, the teacher helps the pupil to reach the stage where he can express himself freely without having to concentrate too much on the process of letter formation, slant, or spacing.

STANDARDS IN HANDWRITING

Children need to see that there are specific standards for writing which may be considered goals. These may be brought to the attention of the pupils in many ways. For example, a teacher who wants to emphasize the matter of height of letters can use an interesting group approach to overcome a common difficulty. Individual papers may be examined for comparison with a blackboard sample or with individual copies of desired letter models. Some teachers have effected motivation through the use of an opaque projector to show writing samples for a shared evaluation or constructive criticism. Boys and girls can be encouraged to compare their handwritings to help establish goals and to see where their efforts should be concentrated to improve their writing style and form. Many teachers have found that higher writing standards can be achieved through the use of such standardized writing scales as the Ayers, Freeman, and Thorndike scales. In one third-grade class, children frequently took their papers to the rear of the room to compare them with the Ayers Scale for their stage of development, and then they returned to their seats to concentrate on a better writing copy for their next comparison of their regular written work.

Children should show a steady increase in the quality of their letter formations and in their writing speed as they grow chronologically. Generally, a quality rating of 60 on the Ayers Scale is considered adequate for the average person. This is a standard set for eighth-grade pupils, but it can be reached by many fifth-, sixth-, or seventh-grade pupils. Pupils who reach this standard early can devote their time and efforts to self-improvement in other areas of handwriting or in other subject fields. A writer's speed should be thought of in terms of its effect on quality. Each pupil should be able to maintain his writing quality along with his increase in speed. Handwriting authorities have said that the average writer expresses himself with a speed of 70 letters a minute on the Ayers Scale. Most sixth graders can attain this rate of speed, although they may not reach the standard of quality designated as satisfactory until they are older. If accepted standards for both quality and speed are reached at the same time, a pupil can continue to work for improvement in his total handwriting pattern, but he should not have to devote a large amount of time and effort to attain only a slight gain.

TABLE 2
Standards for Good Handwriting
in Grades 1 Through 8

	Ayers' Norms		Freeman's Norms	
Grade	SPEED, NUMBER OF LETTERS PER MINUTE	QUALITY OF LETTER FORMATIONS	SPEED, NUMBER OF LETTERS PER MINUTE	QUALITY OF LETTER FORMATIONS
I	20	34	—	—
II	31	38 [35–40]	30	11.0
III	44	42 [40–45]	44	12.5
IV	55	46 [45–50]	51	14.5
V	64	50 [50]	60	16.0
VI	71*	54 [50–55]	63	18.0
VII	76	58 [55–60]	68	20.0
VIII	79	62* [60–70]	73	21.0

* Quality or standard considered desirable for the average writer.

Note: The bracketed numbers indicate desired ranges that may be used to evaluate the quality of the children's letter formations or speed.

The secret of continued growth in handwriting skill will depend upon how much the individual pupil writes. If he writes continuously and at standards of quality designated for his age and grade, his handwriting will continue to improve.

HELPING THE LEFT-HANDED CHILD
WITH HIS HANDWRITING

Research studies have shown that left-handedness may exist in from 2 to 30 per cent of the school population. The authors' study of 1,100 elementary school children in North Arlington, New Jersey, showed 107, or 9.7 per cent, as left-handed, whereas Carrothers' [1] study of 225,000 Michigan pupils showed 10.1 per cent of the first graders as left-handed. Other studies estimate 2 to 8 per cent of children are left-handed; however, most estimates of the prevalence of left-handedness are based on a 6 per cent figure. This latter figure compares favorably with Luella Cole's [2] assumption that 5 out of every 100 girls and 7 out of every 100 boys will be left-handed. Although the authors have seen classes with as many as 5 or 6 left-handed children, the average elementary school teacher may not have more than one or two to work with during a given school year.

Since these children live in a world dominated by right-handed people, many of them need special help or guidance in solving their motor and emotional problems. Pupils and teachers throughout the country can attest that left-handed children have more than their share of difficulty with reading, writing, and speech. While emotionalism for some left-handed children may result from writing and reading frustrations, deep-seated feelings of inferiority and inadequacy may have had their origin in the fact that the pupil has recognized his minority status. Time and time again he has had to be exposed to instruction and activities which were directed to the majority and which have resulted in playground and classroom frustrations. Repeatedly, he has social, educational, and emotional needs which are overlooked by teachers, parents, and peers. Left-handed children who find success in spite of their handicap may owe their success to such compensating factors as high intellect, unusually fine coordination, and a very strong drive factor; other children who are left-handed may be weak in one or more of these areas and require teacher assistance if they are to overcome their handicap.

The Nature of Left-Handedness. The problem of working with left-handed children is often complicated by teacher uncertainty concerning this trait. Some teachers are afraid to do anything to influence a pupil's choice of handedness, because some authorities have indicated that left-handedness is an inherited trait. Actually, the evidence in support of Mendelian factors tends to be obscured by the influence of environmental factors which cannot be ignored. In recent years, many educators have supported the position that the baby is neither right-handed nor left-handed. He is ambilateral until he is about 18 months old, at which time a one-sided pattern begins to emerge as he reacts to his environment. During the first four years of childhood the boy or girl's hand preference may change back and forth, and by the time the child is ready to begin school there is a definite hand preference for certain defined activities.

Since children grow up in a predominately right-handed world, they are exposed to environmental influences which tend to condition them toward right-handedness and right-eyedness. Gesell [5] has indicated that children who are left to select a side for themselves have a 50-50 chance of selecting the wrong side. The evidence seems to support the view that handedness is a motor function which is the result of repeated exposure, habit formation, and training, but many teachers at the lower primary grade levels are afraid to play a part in the redirecting of motor functions. Some of these teachers assume a passive role because: (1) their philosophy calls for guiding the child's natural growth patterns without teacher direction or influence; (2) they still believe that attempts to change pupil handedness will result in an increase in emotionalism, may result in stuttering, and may lead to serious problems in reading and writing; and (3) they want to do something for the child but do not know what steps to take to help the pupil develop a right-hand dominance if he apparently is inclined to favor the left hand for writing activities.

Studies have shown that speech patterns and the body movements of right-handed people are controlled by the right side of the left cerebral hemisphere, but there is little supporting evidence to show that left-handed people have a corresponding dominance on the right side of the cerebrum. *This lack of a central dominance for left-handed people raises the question of whether or not they are really left-sided or merely in a state of partial development or training.* Teachers will find some pupils who are left-handed but who are right-eyed, thus indicating that the pupil may have established a partial left-hand dominance for writing. On the other hand, there are some left-eyed pupils who write with their right hands. This could mean that some right-handed pupils as well as left-handed pupils should be taught to use the opposite hand for writing since there is a close correlation between eyedness and handedness. Since this correlation is a positive one, a test for eyedness as well as handedness can be a means of determining whether or not a pupil is really left- or right-sided.

In view of the difficulties left-handed children have with writing, studies were made to determine whether it was true that stuttering would result from trying to change a pupil's handedness. The results seem to show clearly that the act of changing a pupil's handedness is *not* the cause when the teacher or parent helps the child make the change with an *absence of pressure.* Stuttering is actually the result of emotional turmoil or frustration; therefore, the teacher who does not frighten a child or embarrass him can safely help him make a transfer from apparent left-handedness to right-handedness.

Modern educators now believe that left-handedness is a definite handicap for children who have to live in a right-handed world, and they therefore recommend that left-handed children be changed at an early age. Preferably, the change should be made at the kindergarten and first-grade levels, although changes can be made up through the age of fourteen. If there is an issue here, it is one of *how.* If, for example, a child is only moderately left-sided, the task of the teacher may be relatively easy, but the child who is strongly dominantly left-sided may pose problems for the teacher who lacks understanding and patience. If she is going to upset the child by insisting on right-hand performance, it would be better to allow the pupil to go his own way. The authors recommend the administration of one or more tests to determine handedness and eyedness of five- and six-year-olds, with consideration being given to helping to eliminate crossed eye-hand dominance. If a pupil has not established a hand preference, he should be directed into activities leading to right-hand dominance if he is right-eyed, but he should be directed into activities leading to left-hand dominance if he should be left-eyed. No attempt should be made to change the handedness of children who are strongly left-handed and who fail to show mixed dominance.

In many European countries, notably in Russia, *all pupils* write with their right hand. In Russia, no pupil is permitted to use his left hand to write. American teachers are not asked to emulate such practices, but they are urged to take steps to avoid having children develop a left-handed writing pattern solely on the basis of chance. Our teachers are urged to identify the nature of each child's handedness and direct him to write accordingly. When the pupil shows a definite preference for his left hand, help is given him to enable him to overcome some of the frustrations which frequently perplex left-handed pupils. If the pupil has already learned to write with his left hand, a teacher can change his handedness if she carefully studies the pupil's behavioral patterns. Frequently, bright pupils make the change from left to right with a minimum of direction and extra encouragement, but here, emotional stability can be an important factor. The child who is emotionally insecure, whether slow or bright intellectually, may not be able to make the transition without developing greater emotional tensions. In such a case, the pupil should be permitted to continue writing with his left hand unless he shows an interest and desire to try to write with his other hand. Whenever a change in handedness is to be attempted, the parents should be advised of the teacher's intent in order to secure their approval and cooperation. In addition, the pupil should be made to see the advisability of trying to learn to write with his right hand.

The following are tests a teacher can make to determine a pupil's handedness:

1. *Receiving test.* Stand directly in front of a pupil and offer him an object, such as a pencil, a crayon, a coin, a sheet of paper, and observe which hand takes the object.

2. *The eating test.* Give a child a fork or spoon and ask him to eat something. Since most children will have been trained to eat with their right hands, only the child who has strong left-handed tendencies will resist the training and try to eat with his left hand.

3. *The dot test.* On a paper which has been ruled into small one-inch squares, have the pupil make a dot in the middle of each of the squares while the teacher times the child. She observes the hand the pupil uses to make his dots and counts the number marked in a minute. By comparing his score with those of others in the class, she gets a picture of his manual dexterity and his hand preference. If he changes hands during the test, she may get a clear picture of his hand preference. After trying the test with his right hand, she should repeat the test with the pupil making the dots with his left hand. A comparison of the pupil's two scores will help to show his hand preference.

4.· *Threading-a-needle test.* Here the child is merely asked to thread a needle while the teacher observes him.

5. *Throwing-the-ball test.* Ask the pupil to throw a ball, and observe the hand used to toss it.

6. *The cutting test.* Give the child a small pair of scissors and ask him to cut out a picture from an old magazine. The left-handed child will have more trouble than the right-handed child. A repeat test with the other hand will show whether or not there is a preferred hand. Just cutting along a simple irregular line on a plain sheet of paper can suffice for the cutting test.

7. *Putting puzzles together.* Give the pupil a puzzle with large pieces. As him to put the puzzle together. Observe which hand he uses.

In addition to testing for handedness, the teacher should ascertain which eye is dominant. (The dominant eye is the one which is used for sighting when both eyes are fixed on a common point.) Following are a number of tests which can be used to determine eyedness.

1. The teacher may use a long mailing tube to test a pupil's eye preference. A pupil is asked to look at an object through the tube. He will use his preferred eye to sight the object.

2. Using the same tube, a teacher may refine her test to get a more reliable index by having the pupil hold the long tube about 6 inches from both eyes. With both eyes open, the pupil looks through the tube at a distant object. If he is right-eyed, he will continue to see the object when his left eye is covered. If he is right-eyed, the object will have apparently moved when he looks at it with the right eye covered, and he will not see the object. If he is left-eyed, he will continue to see the object when the right eye is covered.

3. A variation of the tube test calls for the teacher to have a pupil sight through a hole in a sheet of stiff paper. In the center of the

sheet the teacher cuts a hole about an inch in diameter. The pupil holds the card in both hands with his arms stretched out in front of him. The pupil is asked to sight a distant object through the hole with both eyes open. When he sees the object clearly, the teacher covers the left eye. If the pupil reports he can still see the object, he is right-eyed. If he cannot, he is left-eyed. Generally, a single trial may not be sufficient. The teacher should have the pupil try the test from different positions. Four or five tests will give the teacher a clear picture of the pupil's eye preference or dominance.

4. With young children, the teacher may want to try a test calling for a mechanical device, but older pupils or adults can readily be tested for eye dominance through a simple sighting or aiming test. Here the pupil sights a distant object with both eyes open. He brings up his hands and points at the object. If he closes or covers the left eye and finds his fingers still in line with the object, he is right-eyed. If he finds that his fingers have apparently moved out of line, he is left-eyed. If he continues to find his finger pointed at the object when he closes or covers his right eye, he is left-eyed.

Instructional Procedures for the Left-handed Child. When a child has been found to be inherently left-handed, the teacher should direct him in activities which will lead to success with his writing endeavors. He should be helped by guiding him to good posture and a good writing position. Actually, these same instructions for correct posture may be given to *both* left- and right-handed children: (1) Sit well back in the chair, head up, back erect, with feet flat on the floor; (2) lean slightly forward from the waist; (3) support the hand with the third and fourth fingers, elevating the wrist slightly from the paper and making correct contact of the writing fingers with the pen or pencil.

If children are taught to hold pencils as directed in the first grade, left-handed children should have little writing difficulty. Unfortunately, many are not given proper instructions when they begin to write. Many teachers have no understanding of the importance of proper grip on the pencil, and upper grade teachers may have to reteach the child how to hold his writing tool. This can be difficult, because the teacher has to undo years of improper writing habits, but it can be done. In one elementary school, all left-handed children are brought together for special writing instruction. They were taught how to hold pens between their index and middle fingers. Each pupil learned to look directly at the point of his pen. The pupil did not try to look around a broad knuckle or try to turn his hand so the point could more readily be seen (wrists were kept straight). The pupils were also taught how to slant their papers. After a few lessons they were able to return to their regular classrooms where, with continued encouragement by their regular teacher, most of the students showed that they did not need further special writing assistance.

Recent research shows that letters starting with a stroke to the left are most easily executed by the left-handed child. Muscular control can be most readily developed by teaching these letters first: *a, o, d, g*. Since it is more natural for the left-handed child to make all motions from right to left, exercises that develop the ability to move from left to right will not only improve his writing ability, but aid in developing a forward eye sweep. Practice in writing the letters *i, u, w, t, e, l, r, b, f*, and *s* will develop coordination in the forward motion desired.

Teachers must be constantly on the alert to see that all left-handed children who are writing cursive slant their papers toward the left arm—and not imitate those who are right-handed. The top left-hand corner of the desk and both sides of the paper should be parallel with the left arm. All down strokes should pull toward the left elbow. It is imperative that correct writing instruction for the left-handed child be given at the earliest possible opportunity and continued constantly until the pupil has mastered the proper left-to-right motion, letter execution up from the line of paper, and proper position of hand and paper. If this is done, the left-handed pupil can learn to write smoothly and legibly with good speed and a minimum amount of effort, and he will not need to work with mechanical devices to correct the position of his hand or fingers.

REFERENCES

1. George E. Carrothers, "Left Handedness Among School Pupils," *American School Board Journal*, 114 (May 1947), 17–19.
2. Luella Cole, *Handwriting for Left-Handed Children* (Bloomington, Ill.: Public School Publishing, 1955).
3. W. F. Dearborn, "The Nature of Special Abilities and Disabilities," *School and Society*, 1961.
4. Frank N. Freeman, "Teaching Handwriting," *NEA Journal* (November 1954), 482–83.
5. Arnold Gesell, "Handedness," *Journal of American Medical Association*, 155 (August 1954), 1548.
6. Arnold Gesell and Frances L. Ilg, *The Child from Five to Ten* (New York: Harper & Bros., 1946).
7. W. W. Greulich, "Rationale of Assessing the Developmental Status of Children from Roentgenograms of the Hand and Wrist," *Child Development*, 21 (March 1950), 33–44.
8. Frances Ilg and Louise B. Ames, *School Readiness* (New York: Harper & Row, 1965).
9. Irene Marcuse, *A Study of Children's Handwriting as a Guide to Emotionally Disturbed Children* (New York: Noble and Noble, 1957).

CHAPTER 11

Improving Spelling Techniques

Elementals of Teaching Spelling

CHOOSING THE BASIC SPELLING LIST

Children are going to write, and they need to develop proficiency in spelling as a means of communicating with others. The school's problem is essentially one of helping each pupil select the basic core of spelling words necessary for his success. Years ago, the basic core of spelling words for an average child included from 6,000 to 10,000 words. Today, a basic list of 3,000 to 4,000 spelling words will more than suffice for average pupils, while a slow learner may be able to do all the writing he needs if he masters Fitzgerald's [4] 499 basic spelling words, which are considered adequate for 75 per cent of all writing done by average children. Formerly, the word lists contained many meaningless spelling words. Few pupils mastered these words, and fewer used them intelligently in their written work. Modern teachers are more selective in the words they teach, because they emphasize spelling words children can use and will use in their writing.

In an attempt to develop a basic core of spelling words which will have meaning to pupils all their lives, educators have taken words which are considered an essential part of the writings of both adults and children. Although the basic spelling lists taught in many schools today may not be as devastating as those taught at the turn of the century, many of them can still be abbreviated. Research has shown that the law of diminishing returns sets in after children have learned about 2,000 words from the modern basic spelling word lists. Since these 2,000 words include 95 per cent of all the words needed for child or adult writing, the return from teaching additional spelling words diminishes rapidly. After this point the pupil has to learn about 600 new words to increase his knowledge of the basic list by an additional 1 per cent.

Many modern educators recommend the use of a composite word list such as that compiled by Fitzgerald. [4] His core vocabulary includes 2,650 words selected from the most important and commonly used words found in both adults' and children's writings. All the words used occur in the Rinsland [9] and McKee-Fitzgerald [4] children's writing lists, and all but 16 are found in Horn's [7] adult writing list (see pp. 312–14). Fitzgerald divides his list into three sublists for those who need a differentiated curriculum, thus:

> List I includes the 499 spelling words used most often by beginning children and by children throughout the grades, as well as by adults in their writing. These words, with their repetitions, make up 75 per cent of all child writings, and could easily become the basic core of words taught to slow learners.
>
> List II includes 970 spelling words which, with their repetitions, make up 85 per cent of all the words children use in their writing. This list contains the first 499 words plus new words which will be used in adult life as well as throughout their school careers.
>
> List III contains 473 derivatives formed by adding *s, d, ed,* or *ing* to base words. They are the most frequently used derivatives found in the writings of children.

Average children who master a basic word list such as Fitzgerald's will know about 95 per cent of the spelling words they will use all their lives. After having mastered such a list, the individual pupil should learn how to derive alternate forms of the words and to locate in the dictionary the correct spelling of the less usual words for himself. If he has to use technical words which are appropriate for his writing in a more advanced and specialized field, he will have to learn them himself. Since spelling studies have shown that 5,000 spelling words constitute almost 100 per cent of the words children will use in their writings in school and for most of their adult writings, why are the rest of them not recommended for direct teaching? Actually, some of them will never be used by children; others need not be taught, because they will be learned incidentally; and still others will be learned as words derived from the basic core list. Pupils who have mastered the first 2,650 to 3,000 spelling words can continue to study the next level of words, but the total increase in their spelling vocabulary will scarcely be noticed in terms of a percentage gain.

In trying to select spelling words which will have meaning to children at all elementary grade levels, several noted educators have made reference to H. D. Rinsland's [9] famous study based upon a tabulation of 6,012,359 running words taken from children's writings in Grades 1 to 8 from 416 cities in the United States. Hildreth's [6] word list, which was based on the development of a frequency study of words used by Rinsland, has been abbreviated by Dr. Margaret Parke for use in the New York City schools. Here, one finds three lists in use: List A is a listing of the 253 words used most frequently in children's writing; list B includes a listing of 1,000 most frequently used words; while list C includes about 3,000 words divided into frequency usage levels.

Problems of Grade Placement of Spelling Words. The classroom teacher in the average school is not a spelling specialist, so she depends upon others for guidance in the selection of spelling words for her pupils. While she can start with a basic spelling core, the master list may not help her in selecting words considered appropriate for grade usage. If the teacher refers to standard spelling textbooks, she will find that the various authors are not in accord when it comes to grade placement. Moreover, there is an insufficient amount of review of essential words used by upper grade pupils, because spelling words are not mastered in a graded sequence the way children need them in their daily writings. The basic commercial graded textbook gives the teacher, the pupil, and the parent a measure of security, but studies such as that of Betts [1, 2] reveal little agreement in the words selected by various textbook authors. In his 1940 study, Betts found grade placement agreement by seventeen different textbook writers on only 543 of 8,645 different spelling words. In his 1949 study of eight different spellers, he found agreement on grade placement of only 483 words of a total of 8,652. He found considerable agreement in regard to the inclusion of the first 2,000 spelling words in a series even though they were not given the same grade placement. There was considerably less agreement regarding the selection of additional words and their grade placement. This was particularly true of books used at upper grade levels.

In the past, spelling difficulty was a criterion for studying words at designated grade levels, but actual usage may refute this principle. Teachers find primary grade children using difficult words in their writings, and upper grade teachers find their children still need to study and learn words classified as easy. Conflicts develop over a definition of the word "difficult." Actually, whether a word is difficult may depend upon the child's experiences rather than on an adult's interpretation. Frequently, one finds authors omitting spelling words they classify as easy, only to find that the children have failed to learn to spell commonly used words when they encountered them in their reading and writing. About 350 words which are mostly monosyllables and which should be easy to learn continue to give children trouble. Words like "very," "will," "until," "soon," "been," "old," "have," and "come" should be specifically taught to pupils who have not learned them through an incidental approach.

Teachers find little overlap in spelling words designated for particular grade levels. This would be a minor problem if children mastered and retained all the words studied and learned from a graded basic word list or text, but children do not learn that way. First of all, most children are not always ready for the words in a basic speller, and second, children have a tendency to forget spelling words which have no meaning to them or which they do not put to use in their daily work. As a result, one finds a pyramiding of difficult words confronting children when they want to write. A fifth-grade teacher will find pupils who must go back down to second- or third-grade levels to study words they need.

Teachers who feel the need for a gradation of words where a common core list of spelling words has been developed may refer to the recommendation Hildreth makes regarding her six-level list, thus: Grade 2—pupils study the 350 most commonly used words; Grade 3—pupils study the next 500 most commonly used words; Grades 4–6—pupils in each grade study 700 words from levels 3–6.

No Single Graded List Sufficient for All Children's Needs. Individual differences in ability and maturation make it virtually impossible for a teacher to find any *one* spelling list which will meet the spelling and writing needs of all pupils in a given classroom. At lower grade levels, children should not try to spell words they cannot read. As these retarded readers move into higher grades, teachers must make adjustments for them by teaching the words which they missed at earlier grade levels. *At all grade levels* the teacher has to take into account the readiness of children for the spelling words presented. Frequency of use and readiness for use are more important than difficulty as designated by a grade placement level. If children are not going to have any immediate use for words listed in a basic speller, the teacher may try to create a use for them artificially by having the children try to use those words in sentences. This seldom accomplishes anything, since the pupils generally use them incorrectly because they do not understand their meaning and seldom retain them.

Boys and girls often go through the motions of studying spelling words in order to pass a test, but these words are not retained very long. Unless these words are going to be used frequently in the children's writing, they will have to be relearned at a later date. Bright pupils usually know many of the spelling words in a graded speller assignment; therefore, they do not have to study very many words to make their passing score on the spelling test, whereas many of the slower learners who have the least need for the words have to stretch themselves to frustration levels in order to obtain a passing mark. Usually, these pupils memorize the words. In some classes, teachers have found that reversing the dictation order will result in failure for some pupils because a memory sequence was broken. Thus, in classes where a graded spelling text is used, teachers reward the better learners, who make the least effort, and they penalize the slower learners who have had to exert the greatest amount of effort in learning words which they cannot and are not usually ready to apply or use.

FACTORS IN SPELLING SUCCESS

Children learn many words incidentally when they may not be concerned with formal spelling. Frequently, words encountered in language arts, science, and social studies become a part of the learner's writing vocabulary without special spelling drill. In some schools there are teachers who have substituted an "incidental" type of spelling teaching in place of direct (conventional drill) spelling teaching. These teachers often oppose formal spelling approaches, but they do not leave all spelling instruction to chance. They review the word contributions of various subjects in the light of their pupils' writing needs, and they plan activities which call for the use and reuse of words that may have been encountered incidentally. They try to reinforce learning through activities involving writing and spelling as communication skills.

The fact that children study spelling in a special period set aside for that purpose is not a guarantee that spelling objectives will be realized. Poor teaching and the lack of readiness for spelling words can result in a negative attitude toward learning. Many children can learn their spelling in a program where there is regularity and sequence to spelling activities. In addition, teachers must recognize that success in spelling may be greatly influenced by many factors not directly related to the spelling assignment. Basically, the richness of a pupil's nonschool and school experiences contributes to the development of a rich spelling vocabulary.

Spelling Success Dependent on How the Pupil Feels about Learning. Occasionally teachers find themselves with a boy or girl who cannot learn enough in school. The day does not go by that such a pupil does not pore over a new reference or library book. If someone wants the dictionary or encyclopedia, he has it. His questions are always sharp and challenging. He reads new books, avidly in search of new information, new ideas, and new experiences in written language.

Teaching spelling to such a pupil is easy, because he wants to learn! He enjoys discovering the meaning of new words and is challenged when he finds that he can use a new word in his own writing. Unfortunately, such pupils are not as commonplace as teachers would like them to be. Many pupils find satisfaction and even pleasure in school activities, but few of them will go out of their way for new experiences when the going begins to get difficult and they begin to feel insecure about their efforts.

When kindergarten and first-grade children start school, many of them are full of questions. Their natural curiosity makes them susceptible to the teacher's urging, probing, guidance and teaching, but many of them lose their spontaneous interest and desire to learn except when they are under pressure. For example, some of them cannot wait to start writing, reading, or spelling activities in the first grade. All too soon some of them find that there is no short cut to learning. Some types of learning may come easily to them, but the pupils must soon add the word "work" to their vocabulary. They may find teacher directions hard to follow, they may not hear what she says, or they may not understand what she wants. Writing looks so easy when the teacher does it, but when they try to write, their fingers refuse to work for them and what they put on paper is not exactly the way they meant it to look. Sometimes they get very tired. Nobody ever told them that little things like writing, reading, and arithmetic could be so tiring. They look so easy when grownups do them. Teachers who know young children plan a well-balanced program to help avoid fatigue and frustrations; they do not coddle their boys and girls, but they do all they can to preserve that initial spark or interest in learning. Once it is lost, it may never be recaptured.

Spelling Success Related to Writing Success. Few children find success with spelling until they feel secure in their attempts to write and express themselves. Until children obtain good motor control, they may not enjoy writing. Those who find writing tiring and frustrating often try to avoid it. As a result, they have little need for spelling since they do not express themselves very often on paper. In working with such youngsters, some teachers have found that the introduction of the typewriter has been the impetus they need. Some teachers allow children who are having difficulty with the transition to cursive writing to continue their creative efforts in manuscript until they have developed confidence in their new writing form.

One of the prerequisites for spelling readiness is the ability to write the letters of the alphabet. Once the pupil masters the alphabet, he begins to see words or letter groupings. He must then be able to copy words without changing these letter groupings. Until he can copy words and simple sentences correctly, he is not considered ready for formal spelling instruction. After he can copy them without leaving out letters or transposing them, he must be able to demonstrate his ability to write a few words from memory. These may be words dictated by the teacher, based upon prior reading and writing experiences with words considered essential for good writing success.

Spelling Success Related to Reading Success. One of the prerequisites for spelling success is the ability to recognize and pronounce from 300 to 400 common words found in the first-grade reading program. From frequent contact with these words, the pupil should already be able to spell about 75 per cent of them. If he is going to acquire success in written activities where ability to spell is an essential, these words must have *meaning* to the learner and must be words he can use in his oral and reading activities. This means that formal spelling may not be started for many children until they reach the middle of second grade, and it may have to be deferred for other pupils until about the end of second grade. On the other hand, some exceptionally good readers begin second grade without having to review first-grade reading materials; these pupils may be able to proceed directly into a formal spelling program based upon their success in both reading and writing during the first grade. When the teacher has a basic spelling series, her progress with individual pupils should depend upon their ability to learn to write, spell, and use the new words as a means of communication. As a rule, children will not be too successful along these lines until they have mastered the equivalent of the first-grade level reader of the basic reading series. They may go through the motions of memorizing the spelling words, but they may not do too much with them. On the other hand, children who show a need for spelling in order to write may learn how to spell easy words they are encountering in their reading. Here the simple spelling activities will reinforce some of the reading skills. The teacher is reminded that the spelling words must be words that the children can read independently and should be words which are a part of their spoken vocabulary.

Research studies have shown that there is a higher correlation between spelling success and reading success than there is between spelling success and intelligence. Teachers will find that pupils who learn to read readily and who find satisfaction in reading activity tend to have few difficulties with spelling. This does not mean that all good readers are equally good spellers, because other factors can interfere with spelling success. Teachers will find, however, that all poor readers tend to be poor spellers. Teachers will also find that their poorer spellers tend to fall into two categories: the average and good readers who are not good spellers and the poor readers who are also poor spellers. If the teacher is to help these children improve their spelling, two different approaches will have to be used. In working with the former group, the teacher must work on improvement of their method of studying new words. Theirs is essentially a *remedial spelling* problem, while the latter group may require a *remedial reading* approach. Teachers who are working with pupils who are both poor readers and poor spellers will usually find that they can improve children's spelling by helping them improve their basic reading skills.

Spelling Success Related to Pupil's Work-Study Patterns. The pupil who has poor work-study patterns naturally encounters difficulties with spelling. When faced with new words, he does not know what to do. He has never developed a systematic approach to spelling. Instead of concentrating on the word before him, he may try to avoid using it by refraining from writing or by substituting an easier word. If this fails, he may try a trial-and-error approach. This pupil does not know the meaning of organization. He is not particular about details, so he does not look too carefully at new words. He is in the habit of copying words incorrectly, because he has never learned the habit of comparing what he writes with his original source. When he writes a difficult word correctly, it is quite apt to be due to chance.

Frequently, an individual or small-group approach to the pupil's spelling problems will suffice to give the teacher a chance to analyze the nature of his work patterns and then to redirect his activities so that he can see the result of his efforts. Many poor work-study habits may be due to faulty training at lower grade levels. A pupil may have poor listening skills. He may need to learn to listen for such specific things as sounds if he is going to pronounce words correctly. In some cases the pupil's lack of success in spelling and in reading may be based upon a total lack of training in phonetics at lower grade levels. If this is true, a fifth-grade teacher may find that special phonetics lessons are necessary for one or more pupils who may be having trouble with word-attack skills considered essential for success in both reading and spelling. While Horn [7] states that we do not have adequate evidence for making a confident decision as to how much and in what ways the teaching of phonetics can increase efficiency in spelling instruction, he and other authorities see real value in the teaching of phonetics as an aid to spelling as long as it does not substitute for the continuance of a systematic study of spelling. In either case, the problem of work-study patterns goes back to earlier beginnings. One does not acquire facility in working with phonetics or develop a systematic study of spelling without the early establishment of study routines, desirable attitudes to learning, and the development of standards of work.

Individualizing the Teaching of Spelling

Education will have much more meaning to many average and above-average pupils if teachers accept the principle that time spent on the writing or the studying of spelling words which children already know can be directed into other learning channels where there are growth possibilities. For example, at least five sixth-grade pupils in an average class may be counted upon to know the correct spelling for every one of the twenty new words introduced on Monday. Another seven pupils never miss more than two or three words on the practice test. Yet, each pupil has to complete exercises for each word in the graded speller list. This usually means writing each word five times, using the twenty words in a story, writing out meaningless definitions, and then taking at least one additional practice test before the final Friday test. For growth, these pupils should be allowed to work with either more difficult words or words which have meaning and value to them.

One can assume that the spelling exercises were supposed to help improve their spelling; therefore, one has to ask how much growth there is in having these pupils carry out activities that are meaningless to them. These pupils need spelling words and activities which will present a meaningful challenge. The teacher must be able to individualize the spelling assignment by having these children work with different word lists, or work on the mastery of a basic core of essential words up to their own achievement levels. In some classes the teacher works with two or three graded spellers, and in other classes the children all work from a single word list in terms of their own backgrounds and rate of spelling mastery.

READINESS FOR SPELLING INSTRUCTION

Spelling readiness is as important as reading readiness, but it is a stage of learning which is often ignored or overlooked. Children who are introduced to formal spelling before they are ready for it can quickly become discouraged from the frustration which comes with repeated failures. Children who cannot find success when they start to write or spell quickly develop a resistance to or dislike for spelling. Teachers who introduce formal spelling to all children in a class at the same time are ignoring the fact that many of the pupils are not ready for the work that follows. This means that teachers must study their children carefully to ascertain the state of readiness for a formal introduction to spelling. Some of the pupils may have to continue with activities which will give them the background and techniques leading to successful word mastery of the words they use in their writing. In determining spelling readiness, the teacher should give consideration to the following factors:

The pupil should have successfully read one or more books on the first-reader level and be able to recognize and pronounce from 300 to 400 of the words commonly encountered in the first-grade reading program.

The pupil should have had a successful experience with writing: He should have sufficient muscular control to make his writing almost automatic, and he should be able to make a good copy of the letters he needs without strain or tension.

The pupil should be able to see the component parts of the words to be spelled, and he should be able to see them as a whole.

The pupil should be able to hear the sounds of the letters and syllables introduced in reading.

The pupil should have developed a good pattern of work-study skills: He should have a good attention span and be able to concentrate without becoming fatigued.

The pupil should have confidence in himself that comes from some measure of success in his reading and writing activities and acceptance by both his teacher and his peers.

The pupil should have learned how to listen to others.

The pupil should have learned to pronounce words used in reading and other classroom activities.

The pupil should have learned the importance of both following teacher directions and turning in work which represents his best effort.

The pupil should have a desire to write words and sentences: He should have something he wants to say and should see spelling as a prerequisite to this.

The pupil should know the meaning of the words he is going to use in his writing.

The pupil should have developed the ability to express himself in writing with some help from the teacher by first telling a story, then writing it with teacher help.

The pupil should have been taught some technique or method of studying words in order to learn to spell them correctly: He should have been taught to enunciate letter sounds and should have been introduced to names and sounds of the vowels and consonants. The pupil should also have been taught to translate sounds into letters, and letters into sounds. He should be able to look for details in words, such as letter sequence, letter combinations, the length of the word, initial letters or final endings, tall and short letters, etc.

The pupil should understand that written work should be studied or proofread before it is turned in, to ensure that the words are written correctly regardless of whether the words have been copied or written independently.

PROVIDING FOR INDIVIDUAL SPELLING NEEDS
THROUGH PRETESTING

Pretesting is one approach to the problem of individual differences in spelling. In the average classroom the pretest will help the teacher to (1) identify pupils who know all or most of the words in the new lesson; (2) identify pupils who are not actually ready for most of the new words; and (3) discover the extent and nature of individual and group spelling needs. Thus, when there is a common spelling need, she can plan special activities for all pupils working with a similar problem. When there is no pattern, her instruction becomes individualized. Where the pretest plan of teaching spelling is used, the children study only the new words that give them trouble. They may work individually, in teams of two, or in larger groups. If one or more pupils has trouble with specific words, the teacher is available for special instructional assistance.

Educational research favors the test-study method of teaching over the study-test method of teaching as being more beneficial to children. However, Horn [7] says, "The lag between what is known and what is done in spelling is discouraging." Horn is referring to the fact that commercial spelling book directions and teaching practices lead children into a study-test program in the face of a mass of evidence which supports a testing-before-study approach. On the other hand, Gates [5] once advocated the study-test approach in the primary grades, where children have fewer words in their speaking, reading, and writing vocabularies and thus need the study activities before they are tested. This may be true for young children, but all upper grade pupils, with the exception of the slow learners, will find that the test-study method or pretest approach is more efficient and more satisfying to the learner. Horn [7] reports that more recent investigations have shown that the pretest approach is superior to the study-test approach even at the primary grade level.

EVALUATING PUPIL PROGRESS IN SPELLING

When children study spelling, they should have in mind one basic or ultimate purpose, namely, to become better spellers in order to express themselves more effectively. Unfortunately, many pupils fail to look at spelling in this light. If one asks many sixth graders why they are studying a designated list of spelling words, a common answer will be, "We are studying them because we have to pass a test." A few blunt pupils will state, "We will have to write every word we miss, ten times." This feeling that words have to be studied in order to pass a test is a form of *negative learning*. Instead of becoming an evaluative instrument, the test becomes a club. Pupils feel the test is a threat to their security, that if a pupil fails to make a good showing on the spelling test, something drastic will happen to him; therefore, in many instances the pupil resorts to desperate measures to get by. All too often, words are studied until all are memorized, but after the test has been taken, the words are forgotten, with the result that many of them may be misspelled in the pupil's regular work.

Children who study words merely to obtain a mark or to avoid having to do extra work are not looking at a spelling test as a learning situation. The spelling test, whether oral or written, should be considered as a tool for learning. It tells the teacher and the student where the student stands. Under the pressure of marks and a grade standard philosophy, one finds some pupils cheating to avoid a penalty or to maintain status in the eyes of the teacher, his parents, and his peers. Cheating is often an "out" for the pupil who is not prepared or who, after trying repeatedly to master assignments, stops working and tries to get by on his wits. In some classrooms the lack of provision for individual differences leads frustrated children to cheating. In such classes the test fails to prove its worth as an evaluative instrument and is the agent responsible for an *undesirable* and *unacceptable* form of social behavior.

The teacher has to work with pupils on their *attitude* toward spelling just as much as she works on trying to improve their word-analysis skill. They have to see spelling success as an essential to progress in all other fields of endeavor that require writing. Aside from school, the pupil will seldom, if ever, be called on to spell words in isolation the way he does when he takes a test. Yet he will be tested every time he uses words to express himself on paper. Other people may be evaluating his work as he goes through school, college, or the world of business. It is therefore important for the children to see the test, whether it is a pretest or a final test, as a teaching tool which is used to measure growth and to point out areas where special study may be necessary. Children should also realize that spelling test marks are not the only indication of their spelling ability. In fact, they will be penalized every time they turn in papers which are poorly written, or which contain spelling errors in words that pupils have had a chance to study and make part of their speaking and writing vocabulary.

Although spelling tests will continue to be used to evaluate pupil progress, teachers should rely upon other means of evaluation—for example, anecdotal records that show how far students have progressed; review of words listed for study in student notebooks; and written work samples kept by the teacher. Over a period of several months the teacher should see signs of improvement in these papers, but she should not have to wait to see growth. If she is continually observing the children as they work, it should be evident when they are making progress or when they are not. Boys and girls who constantly ask others for the correct spelling of words they are supposed to have mastered will continue to need help. On the other hand, if the teacher sees a pupil referring to the dictionary for help with words when he writes, she can see that the pupil is at least interested in trying to improve his writing and has made a positive step forward.

SPELLING RULES USEFUL
FOR ABOVE-AVERAGE CHILDREN

Bright children can overcome some spelling difficulties through the application of specific spelling rules, but slow learners and many average pupils find rules are of little value because they either never know when to apply them or fail to see the way they operate. Many primary grade classes have studied spelling rules before they were ready for them. With time and maturity, some of the pupils will find the abstract less frustrating. Some students will then find that rules can be applied to solve spelling problems. Generally, teachers will find it wasteful to teach rules on a mass scale, since only a fraction of the pupils in a class will use them to help spell difficult words. If rules are taught, they should be those that will help children learn to spell with a minimum of effort and with accuracy. If rules have many exceptions, they have little place in the average class.

Horn [7] says that

. . . the only rules which should be taught are those which apply to a large number of words and which have few exceptions, such as:

1. Words ending in silent *e* usually drop the final *e* before the addition of suffixes beginning with a vowel, but keep the final *e* before the addition of suffixes beginning with a consonant.
2. When a word ends in a consonant and *y*, change the *y* to *i* before adding all suffixes except those beginning with *i*. Do not change the *y* to *i* in adding suffixes to words ending in a vowel and *y*, or when adding a suffix beginning with *i*.
3. Words of one syllable or words of more than one syllable accented on the last, ending in a single consonant preceded by a single vowel, double the final consonant when adding a suffix beginning with a vowel.
4. The letter *q* is always followed by *u* in a word.
5. Proper nouns and adjectives formed from proper nouns should always begin with capital letters.

In teaching such rules, Horn goes on to state:

> These rules are effectively taught by the following methods:
> (a) Each rule should be taught inductively rather than deductively, the teacher developing it in connection with the study of the words which it covers.
> (b) Only one rule should be taught at a time.
> (c) In teaching a rule, it is important to emphasize both the positive and negative aspects.
> (d) When the rule has been taught, it should be systematically reviewed and applied.
> (e) Both in original teaching and in reviews the emphasis should be upon the use of the rule rather than upon the formal memorizing of its verbal statement.

USE OF STUDY-GUIDE QUESTIONS

When a pupil misspells a word, he is told to study it, but this may pose a problem to him. How does one go about studying spelling words? Suggested procedures advise him to: (1) look at the word; (2) say the word; (3) listen to the word; (4) say it again; (5) try to visualize the word; (6) write the word; (7) check what you wrote; and (8) rewrite the word if you need to do so. Although this may be adequate instruction for some pupils, it does not suffice for others. Studying a word means more than looking, saying, and writing. Many pupils need something to guide them as they look at the word. Some teachers stress the importance of looking at suffixes and prefixes. The pupils may be asked to look for letters which blend together to make a single sound, like *cr, fr, gr, tr, sh, wh, spr, thr*. After learning to look for these initial blends, they may be asked to look for final blends, such as *lf, lp, th, sh, ch, rth, tch, rch,* and *nch*. The pupils may be asked to identify letters within words, note syllable divisions, and then tell how the word is divided. The study of initial consonants, vowels, and vowel sounds will help the pupil in his attack on new words.

Study guides or outlines are often prepared to help pupils remember what to look for as they attack new words. The guide questions may take a number of forms, depending on the age and grade level of the students in a class. Intermediate, upper-grade, and senior high school pupils have found that such guides help them in their independent study of words or lists of words.

Some children find that the study-guide questions help them to study new words. They give purpose and direction to their activities. Independently, or with the help of the teacher, each pupil begins to develop his own spelling attack pattern. Once the pupil learns that

TABLE 1

Study-Guide Questions to Help Pupils Study Words Independently

---

Phonetic analysis questions:

What other words can I write that sound like this word?

What other words can I write that begin like this word? end like this word?

What silent letters are contained in the word?

Which syllable is accented?

Do the vowels have long or short sounds?

Can I pronounce the word correctly?

If the consonants *c, g,* or *s* appear in the word, do they have a hard or a soft sound?

Does the word contain a sound that might be spelled in more than one way?

Structural analysis questions:

Is this a root word for formation of other words? If so, write the new words.

Is there a root word in the new word?

What is the prefix, if any, in this word? Can other prefixes be added?

What is the suffix, if any, in this word? Can other suffixes be added?

Can this word be made plural?

Are there any small words in this word?

Is this a compound word?

Is a new word formed by spelling this word backward?

Can I arrange these words alphabetically?

Can I write this word correctly several times?

Does this word begin with a small or with a capital letter?

How does this word look in configuration?

Does this word contain any double letters?

Is this word a contraction?

Questions regarding meaning:

What is the dictionary definition for this word? Does the word have more than one meaning?

What are some good synonyms for the word?

What are some good antonyms for the word?

Does the word have a homonym?

Is this an action word (verb)?

Is this a telling word (noun)?

Is this a describing word (adjective)?

Can this word be used in more ways than as a verb, noun, or adjective?

Can I find a picture to illustrate the word?

Can I find pictures to illustrate the plural of the word?

Which of the words appear in current events articles I have recently read?

Which words appear in other texts, reference books, and story books I am now studying?

If this is a word which can be dramatized, can I do so?

Can I illustrate the word through art?

Questions regarding word usage

What good article can I write for the class or school magazine using this word or others in the list?

Am I spelling this word correctly in my other work?

(Table 1 continued)

Do I understand the word and its synonyms, antonyms, and homonyms enough to use them in my speech and writing?

What story, poem, announcement, report, letter, or instructions can I write using this word and others in the list?

Keeping a spelling notebook in which examples of the usage of words, stories, sentences, poems, clippings from current events material is helpful. The pupil may ask: Can I illustrate this word in my spelling notebook?

Can I make a crossword puzzle using this word and others on the list?

---

spelling is based not on mere memorization, but rather on a series of specific skills which result in real learning, he will find a study guide helpful.

MEETING SPELLING NEEDS BY DIVIDING THE CLASS INTO SMALL GROUPS

Many teachers have found that they can see greater growth when they divide a class for spelling instruction into two distinct groups, while other teachers work with three spelling groups. In the latter case, the teachers sometimes use pupil assistants to dictate words to one or more groups or to help check on the spelling progress of children in their groups. Usually the pupils are divided into spelling groups on the basis of achievement in spelling. At the beginning of the school year, the teacher may work with a single class group until she can identify the best or the poorest spellers. Sometimes a pretest with a random sampling of words from designated graded spellers or word lists will help the teacher to classify children in terms of their spelling needs. Some teachers have attempted to divide intermediate and upper grade students into spelling divisions on the basis of their reading achievement, but in spite of the high correlation between reading and spelling, one can find some good readers who are poor spellers. Some good readers who spell poorly may need special help in word-attack skills for a short time, but others may need to work on lower spelling levels for a long period of time. When working with spelling groupings, the teacher should continuously check progress. Every six or eight weeks the teacher should evaluate the progress of the children in the various spelling groups, and the pupils should be reassigned to better learning groups in terms of their class achievement or test results.

Many teachers can see values in working with different-level spelling lists, to provide a greater challenge to their better spellers and to avoid frustrating their poorer spellers. Unfortunately, many of these teachers fail to consider the need to vary teaching methods as well as spelling lists in terms of pupil needs or readiness.

Teachers have a habit of starting new spelling activities on Mondays, but this is not necessary. Teachers who cannot dictate the spelling words to two groups at the same time can plan their work so that the groups receive their dictation and instruction on alternate days. In some classes, the teacher will find that the better spellers will not need as many days to study spelling words as the poorer pupils will. If, however, the teacher wants the children to take pretests or final tests at the same time, the children can quickly adjust to the teacher's directions and her alternating dictation of the first word to one group and the second word to the other group, etc. (Teachers have found that spelling words can be dictated in advance with the use of a tape recorder. This helps where multiple groups are considered essential.)

INDIVIDUALIZED SPELLING ACTIVITIES FOR
SELECTED PUPILS

Teaching on the basis of spelling and writing needs and readiness for spelling instruction is not easy. A single textbook or series of graded books may not be adequate for the wide range of differences within a class or group. Therefore, many teachers advocate allowing pupils to progress at their own rate with a single basic common core of spelling words. All pupils will study these words, but will supplement them with words they fail to spell correctly in their daily work. From time to time the pupils will review words which give them difficulty, to ensure that these have been mastered. However, each pupil's forward progress depends on his own individual accomplishment. He keeps his own notebook of words which have proved troublesome. He provides the teacher with a copy of the words he needs to study, so that she can follow his progress and recommend special activities when it becomes evident that there is a repeat pattern in the spelling errors made.

Teachers using an individualized spelling approach often have pupils working together as "buddies" or partners. Two students will study their words both individually and together, then dictate them to each other or to another spelling team, with the teacher occasionally checking on their accuracy and knowledge of word meanings. In a sense, the test-study approach calls for a type of individualized teaching and learning since each pupil is held responsible for the study of only those words missed on his pretest. In a few classes the teacher insists on dictating all the words in an assignment to everyone. In some cases the pupils study the words they miss on the pretest and then, when it is time to take a final test, they prenumber their spelling papers, indicating by number which words they have to spell. Teachers who have worked with individualized spelling programs report that pupil growth in spelling is superior, but Hildreth [6] says that teachers find training pupils to work independently or with partners is their chief problem.

MAKING THE BREAK FROM THE BASIC SPELLER

Several large school systems such as New York City's do not depend upon commercial spelling textbooks since they have developed their own spelling lists from the research done in the field by educators such as Horn, [7] Rinsland, [9] Fitzgerald, [4] and Hildreth. [6] Many small school systems have yet to venture into this new spelling approach. Actually, the break can be made quite simply if the staff of an elementary school is willing to experiment with new approaches that can lead to an individualized spelling program or to a better type of grouping for spelling instruction.

A Gradual Break. Many teachers still enjoy the security of a basic spelling textbook. They know the work has been organized for them and for the children by a reputable spelling expert. They see no reason to dispense with a basic program which meets many of their children's spelling needs—or at least they assume that it does. As a result, these teachers continue to give their weekly lessons from the basic speller but they have found that additional words of an easier or of a more difficult type are essential for some pupils. This leads the teachers to supplement, from other sources, the word lists found in the basic speller. Other teachers will attempt to provide for individual differences by using more than one level of a basic spelling series.

The Combination of a Basic Word List and the Basic Textbook. Some teachers continue to use a graded spelling book, but they supplement it with spelling words taken from a basic word list such as Fitzgerald's (p. 314) or Rinsland's (p. 312). Each week the teacher assigns selected words from the basic spelling list to pupils who have encountered little difficulty with words in the basic text exercise. This may be done by pretesting with words from the basic list in order to approximate their spelling level. Other teachers regularly give all pupils spelling words from the basic list, which they consider essential. Intermediate grade teachers may review with their pupils by giving them words from Rinsland's "One Hundred Most Commonly Used Spelling Words" (see p. 312), since these words reportedly make up more than 60 per cent of the words used in children's written work. Good spellers may review these words at the rate of five to ten words each week, while poor spellers may study three to five of the words as a supplement to their regular spelling lesson. In some classes, teachers delay starting instruction in the basic textbooks until the pupils have presumably studied and mastered a list of essential spelling words.

Some teachers use these 100 most commonly used words as a mere

TABLE 2
Rinsland's 100 Most Commonly Used Spelling Words

a	eat	in	our	there
all	for	is	out	they
am	girl	it	over	this
and	go	just	play	time
are	going	know	pretty	to
at	good	like	put	too
baby	got	little	red	tree
ball	had	look	run	two
be	has	made	said	up
big	have	make	saw	want
boy	he	man	school	was
but	her	me	see	we
can	here	mother	she	went
Christmas	him	my	so	what
come	his	name	some	when
did	home-	not	take-	will
do	house-	now	that	with
dog	how	of	the	would
doll	I	on	them	you
down	I'm	one	then	your

SOURCE: H. D. Rinsland, *A Basic Writing Vocabulary for Elementary School Children* (New York: Macmillan, 1960).

starter, and continue to give pupils additional spelling words from a longer list of commonly used words in either child or adult writings.

Teaching "Spelling Demons" in Addition to the Basic Textbook Words. Research studies have shown that some frequently used words are repeatedly misspelled. These words are sometimes referred to as "spelling demons," because they frustrate children when they write. A few of the words can give children trouble at lower grade levels, but as the children mature and have more writing experience, the words are mastered. However, intermediate and upper grade teachers often find it helpful to review words found in lists such as Fitzgerald's [4] compilation of "220 Spelling Demons" or Johnson's [8] list of the "One Hundred Words Most Often Misspelled by Children in the Elementary Grades." Some teachers compile a list of their own based on observation of the writing difficulties encountered by their own pupils. Many teachers supplement the textbook with words which may be classified as difficult when their children try to use them in their written work. In many instances the children are given special help with the structure of the words.

Using Special Mimeographed Word Lists. Getting away from the traditional spelling textbook is not easy for some teachers. One can find teachers who insist on a basic spelling book, but who teach from it for only a portion of the school year since they make some use of mimeo-

TABLE 3
100 Words Most Often Misspelled by Children in the Elementary Grades

their	you're	because	something	swimming
too	clothes	thought	named	first
there	running	and	came	were
they	looked	beautiful	name	than
then	people	it's	tried	two
until	pretty	went	here	know
our	believe	where	many	decided
asked	little	stopped	knew	friend
off	things	very	with	when
through	him	morning	all right	let's
mother	its	wanted	together	sometimes
another	started	hear	happened	friends
threw	that's	from	didn't	children
some	would	frightened	always	an
bought	again	for	surprise	school
getting	heard	February	before	jumped
going	received	once	caught	around
course	coming	like	every	dropped
woman	to	they're	different	babies
animals	said	cousin	interesting	money

SOURCE: Leslie W. Johnson, "One Hundred Words Most Often Misspelled by Children in the Elementary Grades," *Journal of Educational Research*, 44 (October 1950), 154–55.

graphed spelling lists leading up to mastery of the first 1,000, 2,000, or 3,000 spelling words most frequently used in child and/or adult writings. All pupils may work with the basic word list for a few months. In some schools the better spellers try to master assigned word lists, while the slower or poorer spellers continue to use the standard textbook largely because it contains a wide variety of ready-made spelling activities to guide pupils less ready to work independently or at their own rate of spelling word mastery. Some teachers have found success with a new type of commercial textbook which gives them the basic spelling lists they need. The book, the *Multi-level Speller* by Botel, [10] includes a basic word list of 3,740 words described as the tools needed for good writing. Pupils who use this speller find that they can work with sequential lists or levels of spelling described as follows:

The words in this speller are organized in 11 levels, A through J plus the Extra lists. The words at Level A are more often used than the words in Level B. Words in Level B are used more often than those in Level C. Therefore, it is important to master the words at one level before going to the next. Sometimes we forget words we have once learned, so we must have a way of checking ourselves. The Placement Test tells you your spelling level.

TABLE 4

Fitzgerald's Master List of 220 Spelling Demons, a Useful Core
Vocabulary for Children's Writing

about	didn't	house	our	the
address	dog	how	out	their
afternoon	don't	how's	outside	them
again	down	I	party	then
all right	Easter	I'll	people	there
along	every	I'm	play	there's
already	everybody	in	played	they
always	father	isn't	plays	they're
am	February	it	please	think
an	fine	it's	pretty	thought
and	first	I've	quit	through
answers	football	January	quite	time
anything	for	just	receive	to
anyway	fourth	know	received	today
April	Friday	lessons	remember	together
are	friend	letter	right	tomorrow
arithmetic	friends	like	said	tonight
aunt	from	likes	Santa Claus	too
awhile	fur	little	Saturday	toys
baby	getting	lots	saw	train
balloon	goes	loving	school	truly
basketball	going	made	schoolhouse	two
because	good	make	send	until
been	good-by	March	sent	vacation
before	got	maybe	sincerely	very
birthday	grade	me	snow	want
bought	guest	Miss	snowman	was
boy	had	morning	some	we
boys	Halloween	mother	something	weather
brother	handkerchiefs	Mr.	sometime	well
brought	has	Mrs.	soon	went
can	have	much	stationery	we're
cannot	haven't	my	store	were
can't	having	name	studying	when
children	he	nice	summer	white
Christmas	hear	November	Sunday	will
close	hello	now	suppose	won't
come	her	nowadays	sure	would
coming	here	o'clock	surely	write
couldn't	him	October	swimming	writing
cousin	his	off	teacher	you
daddy	home	on	teacher's	your
day	hope	once	Thanksgiving	you're
December	hospital	one	that's	yours

SOURCE: James A. Fitzgerald, "A Crucial Core Vocabulary in Elementary School Language and Spelling," *American School Board Journal,* 103 (July 1941), 22–24.

Children who use the Botel *Multi-level Speller* work at their own level instead of on a graded spelling book level. Each individual finds his work level through pretesting. The pupil is then supposed to take the responsibility for his own progress. The boys and girls study a number of techniques to assist them as they work with the weekly spelling list. For example, they are required to write a class composition as one method of developing word meaning for the words studied.

A Word of Caution on Using Word Lists. Good word lists lend themselves to a greater individualization of the spelling program. Unfortunately, some teachers and their pupils have been led astray by an overemphasis upon the quantity instead of on the quality of words studied. As a result, some teachers have had to slow down individual students until the pupils could demonstrate their understanding of word meanings and their ability to use the words in a purposeful writing activity.

Teachers who make use of word lists still assist pupils in the mastery of essential rules and word-attack skills. The absence of spelling activities in the textbook may call for originality in the planning of study exercises. One cannot merely turn children loose with a list of spelling words; guidelines and controls must be established. While word lists may be based upon studies of the words children use most frequently, the average word list does not show the words needed by children in a special grade, school, or community. Therefore, children can still spend considerable time spelling words which are not related to their writing needs based on their stage of development or interests.

There is no one way to teach spelling. Good teachers find that they must be prepared to vary their teaching techniques to meet the varied needs of their children. A technique which works well with one class will not necessarily work out satisfactorily with another. Over a period of time, teachers will find themselves experimenting with many methods to stimulate pupil learning and to adapt their instruction to the needs of their boys and girls.

REFERENCES

1. Emmet A. Betts, *Second Vocabulary Study, Grade Placement of Words in Eight Recent Spellers* (New York: American Book, 1949).
2. Emmet A. Betts, *Spelling Vocabulary Study, Grade Placement of Words in Seventeen Spellers* (New York: American Book, 1940).
3. H. F. Bradford, "Afraid to Write? Or Afraid to Spell?" *National Elementary Principal,* 38 (March 1959), 31–32.
4. James A. Fitzgerald, *A Basic Life Spelling Vocabulary* (Milwaukee: Bruce, 1951).
5. Arthur I. Gates, "An Experimental Comparison of the Study-Test and

Test-Study Methods in Spelling," *Journal of Educational Psychology,* 22 (January 1931), 1–19.

6. Gertrude Hildreth, *Teaching Spelling* (New York: Holt, Rinehart & Winston, 1955).
7. Ernest Horn, "Spelling," *Encyclopedia of Educational Research,* rev. ed. (New York: Macmillan, 1960).
8. Leslie W. Johnson, "One Hundred Words Most Often Misspelled by Children in the Elementary Grades," *Journal of Educational Research,* 44 (October 1950), 154–55.
9. Henry D. Rinsland, *A Basic Vocabulary for Elementary School Children* (New York: Macmillan, 1960).
10. Morton Botel, *Multi-level Speller, Grades 3 to 12* (State College, Pa.: Penns Valley Publishers, c. 1959).

CHAPTER **12**

Meeting Individual and
Group Needs in Mathematics

Mathematical proficiency has a high place in the eyes of the general public, so a school can rapidly fall into disfavor if boys and girls fail to learn to use numbers correctly and effectively. Unfortunately for the teachers, full responsibility for arithmetic success or failure rests upon the school, since growth in arithmetic depends upon what is done in the classroom. Up to a point, young children can learn some simple numbers without teacher help, but growth in arithmetic skill stops if the teacher does not introduce the children to higher level phases of arithmetic. This is quite different from reading. Once children start to read, whether it is in school or at home, they can continue to grow on their own because there are so many new vistas open to them. Success in reading opens new doors to learning and to satisfaction or enjoyment from the act of reading. If boys and girls find satisfaction in their first reading experiences, they can and will read in class and at home for information or relaxation. This reading supplements the teacher's instruction and leads to mastery and increased reading skill. In a sense, bright students can learn to read successfully up to a fourth-grade level with little, if any, teacher help; but this is not true for mathematics.

Children's Reactions to
Arithmetic and the Need to Stimulate Them

After the novelty stage of working with numbers has been passed, few young children sit in class working with numbers and number concepts beyond what the teacher has asked them to do. When they go home, one seldom finds them working with number combinations or number problems unless homework has been assigned. While exceptional pupils can and will make a game of numbers, the opportunity to extend their skill or accomplishment outside the class is much less than it is for reading. This is important, because the lack of outside practice limits the range of accomplishment in arithmetic for fast learners or gifted children. A look at the distribution of arithmetic scores from a standardized fifth- or sixth-grade arithmetic test will reveal a clustering of scores just above or below the norm. One will not find the same range in achievement on an arithmetic test as on a reading test, unless the classroom teachers have deliberately helped the faster learners extend themselves through subgrouping for instruction, which permits pupils to move into higher levels of arithmetic when they are ready for them. Most children do not have too much immediate need for arithmetic beyond some easy computational skills, which means that they have to be stimulated to work with higher-level skills. The clustering of scores around the central point is an indication that this has not been done. In most instances, it points to mass teaching of arithmetic with considerable drill activities for both fast and slow learners. For the pupils in the latter category, the drill was essential for memorization of basic facts, and for the former the drill was usually essential to keep them from sitting with nothing to do.

In many arithmetic classes the bright pupils who quickly learn their basic facts and some simple application of these facts are not encouraged to apply their skill and knowledge to the solution of problems not found in textbooks. As a result, these pupils merely become more proficient than the average student in areas taught, but do not acquire proficiency with higher-level skills and principles until some teacher introduces them. These pupils need to be challenged. This *does not* mean merely giving the top fourth or third of a class more examples of the same type once they have demonstrated that they have mastered the skills taught.

Generally, children's reactions to arithmetic vary according to their number experiences. Boys and girls who have had limited success with numbers will often find excuses to avoid the arithmetic class or activities involving number proficiency. On the other hand, many pupils who say, "We do not like arithmetic," are actually trying to say, "We do not like the teacher," or, "We do not like how she teaches." If the teacher has a good relationship with her children, the pupils accept her arithmetic teaching without complaining. Out of respect for their teacher, they will go through the motions of doing arithmetic. They want to please her and may not consciously be able to say they like or dislike arithmetic.

In many cases, social pressures force boys and girls to say they do not like school or a particular subject such as arithmetic. It is the correct thing to say when talking with one's peers. Actually, many children find satisfactions in arithmetic because they enjoy the challenge which comes from working with numbers and because they can see their *own* accomplishment when they have mastered a skill. Studies show that 75 per cent of the average pupils in a class will do arithmetic assignments without question. They do not need to be pressured since they find successes or satisfaction in their accomplishments which are immediate. On the other hand, the remaining 25 per cent have a right to dislike arithmetic, because they are frustrated by arithmetic activities that lack meaning or purpose to them. They face a struggle every time they have to work with numbers unless the teacher recognizes their limitations and begins to teach at their level. A study by Chase, reported by Fehr, [7] states that children actually favor arithmetic over all other subjects. Chase's study involved 16,000 children from Oklahoma and New England. It showed that pupils rated arithmetic as the first or second preferred subject in a list of ten choices. Boys always selected arithmetic as their favorite subject, but girls were more apt to select reading as their first choice.

When some children show a dislike for arithmetic, they may be influenced by the attitude of a teacher rather than by the subject. Some teachers may not realize it, but their *own* dislike for arithmetic is transmitted to their pupils. This dates back to a time when they were in school struggling with arithmetic problems and concepts that were meaningless to them. As adults, they have to teach arithmetic, but they are not always secure in what they do and they fail to show any real enthusiasm about their work. If pupils have unpleasant arithmetic experiences in school, their interest in the subject is quite likely to wane. On the other hand, parents and friends who are enthusiastic about arithmetic can often help some youngsters find themselves. If, however, parents show their dislike for arithmetic, or continually press their youngster to higher achievement without giving him moral support through occasional praise, plus acknowledgement that they are conscious that he is *actually trying* his best to overcome his deficiencies, the pupil will have further cause to dislike the subject.

REASONS WHY SOME BOYS AND GIRLS DO NOT ACHIEVE SUCCESS IN ARITHMETIC

Arithmetic requires an ability to work and think in terms of abstractions. With children who view arithmetic class only as a period of frustration, the teacher will often have to work doubly hard to overcome their resistance to arithmetic, as well as to try to help them find success as they work with numbers. For some it will mean reteaching, but in other instances the boys and girls who are failing to master arithmetic concepts at a given grade level are not actually ready for the ideas or skills as they are presented. The teacher will find it essential to review their arithmetic backgrounds in search of clues which will help her select the best approach to the development of an appreciation for, and an interest in, arithmetic.

For example, she will often find that arithmetic failures may be attributed to one or more of the following factors:

1. The students were introduced to arithmetic principles and processes before they were ready for them. They never took part in an adequate arithmetic readiness program. These children therefore lacked an understanding of the meaning of arithmetic, and they did not receive the concrete backgrounds necessary for the understanding of abstractions.

2. Boys and girls were led through their workbooks or textbooks too rapidly, either from concrete presentations to abstract ones, or from one abstraction to another without sufficient, if any, contact with the necessary concrete experiences to make the abstractions meaningful.

3. Students received little, if any, individual attention when they had to cope with something they did not understand.

4. All students were exposed to the same type of teaching and teaching materials at the same time, regardless of whether or not they were needed or meaningful.

5. The teaching aids, textbook, and methods of instruction used in the past failed to present sufficient challenge to the learner. Arithmetic experiences of an enrichment nature were either nonexistent or inconsequential.

6. Students learned mechanical rules or steps to take in solving arithmetic problems without learning why. When called upon to apply the rules, the students did not know how to do so.

7. Many children cannot understand the meaning of the terms or processes encountered in a textbook because they are unable to read with comprehension. Some pupils have to have problems read to them, because they have never really learned to read arithmetic problems intelligently on their own.

8. Arithmetic was taught very formally with an accent on drill. Arithmetic was taught as a mental discipline, with quantity rather than understanding the chief goal of the teachers.

9. All too often, children have worked only with arithmetic symbols or small pictorial representations of real objects so that arithmetic has been quite removed from real situations.

10. Students have never learned the primary number facts necessary to solve the more difficult and more complicated processes encountered at upper grade levels.

11. Students lack confidence in themselves. Some of them are afraid to make mistakes. They are so insecure that they will not make a real effort to solve arithmetic problems.

Essentially, the teacher's work with these pupils must start at their accomplishment levels. They will not find satisfaction or enjoyment with arithmetic until something positive has been done to help them.

To be successful in arithmetic, each pupil has to develop good work-study patterns. He has to learn to concentrate at a given task until it is completed. This may require an ability to close his mind to activities and thoughts that will distract him from the problem before him. At times he may be able to work examples with others, but essentially each student should know how and when to work independently. He will need to learn the value of perseverance and hard work. He needs to be able to look back at what he has done to try to perceive his errors and then try to re-do the problem—not on a trial and error basis, but on the basis of intelligent reasoning. Again, a school cannot neglect its obligation to teach the values of neatness and accuracy. Without these values, the student will become inhibited in arithmetic. Carelessness is no excuse for errors.

NEED FOR MODERN APPROACHES TO TEACHING ARITHMETIC

Children's problems in arithmetic may be complicated because many arithmetic teachers lack the background and training necessary to teach standard arithmetic and because arithmetic today is in a continual process of change, thus calling for constant teacher learning if she is to teach the "new arithmetic" well. Recent studies have shown that a large proportion of elementary school teachers have had very little, if any, work in arithmetic beyond their own elementary grades. Some of them may have taken a short course in arithmetic teaching in college, but others have not. The result has been a textbook approach to arithmetic teaching by teachers who follow a teacher guide, manual, or textbook until (if they teach the same grade for a number of years) they become familiar with the arithmetic skills or knowledge presented at specific grade levels. And since the standard textbook does not go too far back or too far forward, some of these teachers are not ready to reteach skills ordinarily taught at lower grade levels, nor are they prepared to allow their fast learners to go too far forward, because they will need instruction in higher-level skills than the teacher has mastered. The preceding statements may seem harsh, but many conscientious teachers will admit that they had to relearn their arithmetic as they taught it for the first time.

With the advent of the new teaching approaches in arithmetic, many teachers have become enthusiastic about their teaching and have taken special courses to bring themselves up to date in their thinking, but many others find it difficult to understand the "new language of arithmetic." One has only to ask a group of elementary teachers what they are doing with set theory to throw some of them off balance. Others have trouble trying to teach arithmetic through the use of manipulative devices or visual aids. One group of teachers objected to a sixth-grade textbook because of the emphasis placed upon estimating arithmetic answers. This may seem like a small point, but this was not arithmetic in their minds. When answers are given, they must be exact. Some of these teachers have to learn that arithmetic is taught not for its mental discipline, but because it is an essential part of one's background if one is to live in a world which relies more and more on a mathematical base.

The need for good in-service programs for the experienced arithmetic teacher as well as the new teacher is being recognized as an essential for the security of many elementary and secondary school teachers who have responsibility for teaching some phases of mathematics. Quite often, it will be necessary for these teachers to explore or redevelop their philosophy of teaching in the light of what modern research considers essential for success with arithmetic processes and concepts.

To help these teachers, many school administrators set up arithmetic workshops with teachers, administrators, or consultants who have studied the "new arithmetic" lecturing, demonstrating, explaining, or leading discussions. In some schools professional books are purchased, circulated, and discussed. Teachers are encouraged to read current publications such as *The Arithmetic Teacher* or *The Mathematics Teacher* so that they can see what other teachers are doing and thinking. In one school, a special exhibit of new arithmetic books, including programmed learning materials, was set up for teacher study and use. In another school the teachers were surprised to see what could be done with films and film strips to teach arithmetic. In some schools the Board of Education has paid the cost of having a college instructor give a course in the new arithmetic to interested teachers. In others, the cost of tuition has been paid for teachers taking refresher courses in arithmetic.

When a school system starts to explore a new approach to arithmetic, it may have to start with one or two key teachers. These teachers may have to experiment with the understanding that their administrators will have to support them if they make mistakes or if parents complain that the children appear to be making slow progress.

ARITHMETIC READINESS AS A BASIS FOR
SUCCESS IN ARITHMETIC

The concept of *arithmetic readiness* is not understood by many teachers. *A readiness stage has been reached when the pupil's total background of experiences makes it possible for him to quickly apply a new principle or process to the solving of a problem.* The lack of comprehension of arithmetic readiness is particularly true of intermediate and upper grade teachers, but there are still some primary grade teachers who accept the concept of reading readiness, but who fail to see that arithmetic readiness activities meet the same basic needs of young children when they begin to work with numbers. Actually, arithmetic readiness for beginners may be considered a fairly new innovation in arithmetic, but readiness is more than a series of activities for first or second graders. In a true sense, boys and girls go through a number of readiness stages as they go through school. At every grade level, teachers will find that they have to introduce new skills and concepts which depend upon prior experiences. Therefore, teachers must be prepared to build upon the children's foundations in arithmetic whenever they plan to introduce new number abstractions. They must be prepared to give boys and girls opportunities to take part in a program of functional number experiences leading to the new abstractions which are to be taught. In other words, arithmetic readiness programs are preparatory programs for new learning experiences with numbers at *all* grade levels.

In some schools, this relatively new concept of the need for readiness experiences has led to an actual postponement of the teaching of *formal* arithmetic until the children reach third or fourth grade. In such classes the pupils receive systematic instruction in arithmetic at the second-grade level through a functional experience approach. The teachers will readily admit that their students will not achieve as well as other children on standardized tests, but with their growth in understanding, these pupils surpass the performance of those who have not gone through a comparable readiness program by the time they reach intermediate grades. One finds some teacher and public resistance to what appears to be a neglect of arithmetic fundamentals, so that teachers do not usually defer teaching formal arithmetic until the pupils are older. Instead, primary teachers try to provide more number experiences which will help their children understand the meaning of simple terms and processes.

Continuous growth in arithmetic is dependent upon the teacher's ability to recognize each pupil's stage of readiness for new arithmetic experiences. It is not a stage of growth which one goes through and then has permanently. A fifth-grade pupil may be ready for an arithmetic experience on Monday, but on Thursday the teacher may introduce him to a new phase of arithmetic which is meaningless to him because he is not ready for the new experience. If such a pupil is going to have successful school experiences with numbers, his teacher will have to pace her instruction to the pupil's maturation level, which may mean more than mere arithmetic experience levels. This is what can make arithmetic teaching difficult for teachers who do not see the need to discover the readiness of their children for a new series of arithmetic activities. The teacher goes through the motions of teaching, but there is no actual learning for some boys and girls in the class; they go through the motions of learning with the teacher, but are likely to become frustrated at their lack of success.

Since readiness for arithmetic instruction is a stage of development which is reached by different children at different times, all children are not ready for the same process at the same time. A pupil may be one of the first to understand subtraction, but some months later, owing to a gap in his arithmetic foundation, he may drop to the bottom of the class when he is introduced to the division of whole numbers. Teachers must keep their arithmetic groupings flexible so that they can teach individual pupils when they are ready for a process and not because they belong to a particular group.

Developing Initial Readiness for Arithmetic. Children begin school with different stages of readiness for number experiences. One child's home experiences may have helped him acquire a number of arithmetic skills and concepts. Parents and teachers may assume that the child can begin formal arithmetic without delay because of his *early* interest in numbers and his ability to count to ten, twenty, or thirty (as well as add several numbers not exceeding a total of ten), only to find that learning stops due to unanticipated frustrations.

Too early stimulation and forcing of number experiences on a child can be harmful. He may learn a few preliminary facts to please a doting parent or grandparent, but he may not have the attention span or the physical strength to complete exercises requiring muscular coordination or visual acuity for extended periods of time. As a member of a class, the pupil may have to learn what it means to listen and to follow directions. He no longer receives a personal direction since he is a member of a working group or team. The child may learn a few elementary facts or principles, but he can quickly reach a plateau where he will stay until his total experiential background has been broadened and he can again start to find meaning in what he studies.

The teacher may find that some children come from homes where language experiences were limited and number experiences non-existent. Readiness for some of these boys and girls may have to begin with communication skills and the understanding of the meaning of words. Some of these children may not see any purpose in arithmetic.

At times, these children may need to learn the meaning of independent work since they see nothing wrong in copying another child's answers or even putting their names to other children's papers. The conditions leading to number readiness will not appear without help, and as the child grows older, his lack of readiness for different levels of arithmetic may reflect upon what was or was not done for him at lower grade levels. ,

Recognizing Children's Readiness for New Number Experiences. Effective teaching calls for the pacing of instruction in terms of ever-changing and expanding stages of readiness for number experiences. To do this the teacher must be able to recognize each individual's learning level if she is going to avoid wasting her own and the pupils' time and effort. It will often help her to:

Observe behavioral patterns of pupils as they work in arithmetic and other nonrelated activities. Their work-study skills, interests, and attitudes may be clues to pupil problems or readiness for new learning.

Consult records on background—such factors as home life, physical health, mental ability, previous school experiences, and other data which will describe the pupils' work and behavior patterns.

Use informal and formal tests to pretest children's knowledge, skill, and understanding of numbers and number concepts.

Use an arithmetic skills checklist to keep a record of the individual's accomplishments or experiences in arithmetic.

Interview the pupil to find out how he thinks and what he thinks about. In many instances it is helpful for the teacher to have the student describe each step that he takes in solving a problem.

Investigate the child's previous number experiences, and determine the amount of interest he has in arithmetic and related subjects. Discover whether or not the pupil is ready to understand an abstract presentation without further experiences involving the use of concrete materials or illustrations.

Establish whether or not the pupil can see the mathematical connections in what he has learned or is learning in school with what is going on in or out of school. Also determine whether or not the pupil can see a purpose or meaning in what he does.

Since few teachers can teach children on an individual basis when they have thirty or more pupils in a class, they have to find common learning levels to minimize groupings or to pinpoint instruction in terms of pupil needs in arithmetic. By working with her children and observing them as they work, the teacher can discover collective stages of readiness which lead to group instruction or even all-class instruction for some phases of learning. Actually, the teacher has to discover whether boys and girls are ready for developmental work or a new kind of arithmetic or in need of continued practice or drill in order to fix an understanding and/or skill for ready use.

TEACHING ISOLATED FACTS, RULES, AND
PROCESSES NO FOUNDATION FOR PROBLEM SOLVING

Many educators have espoused the principle that children do not learn to solve problems through mere memorization of isolated facts, rules, and processes, but it took research such as that of Luchins [12] to prove the point. He showed that mechanized procedures for solving problems aided only in the solution of a particular type of problem, and that these same mechanized procedures became an impediment to the solution of problems deviating from that particular type. His study has pointed up one of the main reasons for pupil difficulties in arithmetic. Problem solving is the bane of many teachers' existence because teachers have taught pupils to solve problems *by learning a special rule or process, only to find that pupils have not carried learning over from one problem to another.*

Modern teachers have found that children need to analyze problems and problem situations. Understanding cannot be divorced from the process. This is one of the dangers of textbook and workbook teaching: The pupil is given an illustration. He studies the model and then tries to complete a series of examples similar to the one in the illustration. Up to a point he finds success with his approach, but if a new element is introduced in the problem, the student becomes lost. For effective teaching, boys and girls must learn several methods of attacking problems.

Setting the Stage for
Arithmetic Instruction by Grouping Pupils

Primary teachers use subgrouping techniques to teach reading because they recognize differences in the way children learn and in their rates of learning. These same differences affect pupil growth in other areas of the curriculum, especially arithmetic, but many primary grade teachers and most intermediate grade teachers fail to accept subgrouping for arithmetic instruction as their responsibility. The lack of acceptance of the concept of arithmetic subgrouping is due to uncertainty and misunderstanding on the part of the teachers. All too often, they resist grouping for arithmetic instruction because they do not know how to proceed with it. Or, if they are grouping for reading, they are afraid that they may not have the time to teach two subjects by the group method.

Some teachers are worried about the amount of work they will have to do if they have to divide their arithmetic class into two or three subdivisions. They remember the difficulties they have to face as they plan and teach their three reading groups, each of which may have a different reader throughout the whole year. They see the reading teacher trying to present basic reading skills each day through three different stories which require different types of instruction and work materials for the children. It becomes a frightening prospect, but largely because they visualize all subgrouping in terms of what they have done in the field of reading.

THE NATURE OF ARITHMETIC GROUPING

Arithmetic subgroupings should differ from reading groups in the sense that they do not have to be as "permanent" (unchanged for the school year) as reading groups. A teacher may find it necessary to work with three arithmetic subdivisions of a class, but this does not have to be standard practice. Grouping for arithmetic instruction does not require the same class organization that is used to teach reading. There will be times when common learning needs require an "all-class" approach, as well as times when pupils need individual help.

Teachers can frequently group children for arithmetic instruction through a series of unit activities centering around broad arithmetic topics or problems. At the start of each new field of study, the teacher may begin her work with the whole class. Instruction is differentiated when it becomes apparent that individual pupils need additional review or reteaching of subskills, or when it becomes apparent that the brighter pupils are ready to move into higher levels of instruction due to their advanced arithmetic maturation.

By observation, adequate testing, and frequent reviews, the teacher can determine the pupils' levels of operating and understanding. If there should be no perceptible difference in understanding and achievement, the teacher may continue to work with the entire class for a time. The slower learners may require additional time in mastering some skills, whereas the brighter pupils may be working freely on some cultural or advanced facet of learning.

Some slow-learning pupils may require daily instruction for a week or more before they master a new skill or process. In contrast, some faster learners may master the same skill or process by the end of the second lesson. In working with these students, the teacher may find that they are capable of learning additional ways to solve the same kinds of examples. As a result, the faster learners continue to work in

Team learning: plotting a graph on the blackboard.

Courtesy of the Ford Foundation

the same general area as the slower learners, but by different approaches. If interest on the part of some pupils begins to wane or the students fail to see a logical reason for continued work in a given field, it may even be advantageous to move the whole class on to another topic rather than continue until each subgroup has attained the goals set for it.

Where there is considerable variation in the arithmetic abilities of the pupils in a given class, it may be necessary to meet their needs through differentiation of assignments or by grouping children who have common arithmetic needs. To cope with the problem of grouping, Grossnickle [9] suggests five ways to provide instruction on the pupil's level of operation:

1. Using different materials for the different levels of instruction
2. Employing different ways of performing operations (use of different algorisms)
3. Using different ways to solve verbal problems
4. Teaching estimation to see if answers are sensible
5. Discovery of mathematical principles

Here, pupils may continue to work with common materials, but their goals are not the same. Frequently the same topic or series of examples can continue to serve as the instrument through which the teacher promotes new understandings and skills.

Daily Instruction Not Required in Grouping. How and when children are grouped for arithmetic instruction depend upon the teacher's approach to teaching basic skills or knowledge. In the past, teachers often said, "We teach the kids how to do the work, then the rest is up to them." Today, many teachers guide children as the boys and girls learn how to do the work by discovering for themselves how a problem is to be solved. She has to recognize the different learning levels of the children in her class and see that they have appropriate work materials. Essentially, progress is made by moving steadily from the known to the unknown, from the concrete to the abstract. For each new arithmetic concept, there is a state of readiness. Based upon his past experiences, the pupil is able to work out new exercises or problems.

To some educators this may seem like a waste of time as children work with trial-and-error methods of solving problems, but this is where the teacher steps into the picture. If a crutch is needed, the pupil may use it temporarily, but then it is eliminated. A pupil may have to resort to manipulative devices to solve a problem, but with help he is soon able to use symbols to solve the same kind of problem. The teacher shows him new ways to do an exercise as a means of saving time and effort.

The "Discovery Method" and Grouping. Concepts of subtraction, multiplication, and division are built as the pupils learn to see relationships in a new problem as a result of prior number experiences. Since the four fundamental processes in arithmetic are basically processes of regrouping, all the children learn how to group numbers. Once they understand the way numbers are grouped, they can multiply by adding, or divide by subtracting. After many experiences with problem situations calling for the use of grouping numbers to get a proper solution, the pupils will learn what terms like *multiplication* and *division* mean.

Many teachers will not teach arithmetic as conceived in the foregoing statement, but the principles of learning arithmetic through a discovery approach can be realized in a number of ways. For example, a group of dedicated teachers may learn to teach arithmetic by what has been called the "discovery method." These teachers are prepared to help boys and girls discover for themselves how problems can be solved. Or, program learning may be the answer to individualizing instruction. With careful planning, boys and girls can progress from one skill or subskill to the next with a minimum of teacher instruction. Children may work with teaching machines or specially prepared programmed books. In another approach, many boys and girls can use the modern arithmetic textbooks and workbooks to the point that they are self-instructing even when the teacher does not plan to teach through the "discovery method." Bright pupils and many average children need a minimum of teacher help to go from one stage of learning to higher learning levels. They can discover answers for themselves.

There is a danger that too much emphasis will be placed upon *process* without actually considering *meaning;* therefore, boys and girls must have opportunities to get together in small or large groups to dissect problems orally. They need practice in analyzing and collectively talking out solutions to problems presented on their level of arithmetic maturation. This is important if they are to gain new arithmetic concepts. If the discussion groups are kept small and if the problems are on the children's understanding level, *every* pupil will have an opportunity to participate. As the teacher listens to their oral reasoning, she obtains a clearer picture of their strengths and weaknesses and can help modify pupil activity accordingly.

The "discovery method" will work best if boys and girls can work as individuals or in small groups on materials appropriate to their growth

Photo by Joseph Crescimbeni

Children work with geometrical forms.

levels. In other words, the whole class does not have to work on the same problems, pages, or books. When the textbooks are used, work is modified according to pupil needs. If all children should be working on the same topic, the pupils can work at their own stage of learning. Therefore, everyone may be working on the addition of fractions, for example, with slow learners working with easy fractions they can understand, such as 1/4, 1/2, and 1/3, while the faster learners may be learning to find common denominators for fractions like 3/8, 5/6, and 7/6.

Many teaching aids are used in the "discovery method," especially at lower grade levels. Boys and girls may use bead counters, fractional aid kits, an abacus or counting frame, the flannel board, arithmetic charts, measuring instruments, and geometrical forms. Some of these may be commercial while others are prepared by the teacher or the children. Films and filmstrips may be used to show the meaning of a phase of arithmetic. The pupils are often encouraged to seek solutions requiring some experimentation or work with real objects. In studying measurements, they may try measuring large areas before working out their measuring problems on paper. As they work, the teacher helps them to evaluate their results and to form their own generalizations. She may motivate them to use different solutions to a problem and help them recognize the wisdom of using higher-level solutions to problems as they grow in understanding and skill in working arithmetical processes.

Because the arithmetic teacher cannot always predict the nature of her arithmetic groups, when the class enters into a new phase of arithmetic, she takes an informal inventory or watches them at work on a common problem or lesson. As a rule, the fast learners will generally stay fairly close together and the slow learners will not be too far apart in their arithmetic needs. But the middle 50 per cent may show varying stages of readiness or accomplishment, with the result that some of them may gravitate toward the faster learning section while others have to work with the slower learners on the mastery of subskills and lower-level concepts. This is especially true if the teachers in a school are using the "expanding concept approach" to learning arithmetic. In such cases prior experiences and prior successes will determine pupil placement.

Starting Subgrouping for Arithmetic with the Faster Learners. One approach to grouping consists of dividing a class into two fairly equal divisions based upon class achievement or achievement on a commercial standardized arithmetic achievement test (the Iowa, Stanford, Metropolitan, or California). Under this arrangement, intermediate and upper grade teachers divide a 40- or 48-minute period into two 20- to 24-minute instructional and study-work periods. The grouping arrangement becomes a form of *leveling* instrument, in that the teacher attempts to narrow the range for instruction by the creation of two semipermanent homogeneous groups within the confines of a single classroom. Another point of view has been presented by Johnson, [11] who reports that many teachers have found success with grouping by working alone with rapid learners. By taking a small number of them aside for special instruction at the start, the teacher sets the stage for grouping activities which will involve more of the slow-learning pupils. This is in contrast to the practice so often found which limits special help or some subgrouping for the slow learners.

In some schools where subgrouping is just being tried for the first time, teachers find it highly desirable to keep the average and slow learners together for basic instruction, while the bright or fast-learning students depart from the regular program through individualized assignments or small-group projects. Thus the teacher who is reluctant to let go of her class can test her skill in working with two groups by first setting up special activities for those who can be trusted to work independently.

Another reason for starting grouping with the fast learners lies in the fact that they are usually finished with regular class routines before the other pupils and can afford some time for experimental work. This has the added advantage of avoiding possible boredom by these quicker students.

The first subgroup may be given what may be described as a long-term assignment. The children may work independently for two or three days or even a week. If they are doing arithmetic in the sense that they have to calculate or solve problems, instead of working on research, they may correct their own papers or correct each other's work. If questions arise, they can help each other by discussing possible solutions to a series of examples, or they may turn to a standard arithmetic textbook in search of similar examples. Then, by the process of individual or collective reasoning, they may proceed to solve the problem without having to call upon the teacher for help. During this period the pupils in the fast learning category will not be asked to rejoin the main group unless they have something special to contribute to ongoing activities. While these pupils may be able to work on their own, teachers should make an attempt to check up on them each day to see that every pupil is capable of and ready for independent or semi-independent work. She may meet with the students individually or collectively to review directions, give special help, or to evaluate what they have done or are doing.

Importance of Flexibility in Arithmetic Groups. Many teachers limit their group work in arithmetic at the intermediate and upper grade levels to two semipermanent subdivisions of a class. Other teachers form three learning sections based on a study of standardized test results or on an inventory of pupil skill in various phases of arithmetic. In the latter case, where teachers are working with a definite checklist of the arithmetic skills or goals, instruction should be kept on each pupil's learning level by the reassignment of pupils to new learning groups when they show mastery of designated materials, skills or goals. Thus, pupils are grouped and regrouped in terms of their arithmetic needs. Unfortunately, this is not always done. All too often, teachers are reluctant to *move* students from one group to another once a grouping has been established. This negates the idea that arithmetic groups do not have to be permanent. Again, it fails to acknowledge the fact that children often have common arithmetic needs or that a pupil or group of pupils may have something to contribute to the other students in the class. For example, the pupils in the fast-moving group, who have been conducting research, may have to culminate their work by a report or series of demonstrations to other boys and girls before everyone is ready to move into a new field of study.

Permanency in arithmetic groups is not desired if pupils are working with an arithmetic grouping based upon a unit approach. Here, teacher and pupils may work together before breaking up into work groups based upon interest as well as arithmetic needs. Banking, for example, can become the basis of study for all pupils, with committees working on different phases of the study. Some may do research, while other pupils may complete arrangements with a bank for speakers, films, or even a bank visit. They may want to come together to listen to the speaker, to take the trip, or to work on a study of checks, deposit slips, and other aspects of banking.

Whenever children are assigned to a specific learning group, consideration should be given to the purpose or reason for the action. The children who are placed in a particular grouping should know why they have been assigned to it. If and when they realize the goals established with or for them, they should be free to work in another group or with other pupils on higher learning levels and in enrichment activities.

Sometimes pupils are assigned to a group on a trial basis, to see how they work with other pupils or how they work with certain learning skills. At other times, pupils will want to or need to be a part of two different groups. Other pupils may sometimes not fit into any learning group. Should such individuals not fit into group activity for a prolonged period of time, it may be desirable to make arrangements to transfer the one or more isolate workers to a class more suited to their arithmetic needs. This can be a transfer merely for arithmetic, or it can be a permanent transfer to another class. When a transfer is not feasible, the teacher may have to assign the pupil to a specific group with the understanding that he will still receive differentiated assignments or special assistance.

Small, flexible groups are often desirable when pupils are learning to estimate or obtain approximate answers. They need considerable practice and will not get it in a large group or subdivision. If a lesson is to be effective, the teacher should be able to work with a group that is small enough to permit each pupil to have several opportunities to reason out loud, to tell the teacher and/or other pupils what his thought processes are as he estimates the answer to a problem. By keeping this special grouping small, the teacher can quickly identify pupils whose reasoning is faulty and who may be in need of special assistance.

MEETING CHILDREN'S ARITHMETIC NEEDS
THROUGH A UNIT APPROACH

Some teachers have interpreted the statement, "Arithmetic cannot be taught incidentally" to mean that arithmetic can no longer be taught as a part of a unit. Actually, arithmetic units may be excellent approaches to the problem of individual differences. Again, there are times when arithmetic skills are essential for the understanding of a science or social studies unit. Here, there may be an actual need for arithmetic proficiency, but it may be best to merely explain the arithmetic process without attempting to teach new arithmetic skills or processes, to avoid interrupting the learning of desired social studies concepts. Should the arithmetic skills be essential to progress in the social studies unit, the teacher may set aside time in the regular arithmetic periods to teach the pupils what they need to know, but this teaching is an outgrowth of *pupil needs* and is not a regular part of a unit activity. The exception may be made for bright pupils who have the ability to master the desired skills quickly and easily. The arithmetic encountered in the social studies or science unit may be more exciting and challenging to them than the work in the regular arithmetic class.

From time to time a class can concentrate on a series of unit activities which are *arithmetic-centered*. Here, the group activity may consist of work by several small committees instead of two or three groups. While the general theme and activity are based on an arithmetic problem, language arts and social studies skills may also be brought to bear. At the same time, the unit may call for varied mathematical skills which can be learned collectively by the whole class or by groups of students. Units can be built around such topics as:

Man Learns to Measure Time

Man Learns to Measure Distance

Man Learns to Count

Keeping a Budget

The Role of Banks in the Modern Economy

The Income Tax Problem

Installment Purchasing

How to Stretch an Allowance

Many teachers use the "experience unit" in arithmetic to meet personal needs of their students. If it is a large unit, the boys and girls may assume responsibility for one or more related themes calling for arithmetic skill or knowledge. Instruction continues to be given in flexible groups where pupils show they need help or guidance. If interest is the *basis* for a committee or subgrouping, one may find bright, average, and slow learners working together, with pupils helping each other if special skill is necessary to complete a phase of work. The pupils may draw upon the content or skills acquired in such other subject fields as reading, writing, drawing, social studies, and science. Pupils may have to call upon the industrial arts or home economics teacher for assistance in making models. The arithmetic unit gives pupils opportunity to apply skills they have learned earlier. They may have to think of numbers in many abstract forms. If the unit covers a period of history, they may have to think in terms of abstractions of time and place. Some pupils may find that they are able to assume leadership roles which are not possible in the regular arithmetic class. Again, other pupils may find it possible to pursue interests which will lead to increased pupil activity in a phase of arithmetic *without* the frustration they formerly had when they went to an arithmetic class.

Meeting the Mathematical Needs of Children with Different Learning Abilities

DIFFERENTIATING BETWEEN SLOW AND FAST LEARNERS

Terms such as "slow learner" and "fast learner" should not be used loosely in referring to boys and girls in arithmetic classes. They may not refer to the same pupils to whom the words applied in other classes such as reading or writing. A pupil who is making slow progress in arithmetic need not necessarily have low intelligence. It may merely indicate that he does not have an interest in numbers and number concepts, or it may mean that he has failed to acquire an adequate command of fundamental processes and understandings introduced in the lower grade arithmetic classes. In fact, his lack of arithmetic progress may be traced back to social or emotional immaturity. Other apparent slow learners may be pupils whose earlier education was interrupted by illness or by the migration of their parents from one part of the country to another. For a few, lack of progress may be due to a limited experiential background.

One is not to presume that there are no true slow learners in the average arithmetic class, because they do exist in all classes. The issue is complicated here by the fact that success with numbers requires a different kind of intelligence, one which has not been developed fully for some boys and girls. *Arithmetic requires an ability to work and think in terms of abstractions.* As a result, one finds individuals with high verbal intelligence, especially girls, floundering or at least frustrated when faced by arithmetic problems. In the chapter on reading it was pointed out that most boys who had trouble with reading had average or above-average intelligence. One does find fewer boys having trouble in arithmetic than girls with better than average intelligence. Otherwise intelligent children who do poorly in arithmetic fall into the low achiever category more so than the pupils who have limited mental ability, since these individuals tend to work closer to expectation levels for their potential than their more intellectually gifted peers.

Teachers have to work with a large block of boys and girls who seem to fall into the so-called "average" category. Because of the narrow range in achievement for most children taking standardized arithmetic tests, the number of pupils falling into this category appears much greater than is warranted in terms of comparable studies of actual intelligence. This is because some very bright boys and girls have never been allowed to stretch themselves in arithmetic. These pupils fail to do much more than the minimum and may, as a result, be classified as average students in arithmetic. With proper motivation and some special help, a good portion of these bright pupils could join the fast learner group, or at least those who are working in the slow learning category could move up to the average or high average category. At the same time, one finds some pupils working successfully with average and even fast learning groups, even though they have limited ability or, at best, low average ability. These pupils are not recognized as slow learners, because they are working closer to expected capacity than their peers or because they may have very good work habits which give them an edge over brighter classmates who never acquired good work habits.

The real "slow learner" is the educable pupil who should not be found in the regular classroom. In instances where he cannot be placed in a special class, he will make little, if any, academic progress in arithmetic in terms of grade standards. However, with good sub-grouping and some individual attention, these pupils may achieve successes in arithmetic close to expectation levels for their mental ability by the time they are sixteen. This success will be more pronounced in areas of arithmetic which require routine calculations with everyday numbers. These pupils will not do too well in areas requiring abstract ability. This means that problems can be their undoing. Since educable children tend to learn at about half the speed of average children, teachers who try to have them keep pace with their more intellectually gifted peers will doom them to a life of endless frustration and failure.

The true "fast learner" will be the gifted pupil or the pupil with superior intelligence who has an interest in numbers, as well as the ability to think in terms of abstractions. These pupils will ordinarily command the top marks in the average arithmetic class. If children are grouped, they will gravitate to the top or fastest moving arithmetic section. They are capable of achieving much more in the way of arithmetic skills and knowledge than most teachers will expose them to in their classes. They can work rapidly and should have many opportunities to work with enrichment activities in place of routine drill work when they complete minimum programs. The teacher should be ready to cope with the problem of the truly gifted pupil on a different plane than she does with and for the average, above-average, and even superior pupil. In many schools the teacher is hard-pressed to meet the arithmetic interests and requirements of such children. One teacher said, "I have to go home every night for an hour of study and work to keep ahead of four bright boys in my sixth-grade arithmetic class. I do not know what I would do if the principal assigned that genius in Mr. Dobbin's class to my class." In most small schools the number of pupils who are on the highly gifted side and who are mathematically inclined tends to be small, but the pupils who fit into this category will seldom fit into any regular class or subdivision. At best, they can fit into top arithmetic sections and must then find additional challenge through individualized assignments.

AN ARITHMETIC PROGRAM FOR CHILDREN
WORKING IN THE LOW SECTION

Every class has a bottom group or slow learning section, although the achievement of this group of children will vary from school to school and from community to community. In most arithmetic classes, the distance between the achievement level of the top and bottom classes will be shorter than the distance between comparable sections found in other subject fields. This means that teaching materials and methods used with average and above-average students will often be the same or may overlap in some respects. In the low ability sections, pupils will not be able to progress very quickly, so they may be left behind if some of their peers are able to actually acquire a basic arithmetic foundation. Once this foundation is firmly established, some of the pupils will move from the low section to the average or top arithmetic section, either permanently or for work in areas of related skills and understanding.

When a primary teacher begins a study of time, all the children may work together for several days or even weeks developing concepts involving time measurement. The subject may start with a simple discussion of tardiness. Why do teachers and children have to be in their classrooms when the late bell rings in the morning? Answers to this question may bring out a number of important social values, but ultimately the fact may have to be faced that some of the children do not know when they are late because they *cannot tell time.* Here one may divide a class into those who can tell time and those who cannot. In the latter category one may find children who have yet to learn to tell time in terms of hours, whereas in the former category one may find those who can judge time in terms of hours but who are now ready to begin to learn to tell time in terms of half hours, quarter hours, or even minutes. The children may all work on making clock faces on paper plates, but their work with their clocks can be quite different in view of their varying time concepts or understandings. Children in the slower learning category will need practice in telling time in terms of hours and half hours before they can grasp an understanding of more involved time abstractions. This will keep the two or more arithmetic groups separate for a while, but when the whole class comes together to begin a study of weights and measurements, the teacher may find that some of the boys and girls who had originally been a part of the slow learning section belonged in the middle or top section, since their understanding of measurement of length and liquids was on a much higher plane than that of other pupils in the class. In the new division, the teacher would begin to work with quart measures or foot measures in an attempt to get the slowest learning section visualizing the meaning of concrete terms while the children in the faster learning sections would be working with problems involving symbols representing abstract quantities, or with concrete objects involving smaller numbers of units or fractional parts of wholes such as pint, half-pint, half-foot, quarter-foot, or half-inch.

As the teacher works with her children, she will notice variations in the way the children learn. There will be boys and girls in each section who seem to have trouble comprehending what she is trying to do for and with them, but there will be more pupils in the slower learning section who are slow in grasping concepts. One day they may appear to have it, but the next day she may have to re-introduce them to work with more concrete objects or manipulative devices. By talking with and observing the boys and girls, she tries to learn what their thinking processes are like. She may find some of the slower learners are able to go from objective materials to visual and representative materials, but cannot seem to make the final transition to symbols. With these students she may be able to leave out the use of concrete materials to work on examples illustrated in charts or pictures drawn on the blackboard or shown in a textbook. With others, the difficulty may be one of going from the concrete or objective to the representative. At the same time, the teacher may find one or more pupils in the slow group who can go from the concrete to abstract symbols without having to spend time with representative materials.

TEACHING AIDS ESSENTIAL IN TEACHING ARITHMETIC

If arithmetic teaching is to be socially vital and practical for children at all learning levels, many forms of sensory aids must be used as frequently as possible. Most teachers recognize the utility of such sensory aids—that their application in learning specific concepts helps the child to visualize the relationships involved in a particular arithmetic or problem situation.

Courtesy of the Ford Foundation

Working in groups, some children use colored blocks to solve problems.

Children in the slow learning group require more time and activity with teaching aids if they are to find meaning in their arithmetic. In recent years many commercial teaching aids have become available, but some of them are still expensive and therefore inaccessible to many teachers. This has led some teachers to make their own counting board, number chart, or abacus. If a teacher does not know how to use a hammer and saw, she can frequently get the assistance of older boys or fathers of pupils in the making of a model or demonstration device.

Some types of mechanical devices or manipulative aids used to teach arithmetic are the flannel board, the counter board, the magnetic board, the abacus, the open-end abacus, toy money, the counter or number stick, number pockets, the number chart, measuring cups, fractional discs or fractional cutouts, the pie chart, and simple objects used to help visualize numbers or counters: marbles, blocks, stones or pebbles, matchsticks, tongue depressors, colored discs.

Essentially, the primary pupil (especially the slower learner) is able to learn to understand many phases of arithmetic by the use of teaching aids which permit him to use his hands, to listen as well as look, and to talk instead of sitting and merely trying to do busywork with his pencil and paper. Teachers find children respond in various ways to different approaches, but usually a combination of the sensory, tactile, auditory, and visual will produce better results than any one approach used separately. Thus, the pupil learns through seeing and handling objects as he talks about them. He gets the idea of a number or group of numbers from close association with an object which has reality to him. A picture of a counting frame cannot be visualized as much as one which he is able to hold in his hands as he learns to manipulate it.

Unfortunately, a teaching device can be misused. To some teachers the teaching aid may still be a novelty. The matter of readiness, lack of readiness or post-readiness is not important. The children enjoy the new objects, but real learning may not take place. This is particularly true where the teacher does not understand how the teaching aid should be used. Thus, a large counting frame may stay in the corner most of the year without being used as a teaching tool until someone demonstrates to the teacher the values which lie in using it.

There are those who advocate the wider use of some of the newer teaching machines as a timesaver, and it is implied that large groups of children can use the machines without teacher direction. Up to a point this may be true, especially if one is merely interested in mechanical responses; but the teacher is extremely important if one is concerned about the understanding which goes with the skill or process. Left to themselves, some pupils can cover the "ground" or material without actually retaining very much at the end of the series of drill activities.

The Use of Charts. Bright children can often bridge the gap between concrete objects and abstract symbols, but slower-learning pupils need an intermediate step, namely, through the use of representative materials. Frequently, representative materials are presented by the use of charts. A teacher may mount pictures of objects such as caterpillar tractors, trucks, cars, animals, toys, and the like on large sheets of oaktag (24 x 36 inches) to introduce the concept of a number. If the teacher draws well, she may present illustrative drawings on the chart. The teacher-made chart can become the pupil chart in the upper grades, with students collecting pictures, making pen-and-ink sketches, or using paints and crayons to illustrate mathematical symbols and arithmetic terms. These pupil-made charts can become the basis for their learning important concepts.

If children need concrete experiences, the chart is not the answer. It cannot replace the direct use of objects to give children the feel for objects and the initial understanding they need. However, there are many lessons where the real object is no longer needed. Here, the teacher- or pupil-made chart gives students a contact with numbers in less than abstract form. While charts can be made to show the development of arithmetic processes by the use of number symbols, there are times when the use of mediums other than numbers is more effective. A chart showing geometric forms can be most helpful when students are working in the area of measurement. The chart is available to remind the pupil how rectangles and squares differ. If the processes of finding the area or circumference are outlined on a chart, the slow-learning pupil will find it helpful if he can occasionally refer to it.

The chart has value as a teaching instrument for all-class activity and for small-group instruction. Ideally, one pupil-teacher chart should not be used with another class, because much of the initial learning comes from having the pupils work out the story or illustration as a learning activity. If the chart is put away until another group is ready for that stage of work, some of the material will be helpful—but the meaning will not be as great as if the pupils worked with the teacher in composing their own arithmetic chart to illustrate what the group is actually studying. Their needs will thus be met, and their questions answered. The teacher should use the chart to meet the specific needs of selected students.

Teachers will find that number charts are easily made by intermediate and primary grade children. Every teacher can usually keep a large black drawing crayon or a felt marking pen near where the group meets. If she wants to illustrate a number point, write a story, or review a lesson, a few strokes of the crayon or pen take little time. By working out the details of a chart together, the pupils learn new concepts or strengthen old ones. Number relationships take on a new meaning. The teacher who works closely with her pupils encourages them to think out loud as they do their arithmetic. If she sees that a student does not understand a concept or process, she can reteach it or draw upon other pupils to help the slower learners make progress in their number work. Frequently the pupils demonstrate their ability to compute by working at the chalkboard or at an easel covered with newsprint.

THE USE OF CRUTCHES IN THE ARITHMETIC CLASS

Many of today's manipulative devices fall into the category of a "crutch." The children learn to lean on them for support until they have developed an understanding and feeling of security about a particular process or stage of arithmetic growth. When the pupil has acquired security, the crutch should be eliminated.

At some time in his life, each student uses his fingers as counters. Parents and teachers are apt to get concerned when this happens. Actually, there is no danger in counting on one's fingers when children are beginning to learn to count. The objection comes from their continuing to use their fingers as crutches when they should be "using their heads." Unfortunately, some students continue to use their fingers as counters because they have been forced to memorize isolated facts without ever acquiring an understanding of the principles involved.

The teacher has a responsibility to challenge the pupil who continues to use a specific crutch for too long a period of time. She needs to recognize the need to apply appropriate pressures and motivation so that the child can eliminate the crutch and depend upon his own ability to reason and work out a solution to a problem by the use of more economical means.

Sometimes students learn the use of a crutch as the last step of a process, because they do not know the primary and intermediate steps. They do not relinquish their dependence upon the crutch until they have had a chance to learn the missing steps. This is especially true of the "slow learner." He finds it necessary to use his crutches because he has no alternative, whereas the bright or arithmetic-mature pupil is able to sense relationships and has no need to rely upon such help.

SOME REASONS FOR ARITHMETIC FAILURE

The "Slow Arithmetic Learner" May Have a Reading Problem. Teachers may not realize it, but some of their slow pupils in the arithmetic class know their arithmetic, but cannot demonstrate their skill because they cannot read well. This need for reading proficiency becomes increasingly evident if one looks at the vast amount of reading material found in a modern arithmetic textbook. If pupils have to spend time and effort reading explanations, descriptions, or illustrations, as well as numerous written problems, they may lose interest in arithmetic before they get started because the act of reading is frustrating to them. The pupil who reads slowly and with low comprehension will find that he has to concentrate so hard on reading that he loses the arithmetic concept. Sometimes it becomes discouraging to struggle through an arithmetic assignment and find that everyone else in the class finished the work several minutes earlier and is engaged in another activity. This pupil is always trying to catch up, but just cannot do so.

Some children acquire arithmetic skill through visual and auditory means and can do very good work in fundamental operations which do not require reading skill. As a result, teachers may not realize what has happened when the pupil who has done so well with simple fundamentals in class suddenly fails on a test.

Difficulty with Problems. Problems can be the bane of the pupil's existence when it comes to finding a measure of success in school. This is especially true of pupils in "slow learning" sections of the arithmetic class. Many pupils who can do routine examples which are set up for them fail miserably when they have to select their own process on the basis of study and analysis. This failure with problems may be due to the pupil's poor reading skill, which makes it impossible for him to understand the nature of the problem and what is asked for in the statement of facts. The pupil can read, but he fails to read the problem correctly. He often fails to consider all the steps required to solve the problem, and he generally leaves one out. He fails to pay attention to the explanatory reading matter. He tries to work with numbers taken out of context.

Or, the pupil may have poor work-study habits. He finds it hard to settle down. He lacks the power of concentration, and gives up too easily when the work begins to get difficult or appears different from that to which he has been accustomed. The pupil has too short an attention span. He gets lost before he can finish the problem.

Perhaps the pupil lacks background in the fundamental processes. He does not know how to compute, or he uses the incorrect process or method. He does not know his arithmetic combinations, i.e., multiplication, subtraction, division, or addition. The pupil lacks experience and ability in estimating and judging accuracy of his answers. Thus, he guesses at the answers without trying to obtain reasons for them. He makes no attempt to prove his work.

Often the pupil has no interest in the work since no attempt has been made to motivate him or the class.

Frequently the pupil is careless, working too fast to arrive at accurate solutions to problems. He then fails to look over what he has done. He often copies the work incorrectly.

Finally, the pupil may lack an understanding of the arithmetic vocabulary. He does not know the meaning of the arithmetic terms when he sees or hears them. He fails to do the problem because of a lack of sufficient concrete or enrichment experiences to make the terms encountered in the problem meaningful. The problem may be too abstract or too difficult for the pupil's intellectual level or stage of readiness.

To help such slow learners find success in this phase of arithmetic, a teacher may have to take several paths at the same time. Help may have to be given to the pupil who cannot read his problems. Attention may have to be directed toward the improvement of work-study habits, but essentially the teacher has to get down to the pupil's experience level. Research shows that the pupil's ability to solve arithmetic problems is enhanced by his having experiences with real situations involving numbers. This has led some teachers to assume that one should not teach unless it is possible to work continually with first-hand experiences. This is excellent if it can be done, but it is often impossible to place pupils in situations calling for real and personal experiences. Therefore, the children have to substitute vicarious experiences which will give the same results. Since the number of real situations offering pupils number experiences in the class is limited, the school frequently has to simulate them.

FINDING THE BRIGHT CHILD IN THE ARITHMETIC CLASS

Finding bright children in arithmetic classes may depend upon where one looks for them. It may not take much effort to identify the bright boy or girl in the large city school where the average IQ is only 80 or 90. In this setting, pupils with IQs above average will stand out in many ways. They may be less conspicuous in the average community, with the result that bright pupils who fail to stand head and shoulders above the crowd are not as readily noticed. In more favored communities, where the children come from high socioeconomic levels, there may be so many bright children in the classes that it is the child of average or low-average intelligence who stands out. Because arithmetic achievement ranges tend to be narrow, teachers will be able to screen out those pupils at the very top and at the very bottom of the achievement scale, but many bright pupils will not be noticed in such screenings because they have failed to give the teacher any hint of their brightness.

It is therefore essential that the teacher look for clues to the actual potential of every boy and girl from the first day she begins to work with her or him. By inspecting daily papers, and by special quizzes or teacher-made survey tests, she can tell who has mastered the basic fundamentals. This may be just a beginning, because she is interested in knowing who can do more than compute. She wants to know how well each pupil understands what he has done. Here, the creative teacher will find it necessary to set the stage for the children in her class. She needs to challenge the pupils to demonstrate their own ability to think with numbers.

One approach may be through questioning them in such a way that she stimulates responses which show that they know the meaning of numbers and can apply their knowledge and skill to the solution of realistic problems. With her questioning technique, the teacher can lead the brighter children into the exploration of higher mathematical concepts than she can her slow and average learners. Identification of the bright child in the arithmetic class will depend on how observant the teacher is as she works with them. Frequently, these children give themselves away by their approach to arithmetic. This is especially true when the teacher gives them a chance to take part in activities which allow her to observe their thinking processes as they work with numbers.

A study of the children in the average arithmetic class will show that the student who ranks high in arithmetic ability will have some of the following characteristics:

He needs few, if any, concrete experiences to build understanding. He is able to master a skill or solve a problem with little prompting or direction. He shows that he is able to do assigned work quickly and independently.

He enjoys the challenges he encounters in the arithmetic class. Solving problems gives him a great deal of satisfaction. Mental arithmetic is stimulating to him. Given an example which calls for an estimate, he can quickly arrive at a reasonable answer.

Usually he is able to work out solutions to problems and find the correct method with a minimum of trial and error. If he makes mistakes, he can readily see them when they are called to his attention. Often, if left to his own devices, he may develop short cuts long before the other students have mastered one method.

Frequently he shows an insight into the nature of problems and the procedures required to solve them. He is able to formulate sound generalizations, and if given the opportunity, will test them. He shows an intellectual curiosity and a real desire to learn.

He is able to express himself in mathematical terms. He shows that he knows their meaning, both orally and in writing. He has adopted good work habits and works steadily with little waste motion. His work is well organized and is completed with a minimum of interruptions.

He recognizes basic relationships. He sees the relationship of a skill learned in the arithmetic class and a problem encountered in the social studies class and can use his mathematical skill to solve the social studies problem or any other type of problem.

Finally, he shows tenacity. He is not apt to quit if the arithmetic example is difficult, but will stay with it until he has reached a solution. He will frequently show his resourcefulness by seeking other sources that will give him answers.

Teaching Arithmetic to Bright Children. It should be apparent from the characteristics of bright children described in the preceding paragraphs that methods of teaching used with slower learners may not challenge the more capable students in the arithmetic class. If she is going to meet their basic needs and give them an enriched program, the teacher must be prepared to modify her teaching methods and different work materials. Bright students can enjoy and benefit from the same initial steps of a new procedure based on the use of concrete illustrations or the use of manipulative materials, but they do not need as much repetition or coaching as less capable pupils. In many instances, manipulative materials or arithmetic games should be more complicated or on higher levels than the ones used with children of average or less-than-average intelligence. Since these bright pupils have a good mathematical sense, the teacher can often leave out some of the review steps in presenting new materials or new skills. They will require a minimum of readiness activities in order to grasp new concepts, so that the teacher has to make earlier provisions to separate them from an all-class approach to new arithmetic activities. As a rule, bright children need less contact with concrete materials than slower learners do, in terms of sensing what is happening, but they do find some satisfactions in working with objects or representative materials. They can enjoy and consider as fun the challenge of manipulative devices, arithmetic puzzles, arithmetic games, and other activities which require thinking and some competitiveness.

The observant teacher should give the bright pupils opportunities to review their arithmetic skills or knowledge through application as they work with pupil or teacher problems which supplement those found in the textbook. They may have their own problems, or they may work up their own practice materials. Here is where they may reveal their creativity. Again, as they work in fields such as science or social studies, they will often find their background in arithmetic essential for the understanding of statistics, tables, and charts. These children may be able to take time from their regular arithmetic work to learn the arithmetic processes necessary to solve the problem or see the relationship of the ideas presented in other subject fields. They may even be able to acquire higher-level arithmetic skills as part of activities related to the other subjects. The brighter pupils are much less likely to get "lost" in the process because of the speed with which they see abstractions and number relationships. They can literally see, hear, and think arithmetically when they see an arithmetic problem arising in the midst of their social studies, while the slow learner may have trouble "seeing" just the social studies concepts.

For success with children in the fast learning category, the teacher will find consideration of factors such as the following helpful:

Bright children may need a different type of motivation to challenge them to do more than the minimum.

They need to see the reason or purpose underlying an activity. These pupils need to feel free to grow. Frequently, their resistance to doing additional arithmetic may be due to the rigidity of the teacher. These children can and will do more if they are given an insight as to the values underlying an activity. Work for work's sake can embitter the best arithmetic students; they can see when they are merely doing busywork and can take steps to avoid extra assignments.

They need to understand the principles behind an activity. Success with many bright children depends upon the teacher's ability to introduce the principles underlying an operation. If she can teach these principles realistically, many boys and girls will find the understanding necessary to motivate them to higher level activity.

Bright children need to become adept at mental arithmetic. Bright children readily learn short cuts and find satisfaction in doing so. Estimating answers has meaning to them when they can learn to solve problems mentally. They like to get away from the same approach, so the teacher can make an oral arithmetic lesson meaningful and realistic. The ability to solve arithmetic problems mentally can be an asset to them.

They need to learn to do quality rather than quantity work. Many teachers have a tendency to give bright children the same amount of drill, if not more, than they give to slower learners. This can result in carelessness or an "I don't care" attitude. The children can soon see that it does not pay them to do a good job or to complete their work swiftly. Helping these boys and girls see that it does pay to work for *quality* is a responsibility teachers must recognize.

These children need to be kept busy. Boys and girls need a challenge in the arithmetic class. They need to be kept busy, but they should not be given busywork. New approaches to the same kind of examples or work at higher levels must be substituted for mere repetition of a pattern of examples they have already demonstrated they can solve. The teacher has to help them find new ways to occupy their free time if and when they complete a new learning activity. Team learning may help free the teacher who needs more time to work with slower-progressing pupils.

Interests of bright pupils should be recognized. Many teachers are afraid to allow a class to get too far from the work in a textbook. To do so may mean that the children will not finish the book by the end of the year. But studies have shown that many bright pupils are capable of doing two years' work in a single school year if allowed to proceed at their own pace. Pupil interests should be recognized wherever possible in the field of arithmetic. These children need a constant challenge, so if they show a natural interest in a phase of arithmetic, it need not be ended with a terse reminder that it is time to get back to a basic text that may have no significance for them.

REFERENCES

1. Francis R. Brown, "Arithmetic—Friend or Foe," *The Arithmetic Teacher*, 4 (February 1957), 1–9.
2. Leo J. Brueckner and Foster E. Grossnickle, *Discovering Meanings in Elementary School Mathematics* (New York: Holt, Rinehart & Winston, 1963).
3. William H. Burton, *The Guidance of Learning Activities*, 3rd ed. (New York: Appleton-Century-Crofts, 1952).
4. Clyde G. Corle, *Teaching Mathematics in the Elementary School* (New York: Ronald Press, 1964).
5. Joseph Crescimbeni, *Arithmetic Enrichment Activities for Elementary School Children* (West Nyack, N.Y.: Parker, 1965).
6. Joseph Crescimbeni, *Teaching the New Mathematics* (West Nyack, N.Y.: Parker, 1966).
7. Howard Fehr, "Present Research in Arithmetic," *Teachers College Record*, 52 (October 1950), 11–23.
8. Vincent J. Glennon and C. W. Hunnicutt, *What Does Research Say About Arithmetic?* (Washington, D.C.: Association for Supervision and Curriculum Development, National Education Association, 1958).
9. Foster E. Grossnickle, "Arithmetic for Those Who Excel," *The Arithmetic Teacher*, 3 (March 1956), 41–48; and "Teaching Arithmetic in the Junior High School," *The Mathematics Teacher*, 47 (December 1954), 520–27.
10. Harry F. Harlow, "The Formation of Learning Sets," *Psychological Review*, 56 (January 1949), 51–65.
11. Charles E. Johnson, "Grouping Children for Arithmetic Instruction," *The Arithmetic Teacher*, 1 (February 1954), 16–20.
12. Abraham Luchins, "Mechanization in Problem Solving," *Psychological Monographs*, 54 (1942), 1–95.
13. Ruth H. Nies, "Classroom Experiences with Recreational Arithmetic," *The Arithmetic Teacher*, 3 (April 1956), 90–93.

CHAPTER 13

Helping Children
Discover the World of Science

Teachers may have various reasons for teaching certain phases of science, but the sum total of their activities should result in helping children acquire an awareness of the impact science has upon their daily lives. They should see that science *is not* a field of mystery and that it *is not* too difficult for them to understand. The elementary school teacher is not concerned about the problem of creating future scientists as much as she is in trying to get boys and girls interested enough in science that they will want to continue with the study at higher levels. To do this, the teacher has to present science as a subject which has meaning to the children and which is interesting and enjoyable.

Implications for Instruction

Pupils must see science as a subject that helps answer their questions and solve some of their daily problems. Essentially, an interest in science on the part of the teacher is an important aspect of the learning situation, for her own feelings or interests can influence those of her pupils.

Boys and girls should have many experiences in school with a kind of science that goes *beyond* mere textbook teaching. They can and should do some research and experimentation at all grade levels so that science can become something personal. Science offers some pupils opportunities for leadership in fields where they are willing to exert themselves because of their own interest or desire to get better acquainted with the world about them. Some of these pupils can often help teachers who may be reluctant to get away from a "textbook" kind of science because of their own feelings of inadequacy. These teachers must be ready and willing to learn with their pupils.

In teaching science, the teacher must help children acquire *an inquiring mind*. This is a phase of science that frequently frightens teachers. Actually, much of what one may refer to as scientific thinking is merely good thinking. It involves recognition of the existence of problems, or the identification of a problem, and then the gathering of information necessary to form a generalization or conclusion. The teacher and children can learn to make generalizations and test them on similar problems to see whether their conclusions are basically sound. They should not be ready to accept someone else's answers blindly. They should be ready and willing to question what they see and hear. They should be able, as a result of their experiences, to see likenesses and differences, to make inferences, to classify, to see relationships, and to form conclusions of their own based upon the evidence they have discovered.

ELEMENTARY SCHOOL SCIENCE— THE DOOR TO THE UNKNOWN

Most children are naturally curious about the world around them. They want to know what is going on and why. Life is full of mysteries to them—mysteries a good science program can explain. Young children will have questions about the stars, they will want to know the difference between snow and rain, why objects fall down and not up, and the "why" of hundreds of other things they see about them. In asking their questions, the children may not realize that they are often penetrating into the past and future as well as the present. Some boys and girls find the answers to their questions; others encounter barriers, with the result that the doorway leading to the unknown is closed before they can get a small taste of what lies beyond the barriers of ignorance, superstition, and faulty conjecture.

One has to remember that some of the questions modern children ask have been asked by men since the beginnings of civilization, and it is only recently that answers have been available for many of them. Helping boys and girls find their answers about the expanding world of men as well as of children becomes the new role of the teacher when she teaches science; through her and through science they may find an explanation for the mysteries of their immediate environment and for the universe beyond.

The teacher may have to have a bit of daring in her when she tries to satisfy children's curiosity about the world around them. She may have to explore with them, since most teachers lack the informational background to teach science without further research. However, each teacher should remember that she is not alone. Other adults are seeking answers, and many of them are willing to help children if the school will make the effort to call upon them for help. In every community there are men and women who have hobbies or science interests which they can and would enjoy sharing with children. Numerous companies employing men engaged in research activities are willing to send representatives to the school and, in some instances, will invite older pupils to visit their plants.

Today's teachers can find a wealth of new reading materials dealing with some phase of science, so boys and girls who need enrichment or reading practice can be directed to read and think in terms of science and scientists. Frequently, they will find that science overlaps with many other subjects in the curriculum; therefore, if boys and girls are trying to develop research skills, it may take only a slight "push" in the right direction to get children interested in applying their research skills or reading skills to seeking out answers to their questions in fields involving science. In addition, the teacher will find that she can obtain numerous films and filmstrips to help explain things which are not clear in a textbook, or she can refer children to the daily newspaper or to television. By bringing current science happenings into the classroom, the teacher can help children become increasingly more science-conscious.

Through simple experiments and demonstrations, the pupils can often get closer to the heart of a problem as they get the "feeling of science" by involvement. In many instances the teacher introduces children to science by making them conscious of their environment by encouraging them to ask questions about it. Boys and girls soon discover that science has a content as broad as life itself, but that it is also more than a mere accumulation of knowledge. If taught properly, children's attitudes or outlook upon life should change as they acquire new understandings or concepts regarding how and why things happen in the world around them.

The content of science has certainly expanded enormously during the past few decades, but man is still engaged in activities centering around a number of unchanging principles which have become known as *universal concepts*. It is these principles that have become the framework for the modern elementary school science curriculum. In considering a rich program of activities for children, Craig [3] suggests attention to such themes as the following:

The vastness of space

Time, as evidenced in the age of the world and the universe

The universality of change

Adaption, as shown in the way plants and animals adapt themselves to their environment

Interrelationship, as revealed in the interdependence of living things

Variation, as revealed in the great variety of living and nonliving things found in our environment

These themes have different meaning to different children depending upon their total maturity and experiences. Every teacher, for example, can work with the themes involving time and space concepts. Young children may grope through simple time and space barriers, but as they grow older and have more realistic experiences in social studies, arithmetic, literature, and science, their concept of the terms changes. Sometimes boys and girls can acquire a better understanding of an abstract term such as "a million light years" than they can of terms such as "fathom," "meter," or "kilometer." It all depends upon their experiences. In recent years, modern children have heard and seen much about man's attempts to conquer outer space. They can refer quite easily to terms relating to astronomy and, in many instances, may speak glibly about distant objects in outer space, even though they are not able to visualize the distance between large cities in their own country.

SETTING TEACHING GOALS FOR THE
STUDY OF SCIENCE

In science, as in all subjects, good teachers are motivated by a number of factors. Frequently, they teach in terms of long-range goals which they know cannot be realized in a single year. However, each teacher wants to leave her "mark" on given pupils by helping them adjust to their environment, by helping them to live a rich and full life during the year they spend with her. During this interval she helps them to explore the world around them as they grow in skills, cultural background, attitudes, and behavioral patterns in terms of many short-range goals. At times, progress toward both the short- and long-range goals may appear to be slow, but each teacher must always remember these goals must be realistic and attainable if she is to see noticeable progress. Appropriate long-range goals for science education would include:

1. Teaching boys and girls to develop and use scientific approaches to problem solving.

2. Helping children develop new concepts based upon an understanding of the principles underlying common phenomena, thus eliminating superstition and prejudice.

3. Helping boys and girls acquire a critical attitude. The pupils should learn to speak and act on the basis of their ability to reason from the knowledge they have acquired or can acquire if they set their minds to it.

4. Encouraging boys and girls to use their powers of observation for solutions to problems and the interpretation of observed phenomena. They should learn to relate science to other areas of the curriculum. They should see science as contribution to life through many mediums.

5. Stressing the importance of good health for the individual and the community. Health knowledge is considered as an essential objective of the individual as well as the scientist.

6. Teaching the values and meaning of conservation of resources.

7. Helping pupils to see the social applications of science. Frequently, this is done by studying the contributions of science and scientists to man's life in today's complex social and economic life.

As each pupil studies, he should learn *what* he is doing and *why* he is doing it. He should understand the immediate goals and, ultimately, the long-range ones.

ACQUIRING THE SCIENTIFIC ATTITUDE

Studies have shown that boys and girls can be accelerated through several grades of science with a tremendous gain in science information, yet their attitudes may not undergo much significant change as a result. This points up a problem which confronts dedicated science teachers. Science has to be more than a study of a few facts. Reading about scientific discoveries is easy for teacher and pupil, but the act may not require much physical or mental effort. If pupils are to develop a scientific attitude, they must have opportunities to ask meaningful questions, think constructively and creatively, and in many instances be stimulated to engage in activities that call for exploration and research.

When children leave the classroom, they should be able to recognize many of the phenomena they read about. Thus, a bird, a rock, a tree, or a bolt of lightning should have some meaning to boys and girls who have been studying about such things in class. When they hear the television announcer advising them to purchase a product, they should be able to counter with their own questions: "Is he really telling us the truth?" "Wait, something is wrong here; the body does not react that way." "It is not natural for one single ingredient to suddenly revolutionize our methods of cleaning." Once they start *thinking*, these questioning individuals may conduct their own experiments to verify what they believe. A student may find that he has misjudged the announcer, but with good sound judgment he may save himself a great deal of trouble. In other words, one of the essentials of the scientific attitude is the ability to suspend judgment until all the facts are in, until the individual is able to substantiate an observation or apparent fact by study, experimentation, and questioning.

Teachers and pupils often acquire the faulty idea that the scientific attitude and the scientific method are the same. Actually, the method of thinking may be correct, but the physical process may not be. A boy who can perform every experiment in a textbook or workbook can go through the motions of being a scientist without actually being one. Before he can truly consider himself a scientist, he has to acquire at least one other basic skill—the ability to reason.

The scientific attitude is built upon a *desire to find the truth and upon the willingness of the individual to test and challenge ideas or solutions presented by others*. In going through the physical process of duplicating experiments, the student not only has to sense what it is that he is doing, but also be able to use prescribed techniques to solve other problems. At times he may have to modify them in order to determine scientifically the validity of other hypotheses, or he may test one theory and deduce the answer to other problems from the original experiment when other pertinent information is analyzed in the light of his experience.

For example, a teacher tells the children that plants need sunlight. To prove it, beans are planted in different parts of the room, but all receive the same amount of care. The children are surprised to see the lack of growth on the part of some beans which were kept dry and in the dark, but they are more than surprised when someone discovers that the sprouting beans seem to be bending or turning towards the lighted windows. This is evidence. They can accept the teacher's explanation that they grew because they got the needed sunlight. They see a cause and relation factor in what has happened, until one boy points up the fact that the hot radiators are located under the windows. This raises an interesting question: Perhaps it was the extra heat from the radiators which attracted the plants, and not the sunlight. After examining this element, the children may want to try a more controlled experiment.

The teacher may have to resort to a variety of techniques to give children the experiences necessary for the development of new concepts or understandings. In many cases it will require a planned program of activities if initial impressions or ways of thinking are going to change. The teacher must remember that old concepts are not erased overnight, especially where boys and girls continue to return home to an environment which negates much that the teacher has tried to teach. Helping these children form new concepts based upon their new experiences may call for careful study and direct teaching even when the impetus for the new science experiences originates in what may appear to be a minor or chance learning situation. On the other hand, boys and girls should not be ready to give up their old ideas every time that someone challenges one. The fact that a teacher said something was so should not suffice. The teacher should recognize this, and she must therefore be prepared to help them organize experiences which will help them discover truths for themselves.

TEACHING THE ELEMENTS OF THE
SCIENTIFIC METHOD

When the boy introduced the element of radiator heat as a possible reason for the plant's bending toward the windows, a conclusion had to be reached. Did the plant bend to the light from the sun or toward the radiators beneath the windows? Were the two factors related, or was one element responsible? Could they prove which element was the significant one? The act of recognizing the problem is a step in the scientific approach and is based on their seeing a possible cause-and-effect relationship between two elements which had common ingredients. When the pupils tried to guess which was the significant factor, they were forming hypotheses which they tried to substantiate through research and further experiments. Another experiment was made where there was no question of conflict. Plants were observed turning toward the sunlight in a place where there were no radiators, and the pupils concluded that plants needed sunlight to grow. (See the visual representation of this method shown in Figure 1.)

Children need to observe life about them. They need to recognize problems and see science as a method of solving problems. *Teachers and pupils must get away from a kind of science where everything is too exact, where answers are given them by a textbook or teacher.* They need to engage in activities employing scientific methods, which

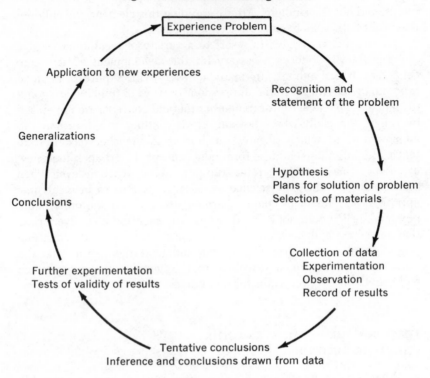
Figure 1. **The Problem-solving Method**

means that they must recognize the elements found in the scientific *method* and the scientific *attitude,* such as those in the following table:

TABLE 1
What Children Learn from Scientific Method and Attitude

Method	Attitude
To recognize a problem when they see one	To see a cause-and-effect relationship
To try to formulate a guess or hypothesis based on one or more clues	To accept a point of view other than their own
To try to solve their problems by exploration and experimentation	To look for reasons
To seek additional information	To accept or reject the evidence they have uncovered
To draw conclusions based on their observations and information	

THE PROBLEM OF SEQUENCE OF
SCIENCE ACTIVITIES

Teaching science in terms of an ever-unfolding process poses a number of problems for teachers at different grade levels. A theme centering about "weather" can become the basis for study at every grade level with new meanings to growing boys and girls. But, if the children are not going to engage in highly repetitious activities, evolution of new understandings at each grade is dependent upon the teacher's awareness of what was taught and learned earlier. To succeed, the teacher must find out what the children have learned and must then be prepared to take them on to higher levels of understanding. Many teachers would prefer to teach a different type of science— one based on a sequence of science activities, but a sequence not necessarily involving the study and restudy of the same topic at different grade levels. Some of them believe that every child should be exposed to the same bodies of knowledge in science and to the same problems in a graded pattern; but attempts to hold to a rigid pattern are complicated both by the varying rates of pupil growth and by learning a subject which is changing as scientists continue to make new advances on different frontiers.

The themes remain the same, but content or understandings will often be changed almost overnight. Since most teachers are concerned about content, they frequently think in terms of a stabilized curriculum. Thus changes in a textbook not only threaten the security of such a teacher, but also make it necessary for her to be prepared to teach aspects of science beyond her own understanding or capabilities. This is one reason for an in-service program—because many teachers need help in keeping up with new trends in science and with new materials.

Science teaching based on pupil interests can be most effective, but here again, one finds teachers facing the problem of sequence in terms of both content and teaching materials. If the curriculum is built upon evolving themes that include the major interests of most children, it does not matter which area is studied at a particular time of the year. However, many teachers like to think in terms of sequences based on the season, so that one can relate a given activity to things which can be seen out-of-doors.

In considering "an interest and pupil needs approach," the teacher with thirty pupils will find that interests vary both in kind and in intensity. She must remember that pupils can ask casual questions without wanting to spend one or two weeks trying to find an answer. Children's interests must be recognized as part of the intangible aspects of growing up; the teacher must always be prepared to recognize the difference between a whim and a sincere interest.

The authors favor a spiral approach to science, with sequence based upon growth, interests, and needs. Children may start a study of a particular theme at a lower grade level with the understanding that they may work on it at succeeding grade levels, but unless circumstances warrant such a continuation, the topic does not have to be reintroduced at *every* grade. The sequence of activities must be based upon continued teacher evaluations of what individual children and groups of children know and think about a particular phase of science. As she works with her children, she can recognize special interests and needs. What she does with the children and how long she works with them on a given science theme depends upon their ability to show growth.

In an attempt to avoid a rigid grade standard sequence, it is recommended that minimum and optional units be outlined in terms of three-year grade sequences (in place of traditional grade sequences), with the teachers being free to enrich the program both vertically and horizontally in terms of the capabilities of their children and their interests. Since no *one* graded science book may meet the needs of these children, succeeding teachers should be able to see, through a more effective record system to supplement their own observations or pretesting, what areas children have studied. Thus, one can have a spiral approach based upon review and reevaluation over long intervals, with teachers being free to take bright or fast-learning pupils into new areas calling for higher-level skills and understanding. Here the teacher uses a *developmental* approach based on taking the children from where she finds them to increasingly higher levels. Each time the pupils return to a broad area for study, it is presumed that they have reached a new stage of science readiness and can go deeper and deeper into the study of a topic. This developmental approach recognizes the fact that children change in their scientific attitudes as they acquire new experiences and background. From year to year their understanding of the world around them increases. Old ideas or concepts change, so the teacher's task becomes more complex unless she is ready to recognize individual differences in the learning stages of given students.

TEACHING SCIENCE IN CORRELATION
WITH OTHER SUBJECTS

The content of a science curriculum is often similar to that included in other subjects, or there may be an overlapping which makes it difficult to separate two subjects. Many teachers like to think of science as an unrelated subject, but in many schools science is taught in combination with other subjects. Thus, weather or climate can be studied as science or as a phase of geography. Similarly, the work of scientists in the study of disease may be considered under science, health, or social studies. Frequently, science units and social studies units are integrated. In some school systems, children are expected to devote up to an hour a day to unit activities. Here, the emphasis tends to be on social studies unit activities, with the understanding that at least one-third of the time be reserved for work on science unit activities. Some of the science and social studies units will overlap. For example, it is hard to say that units on transportation, clothing, communication, conservation, and foods are not related to science, although they are frequently thought of as social studies units.

If a theme or unit is overwhelmingly loaded with science concepts, it may be desirable to develop group activities that may definitely be classified as belonging to a science unit. Actually, the techniques used by the teacher and the students need not be too different in the study of science, social studies, or even mathematics-oriented units. With the exception of the classroom experiment, social studies teachers tend to use the same basic approaches to learning. Audio-visual aids, field trips, pupil-teacher planning, individual projects, committee work, small group and class discussions, wide reading, and reference work involving research skills are all common teaching and learning activities used in both subjects; the differences, if any, depend on the goals or outcomes.

INTELLECTUALLY GIFTED CHILDREN
AND SCIENCE STUDIES

One will find brilliant boys and girls whose interest in scientific activities is merely casual; they may find greater pleasure in reading, writing, music, art, or other fields. But *some* intellectually gifted children do have a special interest in some phases of science. Observing teachers will often notice this interest and will capitalize upon it to stimulate other worthwhile educational activities—some of which may be individual projects, others committee or all-class activities. This interest in science may be due to these children's greater curiosity about the world they see, hear, and read about. These children continually want to know what is happening and why. They are not easily satisfied with general statements or answers and will frequently make an effort to obtain better answers on their own, through questioning, wide reading, experimentation, and other research activities. Frequently, a bright child's hobbies will set the stage for learning, and the classroom teacher should take advantage of these.

While intellectually gifted boys and girls may show their interest in science as pupils, they may show very little interest in science as a

The teacher works with a small accelerated group
while the rest of the class does an assignment.

possible vocational field. This has led some educators to advocate special science programs which will lead them into science careers. The authors are opposed to the idea of forcing young children to make career choices early in life. This does not mean that one ignores the science interests of the students, but rather that one continues to give them experiences which are as rich as possible, so that ultimately they will be able to make their career choices based upon intelligent thinking, true interests, and successful experiences in their chosen area. It is unfair to the bright preteenage youngster to have to make a choice based on a limited exposure to life.

Instead, teachers should encourage bright pupils to cultivate their interests in science by helping them find new and stimulating science books and projects related to science. For example, during the course of the day these pupils' creative writing talents may center about one of a number of science themes. During discussion periods these pupils may serve as discussion leaders when current events reveal new advances in the field of science. In many cases such children may develop science specialties which will allow them to assume a prominent leadership position in the class.

When the student becomes engrossed in a special project, time and fatigue may become meaningless until his goals have been realized. It is this power of concentration and interest that the school has to be prepared to *encourage* and *permit*. If three fifth-grade pupils become so engrossed in a science project that they literally cannot drop it, the teacher should be ready to allow them to postpone some other activity so that they may solve their problem through creative thought and action. Remember, science activities bring out the resourcefulness of bright students. When answers are not apparent through casual study, they will formulate their own hypotheses and then undertake projects to verify them. Thus science helps boys and girls build a background for solving higher-level problems encountered in and out of school.

TAKING CHILDREN WHERE ONE FINDS THEM IN SCIENCE

Trying to find where children are in the field of elementary science is not quite the same as it is in social studies or in arithmetic. A teacher can quiz children regarding their knowledge of science, but getting them to demonstrate the "why" of science can be much more difficult. Frequently, a written test has no value, because the answers fail to show that the individual's thought processes may be faulty. For example, the pupil who can describe or paint the monarch butterfly and tell its life story may have missed the whole point of a lesson if he does not understand the value of protective coloration. Getting past the fact barrier to the understanding level can be more difficult with slow pupils than with bright pupils, because the latter can see cause-and-effect relationships much more easily than pupils in the former category.

By listening to boys and girls talk, teachers can evaluate the nature of their thought processes or type of reasoning. Many children will show that they cannot explain common phenomena. They may show that they are superstitious or that they are relying on "old wives' tales" to explain fairly commonplace events. Again, their reasoning may be faulty because they have been exposed to evidence which was not clear to them. This may call for a *new look* at the evidence, or the teacher may have to help them by referring them to new sources of information. This may call for using special references, talking to authorities, looking at pictures, taking a field trip, conducting an experiment, or engaging in discussion with people who can talk on the basis of facts and experiences rather than on mere conjecture or guessing. Helping these pupils authenticate their sources of information may be considered a basic responsibility of the science teacher.

Children may reveal inner feelings about a phase of science through their emotional reactions. Thus, a fifth-grade teacher saw two distinct reactions when the subject of snakes was introduced. She could see the gleam of excitement in the eyes of some of the boys who could not wait to relate what they knew about snakes, but at the same time she could not ignore the "ugh" which she heard, nor the grimaces on the part of some of the girls. Did the girls really dislike snakes, or were they playing a role for the benefit of the boys? If they were uneasy about the snake in the box on the teacher's desk, what was the basis for their fears? Such teachers cannot ignore the mixed emotions of the children in a class. Frequently, they can dictate how far she can go with a topic. Exuberance can be so widespread that no outside motivation may be necessary to start a discussion or activity. On the other hand, the teacher may have to move slowly with pupils who reveal fears or insecurity as they attempt to work with some phase of science.

Poor readers may have little interest in science as the science books or special materials may be beyond their comprehension. This will create special problems for the teacher who teaches a textbook science based upon the use of an all-class approach, because the content subject may have many more words than the pupils can cope with in terms of their subgroup reading or other language experiences. The slower reader may not feel secure with a science which is essentially based upon their ability to acquire new concepts through reading. These pupils need to take part in many, more sensory type science experiences.

Some slow learners may have had close contact with the world of nature or machines, but are unable to express their feelings or ideas due to poor or ineffective communication skills. These children may be able to make excellent contributions if they can overcome the communication barrier. In one class a boy gained stature when, based upon his own experiences, he vividly portrayed the life of a beaver by way of a mural. Another boy who had trouble with reading was able to receive recognition through his knowledge of electricity and his skill with small motors.

Learning is made easier by words, terms, special expressions, and objects which children know. Science can take on new meaning to boys and girls when they can draw upon their own personal experiences; therefore, the teacher has to understand their backgrounds as a new phase of science is introduced. Where the subject is new to children and they do not understand what they read or hear, the teacher has to make certain that something concrete is done to build up their backgrounds.

What the teacher does with the children in regard to science may depend upon their age and experience levels. Young children may operate on a low scientific level, so the teacher may have to start with little things that they can understand or which excite them. Science may be limited to their immediate world, but as they get older and acquire maturity, the teacher can introduce them to higher level and more abstract concepts.

A fourth-grade science class has an outdoor demonstration and individual observation and recording in an area adjacent to the school.

Updating Elementary School Science

Textbook science is not adequate in a world which is changing because of more scientific advances in a single decade than were made in the previous two thousand years of history! In many schools, the textbooks children use are out of date. While basic principles of science remained fairly static for many years, new developments in science have been so rapid that teachers and pupils must rely upon other sources to supplement the textbook. Intermediate and upper grade pupils must be introduced to science through scientific journals, newsletters, films, radio, and television.

Pupils must see both the interdependence of the various sciences and the impact of what is being done in science upon other fields such as economics, world geography, and history. They must see how the world is "shrinking" with each advance in communication and in space travel. Advances in the field of medicine must be pictured in terms of new life for man, but at the same time the learner may have to see the meaning of this in terms of the world population explosion.

Reading about science will not suffice. Teacher and pupil must be able to understand the significance of what scientists have achieved or are achieving. Man's exploration in outer space, in the depths of the ocean, and in time must be seen as revolutions in travel, communication, and thinking. Young people must learn to use a new vocabulary as they work in the field of science. For example, the story of the atom can be one of interest to all, yet many of our teachers and the parents of modern children need to do considerable studying if they are to talk intelligently about component parts of the atom which were unknown a few years ago. In a broad sense, most elementary science teachers must be prepared to teach a science which leads them to do research as they work with their children. They must learn the new vocabulary as they work with new science concepts and attempt to explain the story of modern mankind to less mature individuals.

Some practical suggestions for improving classroom science teaching are as follows:

A *science corner* can stimulate pupils. This is especially true if the science materials or displays are brought in by the children and are changed frequently. A bulletin board can be helpful if it is kept up to date by teacher and students.

A *"science resource box"* can be challenging to the boys. Many parents will gladly donate wire, light sockets, switches, magnets, nails, pieces of wood, metal, plastic, leather, and other items which can be used in construction work. The box can be the source of many projects, especially if it is added to from time to time with new batteries, litmus paper, and a few test tubes.

A *wide assortment of library books* including paperbacks that deal with aspects of science will answer the children's independent and instructional reading needs. If money is scarce, book collections can often be borrowed from a large county or city library to supplement what may be owned by the school or teacher. Or, an appeal to parents and interested citizens may prove helpful.

An *interest file* including notes on cards or in a notebook can help the teacher to guide individual pupils toward activities related to their interests.

Using *television or radio programs* to alert students to interest-reports or studies related to a class activity.

Planning *demonstrations* by the teacher or by pupils: field trips, slides, films, recordings, discussions, debates, science fairs, science clubs, and a deliberate attempt to correlate science with subjects such as art, mathematics, and creative writing.

An *exchange of classes* between teachers who are uncomfortable with teaching science and those who enjoy it. Other teachers have developed confidence in their own efforts after observing how other teachers teach science. Teacher observation may be made within a school or by visiting other schools.

An attempt to *discover the kind of science experiences* the children have had at lower grade levels. If topics are going to be repeated, the children should find new elements in both content and method of presentation. Testing before the start of a new science project or unit will often help the teacher identify interests, attitudes, or concepts which can lead to new and exciting studies.

Enough *space for activity*. Grouping tables together, providing for a science space corner, and arranging furniture for project activity work enhance the conditions to promote all-class activities.

Constant *evaluation of the progress* of the pupils in a class in the light of both immediate and long-range objectives. Tests may show what they have learned in the way of facts, but it may take considerable observation and special techniques to determine whether pupils have grown in understanding and attitudes.

There is no single answer to the question of how science can be made more modern and more meaningful. Success depends upon the use of common sense and effective teaching methods: Any good teacher can create interest in science, because the content lends itself to activities which developing children can enjoy if they are given the opportunity and the environment to explore them.

And teachers should be able to teach elementary school science with enjoyment, not trepidation, even when their background in science is limited. They can, if they want to do so, learn a great deal of science *with* the children and *from* the children. Many teachers will find it helpful to take special courses in elementary school science as a method of bringing themselves up to date or as a means of getting better acquainted with the areas they teach or can teach. Where this is not possible, teachers can do their own research and study in order to prepare themselves to meet challenging science questions from eager and curious children.

IMPROVING INSTRUCTION THROUGH EXPERIMENTATION

For many years, elementary school science was taught incidentally or, if it was a formal subject, its experimental aspects were ignored even when the textbooks pictured and described fairly simple demonstrations or experiments which teachers and children could perform in the average classroom. In recent years, teachers and administrators have come to recognize the value of an experimental approach to teaching science as a means of improving and updating the quality of instruction. This new approach calls for a wider use of audio-visual aids and experimentation as a supplement to the written word. Unfortunately, many elementary school teachers are not science specialists (or even science-minded). But these teachers must realize that bright or curious children enjoy experimenting, so that the classroom should become a simple laboratory. The equipment necessary for most science experiments is inexpensive and easy to use, and many boys and girls who have worked with a commercial science kit or with simple gadgets will be only too happy to work up a demonstration after school or at home for the benefit of the rest of the class.

But experimentation for the sake of experimenting is not sufficient. Both teacher and learner must understand the nature of the problem and, after observing the results of an experiment, profit by repeating the activity before attempting to formulate conclusions. Again, pupils may be taught to verify their findings by referring to textbooks or other sources of information. The experiment should help the learner discover something he did not know before. It should help explain a phenomenon pupils have encountered and want to know more about. Essentially, the science experiment should be considered as one of several tools to help pupils gain power in problem solving. If experimentation is to have value, these recommendations should be followed:

Science classes should not contain more than 25 to 30 pupils. Individual work and small-group work are an essential for good science teaching. All children should be free to work with the materials and to take part in the experimental phase of science. When class size exceeds these numbers, it becomes impossible to have pupil activity, and teachers have little time to encourage or supervise small-group activity.

Each experiment ought to be built around a well-defined problem.

Boys and girls should work together with the teacher in the planning and preparation of experiments whenever it is possible for them to do so.

Demonstration experiments must be given so that every pupil can observe what happens. If class size interferes with pupil observation or participation, it may be better to divide the class into two sections.

All material needed for an experiment has to be brought together before it starts. There is nothing more embarrassing to a teacher or to a pupil than to start a special activity and then find that some ingredient or piece of equipment is missing.

Science experiments should be kept simple so pupils can observe what happens and understand both the purpose and outcome of the activity. The work should be simple enough for the children to see that there is no mystery in what is being done. They should be able to formulate an opinion about what has occurred before their eyes. If the experiment is too complicated, there is always the possibility that an error can be made or that some unexplainable variable can affect the results.

The directions for conducting an experiment have to be clearly stated. They can be briefly outlined on the board so that the actual steps taken can be followed. Should something go wrong with the experiment, the pupils should be able to decide what may have occurred.

The experiment should cause pupils to think. They should react to the experiment, draw conclusions from their observations, and be prepared to follow them up by further testing, discussion, and reading. A single experiment should never be the basis for a broad generalization or conclusion.

Children ought to learn to use controls in planning experiments. An experiment may be performed with two or three variations in order to study the effect of control factors.

An evaluation should be made of each experiment. First, the evaluation should be made to ascertain whether or not the purpose of the experiment has been realized: Was the problem solved? Second, the experiment should be evaluated in terms of other major objectives: Was pupil behavior affected by the activity? Did it lead to other desirable activities? Were pupil attitudes changed, or did the activity lead to realization of the broad theme or concepts underlying the study? Frequently, the teacher will want to measure the growth of students who played a prominent part in the experiment: Did they show leadership qualities, creativity or originality, resourcefulness, or other desirable traits?

A short summary of the important outcomes of the experiment should be recorded. The summary can be used to show pupils what has been accomplished. It can be used for review purposes or to show what was accomplished during the year.

Television Can Help to Vitalize Elementary School Science. Children need to work with things. They need to experiment, touch, watch, and then talk about what they have experienced. Where possible, the firsthand experience is to be preferred, but when that is not possible, television may be a worthy substitute. In some parts of the country, elementary and secondary school pupils are able to take part in a planned science lesson presented on television by very capable science teachers. These lessons are so well prepared that they cannot be duplicated by the average elementary school teacher, who tends to have a limited science background and who usually has limited equipment or materials to work with. In some schools one may find a closed-circuit television system which enables pupils to ask questions of the science teacher making the television presentation, so the pupils can still become involved in some phases of the program.

Educational television is not a threat to the teacher. Used properly, it can add a new depth to her teaching, as well as enrichment for the children. With a teacher guide to prepare the classroom teacher and the children for what is to come, it is possible to bring new aspects of science to children in designated grade levels. Usually, teachers have all the children in a class observing special science programs, but this is not necessary. Advanced pupils or students with special interests can leave the regular class to look at special programs. In either case, the teacher and the pupils can carry on group or class discussions or proceed with other related science activities.

There will be times when the teacher has no control over the theme presented on television. If it does not meet the needs of her students, she should be free to develop her own program. In other instances, television may be used to supplement what the teacher is doing with a group of children. Good elementary school teachers who know their children and who can teach good science lessons will make use of television to enrich their programs, but will not allow television to replace their science curriculum.

One of the problems teachers have to face with television is that of scheduling. Usually, elementary school teachers do not have to cope with this problem, although television can break established patterns calling for large blocks of time. Television may be helpful in a team-teaching situation, in which large groups of children are brought together with one or two teachers to see a special science program by an outstanding science teacher. In addition, special programs can be viewed by some children while a teacher is working with a reading, writing, arithmetic, or spelling group. Here the teacher substitutes a special program for what is often no more than a busy-work period for many of the pupils when she is engaged elsewhere. Worthwhile television programs can then be seen and heard by interested pupils without interfering with the needs of other children.

Use of Textbooks. Modern elementary school science textbooks are well illustrated, but they vary in terms of content, interest, and readability. Repeated investigations have shown that the average science textbook is too difficult for many children to read with comprehension in the grades designated for their use. In some classes even the better readers will find the science books are above their reading level, either because there is a lack of a controlled vocabulary in them or because the children need reading practice in curricular or special content areas. As a result, many science lessons end up in oral reading by the teacher or by selected bright students while others follow along at their seats as best they can, listening and looking at the "pretty" pictures.

Some elementary school teachers are finding that they can use science books more effectively when they have multiple sets of books from a publisher. Other teachers use multiple books from different publishers, which may or may not all be on the same grade level. In such a class, one may find from two to six science books from each of several publishers, plus numerous library books and special references to give the children and teacher the books necessary for a research type of science teaching. This may or may not supplement a program based upon a laboratory approach. More and more teachers now recognize the values in a research approach to science that calls for wide reading, discussion, and special reports and projects.

In defense of the commercial science textbook, it must be stated that the accompanying teachers manuals have been prepared in such detail and with so much explanation that any teacher who lacks a science background can scarcely make a mistake in her presentation if she follows directions. Used properly, the textbooks in such a series need not result in a strictly textbook science lesson.

Meeting Pupil Needs with a Unit Approach. Studies show elementary school teachers favor a science program based around the development of broad areas or units. Unit teaching is usually related to social studies or social living, but units can be developed which have a strictly science base. Proficiency in writing, reading, drawing, arithmetic, construction, and spelling may be assets for success with some phases of the unit, but the concepts or principles that are learned are related to specific science goals or objectives. A survey of elementary school curriculums shows the ten most commonly listed areas of study that have become the basis for science units are as follows:

1. *The study of the universe.* This includes a study of the moon, sun, stars, planets, and other heavenly bodies. One of the concepts stressed is the vastness of space; that is, the universe is very large. Children are taught to see the relationship of the various bodies in the universe. They may study the causes of day and night, the influence of the tides upon human life, the impact of solar radiation upon modern means of communication, and the reasons for changing seasons in some parts of the world.

2. *The story of the earth.* Different approaches may be used to discover the nature of the world in which we live. Children may study the land, the oceans, and the atmosphere. They may study the age of the earth and its origin, the story of the formation of mountains and seas, along with the changes which have occurred and which are occurring at the earth's surface. The study may include the struggle man has had to combat the forces of erosion and the waste of our natural resources. An interesting phase of the work may center around the study of rocks, minerals, and soil.

3. *The nature of matter.* The class learns the latest developments in the story of the atom. They will learn about the electron, the

proton, and the neutron and should see them as distinct kinds of electricity or particles making up matter. They will study the molecule, nuclear fission, and the uses of radioisotopes. What children study will depend upon their grade and level of maturity.

4. *Kinds of living things.* The children learn of the many kinds of plants and animals found in the world around us. Studies may include the story of their economic importance to man, the way they adapt themselves to their environment, the life cycles of particular plants and animals, and the story of man's conquest of nature.

5. *The survival of living things.* This is a study of the conditions necessary for life. It may include ways plants and animals have adapted themselves to their environment to survive, the role the sun plays in the production of high-energy organic compounds through photosynthesis, and the effects of temperature changes upon plants and animals.

6. *Man's attempts to control his environment.* Children study life on the farm and in the city. They see how man's inventions and discoveries have given him power to harness forces of nature to do his bidding; for example, the building of great dams to contain flood waters, to provide water for irrigation, and to make possible the operation of huge electrical power stations. They may study conservation, types of farming and mining, and the role these resources play in our daily lives.

7. *The importance of good health.* This is the story of health and why it is important. The class learns good health habits, the importance of good foods, adequate rest and exercise, and the proper care of teeth and eyes. They learn about nutrition, good safety practices, and the structure of their bodies.

8. *The human body and how it works.* Here, the structure of the human body and how the various parts work are studied. Children may study about the heart as a part of the story of circulation of the blood. They may study the story of digestion or how food is used by the body. They may study respiration or how the body breathes. Considerable time may be devoted to the study of heredity and how man is influenced by the nature of his genes and by his environment. Disease and man's attempt to control it will be interesting to growing boys and girls.

9. *The story of common phenomena and physical changes.* This concerns such things as sound, light, magnetism, electricity, and gravity. Children see what they are and how they have been mastered to serve mankind. They read about and study how

transportation, communication, and power have been affected by invention. They may study chemical changes which affect us.

10. *How man has learned to use machines to control his environment.* Here, children learn that all of man's powerful and complex machines are adaptions of one of a number of basic machines—the lever, the inclined plane, the wheel, the axle, the wedge, the pulley, and the screw. Children learn the basic principles underlying each type of machine and how they may be combined to make complex machines such as the automobile, the airplane, and the steam shovel.

Some of these major themes may overlap with other themes which have been listed or which have not been described. Teachers may develop other units, such as "The Story of Weather or Climate Changes," along with numerous other exciting and interesting topics which may be included in parts of a major theme. One will frequently find that major units have been broken into subunits. Under the spiral approach the children will begin to study one of these subunits, with succeeding teachers enlarging upon what was started at lower grade levels and introducing new subunits or topics until, by the time the boys and girls have completed their schooling, they have had ample opportunity to study all phases of a complex or broad unit. Unfortunately, the science program in Grades 7, 8, and 9 has not always been too well integrated with the elementary program, with the result that there can be questionable duplication of teacher efforts between the elementary school and the junior high school or between the junior high school grades and the high school. This duplication of effort can destroy pupil interest in further science activity, or it may take away time from enrichment activities that are essential for further understanding and for the development of new science interests on the part of the more rapid learners.

The problem of acceleration in the field of science is complicated by this lack of an awareness or agreement as to what the children will learn in succeeding grades or what they may have learned in preceding grades. In some schools, the problem of what to teach at the intermediate grades may be considered negligible, especially where elementary school teachers at lower grade levels have limited their efforts to incidental science teaching. However, where there has been a concerted effort on the part of teachers at every grade level to teach science units which have meaning to all pupils, one can give bright pupils enough of a science background to enable them to skip either a year of junior high school science or the general science so often taught in the ninth grades of many high schools. Where this has been done, ninth-grade pupils have shown no difficulty in taking biology before it is commonly offered in high school. Many bright pupils have no difficulty mastering advanced science concepts, so they can benefit from activities which call for planned acceleration as a part of broad units or a series of subunits.

In schools where educators have adopted a broad-spiral approach, the same concept areas may be introduced over long time periods, such as a three-year cycle. Here, units are repeated for average children over a span of three years with pupils and teachers making studies in depth which will carry them over to the next cycle where, after a brief review, they can proceed to work with higher-level concepts and applications. In such schools, the faster learners may complete a learning cycle in a shorter period of time or may be allowed to skip one or more intermediate steps of a cycle, if not the whole cycle.

Necessity for Records of Pupil and Class Progress. Where teachers are given a course of study in science with the expectation that each teacher will teach prescribed units at their grade level, succeeding teachers should theoretically have no trouble in planning a science program since nothing has been left to chance. Each teacher knows the curriculum; however, such teaching is no guarantee that the pupils were ready to learn the concepts when they were exposed to them in the graded science curriculum. In a less formal learning situation, where child interests are followed or where pupils are allowed to progress at their own rates of learning, succeeding teachers may be at a loss when it comes to planning, because they do not know to what the children have been exposed at lower grade levels.

To avoid the rigidity of the grade standard curriculum and the duplication of effort in the nondirected program, it is recommended that the science program of a given school be built around large and flexible units, with teachers free to take up a study of one or more optional units if children's interests gravitate in other directions. In addition, it is recommended that the teachers develop a science progress chart which can become a part of the individual's permanent record. The chart can show broad content areas studied and special projects completed. It may include a listing of science concepts taught and presumably learned.

REFERENCES

1. Glenn O. Blough, and others, "Teaching and Evaluating Science in the Elementary School," Chapter VIII, *Fifty-ninth Yearbook of the National Society for the Study of Education,* Part I, in Nelson B. Henry, ed., *Rethinking Science Education* (Chicago: University of Chicago Press, 1960).

2. Glenn O. Blough and Julius Schwartz, *Elementary School Science and How to Teach It*, 3rd ed. (New York: Holt, Rinehart & Winston, 1964).
3. Gerald S. Craig, "Science in the Elementary School," *What Research Says to the Teacher*, No. 12 (Washington, D.C.: National Education Association, 1957).
4. Joseph Crescimbeni, "Science as a Structural Discipline," *Elementary School Notes* (Boston: Ginn, 1966).
5. Robert Heath, *New Curricula* (New York: Harper & Row, 1964).
6. Wendell Johnson, "Speech Handicaps," Chapter X, *Forty-ninth Yearbook of the National Society for the Study of Education*, Part II, *The Education of Exceptional Children* (Chicago: University of Chicago Press, 1950).
7. Paul E. Kambly and John E. Suttle, *Teaching Elementary School Science* (New York: Ronald Press, 1963).
8. National Education Association, *Schools for the Sixties* (Washington, D.C.:National Education Association, 1963).
9. Patricia Sexton, *Education and Income* (New York: Viking, 1961).
10. Abraham Shumsky, *Creative Teaching in the Elementary School* (New York: Appleton-Century-Crofts, 1965).
11. George I. Thomas and Joseph Crescimbeni, *Guiding the Gifted Child* (New York: Random House, 1966).
12. Edward Victor, *Science for the Elementary School* (New York: Macmillan, 1965).

CHAPTER 14

Meeting Individual and
Group Needs in Social Studies

Defining Social Studies

Success with social studies materials will depend to a large extent upon the individual's ability to read and apply basic work-study skills to a body of information that is constantly multiplying beyond man's ability to absorb it. In the child's limited years in school he can only absorb a small sampling of the many fields that are included in a modern definition of social studies. Thus, subjects such as history and geography may no longer be identified when boys and girls attempt to solve realistic problems which may have their base in economics, sociology, political science, history, anthropology, or geography. While the foregoing statement would lead the reader to assume that all social studies teachers follow a problem-solving approach, the truth is that a large portion of the instruction in social studies is based upon day by day recitations of textbook material assigned page by page. Success for these children will be measured in terms of their mastery of or retention of those facts considered significant by the instructor. In such classes one finds teaching is aimed at the masses with little actual consideration being given to the individual.

What the teacher teaches will usually depend upon the philosophy of education found in a given school or school system; however, *how* she teaches will often depend upon her skill in realizing the objectives that have been established for a given grade or class. If, for example, she finds herself with the responsibility to teach children about life in

Egypt, she can set the stage for learning through the use of multiple texts or mixed sets of books instead of limiting herself to a single text. Again, she may make wide use of audio-visual aids and television. She may decide to have students work in committees that have been assigned to or that have elected to complete projects which will result in the attainment of desired goals. When a teacher is new to a school, she may find that materials are inadequate or that the children are not ready for the type of instruction she advocates, but with time she can often overcome these apparent obstacles. In some communities, a teacher's willingness to individualize instruction may seem impossible to put into practice; the teacher has to take into account the readiness of her colleagues as well as the readiness of her students for a type of teaching which will truly reflect her ability to provide the instruction children need.

Unit Teaching—
One Approach to Individual Differences

Traditional social studies was taught from a basic text. For the most part, teaching consisted of a lecture, oral reading by the teacher or by members of the class, and a repetitive routine of questions and answers based upon the text or lecture. While there are times when these approaches satisfy the needs of the moment, the role of the teacher is quite apt to be different where unit teaching is introduced.

Units of study may be built around many types of themes. One may work with science units, mathematics units, literature units, music units, etc., but because social studies lends itself exceptionally well to the unit approach, we have reserved full discussion of the unit as an effective method of individualizing instruction for this chapter.

The unit method of studying a subject—by individual pupils and by groups of pupils who have different degrees of skill, different interests, and different potentialities—lends itself to better mastery of content materials and better understanding of social problems than would any other single method of attack. Unit teaching provides for individual differences in a class and brings together students who need practice in democratic living, sharing, and working. Pupils use all their communication and research skills in good unit activities. In unit work they have opportunities—not possible in a lecture or single textbook approach—to develop creative talents and to demonstrate leadership qualities.

For decades, educators have played with the word "unit." As a result, the word is used rather loosely to describe many kinds of class activities, but teachers may not be talking about the same thing when they use the term. In one school, teachers will talk excitedly about meeting the needs of their children through "experience units." In another school, teachers will proudly demonstrate how interested their children are in a "subject matter unit." Visits to other schools will reveal that teachers are talking about "process units," "resource units," "activity units," "source units," "content units," "topical units," and "textbook units." To dispel any confusion caused by the variation in titles, some definition is necessary. We offer the following:

> A unit is an organized body of knowledge, skills, or concepts considered essential for the realization of a specific objective, e.g., understanding the concept of transportation. A unit may encompass only a small body of knowledge—a study of railroads, for example—or it may include material that requires multiple resources, activities, projects, and the acquisition of complex concepts—for example, a unit on transportation will include automobiles, ships, airplanes, and rockets or space ships as well as railroads.

If unit teaching is to serve as a leveling agent for children with different interests, abilities, and backgrounds, the teacher must know her children by studying them, working with them, and continually evaluating and reevaluating what they are doing. Teachers should forget "educational jargon" and try to be realistic about making their classrooms into living workshops where boys and girls work, alone or together, making full use of research and communication skills. Going to the encyclopedia to copy verbatim a page of data to be read to the rest of the class does not represent real learning from unit teaching. Pupils must absorb ideas from a variety of sources and present them to others in a challenging situation—a situation where the individual knows of what he speaks, and where the receivers can accept or challenge what is given, based on intelligent thinking and acting. Students need opportunities to work with problems which enable them to apply their own knowledge and experience in working out both realistic and practical solutions.

CHOOSING UNIT ACTIVITIES

In selecting a unit, consideration should be given to the needs of the children who are going to work on it. If the interest in the unit is *real* and already there, the teacher may have to adopt approaches different from those used when she is trying to motivate interest. How she guides her pupils' thinking and actions should depend upon their basic needs and her ability to help them see common values in many group activities. Teachers who have to work with mandated units and materials will have to work carefully, in setting the stage for effective learning, by capitalizing on pupil strengths and by developing interests in some phase of the work. If the available resources are too difficult, the teacher may find that it is more rewarding to look for easier source materials or to postpone a study until pupils acquire greater competency with social studies terms and materials.

In teaching a unit, the teacher must try to realize many broad as well as specific objectives. These objectives must be pupil-oriented; children should see a *purpose* in what they do. Some educators have objected to the subject-centered unit, but there is nothing instructionally wrong in such units when the underlying reasons or objectives are understood by the pupils. If subject matter acquisition is deemed important, the teacher will have to see if she can ascertain the readiness of individual pupils to absorb, retain, and understand it. As a rule, only a small number of children in the average class will be ready to engage successfully in a long subject-centered unit unless the teacher has been able to acquire or manufacture materials with the pupils which they can study at their particular learning levels. For example, the teacher who has to teach sixth graders a unit on South America and knows these students are unable to read the assigned textbook independently will waste her time unless supplementary reading materials or audio-visual materials can be procured which they can use effectively as members of a group or class.

Frequently, educators stress the importance of leaving the selection of units to the children on the supposition that pupil interests and needs will result in greater motivation and effort. This approach is commendable if the teacher is certain that the selection of a problem or theme really represents the wishes, desires, and needs of a large segment of the class, and not mere whim. If a class is divided and cannot decide on an appropriate unit, the teacher can have two parallel units going on at the same time; but many teachers would prefer to tip the scale in favor of one segment of the class, because of personal interests or a knowledge of the basic educational needs of most of the children in the classroom.

The Pretest. Most unit outlines, including those presented in this chapter, do not list a step in unit teaching known as the "pretest." Teachers who know their children's abilities, skills, backgrounds, and past school experiences may feel the pretest is an unnecessary step, but it should be noted that teachers who plan to take children from a low learning level to higher levels should base unit selection on the evidence revealed in an inventory or pretest. The pretest can be used as a diagnostic measure which tells the teacher what the children know and where she should begin to work with them. It can be formal or informal, depending upon the teacher. Some teachers use teacher-pupil planning and evaluation meetings, plus a study of previous records to discover what the pupils know about a topic or problem area. If the teachers and pupils have been working closely together, the new unit does not come as a shock or surprise to the students. One series of activities leads naturally into another.

DEVELOPING A UNIT

Teachers can develop their own unit outlines, find them in curriculum study guides, or secure them from commercial sources. But regardless of the nature of the outline or its origin, each unit will have one unifying theme, topic, or problem that gives direction to the teacher and her children. It should, in addition, be built around themes, topics, or concepts that will hold the interest of the learner and still help him acquire higher-level understandings and knowledge. Basically, every unit will require a number of activities of a problem-solving nature if the children are going to achieve their goals and objectives. And because children's growth patterns are affected by so many factors that a concept sequence good for one group of pupils may not be adequate for another, the teacher or teachers must tailor units to the special needs of their children.

Since good unit outlines are not easy to make and can be time-consuming, the authors recommend the accumulation of good resource units that can be adapted to a particular teacher's situation. Although this may appear to be structuring the curriculum, the resource unit file in a school need not limit the teacher; it should be considered as an "idea bank" to which everyone contributes and from which everyone draws only when necessary to meet new interests and challenges.

A number of outline forms may be used to give direction to the teacher who is planning a unit, of which those presented here may be considered typical.

TABLE 1
Typical Outlines for a Unit of Work

Illustration 1	*Illustration 2*
Title of the unit°	The theme or topic°
General purpose, long-range goal	Unit objectives, generalizations
Specific purposes, short-range goals	Specific aims, concepts, or understandings
Steps in initiating the unit	The approach to the unit, introduction to the new field of study
Development of the unit, procedures or directions that may be taken	Questions, problems, and activities for the children
Anticipated outcomes	Anticipated activities
Culminating activities	Culminating activities
Evaluative procedures	Methods of evaluating pupil activity
Bibliography	Instructional resources which may be used to achieve desired goals

Illustration 3

Title of unit or theme   Grade or age

I A descriptive statement

The descriptive statement describes in simple language the content of the unit. It will generally include the purpose or reason for studying the topic.

II A provocative or leading question

Motivation for the study may be promoted by listing one or more provocative or leading questions. A good "how" or "why" question may set the stage for learning by directing the children's attention to a specific topic.

III Suggested disciplines

The title or the provocative question may indicate the subject field or disciplines that may be used to obtain answers to the question, i.e., history, geography, economics, anthropology, sociology.

IV Specific skills to be developed

The teacher may list the social studies skills which will be required of the pupils, i.e., outlining; map reading, sketching or drawing; preparing a bar graph; drawing conclusions; writing a description or a summary; organizing ideas in a sequence.

V Answers to the provocative or leading question

The teacher may briefly outline answers that children may be expected to give to the leading question. The answers may become the basis for generalizations that are to be formulated as a result of the study.

VI Content sources

Books and periodicals may be listed which can be used as reference sources. Films, recordings, etc., may also be listed.

VII Generalizations to be discovered

The study should lead to the development of a number of generalizations. The generalizations may be formulated both individually and collectively in class and should parallel the ones listed by the teacher at the outset of the unitary activity.

° The Negro Struggle for Civil Rights, The Woman Suffrage Movement, Air and Water Pollution, Communication in the World of Tomorrow.

The following material is a slightly condensed version of a unit on Central America prepared for a fifth-grade group by Mrs. Marie Dority of the State University at Albany.

Teaching Unit—Grade 5

Topic:

How the people of Central America live and work and their relationship to us.

Class:

Grade 5; age 10–11; latter part of the year; urban-rural community; heterogeneous group; a unit in the study of the major culture regions of the Western Hemisphere.

I. *General Direction:*

The basic purpose of this unit will be to develop understandings of the culture of the people of Central America. Important aspects of the geography of this area will be stressed, including major climate and vegetational areas, topography, latitude, and prevailing winds. Emphasis will be placed on how history has helped to shape the way in which the people live. Such a study includes an interdisciplinary approach covering the economic and sociological patterns of the nations. Place shall be given to a study of contemporary problems. The unit will take about three and one half weeks.

II. *Generalizations:*

1. Geography, in part, determines the economic and social development of nations.
2. The economic activities of nations are influenced, in part, by their location and natural resources.
3. The form of government of a nation is influenced by its historical development.
4. The historical development of a nation is affected by its neighbors.
5. In any society, specific roles are assumed and enforced upon certain groups.
6. In all nations of the world, there are still many problems that have to be solved.
7. These problems will be solved through cooperative efforts on the part of individuals and nations.

III. *Objectives:*

A. Understandings
   1. Most people who live in Central America are poor.
   2. Central American countries have weak governments.
   3. Central America depends heavily on the United States.
   4. Central America is beginning to change.
   5. Central Americans are moving into the cities and building up power industries.
   6. The relations of different races and classes in Central America are changing.
   7. Central American nations are not certain of the road they will follow in bringing about a social revolution.
   8. The United States will continue to play an important role in the destiny of Central American nations.

B. Attitudes and appreciations
   1. Central Americans have contributed much toward enriching the culture of the Western Hemisphere.
   2. Social cooperation is a saner way of solving common problems than social conflict.
   3. Achieving social democracy has led Central American nations to evolve forms of government different from that of the United States.

    4. Because the people of Central America are different from those in the United States does not mean that they are inferior to us.

C. Skills

    1. To locate and organize information.

    2. To communicate orally and in writing.

       a. To understand terms and abbreviations.

    3. To evaluate and interpret information.

       a. To distinguish between fact and propaganda.

       b. To interpret pictures, charts, graphs and tables.

    4. To understand time and chronology.

       a. To associate seasons with particular months in both Northern and Southern Hemispheres.

       b. To learn to relate the past to the present in the study of change and continuity in human affairs.

       c. To learn to formulate generalizations and conclusions about time in studying the development of human affairs.

    5. To interpret maps and globes.

       a. To understand the significance of relative location as it has affected national policies and international policies.

       b. To compare maps and draw inferences.

          1. To explain the geographic setting of historical and current events.

          2. To infer man's activities or way of living from physical detail and from latitude.

          3. To read into the map the relationships suggested by the data shown, as the factors which determine the location of cities.

IV. *Body:*

Concept. Central America is in the low latitudes.

Activity. Text page 418; read individually.

Show film "Central America, Bridge Between the Americas," Part I and/or II, to observe the geographic significance of Central America as well as how the people live.

Map study—Locate and name the nations; to whom the colony belongs; from whom the U.S. rents land for the Panama Canal and its location; note latitude, point up physical features and stress why people prefer living on the highlands; and point out major cities. Compare it with Mexico.

Plan a trip. Estimate the distance covered and the time required to travel by ship, plane, and car to Central America. Show the routes on a map. Refer to travel folders and timetables. List the countries they want to visit and the things they want to see and buy there. Plan the kinds of clothes they would pack for the trip. What time of year would be best to start the trip?

Concept. Each country in the Western Hemisphere has a rich history of its own.

Activity. Prepare a stamp display using stamps of all the Central American countries. Select several with interesting historical significance and write or tell the story behind it.

Dramatize informally an incident in the history of the Central Americas, e.g., Columbus' discovery, Maya Indians, Panama Canal.

Have the children pretend to be newspaper reporters. Each covers the story of a single historical event. Teach the 5 W's and how to take reporters' notes to be developed into a lead story.

Read individually page 419 in the text, "What has been the history of Central America?"

Concept. Geography partially determines where and how people live.

Activity. Have the children read individually the three paragraphs in the text on page 419 entitled "How the people of Central America live." To supplement particularly the sparse treatment given "bananas," show the film "José Harvests Bananas" or "Honduras, the Banana Republic." Point out other material shown in film which indicates the way the people live.

Do some map exercises utilizing outline maps and the overhead projector. Allow different children to put (draw) in the mountains, rivers and other significant physical features and on the basis of their reading and learnings so far, have them tell what they think the people in that region or city do. Allow the rest of the class to correct or add to the information given.

Concept. People are much alike in feelings and desires though they differ in appearance and ideas.

Activity. To observe more closely how the people live and to learn more about their culture, show the film "People of Guatemala" or "Costa Rica, the Rich Coast."

Arrange a display of flags or pictures of flags from the countries. Discuss the significance and meaning of the symbols on some of these flags. Compare them to the U.S. flag.

Prepare a list of ways in which the Central American countries differ from the United States. Another of similarities. Allow the children access to the library corner if they cannot think of ways. Hold each child responsible for contributing at least one item to the list and do not allow the precocious child to contribute the obvious ways leaving the slower child to search too long for less apparent ways. Someone might like to develop this into his unit project.

Concept. Central Americans are different from people in the United States, but they have contributed much toward enriching the culture of the Western Hemisphere.

Activity. Find pictures of Indian art and craft and arrange a display. Use the full color pictures of Mayan art in the Summer, 1964, issue of *Horizon* magazine.

Collect travel posters, postcards, and other pictures and arrange a display. Have some pupils imagine they are travel agents trying to interest someone in a trip to Central America. Use the posters to illustrate what could be seen. Look for propaganda.

Play the folk song record "Noche Tropical" (Panama) and the game song record "Go Back to Your Cradle" (Honduras). Have the pupils note particularly how the music and games differ from or are like our own.

Concept. Each country in the Western Hemisphere has a rich history of its own, and many forms of social and political organization have grown up out of the past.

Activity. Construct a time line on the chalkboard. Use colored chalk to make it effective and visual. Use directed discussion to elicit volunteer participation and depict major events in the development of Central America. Show such things as: 200–800, peak of Mayan civilization; 1502, Columbus seeks a route to India; 1513, Balboa reaches the Pacific Ocean; 1522, Alvarado rules Central America.

Concept. Change in Central America has been slow and difficult.

Activity. Point out that for many years Central America was ruled by Spain through the chief officer of the district, known as a captain-general. The capital was in what is now Guatemala. Continue developing the time line, including: 1821, break from Spain; 1823, Union of Central American nations; 1838, union fails; 1881, French begin work on the Panama Canal; 1903, Panama Independence; 1914, Panama Canal opens; 1945, democracy for all; 1961, Alliance for Progress.

Concept. National as well as international problems are often caused by geographic conditions.

Activity. Using a string and the globe, measure the distance by sea from NYC around the southern tip of South America to San Francisco. Use a ruler to figure out how much string was used to measure this trip. Now measure the distance between the two cities through the Panama Canal. Have the children figure out how many times longer is the trip around South America. Discuss why they think the U.S. was so interested in renting land and building a canal in a foreign country. See if they can determine from this study why the United States adopted such a policy as the Monroe Doctrine or feels obligated to protect or prevent European countries from interfering in Latin American affairs.

Concept. Latin America depends heavily on the United States.

Activity. Using the *Information Please Almanac,* look up the economic conditions in one of the Central American countries. Develop a list or chart showing the chief occupations, products, main consumers and suppliers (imports and exports), and encourage the children to draw inferences as to their dependence upon the U.S. for markets.

Make an export-import map of goods traded between the United States and Central America. Use wrapping paper to draw it on and paste on pictures of the products traded cut from magazines.

Make a products map showing the main crops for each country in Central America and other products which are mined, grown, or manufactured. Guide the children in discussing what use is made of these products.

Concept. The historical development of a nation is affected by its neighbors.

Activity. Have pupils write a short story about which Americans "made history" in their dealings with Central America. Leaders in such events as the Panama Canal and the Monroe Doctrine. How each of these people or events helped to set policy for our relationships.

Take a field trip to the locks of the Barge Canal and compare this canal to the Panama Canal.

Have pupils give a brief oral report of a phase of development or how a particular problem was solved of the construction of the Panama Canal. Collect material on the Canal and encourage the children to bring in pictures. Have someone report on the need for and possibility of a new canal.

Concept. Most of the people of Central America are of Spanish or Indian heritage, and Spanish is the common language.

Activity. Find illustrations of the types of architecture found in Central America and discuss how it depicts their heritage.

Read about the Indians of Central America. Have the pupils report orally on what was learned, the book used, and how the Indians live today.

Have each child select one foreign word he has found either in the textbook or in any of the other literature he has read and develop a definition chart for it. His chart should tell the history of the word, the meaning, and a cut out or drawn picture to show its meaning.

See if there is any possibility of having someone from Central America or someone who has been in Central America visit the class. If no one is available in the immediate community, see if arrangements can be made to have a guest visit the school. Arrange with the PTA or Grade Mother to transport the guest.

Concept. Central America is beginning to change.

Activity. Collect a week's newspaper clippings or pictures dealing with events in Central America. Organize them according to different categories and relate events to past conditions to infer change if any in industry, defense, politics, or social customs.

View film "Guatemala Tells a New Story—Palestine Refugees." Use guided discussion to see what, if any, inferences the pupils are able to draw as to what effect this may have on the country and how these people differ from Central Americans.

Concept. Social cooperation is a saner way to solve common problems than social conflict.

Activity. Conduct a mock meeting of the Organization of American States with one child representing each country. Suggest a current problem which affects all the members which they will be able to discuss.

Have the children locate and report on Peace Corps activities in Central America. Have someone find out why one Central American country has refused to accept Peace Corps aid.

V. *Initiation:*

A. View film "The Faces Behind the Masks"
   1. To give the students an understanding of class conditions in Latin America.
   2. This film could serve to culminate the preceding unit on Mexico.

B. Background for film:
   All people like to go to parties and celebrations to have fun and let off steam. Many of the holidays we celebrate now as Christian holidays are continuations of pagan celebrations. Halloween is a celebration honoring all saints so that those who do not have special days will not be angered. Children wear masks on that day and sometimes use the celebration as an excuse to be rowdy and do mischief. In Latin America, grown people wear masks and work off their frustrations in gay festivals which are held several times a year. Through these religious festivals, the people work off some of the frustration of their poverty and discontent.

C. Things to note:
   Why the mask is symbolic of Latin America.
   The classes in Latin American society.
   The pagan aspect of Latin Christian festivals and dances.
   The way in which Latin Americans view death.
   The new meaning taken on by the festivals today.
   The necessity of festivals in Latin American life.

D. Develop a meaningful understanding of the new words which will be found in the unit and check their understanding of the words from the preceding unit on Mexico. Words: mestizos, jungle, miniature, colony, republic, cacao bean, volcanoes, earthquake, abode, dictator.

VI. *Culminating Activity:*

A. Class discussion to summarize the learnings with adequate opportunity to view and discuss each child's unit activity.

B. Each child will be required to complete a written report or project. They may be individual, or two or three pupils may do a cooperative report-bibliography-project. Subjects might include (g = generalization from list in item II which the subject would develop):

 1. A report on an individual country (g 1–7).
 2. On the building of the Panama Canal (g 1, 2, 4, 6, 7).
 3. How bananas are grown and shipped (g 1, 2, 5).
 4. How coffee is grown and shipped (g 1, 2, 5).
 5. Early history of Central America (g 1, 2, 3, 4, 5).
 6. The Pan-American Highway (g 1, 2, 4, 7).
 7. Famous volcanoes in Central America (g 1, 2).
 8. How a canal across Nicaragua may be built some day (g 2, 4, 6, 7).
 9. Peace Corps activities in Central America (g 6, 7).
 10. A bibliography and exhibit of literature on Central America.
 11. Projects might include a *papier-mâché* map showing:
   a. Panama Canal.
   b. Possible route for new canal.
   c. Pan-American Highway.
   d. Relief map of countries or the entire region.
 12. A mural might depict any of the above topics or even the types of architecture found in Central America, such as hut, abode, Spanish, modern.
 13. An illustrated time line could be developed.

VII. *Evaluation:*

A. Evaluation of knowledge, information, and skills.
 1. A short quiz in essay or objective form.
 2. Note by observation which students participated in informal discussions and seemed aware of the ideas presented in class.
 3. Correct unsupervised written work to note comprehension of understandings.
 4. Direct "why" questions to the students to draw out specific generalizations such as why most of the people live on the higher plateaus.
 5. Evaluate the final report or project in terms of the pupil's level of understanding of the generalizations which apply to his particular study.
 6. Use an objective test to measure the student's ability to memorize facts with understanding.
 7. The travel agent activity would evaluate the student's ability to express ideas.
 8. Check for understanding of terms in both daily and written work.
 9. In their other class work or in units of study which follow, watch for indications of transfer of both understandings and skills.

B. Evaluation of the unit; observation.
   1. Did the activities involve the pupils and hold their interest?
   2. Would a rearrangement of the activities improve the unit?
   3. Should it be shortened or lengthened?

VIII. *Resources:*

A. Books for children:
   1. Walter Buehr, *Through the Locks: Canals Today and Yester-day*, Putnam, 1954. 64p.
   2. Ann N. Clark, *Magic Money*, Viking, 1950. 121p. (Culture conflict of a Guatemala Indian boy—for advanced readers).
   3. Robert B. Consodine, *Panama Canal*, Random House, 1951.
   4. Delia Goetz, *Neighbors to the South*, Harcourt Brace, 1956. 179p.
   5. Anne Merriman Peck, *The Pageant of Middle American History*, Longmans, 1947. 496p.
   6. Vernon Quinn, *Picture Map Geography of Mexico, Central America, and the West Indies*, Lippincott.
   7. A. E. Rothery, *Central America Roundabout*, Dodd, 1944.
   8. Karena Shields, *Three in the Jungle*, Harcourt, 1944.
   9. Howard O. Yates, *How People Live in Central America*, Benefic Press, 1964.
   10. E. J. Coatsworth, *Boy with a Parrot*, Macmillan, 1930.
   11. Pachita Crespi, *Wings over Central America*, Scribners, 1947 (Air trip through 6 countries—factual material).
   12. Dee Day, *Getting To Know Panama*, Coward-McCann, 1958 (Land, history, and people).
   13. N. A. Frey, *The River Horse*, W. R. Scott, 1953 (Guatemala).
   14. Patricia Markum, *The First Book of the Panama Canal*, Watts.
   15. Lupe de Osma, *The Witches Ride and Other Tales from Costa Rica*, Morrow, 1957.

B. Books for teachers:
   1. Ralph Hancock, *Rainbow Republics: Central America*, Invitation to Travel Series, Coward-McCann, 1948.
   2. Tod Wallstrom, *Wayfarer in Central America*, Roy, 1955.
   3. Richard N. Adams, John P. Gillin, Allan R. Holmberg, Oscar Lewis, Richard W. Patch, Charles Wagley, *Social Change in Latin America*, Vintage Press, 1960.
   4. Miguel Covarrubias, *Indian Art of Mexico and Central America*, Knopf, 1957.
   5. A. Curtis Wilgus, *Latin America in Maps*, Barnes and Noble, 1943.

C. Supplementary texts:
   1. *Understanding Latin America*, Edmund Lindop, Tiegs-Adams Series, Ginn and Co., 1960. pp. 129–163.
   2. *Journeys Through the Americas*, Drummond, Allyn & Bacon, 1960. pp. 315–333.

3. *Latin America,* Scholastic World Affairs Multi-text, Robert J. Alexander, Scholastic Book Services, 1964.

D. Magazines:
1. *Americas:* Diaz, A. S., "Managua Revisited," December 1958, 10, pp. 29–32.
2. *Holiday:* "El Salvador: Its Fountain of Firs," May 1957, 2, pp. 162–163.
3. *Rotarian:* "Family of Costa Rica: Miguel Castro Family," November 1958, 93, pp. 18–23.
4. *Horizon:* "Rediscovering America," Summer 1964, 6, pp. 73–93.

E. Films:
1. United Nations Films, Screen Magazine #10, "Guatemala Tells a New Story—Palestine Refugees."
2. CUE film #12, Cultures and Continents, "The Faces Behind the Masks."

F. Filmstrips:
1. "Central America, Bridge Between the Americas," Part I, "Guatemala, British Honduras, and El Salvador," #6458, Stanley Bowmar Co., Valhalla, N.Y. Part II, "Nicaragua, Costa Rica, Panama, Honduras," #6459.
2. "José Harvests Bananas," Guatemala #4242, Stanley Bowmar Co., Valhalla, N.Y.
3. "Costa Rica, The Rich Coast," #5745, Stanley Bowmar Co., Valhalla, N.Y.

G. Records:
1. *Latin American Folk Songs* #B102, Stanley Bowmar Co., Valhalla, N.Y.
2. *Latin American Game Songs* #FL6, Stanley Bowmar Co., Valhalla, N.Y.

CREATING PUPIL INTEREST IN A UNIT

Many teachers depend upon a variety of techniques to foster pupil interest in a new unit. Some teachers cannot wait for the fall term to show what they have picked up as souvenirs during a vacation period. Teachers who have traveled to new places will frequently find their own enthusiasm may suffice to spur children to new activity.

Some teachers set the stage by reading or having the pupils read about the people of a country which is to be studied in detail. As the children ask questions and show a curiosity about the life of the people, she leads them to the point where they ask for a chance to study more about these people and their land. One teacher interested her class in a study of Central Europe by bringing in her collection of European dolls. A seventh-grade teacher literally raided a nearby museum in order to present an exhibit of Indian relics. Once the pupils

As part of a unit of study on the Vikings, these fourth-graders are weaving their own Viking belts.

Photo by Margot Kaiser, courtesy of Ethical Culture Schools, New York City

began examining her display, there was no question about selecting the next unit of study. A fifth-grade teacher used a film about a forest fire to stimulate interest in a conservation unit. A third-grade teacher found her collection of toy trucks, trains, and boats could be used to stimulate interest in a transportation unit. Another teacher accomplished the same end by putting out a display of books dealing with various phases of transportation.

Some educators claim that it is not fair to overwhelm children with stories, books, pictures, and talk about a country to the point that the pupils unanimously agree to a study of the theme represented by the teacher's "prevue of the next attraction." If the teacher is alert and has any freedom of choice, she will take advantage of children's basic interests and will capitalize on events which lead naturally into a study appealing to most pupils. Studies have shown that, when the teacher can discern pupil problems which are realistic and meaningful to the whole class, there is merit to following the lead of the children.

On the other hand, the teacher must remember that a large number of children do not know what they want, because they have not had enough experience to acquire interests of depth. Left to themselves, some pupils will not proceed down new trails. The teacher has a responsibility to open up new vistas for them. If she is going to get them to follow her lead, she has to make their first taste a good one. She has to excite their curiosity so that they will want more of the same.

When the teacher introduces the new unit, she has to give children sufficient background to get them to see where they are going. Without this, children can be completely bewildered if they are led into a discussion about a topic which has no meaning to them. The teacher will also have to consider the maturity of her pupils when she sets the stage for a new unit. A group of very bright pupils will quickly see where her efforts are leading, but a group of slow learners will have difficulty anticipating what may be forthcoming.

VARIETY OF ACTIVITIES OFFERED IN
A SUCCESSFUL UNIT

One of the advantages of unit teaching is that good units include a number of types of activities which can be carried out by pupils with varying degrees of ability and skill. If children lack the skills needed for success in an activity, the teacher has to either teach them these skills or direct them to take part in activities which will challenge them, but which will be within their capacity to achieve progress leading to higher levels of success. At the same time she will see that more capable pupils refrain from starting activities which present no real challenge to them or which duplicate one which they may have just completed. The teacher tries to encourage a wide participation in activities which will be both educationally significant and on higher educational levels.

The work period can be very trying to the teacher who is trying to promote maximum growth for all. Some teachers are satisfied to start children in a given direction, then leave them on their own, but conscientious teachers never turn the children free. They want to see what pupils are accomplishing and they want to be able to give them special help when and where they need it.

Since the average unit will most likely run from three to four weeks, the children should have an ample opportunity to engage in *several* meaningful activities. This is a time when some of the children can work individually or collectively, with or without the teacher. Sometimes they will do research, or they may work intensively in their textbook. They may have time for listening, conversing, discussing. They may be creative individuals one day and copyists the next. In some activities, certain pupils will assume leadership roles; in others, they will be followers.

If committees have been formed, the teacher will see that committee members know their responsibilities and can carry them out properly. She will coordinate the work of several committees to prevent conflict and overlapping. She observes the committees in action and tries to help students with committee assignments so that they can resolve their problems with a minimum of frustration and move in the desired direction. As children complete activities, they make reports to the whole class or to other groups of pupils. If work teams complete assignments satisfactorily, they may go on to other activities; but if the children show that they do not know their material, cannot carry out specific duties, or have not mastered desired and essential skills, they may be taken in hand by the teacher for special help and additional practice in the areas of deficiency.

Continuous Evaluation of Pupil Activities. Teachers and students are accustomed to thinking of evaluation in terms of testing. While tests can be used to measure some phases of growth and progress at the end of a series of unit activities, the formal test should not be the only evaluative device used. How children work with others and how they work with individual tasks or responsibilities is, frequently, more important than what pupils do on a test. Actually, there should be a relationship between test scores and work patterns. Pupils who know how to follow directions and can work independently as well as cooperatively, and who can be depended upon to assume responsibility and to complete assignments on time, are students who tend to stand out in most classes. The teacher should be able to anticipate what growth they have made without looking at test papers.

In evaluating individual pupil or group work, the teacher does not wait until the end of the unit to make a decision about their progress or achievement. The teacher should be working with pupils in terms of her daily observations, notes, and records of student needs and accomplishments. At times the responsibility for evaluation can be shared with the students. They can learn the importance of evaluating individual or group work. As the pupil works with the teacher, she tries to help him see where he is going in terms of where he was and where he wants to be. Sometimes this is done individually, but it is often a group activity. Teacher-pupil meetings for evaluation purposes can be highly significant phases of unit work. After the initial planning meetings, there should be a fairly frequent series of "progress" meetings to review objectives and to consider individual and group progress.

Teachers often fail to let pupils evaluate their own work or that of others. With supervision and standards to guide them, most pupils can be objective in their observations, comments, and conclusions. Personal feelings do not get hurt when the children are taught to make positive statements in oral evaluations. There is no place in the classroom for ridicule or sarcasm by either the teacher or pupils. It will help if everyone understands from the beginning that mistakes are going to be made, but these mistakes do not have to be repeated. If they are, it may mean that the evaluative process has been ineffective or that the goals are too high for the individual who continues to make the same mistakes.

Culminating Activities. A major culminating activity is not a prerequisite in unit teaching, but many pupils look forward to taking an active part in a play, recital, dance, debate, fair, or field trip as the concluding phase of an intensive study. If these become culminating activities, they should be worth both pupil and teacher time and effort to let others see what has been learned or accomplished. Sometimes this may result in a presentation to the whole class or to pupils in another class. Then again, it may call for a special assembly before the rest of the pupils in the school. If the activity is meaningful, parents may be invited to see what the children have done. Although pupil assemblies can be most trying to some teachers, the social and academic learnings acquired in preparation for the culminating activity may last long after children have forgotten specific facts or bodies of knowledge they had to master along the way. Parents enjoy seeing their children take part in special programs, so it helps to promote better home and school relations *if* the programs are the natural outgrowth of a series of purposeful activities instead of merely productions put on because they were considered entertaining.

When the curtain falls and the applause has died away, the teacher should not sit back with a feeling that "This is the end of Holland." The culminating activity should be a *high point* in the unit study, but it should not be construed as meaning the *end* of a study. Neither the teacher nor the children should let the culminating activity cut off all further activity related to the realization of the unit objectives. In many cases, it can even lead to other areas of study. The pupils should have learned skills that will continue to be important to them as they work with other problem areas. The facts they learned and the social graces they acquired should help them become better citizens in the class and in the world about them.

Field Trips Should Be Related to Ongoing Activities. Field trips can be important if they are planned in relation to ongoing unit activities. They should be considered a means of enriching a study by bringing pupils close to a learning situation which is not easily visualized through reading or talking. Some field trips may be taken to gather information on specific topics or projects, and as such they may give the pupils new motives or directions. For example, children who are trying to depict life during colonial days may find a museum opens up a new world to them. Frequently, boys and girls fail to recognize the accomplishments of people who lived in the early American colonies. Some of them find it difficult to picture the substantial homes which were built in numerous New England towns; others cannot imagine the quality of the furniture and decoration found on old southern plantations. Their lack of a "time sense" gives them a faulty picture of life in colonial times. Many fifth-grade pupils might find their concept of life in the 1850s quite different if they could make the short trip from New Salem, Illinois, where Lincoln spent a period of his youth, to see Lincoln's home in Springfield, from which he departed for the White House.

Pupils who can visit places like Sturbridge Village (Massachusetts), The Shelburne Museum (Vermont), Dearborn Village (Michigan), Williamsburg (Virginia), and other restored sites can see that although those men and women did not have many of our conveniences, they did have furniture and furnishings which show high craftsmanship, beauty, and creativity, as well as utility.

Sometimes it is difficult to assess the value of a field trip, because many intangible objectives are realized through the whole process of planning the activity, taking the trip, and evaluating it. To some pupils, the information acquired may be of less significance than the socializing values derived from the multiple activities engaged in by the pupils as they worked together. For example, discussion and writing activities may reveal needs in the communication skills areas. Teachers will find that pupils who have visited a museum with their parents find new interests when they go with classmates. Some of these pupils may play an important leadership role in the planning and guiding of other

A sixth-grader experiments with a colonial printing press during class visit to Sturbridge Village, Massachusetts.

Photo by Andrew Schulz, courtesy of Ethical Culture Schools, New York City

pupils to a place they know. Other pupils may find that the new group experience helps them realize a need for a friend or an opportunity to get to know others in a non-classroom situation. Many teachers become "human" to their pupils on a school trip, and in return the teacher can learn a great deal about her pupils as she rides with them on a bus and listens to their conversations or watches their behavior. Children can play far different roles on a school trip than they do when they are confined to their desks in the classroom. In some areas of study, the field trip may become the basis for a number of further studies, whereas in other classes the field trip may be the climax of the study, with all other activities leading up to it.

Most teachers of younger children will limit themselves to short trips with a central point of interest—for example, a visit to a neighborhood bakery, to a farm, to a firehouse, to the police station, to the post office, or even just to watch the construction of a new house. With older pupils, the trip may be to more distant places to see more complex activities. These pupils may benefit from visiting a factory to see an assembly line operation. They may visit a railroad roundhouse, an airport, an automobile assembly plant, a museum, a planetarium, a granary, a meat-packing plant, a newspaper plant, or a reservoir. In each case, however, the field trip should be based on something that will be of interest to the pupils and that will meet some of the needs of individual pupils for firsthand experiences.

Meeting Individual Needs by Approaches Other Than Unit Teaching

The teacher may help students acquire fundamental ideas or social studies concepts without relying upon the unitary approach. Since many of these approaches have been described elsewhere in the book, they will be mentioned here briefly only for review purposes.

1. *Subgrouping.* Subgrouping plans similar to those used to teach such basic skills as reading and writing may be followed for social studies when individual children require extra help in the mastery of essential work-study skills. Such groupings will often be temporary. Once a skill has been mastered, the individuals receiving special assistance may rejoin the entire class or they may begin to work with other students who require help in specialized areas.

2. *Homogeneous grouping.* Boys and girls may be assigned to social studies classes homogeneously. Students with common experiential backgrounds will often find themselves placed together. Reading achievement and intelligence are the usual criteria used for making homogeneous assignments, although social studies classes

may be formed on the basis of interest. Success or level of accomplishment on a test attempting to measure work-study skills ability may be the basis of pupil assignment.

3. *Cross-grade grouping.* Traditional grade lines may be broken in order to bring together children with common skill needs. Thus, fourth-, fifth-, and sixth-grade pupils may work with the same teacher on the mastery of essential work-study skills.

4. *Buzz sessions.* Mass instruction may be modified through the division of a class into four, five, or six buzz session groups. Book reports may be given to members of the buzz session team, but the buzz session is frequently devoted to discussions of common problems.

5. *Team teaching.* Students may work with a team of teachers who collectively plan programs of studies or activities. With good team planning prior to the actual team teaching activity, instruction may be varied in terms of the stages of readiness of the pupils. Thus, a special lecture to 150 pupils may be followed by the division of students into small learning groups where concepts and generalizations are formulated in terms of the pupils' levels of understanding.

6. *Team learning.* Teachers may encourage pupils to work together in small work teams. Two or three pupils will help each other solve common problems as they seek answers to their questions. Team learning will often make the members of a team much less dependent upon the teacher for solutions to problems than is possible in the teacher-dominated classroom.

7. *The mixed set approach.* Since reading is one of the primary sources of social studies information, children who have difficulty with reading skills may work with different-level books. Bright students or fast readers will often read independently, while poor readers will be assigned work in easier social studies textbooks.

8. *The multiple text approach.* Children learn to work with a wide variety of textbooks and reference sources. As a rule, boys and girls learn to work independently of each other. They tend to work from topical references rather than from page-by-page assignments.

9. *The multi-media approach.* Since children learn through a variety of approaches, there is an increased emphasis upon the use of multi-media learning materials. Tape recordings, films, records, programmed units of study, slides, and filmstrips can help meet the challenge of individual differences. Similarly, television, newspapers, magazines, pamphlets, and other reference materials may be used to supplement the social studies text.

10. *Differentiated assignments.* While mixed or multiple texts may be considered good approaches to the need for individualized

assignments, most social studies teachers still need the security that comes from having one basic social studies textbook. In such classes the teachers can meet the needs of different students through differentiated assignments. For example, fast learners may be given assignments that call for considerable study in depth. They can take a long-range assignment and work on it early enough in the year to become experts or authorities in a particular phase of study.

11. *Committees*. Teachers can make use of committees to differentiate instruction and to provide outlets for individual students who can benefit by a division of labor and responsibility. Students who need opportunities for leadership will often find the chairmanship of a social studies committee gives them the incentive to stretch themselves. Other students learn the meaning of research and responsibility. Heterogeneity in a classroom can be an asset when a number of committees are formed. For example, the creative student may use his artistic talents to make posters or stage scenery. Another pupil may use his dramatic ability to portray incidents which would otherwise have been drab and lifeless to those who have limited skill with reading materials.

12. *Special counseling*. Children who become disciplinary problems or who fail to make satisfactory social and academic growth because they have personal problems may be assisted through study of special units—units devoted to topics of special interest to the pupils. Although such units may stem from normal pupil-teacher relationships, valuable suggestions regarding teaching methods may be provided by teacher counselors or guidance workers who are assigned responsibility to work with these children.

13. *Extended learning periods*. The daily time schedule should be kept flexible in order to permit boys and girls to plan and use time in terms of their basic needs. For example, the student who is preparing a good social studies report, writing a story, or making a model will be handicapped if all his activities are limited to a basic thirty- or forty-minute period. To correct this, optional work periods may be built into the program or teachers may plan their days around double periods that can be used to extend a learning activity.

14. *Post-school or pre-school sessions*. Some schools have what is known as zero period. This is a special period before the regular opening of school that can be used by students desiring extra help. In one school, the pre-school sessions were considered as time for makeup work, remedial help, or counseling. Slow students and low achievers were supposed to come to school early, but teachers

found that many of the bright students also came in to work on special social studies and science projects. A number of schools have post-school sessions for students who need or want extra help or just more time to complete regular activities.

Helping Pupils Find Themselves
Through Social Studies

Many boys and girls look forward to social studies activities, but research has shown that there is a resistance to social studies in the minds of some elementary school pupils. Surprisingly enough, social studies has more of an appeal to boys than to girls. This is evident in surveys made by Chase and Wilson, [1] which showed the subject preferences of 13,483 fifth graders in 1947 as compared with the preferences of a comparable group of 19,135 fifth graders in 1957. In both surveys it was evident that boys ranked social studies as a *pre-ferred* subject more than girls did. The boys' responses in both cases showed social studies ranked fourth in their choice of elementary school subjects, while it ranked sixth in the minds of the girls. What makes the results significant is the fact that twice as many boys as girls showed a preference for social studies.

Classroom teachers should be interested in the results of such studies, because they place considerable emphasis on the teaching of basic concepts and the application of reading skills and principles through the medium of social studies. Since pupils and teachers have devoted a great amount of time to social studies activities, it is wise to ask why it is a subject not preferred by so many pupils. Have we driven pupils away from the subject by faulty teaching and materials which lack challenge? Is the problem one of content or of method? While there may be many reasons to challenge the statement that poor teaching is probably the most important factor in developing negative attitudes toward social studies, one cannot ignore the fact that understanding or comprehension has often been a missing element in many social studies classrooms.

It is easy to find upper grade pupils who will ask, "Why do we have to study social studies?" or "What good is all of this material going to do us?" In many cases these pupils are serious. They do not seem to sense a value or purpose in what they are studying. In many classrooms, pupils are clever enough to assume a superficial interest in the subject in order to please the teacher. They go through the motions of reading the text, answering a few questions, taking a few tests, and then are content to forget the major portion of what has been taught.

Although pressure groups have frequently made social studies required in many high schools, one finds college-bound students con-

centrating more on other subjects. This one subject, which can do more
to bring about an understanding of economic, political, and social
problems, is frequently downgraded by adults who are considering the
basic needs of boys and girls and adolescents. Unfortunately, in many
classrooms the subject has never been taught as anything but a textbook subject. Many teachers have never lost the habit of teaching by
oral and silent reading, followed by question-and-answer periods.
Again, an overemphasis upon memorital learning has helped to create
a decreased interest in social studies by pupils who have never learned
to understand either the vocabulary or the concepts of social studies.

FACTORS IN THE TEACHING AND LEARNING
OF SOCIAL STUDIES

This subject, which covers many fields of knowledge, requires that
certain fundamental skills be mastered by the students. Among these
fundamentals are the development of time, space, and quantitative
concepts and skill in reading and interpreting maps, as well as the
development of work-study skills basic to success in the study of any
subject area.

Development of Time, Space, and Quantitative Concepts. While
memory work is not the only reason pupils fail to show interest in
social studies, the authors have reason to believe that growing boys and
girls fail to get excited about social studies because it is often introduced to them before they have acquired a sense of "time and place."
Many children begin to develop *time* concepts long before they begin
school, but many of them never acquire a meaningful concept of time.
All too often children get lost in the world of "today" and never get to
really understand the broad meanings of "yesterday" and "tomorrow."
A study of time concepts of young children will reveal differences in
their view of time. Some will think of time in relation to day and night
activities: when it gets dark, you go to bed; when it gets light, you get
up. Other children will have reached the stage where the clock dictates
their actions: it tells them when to go to bed, when to get up, when to
eat, or when to go to school. Some of these young "clock-conscious"
children may not be able to tell time in terms of exact hours and
minutes, but time has more meaning to them than it does to those who
let the sun guide their lives.

Teachers of young children must recognize these differences and
must help children extend their time concepts by experience. By
learning to pace their rate of reading, writing, and computation in
terms of suggested intervals, pupils may obtain a feeling for immediate
time. At first the teacher may work hard to get pupils to think in terms of

short time units like a second or a minute. Developing the concept of an hour will be more difficult, but they can begin to sense the nature of this time interval with teacher assistance.

In addition to learning to pace activities in terms of minutes and hours, the children need to think in larger time blocks. They can learn to plan in terms of days, weeks, and then months; but young children are more apt to think of months in terms of special holidays or events, rather than as time intervals, and this is essentially a part of their problem in social studies. Time is too frequently limited to immediacy and to something personal. Many young children struggle with the days of the week, thinking first of days that have special significance rather than days like Wednesday, Thursday, and Friday. Teachers will have to help them distinguish between days. Second-grade boys, for example, may learn to associate Thursday with the visit of the physical education teacher, while Friday is easily learned because it is the last day of school before the weekend. Children need many calendar experiences if they are going to learn the names of the months and the number of weeks during a month or year. As often as possible, the children need to associate incidents with specific calendar days or dates.

Children can work with learning activities involving time in all their school subjects. Gradually, they must learn the meaning of terms such as "long ago," "yesterday," "tomorrow," "a week ago," "last month," "last year." Unfortunately, there are many pupils who have not acquired a vivid time sense by the fifth and sixth grade, so that their social studies work may involve time concepts which are beyond their comprehension. If sixth graders have not acquired an understanding of the amount of time involved in a decade or a century, it may be difficult for them to place historical incidents in a chronological sequence. Did the Civil War precede or follow the American Revolution? What do the words "medieval period" mean to pupils who cannot conceive of large time intervals involving hundreds of years? Until they do develop a greater sense of time, they will fail to acquire a true feeling of what we think of as the cultural heritage of man.

Similarly, children have trouble developing *space* concepts. Modern methods of communication and transportation have brought people and places closer together, but time and space relationships are difficult for many intermediate and upper grade pupils to perceive. Pupils who cannot conceive of the nature of a yard, a mile, or ten miles, even when they are looking at objects which are within one of these space limits, will have trouble with map studies involving people and places who live many miles from a known center of interest. It is difficult for some pupils to read the word "France" and place it in its proper geographic setting unless they have developed their space concepts in terms of place and space relationships. All too often, boys and girls read words and learn to describe people and places without really being able to distinguish events that occurred in the distant past from those that occurred in the recent past.

In addition to understanding time and place, children need to understand quantitative concepts. Fourth graders become more subject matter conscious because they are spending less time on basic reading, writing, and arithmetic skills in order to devote more time to the application of skills and the acquisition of knowledge. In social studies materials they encounter a new type of reading which can be both challenging and frustrating. Even good readers find trouble studying social studies, because their textbooks contain numerous words, phrases, or special terms which involve the ability to understand quantitative concepts. Jarolimek and Foster [8] studied fifth-grade geography, history, and social studies and found that six categories of quantitative concepts were contained therein, namely:

> Definite references to quantities of objects, i.e., *500 bushels of wheat;*
> Indefinite references to quantities of objects, i.e., *a large number of buffalo;*
> Definite references to space, i.e., *93,000,000 miles;*
> Indefinite references to space, i.e., *several feet above sea level;*
> Definite references to time, i.e., *four centuries previously;*
> Indefinite references to time, i.e., *a short time later.*

Some pupils try to figure out what is meant by such terms by looking for pictures, charts, and illustrations, plus past experience, but many average readers have trouble with words or terms calling for the ability to answer questions asking "how much," "how far," and "how many." These pupils may be in a quandary only half the time, but many slow readers or slow learners find it impossible to obtain any meaning in their reading. They find it takes so much time to look up these words that they lose the thought of what preceded the frustration. Jarolimek and Foster reported that average and above-average pupils could understand about half of the quantitative concepts encountered in the average fifth-grade social studies book, with below-average pupils finding a lack of understanding with two-thirds of them.

The statement has been made that modern children have been exposed to more through better books and new methods of communication and travel. But exposure is not education. There has to be more unity and understanding along with increased exposure. Young children are not going to work with social studies materials that are too abstract for them. They want to work with concrete materials so that they can see their own growth and progress as they work.

Developing Skill in Reading and Interpreting Maps. A good social studies program depends upon an early introduction to locational skills, with a steadily increasing emphasis upon the mastery of maps, map terms, and the significance of the story they tell about man and how and where he lives. How far a teacher goes with map work depends upon the experiences she has with maps and upon the past experiences of the pupils. There should be a sequence of map activities, with continued use of maps and globes supplementing direct instruction in geographic or scientific principles essential for a full understanding of the significance of size, distance, and position. In the primary grades children can start with neighborhood maps and work up to develop a world consciousness. Maps are frequently introduced formally in many fourth-grade classes, but map study also ends there. This is especially true where the upper grade teachers teach a social studies that is history-oriented. In many such schools the teacher cannot work a program of map studies into their curriculum without breaking into a chronological time sequence. In some such schools the authors have recommended an introductory unit at the fifth-, sixth-, and seventh-grade levels which will give children a chance to master essential map and geography skills. Teachers and children have found satisfaction in optional units entitled, "This Is Our World," "Getting Acquainted with Maps and Globes," and "Life in the Modern World Without Maps and Globes To Guide Us." Sixth-grade teachers will find that the last title can lead to considerable creative thinking and acting in subject fields other than social studies.

Success with maps often depends upon the development of an understanding of a number of symbols and special terms which Odell [14] refers to as the "language of maps." Until children can read meaning in the colors, symbols, and terms, the study of maps can be as difficult as learning a foreign language. Pupils who have had little contact with maps need to start working with maps that contain few details and symbols. These will have much more meaning to them than will the maps with various colors and multiple symbols. Thus, a beginner who starts with a map showing only two colors may acquire the concept that "Much of the world is covered by water." This may be followed by the concept, "Man lives on only a small part of the world's surface." With added experience and an acquaintance with many kinds of maps, his concept of the world, people, and places will change. Gradually, he learns to read the "international color scheme for maps" and is able to determine land elevations and sea depths by interpreting the various colors. When he reaches this stage, he is ready to study ocean currents, the location of fishing grounds, and other technical data.

Success with Reading. Unless they have learned how to read independently and can find enjoyment in their reading activities, few pupils will find social studies appealing and challenging when they are required to dig deep beneath the surface in search of knowledge and the answers to problems. Children who do not like to read will not do the extra reading which gives life and meaning to social studies. Children who have not learned to read both fiction and nonfiction will find the technical vocabulary and content an obstacle to continued progress with social studies materials. While such children may secure help through auditory approaches, they should be given special assistance in the mastery of silent reading at their reading levels before they can be expected to find much success with advanced studies materials.

Ability to Use Basic Work-Study Skills to Locate Information and to Solve Problems. Many boys and girls have failed to find satisfaction in social studies activities because they have not been taught desired work-study skills or have not had ample opportunity to practice using skills introduced at lower grade levels. Reading a single textbook with or without the teacher does not make any pupil an authority. He must be prepared to go beyond a single source for data or ideas. Usually, this means that he will have to work on his own if he is to supplement the basic textbook. The student must know when and where to look for answers as well as how. This is evident in the work patterns of many college pupils who find that the doors to continued higher education are closed to them because they never learned at lower educational levels to practice research and organizational skills. Essentially, the individual who is to grow in the field of social studies must be able to master the work-study skills described in a previous chapter.

Use of Social Studies Textbooks. Teachers should not acquire the feeling that emphasis upon unit work and library materials means the end of the social studies textbook. Good textbooks have been and will continue to be important guides to teacher-pupil activity. If there has been an objection to them, it has been in the manner in which social studies textbooks have been used in too many classrooms. Good teachers could not get along without a wide collection of textbooks. While the authors prefer the use of multiple sets of textbooks to the use of the single textbook, every principal must remember that many elementary school teachers do not feel secure unless they have a basic social studies textbook for each pupil. This element of teacher security may call for the expenditure of a few more dollars, but it is an aspect of teaching which must be recognized. If, in addition to the basic textbook, the teacher has a rich collection of supplementary textbooks and other teaching aids, she may be induced to experiment with the use of multiple books or multiple sets of books in the study of some aspects of social studies.

Combining learning skills in a self-contained classroom may be a minor problem for some teachers. For example, dictionary skills may be taught as a part of spelling, reading, language, or social studies. The art of making a good oral or written report may be a part of the English work taught at various grade levels, but the social studies teacher may need to work on the improvement of this skill.

TABLE 2

Types of Classifications of Learning Skills in
Social Studies Textbooks

Locational skills:

    Locating information within individual books
    Locating other books and magazines
    Using ready references in the classroom

Acquisition skills:

    Reading printed materials
    Interpreting pictures, drawings, charts, graphs, etc.
    Interviewing, listening to speeches, etc.
    Observing firsthand

Recording skills:

    Simple note-taking
    Filling in outlines and outline maps
    Completing chart and graph forms
    Using mechanical recorders

Arranging, outlining, and organizing skills:

    Arranging events in proper sequence
    Comparing data from different sources
    Distinguishing between important and unimportant ideas
    Listing important details in logical order
    Filling in related supporting data

Communicative skills:

    Discussing
    Reporting, oral and written
    Establishing rapport and creating a favorable impression
    Handling criticisms and reconciling differences
    Handling interruptions and answering questions
    Admitting shortcomings as well as handling the errors of others

Evaluative skills:

    Judging sources of materials or assertions
    Judging data
    Judging qualifications of speakers and writers
    Evaluating methods of recording, outlining, and organizing
    Evaluating communicative skills

Selection of Problem Areas from Current News Sources. The social studies curriculum is expanding at such a rapid rate that many teachers could continually select problems to study from current news sources without having to make use of standard history or geography textbooks. However, one of the dangers of such an approach lies in the slowness with which current problems are solved after they arise. Boys and girls who get excited about a new legislative act may find that it will be tied up for months in endless wrangling and debating. On the other hand, there are many items in the news today which will be history tomorrow. Teachers cannot ignore some of these current headlined stories when they affect American life and the lives of vast numbers of peoples in other parts of the world. But because most teachers have a responsibility to finish a textbook or cover a prescribed number of units of study, they find a conflict between problems from the standard curriculum and problems from current news sources. Since there is so much that could be taught in the field of social studies, the teacher must learn to be selective in choosing what problems become the basis of study.

There are times when current news and the standard curriculum complement each other. When this occurs, the teacher who fails to direct children to newspapers, magazine and radio or television sources to supplement the textbook is wasting an opportunity to challenge her pupils and enrich the program. If the curriculum is flexible, the teacher can deviate from routine studies to study critical world or national problems. The optional unit plan allows the teacher freedom to explore new areas as well as to concentrate on problems of special interest to the pupils or to herself.

SOCIAL STUDIES AS EDUCATION
FOR DEMOCRACY AND GOOD CITIZENSHIP

The problem of giving meaning to social studies is found in the need to promote an understanding of democracy and good citizenship. For a time citizenship was identified with the study of national, state and local government, but this type of citizenship training is not enough. Children need to learn the structure of our government, but they have to do more than read about it. They need to see it work and feel it as it relates to their own lives. They need to have experiences which make such terms as "democracy," "freedom," "interdependence," "responsibility," "equality," and "rights" be more than clichés. The ability to define these terms from memory is not enough. We are not interested in verbal mouthings when actions show that pupils do not understand the real meaning of the words they use, or just do not care. In many instances pupils talk about democracy in school settings which ignore the basic principles underlying the words; therefore, one may ask whether the pupils can really understand the true meaning of democracy.

The recognition of the importance of helping to train children for citizenship has led some educators to the adoption of the term "citizenship education" in place of social studies. In these new programs one finds increased emphasis placed upon trying to develop better citizens. Some of the major concepts stressed in the program recommended by the New York State Department of Education are as follows:

1. People become social through group life and shared experience.

2. People's ways of living are conditioned by their natural environment.

3. People work to satisfy their needs and desires.

4. People strive through laws and organizations to gain justice and security.

5. People have struggled through the ages to achieve a better life.

These concepts are not hard to read; it is getting boys and girls to understand them as essentials to democratic citizenship that is the problem. Teachers work with boys and girls at different grade levels, teaching and leading pupils in varied activities in hopes that each pupil will acquire the understandings and feelings that will make him into a good citizen. Different teachers will use different methods to achieve the desired end, but underlying all that they do will be the class organization.

In setting the stage for learning, controls and standards that *children* understand must be established. The children must have opportunities to assume many kinds of responsibilities. Too often, democracy is thought of in terms of freedom, but this is something which can be lost when men and women do not exercise their rights as citizens in the continuing struggle to protect and guarantee the freedom of others as well as their own. Boys and girls must continue to see their freedom as something which they must help fight for all through their lives. Helping pupils see democratic living as a sharing process, with giving as well as receiving, is a worthy purpose for the teaching of social studies.

Again, each pupil must learn to accept the consequences of his own actions, both as an individual and as a member of a group. Frequently, group pressures become a motivating force when one person is responsible for the loss of rights and privileges of others, but essentially each individual should be able to operate from within his own consciousness of what is right and proper instead of having to bend to group pressures. The teacher helps along these lines when she helps a pupil to feel that he is accepted as a member of a working team. He has the right to initiate ideas or projects, to have a say, to make a choice, or to assume a large measure of the responsibility necessary for successful group and individual progress.

Attempts to promote better citizenship through character studies have not been successful. In many instances, biographies have tried to create artificial images of important people, but children do not emulate these ideal figures unless they represent a model that appeals to them and to their classmates. One of the dangers in this kind of education lies in the fact that the school is helping to train followers instead of creative and independent leaders. Also, as they mature, pupils may just as easily try to emulate other heroes who have undesirable characteristics. This does not mean that the study of biographies is bad, but it does imply that the teacher may be placing too much emphasis upon an approach to good citizenship which is not too effective. By reading about the lives of great men and women, the pupils may get a better picture of the past and the struggles which men and women faced to make our country what it is, but the actual reading may be less important than what the pupil does to acquire the information or relay it to others.

Actually, citizenship is a process of living based upon a *sound philosophy of life.* Many people play a role in helping to form this philosophy. Sometimes it may be only a small thing which affects the pupil's way of thinking or living. A teacher may say a few words that make all the difference, or he may be affected by something he has read or done. As the individual matures, his goals or ideals may change as he acquires new experiences. If these experiences are good, rich, and healthy ones, the individual has a better chance of becoming an acceptable, if not leading, citizen than if he were to grow up in an environment where he could not find himself, where he could not explore the world about him, or where he could not find realistic answers to his problems.

Necessity for Critical Thinking. To some people, education implies the constant feeding of facts, figures, rules, and general information, with the implication that the pupil will be able to give back, orally or in writing, what he has learned. While a nation needs citizens who have a cultural background along with knowledge and skills to support their arguments and actions, the fact remains that our way of life calls for individuals who have done more than accumulate knowledge. American schools have an obligation to do more than train a race of automatons or individuals who make good followers, but seldom leaders. The nation needs citizens who have been taught to think critically. It needs an intelligent and informed citizenry, individuals who have been taught to think for themselves. It needs citizens who will not blindly follow a demagogue, because they have been taught to ignore appeals to their emotions and prejudices. It needs citizens who, as a result of their education, have learned to weigh statements which they hear or see in print and then make their own decisions, regardless of how others attempt to influence their actions.

Teaching pupils to think critically is much more difficult than teaching them isolated facts and figures. The former calls for the use of "active" intelligence, the latter for a "passive" intelligence. It calls for memorital and drill learning, but it does not guarantee that pupils will be able to see the relationships between what they have learned and problems which have to be solved. Actually, pupils with high intelligence may be able to reason with little outside help, but the great mass of students who have average or below-average intelligence will not be able to apply what they have learned unless the school makes a direct attempt to teach them the value of critical thinking and analysis throughout their school careers.

This requires time and may get in the way of some of the more dramatic results which the traditional educational program may appear to achieve. Some critics will cry out that "fundamentals are being sold down the river." This is not so. Children can learn more and in less time with modern methods of teaching if teachers will use the best available techniques and teaching aids to give *meaning* to their teaching. On occasion, other critics will resist a problem approach, because there are still some individuals who are afraid that too many critical-thinking citizens can use their knowledge to upset the status quo. As a result, teachers have been subjected to direct and indirect pressures to get them to temporize and refrain from teaching about issues which may be classified as critical or controversial. With public support, children can be taught to think creatively, without the teachers' allowing themselves to become personally involved in the controversies.

REFERENCES

1. W. Linwood Chase and Gilbert M. Wilson, "Preference Studies in Elementary School Social Studies," *Journal of Education*, 140 (April 1958), 2–48.
2. Robert E. Chasnoff, *Elementary Curriculum* (New York: Pitman, 1964).
3. Education Policies Commission, *The Purposes of Education in American Democracy* (Washington, D.C.: National Education Association, 1938).
4. Robert Fleming, *Curriculum for Today's Boys and Girls* (Columbus, Ohio: Chas. E. Merrill, 1963).
5. *A Guide to Elementary Education* (Baltimore: Baltimore Public Schools, 1955).
6. John Holt, *How Children Fail* (New York: Delta Books, 1965).
7. Frances Ilg and Louise B. Ames, *School Readiness* (New York: Harper & Row, 1965).

8. John Jarolimek and Clifford D. Foster, "Quantitative Concepts in Fifth Grade Social Studies Textbooks," *The Elementary School Journal,* 59 (May 1959), 437–42.
9. John Jarolimek and Huber Walsh, *Readings for Social Studies in Elementary Education* (New York: Macmillan, 1965).
10. Newell C. Kephart, *The Slow Learner in the Classroom* (Columbus, Ohio: Chas. E. Merrill, 1960).
11. Arthur D. Morse, *Schools of Tomorrow—Today* (Garden City, N.Y.: Doubleday, 1960).
12. New York State Department of Education, *A Chart for Citizenship Education in the Elementary Schools* (Albany, N.Y.: Department of Education, 1957).
13. New York State Department of Education, *The Elementary School Curriculum, An Overview* (Albany, N.Y.: Department of Education, 1954).
14. Clarence B. Odell, "The Use of Maps, Globes, and Pictures in the Classroom," *Twenty-ninth Yearbook of the National Council for the Social Studies,* in Preston E. James, ed., *New Viewpoints in Geography* (Chicago: University of Chicago Press, 1959).
15. Willard Waller, *The Sociology of Teaching* (New York: John Wiley, 1965).

BIBLIOGRAPHY

American Textbook Publisher Institute. *Textbooks in Education*. Chicago: Lakeside Press, 1949.

Anderson, Robert H. "Ungraded Primary Classes—An Administrative Contribution to Mental Health," *Understanding the Child*, 24 (June 1955), 66–72.

Andre, Robert G. "How to Improve Instruction with Teaching Teams," *School Management*, 4 (November 1960), 50–54.

Andreen, Earl P. "A Study of Workbooks in Arithmetic," *Journal of Educational Research*, 32 (October 1958).

Art Education, Part II, *Sixty-fourth Yearbook of the National Society for the Study of Education*. Chicago: University of Chicago Press, 1965.

Barbe, J. W. "Evaluation of Special Classes for Gifted Children," *Exceptional Children*, 22 (November 1955), 60–62.

Barron, Frank. "Creativity, What Research Says About It," *National Education Association Journal*, 50 (March 1961), 17–19.

Beauchamp, George. *The Curriculum of the Elementary School*. Boston: Allyn and Bacon, 1964.

———. *The Basic Dimensions of Elementary Method*. Boston: Allyn and Bacon, 1959.

Belth, Marc. *Education as a Discipline*. Boston: Allyn and Bacon, 1965.

Best, John W. *Research in Education*. Englewood Cliffs, N.J.: Prentice-Hall, 1959.

Bettelheim, Bruno. "Segregation: New Style," *School Review*, 66 (September 1958), 251–72.

Betts, Emmet A. *Second Vocabulary Study, Grade Placement of Words in Eight Recent Spellers*. New York: American Book, 1949.

———. *Spelling Vocabulary Study, Grade Placement of Words in Seventeen Spellers*. New York: American Book, 1940.

Biddle, Bruce J., and William J. Ellena. *Contemporary Research in Teacher Effectiveness*. New York: Holt, Rinehart & Winston, 1964.

Bish, Charles E. "Teaching the Upper 15 Per Cent," *The Clearing House*, 33 (May 1959), 515–18.

Blough, Glenn O., and others. "Teaching and Evaluating Science in the Elementary School," Chapter VIII, *Fifty-ninth Yearbook of the National Society for the Study of Education*, Part I, in Nelson B. Henry, ed., *Rethinking Science Education*. Chicago: University of Chicago Press, 1960.

————, and Julius Schwartz. *Elementary School Science and How to Teach It*, 3rd ed. New York: Holt, Rinehart & Winston, 1964.

Bohnhorst, Ben A., and Sophia N. Sellars. "Individual Reading Instruction vs. Basal Textbooks Instructions," *Elementary English*, 36 (March 1959), 185–90.

Botel, Morton. *Multi-Level Speller, Grades 3 to 12*. State College, Pa.: Penns Valley Publishers, 1959.

Bradford, H. F. "Afraid to Write? Or Afraid to Spell?" *National Elementary Principal*, 38 (March 1959), 31–32.

Bremer, Neville. "First Grade Achievement Under Different Plans of Grouping," *Elementary English*, 35 (May 1958), 324–26.

Brown, Francis R. "Arithmetic—Friend or Foe," *The Arithmetic Teacher*, 4 (February 1957), 1–9.

Brueckner, Leo J., and Foster E. Grossnickle. *Discovering Meanings in Elementary School Mathematics*. New York: Holt, Rinehart & Winston, 1963.

————, and ————. *Making Arithmetic Meaningful*. New York: John C. Winston, 1953.

Bruner, Jerome. *The Process of Education*. Cambridge, Mass.: Harvard University Press, 1963.

Bruns, Richard F. "Improvement of Reading Through Ability Level Assignments," *Curriculum Bulletin* 57CBM. Houston, Tex.: Houston Independent School District, February 1957.

Bulletin of National Association of Secondary School Principals. Washington, D.C.: The Association, January 1961.

Burr, Marvin Y. "A Study of Homogeneous Grouping," *Contributions to Education*, No. 457. New York: Bureau of Publications, Teachers College, Columbia University, 1931.

Burton, William H. *The Guidance of Learning Activities*, 3rd ed. New York: Appleton-Century-Crofts, 1952.

California Test Bureau. *Manual—California Short-Form Test of Mental Maturity, Elementary, Grades 4–8*, S-Form. Los Angeles: California Test Bureau, 1957.

Cameron, Norman. *Personality Development and Psychopathology*. Boston: Houghton Mifflin, 1963.

Capra, James. "Individualizing Instruction," *American School Board Journal*, 137 (December 1958), 17–18.

Carrothers, George E. "Left Handedness Among School Pupils," *American School Board Journal*, 114 (May 1947), 17–19.

Carter, Robert S. "How Invalid Are Marks Assigned by Teachers?" *Journal of Educational Psychology*, 43 (1952), 218–28.

Cay, Donald F. *Curriculum: Design for Learning*. Indianapolis: Bobbs-Merrill, 1966.

Charles, Don C. *Psychology of the Child in the Classroom*. New York: Macmillan, 1964.

Chase, W. Linwood, and Gilbert M. Wilson. "Preference Studies in Elementary School Social Studies," *Journal of Education*, 140 (April 1958), 2–48.

Chasnoff, Robert E. *Elementary Curriculum*. New York: Pitman, 1964.

Christensen, Anne. "Age-Graded Elementary School," *Educational Leadership*, 18 (November 1960), 76–78.

Clark, John R., and Laura K. Eades. *Guiding Arithmetic Learning*. New York: World Book, 1954.

Cole, Luella. *Handwriting for Left-Handed Children*. Bloomington, Ill.: Public School Publishing, 1955.

Combs, Arthur. *The Professional Education of Teachers*. Boston: Allyn and Bacon, 1965.

Conant, James B. *Shaping Educational Policy*. New York: McGraw-Hill, 1964.

————. *The American High School Today*. New York: McGraw-Hill, 1959.

Corle, Clyde G. *Teaching Mathematics in the Elementary School*. New York: Ronald Press, 1964.

Craig, Gerald S. "Science in the Elementary School," *What Research Says to the Teacher*, No. 12. Washington, D.C.: National Education Association, 1957.

Cram, David. *Explaining "Teaching Machines and Programming."* San Francisco: Fearon, 1961.

Crescimbeni, Joseph. "Science as a Structural Discipline," *Elementary School Notes*. Boston: Ginn, 1966.

————. *Teaching the New Mathematics*. West Nyack, N.Y.: Parker, 1966.

————. *Arithmetic Enrichment Activities for Elementary School Children*. West Nyack, N.Y.: Parker, 1965.

Cronbach, Lee J. "What Research Says About Programmed Instruction," *National Education Association Journal*, 51 (December 1962), 45–47.

Cummings, E. W. "Grouping: Homogeneous or Heterogeneous," *Educational Administration and Supervision*, 44 (January 1958), 19–26.

Cutts, Norma, and N. Mosely. *Teaching the Bright and Gifted*. Englewood Cliffs, N.J.: Prentice-Hall, 1957.

Dahl, L. A. *Public School Audiometry: Principles and Methods*. Danville, Ill.: Interstate Printers and Publishers, 1949.

Dallman, Martha. "Homework," *Grade Teacher*, 79 (November 1961), 36, 114–15.

Dearborn, W. F. "The Nature of Special Abilities and Disabilities," *School and Society*, 1961.

deGrazia, Alfred, and David A. Sohn. *Revolution in Teaching*. New York: Bantam Books, 1965.

DeHaan, R. F., and R. J. Havighurst. *Educating Gifted Children*. Chicago: University of Chicago Press, 1957.

Delaney, Eleanor C. "The Case for the Ungraded Primary Unit," *Council Schools at Work*, 6 (December 1961).

Derby, Orlo L. "Towards a Rational View of Promotion," *Understanding the Child*, 23 (April 1954), 43–45.

Doll, Ronald. *Curriculum Improvement*. Boston: Allyn and Bacon, 1964.

Downing, John. *The Initial Teaching Alphabet*. New York: Macmillan, 1964.

Dunn, Harry. *The School Teacher's Manual Containing Practical Suggestions on Teaching and Popular Education*. Hartford, Conn.: Reed and Barber, 1838.

Durrell, Donald D., and Viola Palos. "Pupil Study Teams in Reading," *Education*, 76 (May 1956), 552–56.

Ebel, Robert L. *Measuring Educational Achievement*. Englewood Cliffs, N.J.: Prentice-Hall, 1965.

Educational Policies Commission. *The Purposes of Education in American Democracy*. Washington, D.C.: National Education Association, 1938.

Elam, Stanley, ed. *Education and the Structure of Knowledge*. New York: Rand McNally, 1964.

Fehr, Howard. "Present Research in Arithmetic," *Teachers College Record*, 52 (October 1950), 11–23.

Fendrick, P. A. "Visual Characteristics of Poor Readers," *Teachers College Record*, 37 (February 1936), 452–53.

Finn, James D., and Donald G. Perrin. "Teaching Machines and Programmed Learning, 1962: A Survey of the Industry," *Occasional Paper #3*, Technological Development Project. Washington, D.C.: National Education Association, 1961.

Fitzgerald, James A. *A Basic Life Spelling Vocabulary*. Milwaukee: Bruce, 1951.

————. "A Crucial Core Vocabulary in Elementary School Language and Spelling," *American School Board Journal*, 103 (July 1941).

Fleming, Robert. *Curriculum for Today's Boys and Girls*. Columbus, Ohio: Chas. E. Merrill, 1963.

Ford, G. W., and Lawrence Pugno. *The Structure of Knowledge and Curriculum*. New York: Rand McNally, 1964.

Freedman, Leonard, and Cornelius Cotter. *Issues of the Sixties.* Belmont, Calif.: Wadsworth, 1965.

Freeman, Frank N. "Teaching Handwriting," *NEA Journal* (November 1954), 428–83.

Gans, Roma. *Fact and Fiction About Phonics.* Indianapolis: Bobbs-Merrill, 1964.

Gates, Arthur I. "An Experimental Comparison of the Study-Test and Test-Study Methods in Spelling," *Journal of Educational Psychology,* 22 (January 1931), 1–19.

Gesell, Arnold. "Handedness," *Journal of American Medical Association,* 155 (August 1954), 1548.

———, and Frances L. Ilg. *The Child from Five to Ten.* New York: Harper & Bros., 1946.

———, and ———. *The Infant and Child in the Culture of Today.* New York: Harper & Bros., 1943.

———, ———, and Louise B. Ames. *Youth, the Years from Ten to Sixteen.* New York: Harper & Bros., 1956.

Ginther, John. "Man, Values and the Machine," *Elementary School Journal,* 60 (January 1960), 179–89.

Glennon, Vincent J., and C. W. Hunnicutt. *What Does Research Say About Arithmetic?* Washington, D.C.: Association for Supervision and Curriculum Development, National Education Association, 1958.

Good, Carter V. *Introduction to Educational Research,* 2nd ed. New York: Appleton-Century-Crofts, 1962.

Good, Harry G. *A History of American Education,* 2nd ed. New York: Macmillan, 1962.

Goodlad, John I. "Individual Differences and Vertical Organization of the School," *Sixty-first Yearbook of the National Society for the Study of Education,* Part I, *Individualizing Instruction.* Chicago: University of Chicago Press, 1962.

———, and Robert I. Anderson. *The Nongraded Elementary School.* New York: Harcourt, Brace & World, 1959.

Goodman, Paul. *Compulsory Mis-Education.* New York: Horizon Press, 1964.

Grand Rapids Public School Teachers. *Growing by Doing.* Grand Rapids, Mich.: Board of Education, September 1951.

Green, Edward J. *The Learning Process and Programmed Instruction.* New York: Holt, Rinehart & Winston, 1962.

Greene, Maxine. *The Public School and the Private Vision.* New York: Random House, 1965.

Greulich, W. W. "Rationale of Assessing the Developmental Status of Children from Roentgenograms of the Hand and Wrist," *Child Development,* 21 (March 1950), 33–44.

Gronlund, Norman. *Sociometry in the Classroom.* New York: Harper & Bros., 1958.

Gross, Ronald, and Judith Murphy. *The Revolution in the Schools.* New York: Harcourt, Brace & World, 1964.

Grossnickle, Foster E. "Arithmetic for Those Who Excel," *The Arithmetic Teacher,* 3 (March 1956), 41–48.

———. "Teaching Arithmetic in the Junior High School," *The Mathematics Teacher,* 47 (December 1954), 520–27.

A Guide to Elementary Education. Baltimore: Baltimore Public Schools, 1955.

Hanson, Lincoln F., ed. *The Journal of Programmed Instruction,* New York: Center for Programmed Instruction, 1962.

Harlow, Harry F. "The Formation of Learning Sets," *Psychological Review,* 56 (January 1949), 51–65.

Harris, Irving D. *Emotional Blocks to Learning.* New York: Free Press, 1961.

Havighurst, R. J., ed. *Education for the Gifted.* Chicago: University of Chicago Press, 1958.

Heath, Robert. *New Curricula.* New York: Harper & Row, 1964.

Heffernan, Helen. "Grouping Pupils for Well-rounded Growth and Development," *California Journal of Elementary Education,* 21 (August 1952), 42–50.

Hildreth, Gertrude. *Teaching Spelling.* New York: Holt, Rinehart & Winston, 1955.

Hilgard, Ernest R., and David H. Russell. "Motivation in School Learning," *Forty-ninth Yearbook of the National Society for the Study for Education,* Part I, *Learning and Instruction.* Chicago: University of Chicago Press, 1950.

Hillson, Maurie. *Change and Innovation in Elementary School Organization.* New York: Holt, Rinehart & Winston, 1965.

Holt, John. *How Children Fail.* New York: Delta Books, 1965.

Horn, Ernest. "Spelling," *Encyclopedia of Educational Research,* rev. ed. New York: Macmillan, 1960.

————. "Teaching Spelling," *What Research Says to the Teacher.* Washington, D.C.: American Educational Research Association of the National Education Association, 1954.

Ilg, Frances, and Louise B. Ames. *School Readiness.* New York: Harper & Row, 1965.

Jarolimek, John, and Clifford D. Foster. "Quantitative Concepts in Fifth Grade Social Studies Textbooks," *The Elementary School Journal,* 59 (May 1959), 437–42.

————, and Huber Walsh. *Readings for Social Studies in Elementary Education.* New York: Macmillan, 1965.

Jenkins, Marion. "Selected References on Reading, with Special Emphasis on Self-selection in Reading," *California Journal of Elementary Education,* 27 (February 1959), 188–92.

Johnson, Charles E. "Grouping Children for Arithmetic Instruction," *The Arithmetic Teacher,* 1 (February 1954), 16–20.

Johnson, Leslie W. "One Hundred Words Most Often Misspelled by Children in the Elementary Grades," *Journal of Educational Research,* 44 (October 1950), 154–55.

Johnson, Wendell. "Speech Handicaps," *Forty-ninth Yearbook of the National Society for the Study of Education,* Part II, *The Education of Exceptional Children.* Chicago: The University of Chicago Press, 1950.

Jones, Arthur J., E. D. Grizzell, and Wren Jones Grinstead. *Principles of Unit Construction.* New York: McGraw-Hill, 1939.

Journal of Educational Sociology, 34 (April 1961).

Kambly, Paul E., and John E. Suttle. *Teaching Elementary School Science.* New York: Ronald Press, 1963.

Kenworthy, Leonard. "Education for the Community of 1985," *Educational Leadership,* 17 (May 1960), 470–74.

Kephart, Newell C. *The Slow Learner in the Classroom.* Columbus, Ohio: Chas. E. Merrill, 1960.

Kerber, August, and Wilfred Smith. *Educational Issues in a Changing Society.* Detroit: Wayne State University Press, 1964.

Kimball, Solon, and James E. McClellan. *Education and the New America.* New York: Random House, 1963.

Klausmeier, Herbert J., and Katherine Dresden. *Teaching in the Elementary School,* 2nd ed. New York: Harper & Bros., 1962.

Komoski, P. Kenneth. "Teaching Machines—An Interview," *Instructor,* 70 (March 1961), 32ff.

Lieberman, Myron. *The Future of Public Education.* Chicago: University of Chicago Press, 1963.

Lowenfeld, Viktor. "Current Research on Creativity," *National Education Association Journal,* 47 (November 1958), 538–40.

————. *Creative and Mental Growth.* New York: Macmillan, 1952.

Luchins, Abraham. "Mechanization in Problem Solving," *Psychological Monographs,* 54 (1942), 1–95.

Lysaught, Jerome P., and Clarence M. Williams. *A Guide to Programmed Instruction.* New York: John Wiley, 1963.

Mackie, Romaine P., and Wendell Johnson. *Speech Correctionists: The Competencies They Need for the Work They Do.* Office of Education, U.S. Department of Health, Education, and Welfare. Bulletin No. 19, OE-35010. Washington, D.C.: Government Printing Office, 1957 and 1960.

Manning, Duane. *The Qualitative Elementary School.* New York: Harper & Row, 1963.

Marcuse, Irene. *A Study of Children's Handwriting as a Guide to Emotionally Disturbed Children.* New York: Noble and Noble, 1957.

Martinson, Ruth, and others. "Special Programs for Gifted Pupils," *California State Department of Education Bulletin,* 30 (January 1962).

Mazurkiewicz, Albert J. *New Perspectives in Reading Instruction.* New York: Pitman, 1964.

McDonnell, Kenneth A. "A Dual Mark for Reporting Pupil Subject Accomplishment," *American School Board Journal,* 131 (August 1955), 19–20.

McSwain, E. T. "Intermediate School Grouping." *Portfolio for Intermediate Teachers,* Leaflet No. 5. Washington, D.C.: Association for Childhood Education, 1946.

Meitner, John G. *Astronautics for Science Teachers.* New York: John Wiley, 1965.

Metropolitan School Study Council. "Grouping Within a Classroom," *A Study of Grouping Practices Designed to Improve Individualization of Instruction Based on Experiences of Teachers in Council Schools.* New York: Metropolitan School Study Council, 1952.

Meyer, Adolph. *An Educational History of the American People,* 2nd ed. New York: McGraw-Hill, 1965.

Mohr, Louise, and others. *Winnetka Child Development Summary.* Winnetka, Ill.: Winnetka Public Schools, 1960.

Mok, Paul. *Pushbutton Parents and the Schools.* New York: Delta Books, 1965.

Morrison, Nellie C. "Instead of Ability Grouping—What?" *Childhood Education,* 36 (April 1960), 371–73.

Morse, Arthur D. *Schools of Tomorrow—Today.* Garden City, N.Y.: Doubleday, 1960.

Myers, Louise Kifer. *Teaching Children Music in the Elementary School,* 3rd ed. Englewood Cliffs, N.J.: Prentice-Hall, 1961.

Nakosteen, Mehdi. *The History and Philosophy of Education.* New York: Ronald Press, 1965.

Nally, T. P. F. "The Relationship Between Achieved Growth in Height and the Beginning of Growth in Reading," *Journal of Educational Research,* 49 (October 1955), 153–54.

The National Association for Mental Health. "Mental Health Is 1, 2, 3." New York: The National Association for Mental Health, 1951.

National Education Association. *Schools for the Sixties.* Washington, D.C.: National Education Association Office, 1963.

———. *Unifying Factors in American Education.* Ninth Yearbook of the Department of Superintendence, National Education Association, pp. 121–26. Washington, D.C.: The Association, February 1931.

New York State Department of Education. *The Use of Textbooks.* Circular No. 3, Informal Teaching Series. Albany, N.Y.: Department of Education, 1958.

———. *A Chart for Citizenship Education in the Elementary Schools.* Albany, N.Y.: Department of Education, 1957.

———. *Child Development Guides.* Albany, N.Y.: Department of Education, c. 1955.

———. *The Elementary School Curriculum, An Overview.* Albany, N.Y.: Department of Education, 1954.

Nies, Ruth H. "Classroom Experiences with Recreational Arithmetic," *The Arithmetic Teacher,* 3 (April 1956), 90–93.

Odell, Clarence B. "The Use of Maps, Globes, and Pictures in the Classroom," *Twenty-ninth Yearbook of the National Council for the Social Studies,* in

Preston E. James, ed., *New Viewpoints in Geography.* Chicago: University of Chicago Press, 1959.

Olson, Waldemar. "Homework: Friend or Foe to Children?" *Instructor,* 71 (January 1962), 6, 76, 82.

Otto, Henry J. *Elementary School Organization and Administration.* New York: Appleton-Century, 1944.

Parkhurst, Helen. "The Dalton Plan," *Twenty-fourth Yearbook of the National Society for the Study of Education,* Part II, *Adapting the Schools to Individual Differences.* Bloomington, Ill.: Public School Publishing, 1925.

Petersen, Dorothy G. *The Elementary School Teacher.* New York: Appleton-Century-Crofts, 1964.

Petty, Mary Clare. *Intraclass Grouping in the Elementary School.* Austin: University of Texas Press, 1953.

Popham, W. James. "The Changing Face of Programmed Instruction," *California Journal of Elementary Education,* 31 (November 1962).

Public Schools of the District of Columbia, Washington, D.C. *Child Growth and Development, Characteristics and Needs.* New London, Conn.: Arthur C. Crofts, 1953.

Rinsland, Henry D. *A Basic Vocabulary of Elementary School Children.* New York: Macmillan, 1960.

Rogers, Carl R. "Toward a Theory of Creativity," in M. Barkan and R. L. Mooney, eds., *Conference on Creativity: A Report to the Rockefeller Foundation.* Columbus, Ohio: Ohio State University Press, 1953.

Rudy, Willis. *Schools in an Age of Mass Culture.* Englewood Cliffs, N.J.: Prentice-Hall, 1965.

Russell, James E. *Change and Challenge in American Education.* Boston: Houghton Mifflin, 1965.

Sexton, Patricia. *Education and Income.* New York: Viking, 1961.

Shaplin, Judson T., and Henry F. Olds, Jr. *Team Teaching.* New York: Harper & Row, 1964.

Shumsky, Abraham. *Creative Teaching in the Elementary School.* New York: Appleton-Century-Crofts, 1965.

Shuster, Albert E., and Milton H. Ploghoft. *The Emerging Elementary Curriculum.* Chicago: Chas. E. Merrill, 1963.

Smith, Louis M., and Bryce B. Hudgins. *Educational Psychology.* New York: Knopf, 1964.

Stephens, John M. *The Psychology of Classroom Learning.* New York: Holt, Rinehart & Winston, 1965.

Stern, Catherine, and Toni Gould. *Children Discover Reading.* New York: Random House, 1965.

Stinnett, T. M., and Albert Huggett. *Professional Problems of Teachers.* New York: Macmillan, 1963.

Stulurow, L. M. *Teaching by Machine.* Washington, D.C.: Government Printing Office, 1961.

Sumption, Merle R., and Evelyn M. Luecking. *Education of the Gifted.* New York: Ronald Press, 1961.

Taba, Hilda. *Curriculum Development.* New York: Harcourt, Brace & World, 1962.

Thayer, V. T. *Formative Ideas in American Education.* New York: Dodd, Mead, 1965.

Thelen, Herbert A. "Group Dynamics in Instruction, Principle of Least Group Size," *The School Review,* 57 (March 1962), 142.

Thomas, George I. "A Study of Reading Achievement in Terms of Mental Ability," *The Elementary School Journal,* 47 (September 1946), 28–33.

———, and Joseph Crescimbeni. *Guiding the Gifted Child.* New York: Random House, 1966.

Thomas, R. Murray, and Shirley Thomas. *Individual Differences in the Classroom.* New York: David McKay, 1965.

Thorndike, Robert L., and Elizabeth Hagen. *Measurement and Evaluation in Psychology and Education.* New York: John Wiley, 1961.

Thut, I. N. *The Story of Education.* New York: McGraw-Hill, 1957.

Torrance, Paul. "The Creatively Gifted Are Cause for Concern," *The Gifted Child Quarterly,* 5 (August 1961).

Travers, Robert M. *Essentials of Learning.* New York: Macmillan, 1963.

Traxler, Arthur E. *Techniques of Guidance.* New York: Harper & Row, 1957.

Victor, Edward. *Science for the Elementary School.* New York: Macmillan, 1965.

Waldman, J. L., F. A. Wade, and C. W. Aretz. *Hearing and the School Child.* Philadelphia: Temple University Press, 1930.

Waller, Willard. *The Sociology of Teaching.* New York: John Wiley, 1965.

Washburne, Carleton. "Burke's Individualized System as Developed at Winnetka," *Twenty-fourth Yearbook of the National Society for the Study of Education,* Part II, *Adapting the Schools to Individual Differences.* Bloomington, Ill.: Public School Publishing, 1925.

Watson, Robert I. *Psychology of the Child.* New York: John Wiley, 1965.

West, Paul. "A Study of Ability Grouping in the Elementary School in Terms of Variability of Achievement," *Contributions to Education,* No. 588, *The Teaching Problem and Pupil Adjustment.* New York: Bureau of Publications, Teachers College, Columbia University.

Wetzel, N. C. "The Role of the Grid Technique in a Physical Fitness Program," *Medical Woman's Journal,* 55 (1948), 19–37.

———. "Physical Fitness in Terms of Physique, Development, and Basal Metabolism," *Journal of the American Medical Association,* 116 (1941), 1187–1195.

White, Dorothy. "Individualized Reading," *National Education Association Elementary Instructional Service Leaflet.* Washington, D.C.: National Education Association, November 1958.

Wigren, Harold, and others. "Which ETV for Your School System?" *National Education Association Journal,* 52 (February 1963), 40–42.

Wilhelms, Fred T., and Dorothy Westby Gibson. "Grouping: Research Offers Lead," *Educational Leadership,* 18 (April 1961), 410–13.

Williams, Harold M. *Education of the Severely Retarded Child—Classroom Programs.* Washington, D.C.: Government Printing Office, 1961.

Wilson, Robert C. "Creativity," Chapter VI, *Fifty-seventh Yearbook of the National Society for the Study of Education,* Part II, in Nelson B. Henry, ed., *Education for the Gifted.* Chicago: University of Chicago Press, 1958.

Wrightstone, J. Wayne. *What Research Says to the Teacher About Classroom Organization for Instruction.* Washington, D.C.: National Education Association, 1957.

INDEX

A

Ability
  evaluations based on, 138–40
  marks based on, 136–38
    parental dissatisfaction with, 140–41
  translating test norms in terms of group's level of, 130
Ability grouping, *see* Homogeneous grouping
Ability levels for pupils, establishing, 143
Abstractions, arithmetic and, 336
Academic achievement, *see* Achievement
Academic progress, *see* Progress
Acceptance levels in schools not recognizing continuous progress, 222–24
Achievement (academic)
  code for, 152
  elimination of as basis for promotion and nonpromotion, 157–60
  measurement of, 262–63
  in ungraded schools, 37
  See also specific subjects

Achievement level
  anticipated, adjusting instructional level to, 129
  progress in terms of, 134
Achievement quotient, 118–19
Achievement tests
  in arithmetic, 120, 331
  intelligence tests and, 114–17
  in music, 182
  for placement in ungraded schools, 42–43
Activity movement, 28
Adjustment classes, 59
Adjustment of teachers, 68–69
Administrative patterns, as obstacles to student progress, 68
Age, *see* Chronological age; Mental age
Age equivalents, 116
All-class sessions, importance of, 256–257
American education, changes in pattern of, 17–19
American Medical Association Rating Reading Chart, 95
American Precepter (Bingham), 15
American Selection, An (Webster), 15

Anderson, Robert H., 155
Anticipation achievement charts, 128–129
Area teaching, 59–61
Arithmetic, *see* Mathematics
Arithmetic Teacher, The, 322
Art activities, 177–81
tests in, 180–81
Audiometers, 98

B

Barnard, Henry, 21, 23
Basic spelling list
caution in using, 315
choice of, 294–98
mimeographed, 312–13
with speller, 311–12
tables of, 312, 313, 314
Basic Writing Vocabulary for Elementary School Children, A (Rinsland), 312
Batavia Plan, 29
Battledoor, 13
Beginning group
duration of initial activities in, 190–191
need for careful supervision in, 191–92
outlining responsibilities for, 192–193
Bell, Andrew, 17
Betts, Emmett A., 296
Bingham, Caleb, 15
Block scheduling, 6
compared to flexible scheduling, 62
Blue Back Speller (Webster), 14
Bond, George, 216–17
Books
individualized reading program and, 260–61
learning parts of, 200–1
value of knowing, 73–74
See also Textbooks
Botel, Morton, 313, 315
Bright children, *see* Fast learners

Buzz sessions, 208–9
in social studies, 395

C

California Achievement Tests, 129, 130
Cambridge Plan, 26
Catechism, 13
Chalkboard writing experiences, need for, 275–76
Charts, use of in mathematics teaching, 340–41
Chase, W. Linwood, 319, 397
Checklist in reading, use of, 237
Child-centered curriculum, structured curriculum vs., 34
Chronological age
as educational statistic, 107
grouping by, 35, 42
Citizenship, social studies as education for, 404–7
Citizenship code, 152
Cliques, 102
See also Sociogram
Closed-circuit television as form of programmed learning, 55–57
Commission on Reorganization of Secondary School, 66
Committee work
duration of initial group activities in, 190–91
need for careful supervision in, 191–92
outlining responsibilities for, 192–193
in social studies, 396
Conferences
with parents, 146–47
reading sessions as, 259
Continuous progress
acceptance levels in school not recognizing, 222–24
continuous promotion and, 155–56
in teaching of reading, 221–27
in ungraded schools, 38–40

Continuous progress (*continued*)
  ungraded schools as solution to problem of, 156–57
Cooperative group plan, 28–29
Corrective phase of reading program, 217–19
Counseling in social studies, 396
Creative dramatics, 183–84
Creative planning in area teaching, 60
Creativity, 161–84
  art activities, 177–81
  boys and girls compared, 169–70
  classroom development of, 162–71
  defining, 162
  discipline and, 170–71
  dramatics, 183–84
  inner feeling and, 177
  music activities, 181–83
  recognizing need for, 161–84
  as teacher's responsibility, 161–72
  testing patterns and, 171–72
  writing activities, 172–77
Critical reading phase of reading program, 220
Critical thinking
  necessity for, 406–7
  teaching of, 34
Criticism of children, effects of, 167
Cross-grade grouping in social studies, 395
"Crucial Core Vocabulary in Elementary School Language and Spelling" (Fitzgerald), 314
Curricular reading phase of reading program, 219–20
Curriculum
  enriched, 49
  structured vs. child-centered, 34
Cursive writing, 284–93
  standards in, 286–87

Dedham, Mass., experiment in, 47–48
Delinquent behavior, significance of, 87
Democracy, education for, 34
  social studies and, 404–7
Departmentalized elementary schools, 29
Departmentalized teaching, 45–46
Derby, Orlo L., on nonpromotion, 158
Developmental approach to science, 358
Developmental phase of reading program, 217
Dewey, John, 33, 66
Dictionary use
  skills in, 249
  value of systematic training in, 201–2
Differences, *see* Individual differences
Differentiated assignments in social studies, 395–96
Dilworth's *A Guide to the English Tongue*, 14
Discipline, 21
  mental, theory of, 35
  team learning and, 49–50
"Discovery method" in arithmetic, grouping and, 329–31
Discussion techniques, improvement of, 204–9
Distribution, normal, 108–9
Divisions in schools, 21
Dority, Marie, 379
Drive, 193–94
Dramatics, creative, 183–84
Dual marking systems
  identifying under- and over-achievers with, 142–43
  use of, 141
Durrell, Donald D., 48

D

Dalton Plan, 26–27
Dearborn Village (Mich.), 393

E

E Chart, *see* Snellen Chart
Eames Eye Test, 95

Economic background, effect of, 87–91

Educational growth, total growth and, 91–93

Educational philosophy, 65
  goals and, 66–78

Educational Policies Commission, 66

Educational quotient, 116–17

Effort, relationship between interest and, 33

Elementary and Secondary Education Act, 7

Enriched curriculum, 49

Established policies, need for, 67

Examinations, success and, 25

Expectation levels, 143–44
  in reading, 239–43

Experimentation in science instruction, 365–73

Extended learning periods in social sciences, 396

Eye difficulties, 94–96
  learning manuscript writing and, 281

F

Fast learners (rapid learners), 63
  in arithmetic, 335–48
  in reading, 224–25
  in science, 359–61
  See also Grouping; Subgrouping

Fehr, Howard, 319

Field trips in social sciences, 392–94

Fitzgerald, James A., 294, 295, 311, 312, 314

Flexible scheduling, 61–63

Fundamental education, belief in, 33

G

Gates, Arthur I., 304

Geometrical forms, 330

Gesell, Arnold, 288

Goals
  applying, 67–78

establishing, 66–67
  need for written policies on, 67

Good citizenship, social studies as education for, 404–7

Grade equivalents, 114–16

Grade standards, 24–25
  vs. continuous progress in reading, 221–24
  evaluation in terms of, 133
  report cards based on, 134–36

Graded schools
  concepts of education in, 31–35
  evolution of, 12–24
  individual differences in, 24–29
  patterns of organization of, 22

Grossnickle, Foster E., 328

Group approach, teacher adjustment and, 68–69

Group instruction
  individualized reading within, 255–256
  See also Grouping; Subgrouping

Group intelligence tests, 42–43

Grouping, 4–6
  by achievement test results, 42–43
  in arithmetic, 326–35
  by chronological age, 35, 42
  by mental age, 42
  random, 42
  reading as basis for, 40–41
  in social studies, 394–95
  in spelling, 309–10
  See also Homogeneous grouping

Growth
  educational and total, 91–93
  mental, see Mental age
  physical, 94
    table, 84

Guide to the English Tongue, A (Dilworth), 14

H

Hagen, Elizabeth, 110

Hands, anatomy of, and readiness for reading, 272–73

Handwriting, 267–93
  chalkboard experiences and, 275–276
  cursive, 284–93
    standards in, 286–87
  left-handedness and, 287–93
  manuscript, 277–84
  paper standards by grade, 276
  readiness for, 269–76
    anatomy of children's hands, 274–275
    cursive writing, 285–86
    meaning of "left" and "right," 272
    mental age and, 273–74
    writing of stories dictated by children, 272–73
  spelling success related to success in, 299–300
Harris, William T., 25
Health, see Mental health; Physical health
Hearing deficiencies, 96–98
Heffernan, Helen, 158
Help periods, 58–59
Heterogeneous grouping, 41–42
Higher Education Act, 7
Hildreth, Gertrude, 296, 297, 310–11
History of elementary schools, 12–24
Holland, J. L., 172
Homework
  failure to complete, 128
  pupil responsibilities for, 211
  role of parent in, 211–12
  setting a policy for, 209–12
  talented children and, 182
  teacher's responsibilities in, 210–11
Homogeneous grouping, 4–6
  defined, 4
  evaluating children assigned to, 144–45
  popularity of, 3
  in social studies, 394–95
Honors classes, evaluating children assigned to, 144–45
Horace Mann School, 279

Horn, Ernest, 295, 301, 304, 306–7, 311
Hornbook, 13
Hosic, James F., 28

I

Independent seat activities in reading, 231–33
Individual differences
  early attempts to provide for, 24–29
  grouping as solution to problem of, see Grouping; Subgrouping
  mathematics teaching and, 335–48
  promotion and, 155–56
  recognition of, 35
  social-science unit teaching and, 375–94
  ungraded schools and, 37
  See also Growth
Instructional level, anticipated achievement level and, 129
Intellectually gifted children, see Fast learners
Intelligence quotient
  constancy of, 110–11
  creativity and, 171–72
  descriptive classification of, 109–10
  as educational statistic, 108
Intelligence tests
  achievement tests and, 114–17
  art ability and, 180–81
  group, 42–43
Interest
  relationship between effort and, 33
  successful reading experiences and, 250–52
Iowa Basic Skills Test, 131
Iowa Every-Pupil Tests of Basic Skills, 194

J

Jackson, Andrew, 19
Jenkins, Marion, 258

Johnson, Charles E., 331
Johnson, Leslie W., 312
Johnson, Wendell, 99

K

Kennedy, John, 29
Keystone Visual Survey Telebinocular, 95
Kindergarten, 20
    growth patterns and, 91–92

L

Lancaster, Joseph, 17
Language arts program, handwriting as functional part of, 268–69
Leaders, pupil, importance of, 206–8
Learning
    economic background and, 87–91
    mental health and, 85–87
    physical health and, 93–100
Learning experiences, need for, 34
"Left," meaning of, 272
Left-handedness
    handwriting and, 287–93
    tests for, 290–91
Letter formation in manuscript writing, 280–81
Library, use of, 199–200
Lincoln School, 279
Long-range assignments, 165
Lowenfeld, Viktor, 162, 180
Luchins, Abraham, 326
Luther, Martin, 182

M

McGuffey *Readers,* 19–21, 214
McGuffey *Spelling Book,* 20
Maico audiometer, 98
Malnutrition, children suffering from, 94

Mann, Horace, 21, 23
Manuscript writing, 277–84
    See also Handwriting
Maps, reading and interpreting, 401
Marking codes on report cards, 137
    dual, 141–43
Massachusetts Vision Test, 95
Mathematics (arithmetic), 317–48
    achievement tests in, 120, 331
    children's reactions to, 317–26
    crutches in, 341–42
    grouping in, 326–35
    modern approaches to teaching of, 321–22
    problem solving in, 326
    readiness in, 323–26
    reasons for failure in, 319–21, 341–342
    teaching aids for, 339–41
Mathematics Teacher, The, 322
Meaning of words, questions on, 308
Mental age, 37, 111–14
    grade conversion table, 123–24
    grade level expectancy for, 112
    grouping by, 42
    levels of reading and, 121–25
    writing readiness and, 273–74
Mental development, table on, 82–83
Mental health, learning and, 85–87
Mixed textbook teaching, 75
    in social studies, 395
Monitorial schools, 16–17
Multilevel assignments, 44–45
Multi-level Speller (Botel), 313, 315
Multi-media approach in social studies, 395
Multiple textbook teaching, 74–75
    in social studies, 395
Multitrack grouping, 26
Music activities, 181–83

N

National Merit Examinations, 172
Negative learning, 304–5
New England Primer, 13–14

New York State Department of Education, 405
Nonpromotion, 154–55
    elimination of academic achievement as basis for, 157–60
Normal distribution, 108–9
Number experiences
    readiness for, 325–26
    See also Mathematics

O

Odell, Clarence B., 401
"Old Deluder Satan Act," 12
Olney, Jesse, 16
"One Hundred Most Commonly Used Spelling Words" (Rinsland), 311–12
"One Hundred Words Most Commonly Misspelled by Children in the Elementary Grades" (Johnson), 312–13
Organization of graded schools
    breaking from pattern of, 25–29
    table of patterns of, 22
Originality, encouragement of, 165–166
Ortho-Rater, 95
Outlines, teaching children about, 202–3
Overachievers, identification of, with dual marking system, 142–43

P

Panel discussions, 208
Paper standards by grade for children, 276
Parents
    dissatisfaction with marking by, 140–41
    homework and, 211–12
    importance of conferences with, 146–47

letter reports to, 147–49
    pupil reaction to behavior of, 86
Parke, Margaret, 296
Parkhurst, Helen, 26
Percentile, defined, 115
Performance ranges, 143–44
Philadelphia, Pa., 17
Philbrick, John D., 23
Philosophy of education, 65
    goals and, 66–78
Phonetics
    comprehension of, 248
    in spelling, 308
Physical growth and development, 94
    table of, 84
Physical health
    effect on learning of, 93–100
    hearing deficiencies, 96–98
    responsibility of teacher for, 94–95
    speech deficiencies, 98–100
    visual deficiencies, 94–96
        learning handwriting and, 281
Placement, *see* Grouping
Platoon school, 28
Post-school sessions in social studies, 396–97
Preplanning in area teaching, 60
Pre-school sessions in social studies, 396–97
Pretesting
    in spelling, 304
    unit approach and, 377–78
Problem solving, foundation for, 326
Program, planning a, 82–84
Programmed learning, 51–57
    advantages and disadvantages of, 53, 55
    television as a form of, 55–57
Progress, academic, 37
    continuous, *see* Continuous progress
    evaluation and reporting of, 133–60
    See also specific subjects
Promotion, 154–60
    continuous, 155–56
    elimination of academic achievement as basis for, 157–60
Puritans, 12–14

Q

Quantitative concepts
  in social studies, 398–400
  See also Mathematics
Quincy Grammar School, 12, 23–24

R

Rapid learners, *see* Fast learners
Reader (Bingham), 15
Readers, 214–17
  McGuffey, 19–21, 214
  problems created by teachers by
    basic, 220–21
  reinforcement, 39
Reader's Guide, 200
Readiness
  for arithmetic, 323–26
  for handwriting, *see* Handwriting,
    readiness for
  for spelling, 302–3
Reading, 213–66
  accelerated, 224–25
  arithmetic failure related to, 342–
    344
  as basis for grouping, 40–41
  developmental phase of program
    for, 217
  early teaching of, 12–13
  gradedness vs. continued progress,
    221–27
  independent seat activities in, 231
  individualized, 4, 252–66
  levels of, 234–43
    determination of, 238–43
    inventory to establish, 236–37
    mental age and, 121–25
    teacher's guide in identifying, 234
  oral, 245–47
    list of deficiencies in, 240–41
  phonetics in, 248
  recommendations for good program
    in, 263–66

recreational phase of program for,
  217, 259
remedial phase of program for, 217–
  219, 301
silent, 245
  list of deficiencies in, 240–41
social studies and, 402
specific skills to be taught (table),
  216
spelling success related to success
  in, 300–1
structural analysis in, 248–49
subgrouping for, 227–43
test rating vs. independent level of,
  127–28
in ungraded schools, 37
word recognition in, 247–48
Reading lessons, 243–52
Reading quotient, 239
Recitations
  discussion and, 204–6
  learning and, 15–16
Recreational phase of reading program, 217, 259
Regimentation in graded schools, 11–
  30
Remedial phase of reading program,
  217–19, 301
Remedial spelling, 301
Report cards
  based on ability, 136–41
  based on grade standards, 134–36
  dual marking system in, 141–43
  newer types of, 150–52
  sample of making codes used on,
    137
Reporting system, 133–60
  basic principles for setting up, 152–
    154
  See also Report cards; Reports,
    written
Reports, written
  by children, 203
  to parents, 147–50
Responsibilities of teachers, 69–70,
  187–99

Rice, J. M., 34
"Right," meaning of, 272
Rinsland, Henry D., 295, 296, 311

S

St. Louis Plan, 25–26
Scheduling, 6
  flexible, 61–63
Science, 349–73
  acquiring scientific attitude, 353–55
  children's curiosity and, 350–52
  in correlation with other subjects, 358–59
  experimentation in, 365–73
  intellectually gifted child and, 359–361
  records of progress in, 372
  scientific method and, 355–57
  sequence of activities in, 357–58
  setting teaching goals for study of, 352–53
  television and, 367–68
  textbooks in, 368–69
  understanding level and, 361–63
  unit approach in, 369–72
  updating, 363–73
Seashore Measures of Musical Talent, 182
Seat activities, independent, in reading, 231–33
Self-discovery, pupil's, 169
Sequence of learning skills, 40–41
Sex differences in creativity, 169–70
Shelburne Museum (Vt.), 393
Slow learners
  ability marking and, 140
  in arithmetic, 335–45
  handwriting and, 281–82
  in ungraded schools, 37
  See also Grouping; Subgrouping
Slow starters, 39, 135–36
Snellen Chart, 95
Social-emotional growth, table of, 83–84

Social studies, 374–408
  buzz sessions in, 395
  committees in, 396
  continuous evaluation of activities in, 391–92
  culminating activities in, 392
  defining, 374–75
  differentiated assignments in, 395–396
  as education for democracy and citizenship, 404–7
  extended learning period in, 396
  factors in teaching and learning of, 398–404
  field trips in, 392–94
  helping pupils find themselves through, 397–407
  mixed-set approach in, 395
  multi-media approach in, 395
  multiple text approach in, 395
  post-school or pre-school sessions in, 396–97
  special counseling in, 396
  team learning in, 395
  textbooks in, 395, 402–4
  unit in, 376–94
Sociogram, use of, 100–6
Sonotone audiometer, 98
Space, concept of, in social studies, 398–400
Special adjustment classes, 59
Special help periods, 58–59
Special teachers, 269
Speech deficiencies, 98–100
Spellers
  combination of basic word list and, 311–12
  making break from basic, 311–15
Spelling, 294–315
  basic word list in
    caution in using, 315
    choice of, 294–98
    mimeographed, 312–13
    with speller, 311–12
    tables of, 312, 313, 314
  evaluating progress in, 304–6
  factors in success in, 298–301

Spelling (*continued*)
    feelings about learning, 298–99
    pupil's work-study pattern, 301
    reading success, 300–1
    writing success, 299–300
  grouping in, 309–10
  individualizing teaching of, 301–16
  pretesting and, 304
  readiness in, 302–3
  remedial, 301
  use of rules in, 306–7
  use of study-work questions in, 307–9
"Spelling demons," 312
Standardized tests, 107–32
  actual instructional activities vs. ideal test score, 126–27
  adjusting instructional level to anticipated achievement level, 129
  anticipation achievement charts, 128–29
  danger of accepting single test score, 130–31
  determining expected achievement level through, 117–26
  independent reading level vs. test ratings, 127–28
  as measure of pupil capacity, 126
  as measures of strengths and weaknesses, 131–32
  test norms in terms of group level, 130
  See also specific types of tests
Stanford-Binet Intelligence Scale, 114
Statesman's Yearbook, 200
Statistics, educational, 107–26
Structural analysis, 248–49, 308
Structured curriculum, child-centered curriculum vs., 34
Student progress, *see* Progress
Study, teaching children how to, 193–99
Study-guide questions in spelling, 307–9
Study skills phase of reading program, 219

Sturbridge Village (Mass.), 393
Subgrouping, 5
  in arithmetic, 331–32
  in reading, 227–43
  in social studies, 394
Subject matter, overemphasis on, 73
Symbol patterns, ability to see differences in, 270

T

Teacher aides, 57–58
Teachers
  adjustment to group approach by, 68–69
  responsibilities of, 69–70, 187–99
  reviewing of work by, 70–71
  special, 269
  textbook, 72, 73, 76–77
  two-teacher classes, 43–44
Teaching
  challenges of, 6–8, 79–80
  departmentalized, 45–46
  need for consistency in, 67–68
Teaching aids, 32–33
  in arithmetic, 339–41
Team learning, 47–50, 328
  discipline and, 49–50
  in social studies, 395
Team planning, 47
Team teaching, 45–46
  in social studies, 395
Television
  as form of programmed learning, 55–57
  science teaching and, 367–69
Tests
  acceptance of, 34–35
  of art ability, 180–81
  group level of ability and test norms, 130
  independent reading level vs. test ratings, 127–28
  for left-handedness, 290–91
  for musical talent, 182

Tests (*continued*)
  scores of
    actual instructional activities vs., 126–27
    danger of accepting single test scores, 130–31
  See also Intelligence tests; Standardized tests
Textbook teachers, 72, 73, 76–77
Textbooks, 72–78
  effective use of, 71–72
  emergence of, 13–15
  lack of consistency in assigning, 76
  overdependence on labels of, 75–76
  programmed, 53, 55
  role of, 72–73
  science, 368–69
  social studies, 402–4
  See also Readers; Spellers
Thorndike, E. L., 35, 110
Time, concept of, development of, 398–400
Time limits, reasonable, 166
Total growth, educational growth and, 91–93
Transfers in ungraded schools, 41
Traxler, Arthur E., 140
"220 Spelling Demons" (Fitzgerald), 312, 314
Two-teacher classes, 43–44

U

Underachievers, identification of, 142–143
Understanding level, science and, 361–63
Ungraded school, 36–43
  adaptability of, 38
  advantages of, 36–38
  continuous progress in, 38–40
  grouping in, 41–43
  reading as basis for grouping in, 40–41
  as solution to problem of continuous progress, 156–57
  transfers in, 41

Units
  activities offered in successful, 390–394
  in arithmetic, 334–35
  creating interest in, 388–90
  developing, 378–88
  in science, 369–72
  in social studies, 375–94
Universal concepts in science, 351–52

V

Visual deficiencies, 94–96
  learning manuscript writing and, 281
Volunteer teacher aides, 58

W

Warm-up period, 165
Washburne, Carleton, 27
Webster, Noah, 14–15
Wechsler Intelligence Scale, 114
Western Electric audiometer, 98
White, Dorothy, 253
Who's Who in America, 200
Williamsburg (Va.), 393
Wilson, Gilbert M., 397
Winnetka Plan, 27–28
Wirt, William A., 28
Word list, basic
  caution in using, 315
  choice of, 294–98
  mimeographed, 312–13
  with speller, 311–12
  tables of, 312, 313, 314
Word recognition, 247–48
Word usage, questions regarding, 308–9
Work materials in area teaching, 60–61
Workbooks, standards for selecting, 77–78

Work-study code, 152
Work-study patterns
  creativity and, 402
  developing, 187–212
  responsibility and, 189–90
  social studies and, 402
  spelling success related to success
    in, 301

types of, 199–212
World Almanac, 200
Writing, *see* Handwriting
Writing activities, 172–77
Written policies, need for, 67
Written reports
  by children, 203
  to parents, 147–50